Solaris™ 10 System Administration Essentials

Solaris™ 10 System Administration Essentials

Solaris System Engineers

Sun Microsystems Press

PRENTICE
HALL

Upper Saddle River, NJ • Boston • Indianapolis • San Francisco
New York • Toronto • Montreal • London • Munich • Paris • Madrid
Capetown • Sydney • Tokyo • Singapore • Mexico City

The publisher offers excellent discounts on this book when ordered in quantity for bulk purchases or special sales, which may include electronic versions and/or custom covers and content particular to your business, training goals, marketing focus, and branding interests. For more information, please contact:

U.S. Corporate and Government Sales
(800) 382-3419
corpsales@pearsontechgroup.com

For sales outside the United States please contact:

International Sales, international@pearsoned.com

Visit us on the Web: informit.com/ph

Library of Congress Cataloging-in-Publication Data

Solaris 10 system administration essentials / Solaris system engineers.
    p.   cm.
  Includes index.
  ISBN 978-0-13-700009-8 (pbk. : alk. paper)
  1. Electronic data processing—Management. 2. Systems software. 3.
Solaris (Computer file) I. Sun Microsystems.
  QA76.9.M3S65 2009
  005.4'3—dc22

                                             2009034498

Copyright © 2010 Sun Microsystems, Inc.
4150 Network Circle, Santa Clara, California 95054 U.S.A.
All rights reserved.

ISBN-13: 978-0-13-700009-8
ISBN-10:   0-13-700009-X
Text printed in the United States on recycled paper at RR Donnelley in Crawfordsville, Indiana.
First printing, November 2009

Contents

Preface

Solaris™ 10 System Administration Essentials

Solaris™ 10 System Administration Essentials is the centerpiece of the new series on Solaris system administration. It covers all of the breakthrough features of the Solaris 10 operating system in one place. Other books in the series, such as *Solaris™ 10 Security Essentials* and *Solaris™ 10 ZFS Essentials*, cover specific features and aspects of the Solaris OS in detail.

Solaris™ 10 System Administration Essentials is the most comprehensive book about Solaris 10 on the market. It covers the significant features introduced with the initial release of Solaris 10 and the features, like ZFS, introduced in subsequent updates.

The Solaris OS has a long history of innovation. The Solaris 10 OS is a watershed release that includes features such as:

- **Zones/Containers,** which provide application isolation and facilitate server consolidation
- **ZFS,** the file system that provides a new approach to managing your data with an easy administration interface
- The **Fault Management Architecture,** which automates fault detection and resolution

- The **Service Management Facility,** a unified model for services and service management on every Solaris system
- **Dynamic Tracing (DTrace),** for troubleshooting OS and application problems on production systems in real time

The Solaris 10 OS fully supports 32-bit and 64-bit x86 platforms as well as the SPARC architecture.

This book is the work of the engineers, architects, and writers who conceptualized the services, wrote the procedures, and coded the rich set of Solaris features. These authors bring a wide range of industry and academic experience to the business of creating and deploying operating systems. These are the people who know Solaris 10 best. They have collaborated to write a book that speaks to readers who want to learn Solaris or who want to use Solaris for the first time in their company's or their own environment. Readers do not have to be experienced Solaris users or operating system developers to take advantage of this book.

The book's key topics include:

- Installing, booting, and shutting down a system
- Managing packages and patches (software updates)
- Controlling system processes
- Managing disks and devices
- Managing users
- Configuring networks
- Using printing services

Books in the Solaris System Administration Series

Solaris™ 10 Security Essentials

Solaris™ 10 Security Essentials describes how to make Solaris installations secure and configure the operating system to the particular needs of an environment, whether the systems are on the edge of the Internet or running a data center. It does so in a straightforward way that makes a seemingly arcane subject accessible to system administrators at all levels.

Solaris™ 10 Security Essentials begins with two stories that highlight the evolution of security in UNIX systems and the particular strengths that Sun Microsystems has added to the Solaris operating system that make it the best choice for meeting the present-day challenges to robust and secure computing.

Solaris™ 10 ZFS Essentials

Solaris™ 10 ZFS Essentials presents the revolutionary Zettabyte File System introduced in Solaris 10. It is a file system that is elegant in its simplicity and the ease with which it allows system administrators to manage data and storage.

ZFS is an all-purpose file system that is built on top of a pool of storage devices. File systems that are created from a storage pool share space with the other file systems in the pool. Administrators do not have to allocate storage space based on the intended size of a file system because file systems grow automatically within the space that is allocated to the storage pool. When new storage devices are added, all file systems in the pool can immediately use the additional space.

Intended Audience

The books in the Solaris System Administration Series can benefit anyone who wants to learn more about the Solaris 10 operating system. They are written to be particularly accessible to system administrators who are new to Solaris, and people who are perhaps already serving as administrators in companies running Linux, Windows, and/or other UNIX systems.

If you are not presently a practicing system administrator but want to become one, then this series, starting with the *Solaris™ 10 System Administration Essentials*, provides an excellent introduction. In fact, most of the examples used in the books are suited to or can be adapted to small learning environments like a home setup. Even before you venture into corporate system administration or deploy Solaris 10 in your existing IT installation, these books will help you experiment in a small test environment.

OpenSolaris

In June 2005, Sun Microsystems introduced OpenSolaris, a fully functional Solaris operating system release built from open source. While the books in this series focus on Solaris 10, they often incorporate aspects of OpenSolaris. Now that Solaris has been open-sourced, its evolution has accelerated even beyond its normally rapid pace. The authors of this series have often found it interesting to introduce features or nuances that are new in OpenSolaris. At the same time, many of the enhancements introduced into OpenSolaris are finding their way into Solaris 10. Whether you are learning Solaris 10 or already have an eye on OpenSolaris, the books in this series are for you.

About the Authors

This book benefits from the contributions of numerous experts in Solaris technologies. Below are brief biographies of each of the contributing authors.

David Bustos is a Senior Engineer in the Solaris SMF team. During seven years at Sun, he implemented a number of pieces of the SMF system for Solaris 10 and is now designing and implementing enhanced SMF profiles, which is a major revision of the SMF configuration subsystem. David graduated from the California Institute of Technology with a Bachelor of Science degree in 2002.

Stephanie Brucker is a Senior Technical Writer who enjoys documenting networking features for system administrators and end users. Stephanie worked for Sun Microsystems for over twenty years, writing tasks and conceptual information for the Solaris operating system. She has written Wikipedia and print articles on computer networking topics, as well as articles on ethnic dance for specialty magazines. Stephanie lives in San Francisco, California. She has a Bachelor of Fine Arts degree in Technical Theater from Ohio University.

Raoul Carag is a Technical Writer at Sun. He belongs to the System Administration writers group and documents networking features of the Solaris OS. He has been involved in projects that enhance network administration such as IP observability, rearchitected multipathing, and network virtualization.

Penelope Cotten is a Technical Writer at Sun Microsystems, working on Solaris Zones/Containers and the Sun xVM hypervisor.

Scott Davenport has been at Sun for eleven years, the last five of which have been focused on fault management. He is a leader of the OpenSolaris FM Community (http://opensolaris.org/os/community/fm) and issues periodic musings about fault management via his blog (http://blogs.sun.com/sdaven). Scott lives in San Diego, California.

Alta Elstad is a Technical Writer at Sun Microsystems, working on device drivers and other Solaris and OpenSolaris operating system features.

Eric Erickson is a Technical Writer and a professor of English at Mt. San Antonio College, Walnut, California. He has a Master of Fine Arts degree in English from the University of Iowa.

Juanita Heieck is a Senior Technical Writer in the Sun Learning Services organization at Sun Microsystems. She writes basic and advanced system administration documentation for a wide range of Solaris features including booting, networking, and printing.

Puneet Jain works as a developer at Sun Microsystems in the Diagnostics Engineering Group. He works on design and development of system-level diagnostics using C on Solaris. These diagnostics are used across all the Sun hardware products during engineering, manufacturing, and field usage. His major responsibilities include developing new diagnostics and enhancing the existing diagnostics in I/O space to ensure that Sun Systems shipped to the customers are of the highest quality. For his academic and leadership excellence, he has been awarded with the Gold Medal from his college and The Best Student of State Award, 2006 from the Indian Society of Technical Education (ISTE), New Delhi. Puneet lives in Bangalore with his parents, Mr. Surendra Kumar Jain and Ms. Memo Jain. His father likes writing poems in his spare time and Puneet enjoys listening to his father's poems in his spare time.

Narendra Kumar.S.S earned his Bachelor of Science in Computer Science & Engineering and Master of Science in Software Systems. He has over ten years of experience and has worked in varied areas such as networking, telecom, embedded systems, and Operating Systems. He has worked for Sun for the last four years. Initially he joined the "Solaris Install" team and later was moved to the "Solaris Sustaining" team. Currently he is responsible for sustaining the sysidtools part of the Solaris Install. He is based in Bangalore and lives with his wife, Rukmini, and daughters, Harshitha and Vijetha.

James Liu is a Senior Staff Engineer at Sun. He joined Sun in 1995 and has helped countless ISVs and IHVs to develop Solaris and Java software. James has a broad range of expertise in UNIX, Java, compilers, networking, security, systems administration, and applications architecture. He holds multiple software patents in performance tuning, bug management, multimedia distribution, and financial derivatives risk management. Prior to coming to Sun, James did research in inertial confinement fusion, and then worked as a consultant building trading- and risk-management systems in the Tokyo financial markets. James holds a Bachelor of Science and Doctorate of Philosophy from UC Berkeley in Nuclear Engineering, specializing in Shockwave Analysis and Computational Physics. At present, James is a kernel engineer helping IHVs write device drivers. In his spare time, he likes to blog about how to build cheap Solaris x86 boxes.

Alan Maguire is a Software Engineer at Sun Microsystems. He has ten years of experience in Solaris—covering both test and product development—primarily focused on networking components in the Solaris Operating System. These include the open-source Quagga routing protocol suite, the Network Auto-Magic technology, and the Service Management Facility (SMF). He graduated with a Bachelor of Science in Computer Science and obtained a Master of Science in Cognitive Science from University College, Dublin, Ireland.

Cathleen Reiher is a Senior Technical Writer at Sun Microsystems. She has over seventeen years of experience working with and writing about the Solaris operating system. Her work is primarily focused on helping system administrators and developers to effectively use Sun technologies to support their endeavors. She graduated with a Bachelor of Arts degree in Linguistics from the University of California, Los Angeles.

Vidya Sakar is a Staff Engineer in the Data Technologies group of Solaris Revenue Product Engineering. Vidya Sakar has about ten years of technical and management experience in Solaris Sustaining and Engineering. During this period he has worked on different file systems, volume managers, and various kernel subsystems. He was a part of the team that ported the ZFS file system to Solaris 10 and has delivered talks on Internals of file systems at various universities in India and at technology conferences. He is a Kepner Tregoe certified Analytic Trouble Shooting (ATS) program leader and has facilitated on-site trouble-shooting sessions at customer sites.

Michael Schuster earned his degree ("Diplom-Ingenieur") at the Technische Universität in Vienna in 1994. Since the early 1990s, he has been working with and on UNIX systems, mainly Solaris, but also HP-UX and AIX. After several years of software engineering work in Austria, Michael moved to Munich to join Sun Microsystems' Services organization, where he specialized in kernel internals-related work and performance analysis. He joined the Solaris Engineering group in late 2006, where he currently works in the networking team, and moved to the San Francisco Bay Area in early 2007.

Lynne Thompson is a Senior Technical Writer who has written about the Solaris operating system for more than fourteen years. She is a twenty-year veteran of writing about UNIX and other technologies. To enhance the understanding of Solaris for system administrators and developers, she has written extensively about Solaris installation, upgrading, and patching, as well as many Solaris features related to installing, such as ZFS, booting, Solaris Zones, and RAID-1 volumes. Lynne is a contributor to OpenSolaris. She has a Master of Arts in English (Writing). When she's not learning and writing about technology, Lynne is traveling, designing art-jewelry, or tutoring reading for people with learning disabilities.

Sowmini Varadhan is a Staff Engineer at Sun Microsystems in the Solaris Networking group. For the last nine years, she has been participating in the implementation and improvements of routing and networking protocols in the Solaris TCP/IP stack. Prior to working at Sun, Sowmini was at DEC/Compaq, working on Routing and IPv6 protocols in the Tru64 kernel, and on Sun RPC interfaces at Parametric Technology Corp.

1

Installing the Solaris 10 Operating System

The chapter explores the key methods for installing and updating the Solaris oper-
ating system. It takes the reader from simple installation on a single system
through the options for installing and upgrading systems in a networked environ-
ment where multiple machines can be managed automatically.

1.1 Methods to Meet Your Needs

The Solaris 10 operating system offers a rich installation experience with a number of options to meet the needs of a variety of users and environments. The
Solaris OS can be installed easily on a single system using a CD or DVD, it can be
installed over a network, update installations can be performed while the system
is running without interruption, and installation on multiple machines can be performed hands-free with JumpStart. You can even clone a system for installation on
other machines using the Solaris Flash archive feature.

The first thing a new Solaris user needs is the DVD or an image of the DVD
from which the Solaris OS can be installed. The DVD image can be downloaded
from `http://www.sun.com/software/solaris/10/`. Once you have downloaded that image, you can burn an ISO format disk image and then install that
image on one or more systems. This method provides a simple GUI installation
process, though you can always use the text-based installation interface.

It is not necessary to create a DVD, though. You can install the Solaris OS
directly from the image you downloaded. That can be done from the image stored

on the machine you wish to install on or from another system in the network of which your target system is a part.

When you get to installing multiple machines, you will want something more versatile than a DVD, which must be carried to each machine. A network-based installation is obviously a useful alternative. You can use all of the Solaris installation methods to install a system from the network. You can point each machine at the installation image on the network and install almost as if you had inserted a DVD. However, by installing systems from the network with the Solaris Flash installation feature or with a custom JumpStart installation, you can centralize and automate the installation process in a larger environment.

An upgrade installation overwrites the system's disk with the new version of the Solaris OS. If your system is not running the Solaris OS, then you must perform an initial installation.

If the system is already running the Solaris OS, then you can choose to perform an initial installation. If you want to preserve any local modifications, then you must back up the local modifications before you install. After you complete the installation, you can restore the local modifications.

You can use any of the Solaris installation methods to perform an initial installation.

To upgrade the Solaris OS, there are three methods: standard installation, custom JumpStart, and Solaris Live Upgrade. When you upgrade using the standard installation procedure or JumpStart, the system maintains as many existing configuration parameters as possible of the current Solaris OS. Solaris Live Upgrade creates a copy of the current system. This copy can be upgraded with a standard upgrade. The upgraded Solaris OS can then be switched to become the current system by a simple reboot. If a failure occurs, then you can switch back to the original Solaris OS with a reboot. Solaris Live Upgrade enables you to keep your system running while you upgrade and enables you to switch back and forth between Solaris OS releases.

1.2 The Basics of Solaris Installation

Many terms and options make Solaris widely configurable for the large install-base administrator; however, a basic understanding of these terms and options will help an administrator installing even a single instance of Solaris get all that one can from their system.

When you start off small with only a single system to install, the GUI and console mode text installers are the simplest ways to install a single instance of the Solaris OS. Because Solaris systems are optimized for networking, this installation method focuses on setting up network parameters and file sharing identification to accommodate user home directories on numerous Solaris systems in the network.

The minimum memory requirement for installing Solaris is 128MB. The recommended size is 256MB. If you install with the GUI installer, then you need 512MB. If the system has less than 384MB, then the text installer will be used automatically. These limits change slightly between the SPARC and x86 architectures (see Table 1.1).

Table 1.1 Memory Requirements for "Solaris Install Display Options"

SPARC: Memory	x86: Memory	Type of Installation	Description
128–383 MB	256–511 MB	Text-based	Contains no graphics, but provides a window and the ability to open other windows. If you install by using the `text` boot option and the system has enough memory, you are installing in a windowing environment. If you are installing remotely through a `tip` line or using the `nowin` boot option, you are limited to the console-based installation.
384 MB or greater	512 MB	GUI-based	Provides windows, pull-down menus, buttons, scrollbars, and iconic images.

In a single-system install installation, the primary objective is to get the system to boot up usably. This means specifying which of the system network interfaces should be used as the primary interface for network traffic, and nowadays even which version of the Internet Protocol to use (IPv4 or IPv6) needs be specified. After figuring out which protocol to use, you need to specify how large the machine's network segment or subnet is and a default route for traffic destined for another subnet. Solaris has support for Kerberos authentication and credential support; if you wish to set it up, then you can do that at install as well. One of the last network services to set up is the naming service to be used for mapping hostnames to Internet Protocol (IP) addresses. Solaris supports the Network Information Service (NIS), the no longer recommended NIS+, the Lightweight Directory Access Protocol (LDAP), and the Domain Name System (DNS). During installation, only one service can be specified. Each service requires specific information for setup (see Chapter 13, "Using Naming Services"). In the home or small business case, DNS will be used because it requires only a DNS server IP address. Lastly, for network configuration, NFS version 4 now supports domain based identification, so you can configure which domain to use, if necessary (see Section 5.4, "NFS File System Administration," for more info).

After you specify the network settings, the installation program focuses on system configuration. First, you specify the date and time, a root user password (also known as an administrator password), and the last networking question about whether the system should be "Secure by Default." Solaris' Secure by Default provides security for the system without requiring you to do a lot of configuration or know a lot about security. See "Solaris Security Essentials" in the *Solaris System Administration* series for more information about Secure by Default and the many other security features of the Solaris OS.

Packaging and package metaclusters (also known as Software Groups) are a key idea in a Solaris installation. You must specify the parts of Solaris to be installed or specifically left off a system. Package metaclusters are designed as groups of packages for designating a system's intended use after installation. In this day of big disks, it is recommended that you install the *Entire Distribution plus OEM support* metacluster. However, you can use the customize feature in the GUI or text installers to specify which metaclusters are to be installed. Table 1.2 describes each Software Group and the disk space recommended for installing it.

Table 1.2 Disk Space Recommendations for Software Groups

Software Group	Description	Recommended Disk Space
Reduced Network Support Software Group	Contains the packages that provide the minimum code that is required to boot and run a Solaris system with limited network service support. The Reduced Network Support Software Group provides a multi-user text-based console and system administration utilities. This software group also enables the system to recognize network interfaces, but does not activate network services.	2.0 GB
Core System Support Software Group	Contains the packages that provide the minimum code that is required to boot and run a networked Solaris system.	2.0 GB
End User Solaris Software Group	Contains the packages that provide the minimum code that is required to boot and run a networked Solaris system and a Desktop Environment.	5.3 GB

Table 1.2 Disk Space Recommendations for Software Groups (*continued*)

Software Group	Description	Recommended Disk Space
Developer Solaris Software Group	Contains the packages for the End User Solaris Software Group plus additional support for software development. The additional software development support includes libraries, "include files," "man pages," and programming tools. Compilers are not included.	6.6 GB
Entire Solaris Software Group	Contains the packages for the Developer Solaris Software Group and additional software that is needed for servers.	6.7 GB
Entire Solaris Software Group Plus OEM Support	Contains the packages for the Entire Solaris Software Group plus additional hardware drivers, including drivers for hardware that is not on the system at the time of installation.	6.8 GB

When installing any software, the amount of space it takes up is always a question. With an operating system another choice is available: the way you would like to use your system's disk space. Solaris supports several file systems. During installation, you can choose UFS, the traditional file system for Solaris; or ZFS, the new and future file system for Solaris. ZFS is usually the best option. See Chapter 5, "Solaris File Systems," for more information on file systems. Selecting ZFS over UFS will change how much control you have during installation for laying out disks, but ZFS is more flexible after an install.

If ZFS is selected as the system's boot file system, then you can choose the size of the root pool (or storage space available) and the space set aside for system swap and memory dump locations. Also, you may opt for separate root (/) and /var datasets to make quota enforcement easier, or you can choose a monolithic dataset.

If UFS is selected as the system's boot file system, then there are more choices you need think about during installation. UFS is less flexible once the system is installed. There is, however, an automatic layout option that enables you to pick which directories should live on their own file systems versus which should reside on the root file system. Where such large disks are available today, it is only recommended to select swap to be separate unless the system will otherwise have specific security or application requirements.

1.2.1 Installing Solaris on a SPARC System

These steps for SPARC and x86 differ slightly. We will first see how Solaris is installed on a SPARC system.

1. Insert the Solaris 10 operating system for SPARC platforms DVD.
2. Boot the system.
   - If the system is already running, execute `init  0` to halt it.
   - If the system is new, then simply turn it on.
3. When the OK prompt is displayed, type `boot  cdrom`.
4. When installation begins, you are asked to select a language. Select a language and hit Enter.

   After a few moments the Solaris Installation Program Welcome Screen appears. Figures 1.1 and 1.2 show the graphical and text versions of those screens.
5. Click Next to start entering the system configuration information.

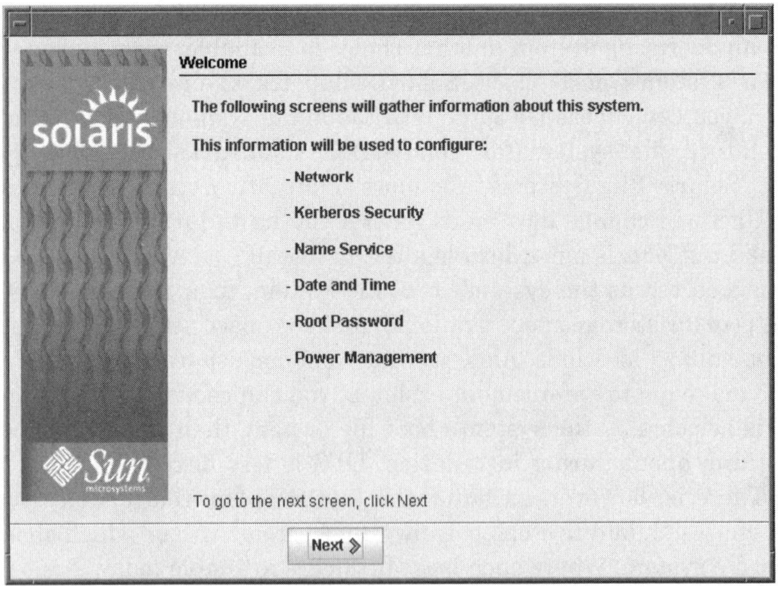

Figure 1.1 Solaris Installation Program Welcome Screen (GUI)

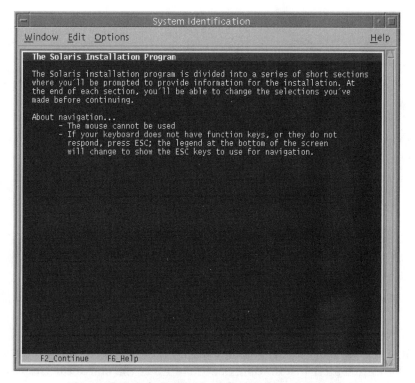

Figure 1.2 Solaris Text Installer Welcome Screen

After getting all the configuration information, the Solaris Installation Screen appears (see Figure 1.3).

After this the actual installation related questions will be asked. What follows are the questions that typically will be asked:

1. Decide if you want to reboot the system automatically and if you want to automatically eject the disc.

2. The Specify Media screen appears. Specify the media you are using to install.

3. The License panel appears. Accept the license agreement to continue the installation.

4. The Select Upgrade or Initial Install screen appears. Decide if you want to perform an initial installation or an upgrade.

5. When you are prompted to select initial installation or upgrade, choose Initial Install.

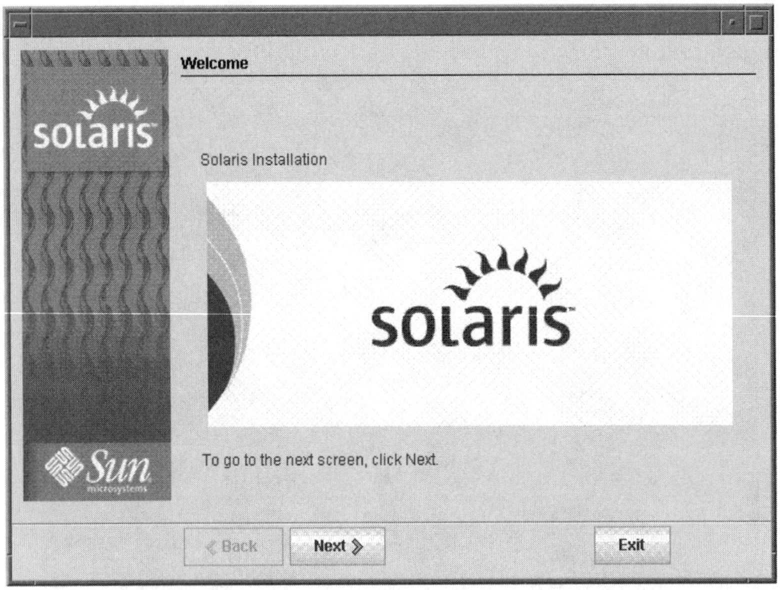

Figure 1.3 Welcome to Solaris Installation Screen

6. Fill in the sequence of screens that ask for information about the system configuration after installation. See Table 1.3 at the end of the chapter for a checklist of information you need on these installation screens.

After you provide all the necessary information on the installation, the Ready to Install screen appears as in Figure 1.4.

Click the Install Now button to start the installation.

When the Solaris installation program finishes installing the Solaris software, the system reboots automatically or prompts you to reboot manually (this depends on what you selected initially).

If you are installing additional products, then you are prompted to insert the DVD or CD for those products. After the installation is finished, installation logs are saved in a file. You can find the installation logs in the /var/sadm/system/ logs and /var/sadm/install/logs directories.

If you are performing an initial installation, then the installation is complete. You can reboot the system.

If you are upgrading to a new version of Solaris operating system, then you might need to correct some local modifications that were not preserved. Review the contents of the upgrade_cleanup file located at /a/var/sadm/system/data to determine whether you need to correct local modifications that the Solaris installation program could not preserve. Then you can reboot the system.

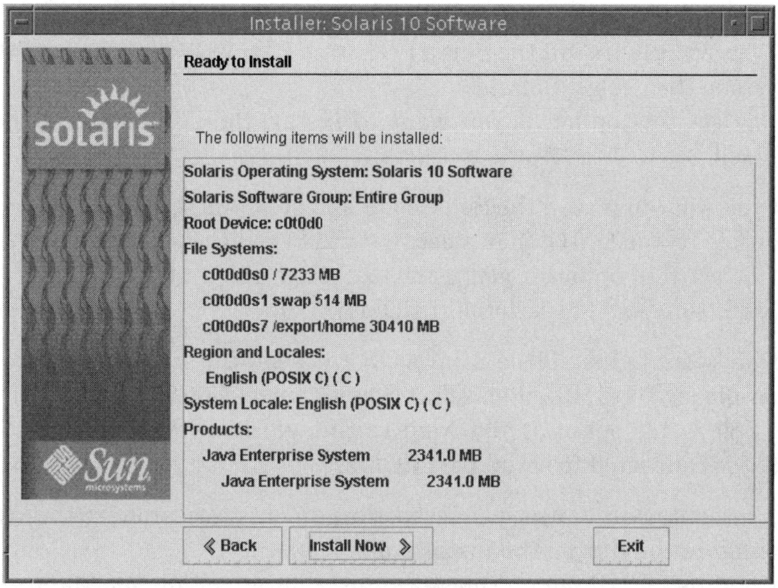

Figure 1.4 Solaris Installation Ready to Install Screen

1.2.2 Installing Solaris on an x86 System

As mentioned, the installation for an x86 system differs slightly from a SPARC Solaris installation.

On an x86 system, when the booting starts, go inside the BIOS (by selecting F2) and change the booting sequence by selecting CD/DVD to boot first. Check your hardware documentations to learn how to enter BIOS and make changes. After making the changes, save and come out. Now, the system will boot with the x86 Solaris 10 Operating System media placed in the disk drive.

The first screen to appear is the GRUB menu:

```
GNU GRUB version 0.95 (631K lower / 2095488K upper memory)
+--------------------------------------------------------------------------+
| Solaris                                                                   |
| Solaris Serial Console ttya                                               |
| Solaris Serial Console ttyb (for 1x50, v60x and v65x)                     |
|                                                                           |
|                                                                           |
+--------------------------------------------------------------------------+
Use the ^ and v keys to select which entry is highlighted.
Press enter to boot the selected OS, 'e' to edit the
commands before booting, or 'c' for a command-line.
```

1. Select the appropriate installation option.

   - If you want to install the Solaris OS from CD or DVD on your current
     system, then select Solaris.
     Select this option if you want to install the system using the default
     values.

   - If you want to install the Solaris OS and send the screen output to serial
     console ttya (COM1), then select Solaris Serial Console ttya.
     Select this option if you want to change the system display to a device
     that is connected to serial port COM1.

   - If you want to install the Solaris OS and send the screen output to serial
     console ttyb (COM2), then select Solaris Serial Console ttyb.
     Select this option if you want to change the system display to a device
     that is connected to serial port COM2.

   - You might want to use specific boot arguments to customize the system
     configuration during the installation.
     On the GRUB menu, select the installation option you want to edit and
     then press Enter.
     Boot commands that are similar to the following text are displayed in
     the GRUB menu.

   ```
   kernel /boot/multiboot kernel/unix -B install_media=cdrom
   module /boot/x86.miniroot
   ```

2. Use the arrow keys to select the boot entry that you want to edit and again
   press Enter.
   The boot command that you want to edit is displayed in the GRUB edit window.

3. Edit the command by typing the boot arguments or options you want to use.
   The command syntax for the Grub edit menu is as follows.

   ```
   grub edit>kernel /boot/multiboot kernel/unix/ \
   install [url|ask] -B options install_media=media_type
   ```

4. To go back to the GRUB menu, press Enter.
   The GRUB menu is displayed. The edits you made to the boot command
   are displayed.

5. To begin the installation, type b in the GRUB menu.
   The Solaris installation program checks the default boot disk for the
   requirements to install or upgrade the system. If the Solaris installation
   cannot detect the system configuration, the program prompts you for any
   missing information.

When the check is completed, the installation selection screen is displayed. Select an installation type.

The installation selection screen displays the following options:

```
Select the type of installation you want to perform:
        1 Solaris Interactive
        2 Custom JumpStart
        3 Solaris Interactive Text (Desktop session)
        4 Solaris Interactive Text (Console session)
        5 Apply driver updates
        6 Single user shell

        Enter the number of your choice followed by the <ENTER> key.
        Alternatively, enter custom boot arguments directly.

        If you wait 30 seconds without typing anything,
        an interactive installation will be started.
```

To install the Solaris OS, choose from the following options.

- To install with the Solaris interactive installation GUI, type 1, then press Enter.

- To install with the interactive text installer in a desktop session, type 3, then press Enter. You can also type `b - text` at the prompt.

  Select this installation type to override the default GUI installer and run the text installer.

- To install with the interactive text installer in a console session, type 4, then press Enter. You can also type `b - text` at the prompt.

  Select this installation type to override the default GUI installer and run the text installer.

The system configures the devices and interfaces and searches for configuration files. The `kdmconfig` utility detects the drivers that are necessary to configure the keyboard, display, and mouse on your system. The installation program begins.

If you want to perform system administration tasks before your installation, choose from the following options.

- To update drivers or install an install time update (ITU), insert the update media, type 5, and then press Enter.

  You might need to update drivers or install an ITU to enable the Solaris OS to run on your system. Follow the instructions for your driver update or ITU to install the update.

- To perform system administration tasks, type 6, then press Enter.

  You might want to launch a single user shell if you need to perform any system administration tasks on your system before you install.

After you perform these system administration tasks, the previous list of options is displayed. Select the appropriate option to continue the installation.

Decide if you need to modify the configuration settings.

> **Note**
>
> If the `kdmconfig` utility cannot detect the video driver for your system, the `kdmconfig` utility selects the 640x480 VGA driver. The Solaris installation GUI cannot be displayed with the 640x480 VGA driver. As a result, the Solaris installation text installer is displayed. To use the Solaris installation GUI, use the `kdmconfig` utility to select the correct video driver for your system.

If you do not need to modify the configuration settings, then let the Window System Configuration for Installation screen time out.

If you need to modify the configuration settings, then follow these steps.

1. Press the ESC key. (Note that you must press the ESC key within five seconds to interrupt the installation and modify device settings.)

   The kdmconfig – Introduction screen is displayed.

2. Examine the configuration information on the kdmconfig – View and Edit Window System Configuration screen and determine which devices you need to edit.

3. Select the device you want to change and press F2_Continue.

4. Select the appropriate driver for the device and press F2_Continue.

5. Repeat the steps for each device you need to change.

6. When you are finished, select No changes needed – Test/Save and Exit and press F2_Continue.

7. The kdmconfig Window System Configuration Test screen appears. Press F2_Continue.

   The screen refreshes and the kdmconfig Window System Configuration Test palette and pattern screen appears. Move the pointer and examine the colors that are shown on the palette to ensure that they are displayed accurately.

   If the colors are not displayed accurately, click No. If possible, press any key on the keyboard or wait until `kdmconfig` exits the kdmconfig Window System Configuration Test screen automatically. Repeat the steps until the colors are displayed accurately and you can move the pointer as expected.

If the colors are displayed accurately, then click Yes.

8. After a few seconds, the Select a Language screen is displayed. Select the language you want to use during the installation, and press Enter.

After this, the screens and the steps are the same as those for the SPARC based Solaris Installer.

1.3 Solaris JumpStart Installation

The custom JumpStart installation method is a command line interface that enables you to automatically install or upgrade several systems based on profiles that you create. The profiles define specific software installation requirements. You can also incorporate shell scripts to include preinstallation and postinstallation tasks. You choose which profile and scripts to use for installation or upgrade. The custom JumpStart installation method installs or upgrades the system, based on the profile and scripts that you select. Also, you can use a `sysidcfg` file to specify configuration information so that the custom JumpStart installation is completely hands-off. The key features of JumpStart install can be summarized as follows:

- Useful for unattended installation of Solaris
- Supports multiple OS releases
- Supports both Sparc and Intel based processors
- Supports multiple configurations for hosts based on a variety of criteria
- Allows for customization via pre/postinstall Bourne shell scripts

1.3.1 Setting up a JumpStart Server

The JumpStart Server performs three separate functions, which can be performed by a single machine or can be spread out across several machines, depending on user requirements.

- Boot Server
  - Uses RARP & BOOTP or DHCP to set the basic network parameters for the machine.

- Uses tftp to load a boot kernel to perform the more complex task of mounting the appropriate directories used to install the Solaris packages.
- Boot server must exist on the same network as client (in other words, they should have the same netmask). Once client has loaded its boot kernel, it can access an Install server across routers.

- Install Server
  - Contains Solaris packages, copied from the Solaris installation CDs or DVD, to be installed.
  - Contains a Solaris miniroot, which the client mounts via NFS. The OS install is performed while running from this miniroot.
  - Multiple Install servers can be used to distribute the load.
    The items mentioned above are together called the Solaris Install Image.

- Configuration Server
  - Contains site-specific information used for a custom JumpStart installation.
  - `sysidcfg` file used to set basic network configuration; this is needed to perform an unattended install. A different `sysidcfg` file is needed for each architecture and OS release.
  - Single configuration server can be used to install on multiple clients, which will be easy to manage.

1.3.2 Creating a Profile Server for Networked Systems

When setting up custom JumpStart installations for systems on the network, you will have to create a directory called a JumpStart directory on the server. The JumpStart directory contains all of the essential custom JumpStart files, for example, the `rules` file, profiles, and pre/postinstall scripts.

The server that contains a JumpStart directory is called a *profile server*. A *profile server* can be on the same system as an *install server* or a *boot server*, or the server can be on a completely different system. A profile server can provide custom JumpStart files for different platforms. For example, an x86 server can provide custom JumpStart files for both SPARC based systems and x86 based systems.

The sequence of commands to create a JumpStart directory follows:

1. `mkdir -m 755 <JumpStart directory>`
2. `share -F nfs -o ro,anon=0 <JumpStart directory>`

3. `cp -r <media_path>/Solaris_10/Misc/JumpStart_sample/*`
   `<JumpStart directory>`
   Where, `<media_path>` is the path to the Solaris Install CD/DVD or
   Solaris Install Image on the local disk.

4. Copy the configuration and profile files to this directory.

The next step is to ensure that the systems on the network can have access
to the profile server. The command that comes in handy to get this done is
`add_install_client`. There are various options for this command. For this
reason, refer to the corresponding man pages to get all of the relevant details.

1.3.2.1 `rules` and `profile` file

The `rules` file is a text file that contains a rule for each group of systems on which
you will install the Solaris OS. Each rule distinguishes a group of systems that are
based on one or more system attributes. Each rule also links each group to a profile. A `profile` is a text file that defines how the Solaris software is to be installed
on each system in the group. This `rules` file will be used to create a `rules.ok` file,
which will be used during JumpStart.

1.3.2.2 Syntax of the `rules` File

The `rules` file must have the following attributes:

- The file must be assigned the name `rules`.
- The file must contain at least one rule.

The `rules` file can contain any of the following:

- Commented text
- Any text that is included after the # symbol on a line is treated by Jump-
  Start as a comment. If a line begins with the # symbol, then the entire line is
  treated as a comment.
- One or more blank lines
- One or more multiline rules

To continue a single rule onto a new line, include a backslash character (\) just
before pressing Return.

1.3.2.3 Creating a `rules` File

To create a `rules` file, do the following:

1. Use a text editor to create a text file that is named `rules` or open the sample `rules` file in the JumpStart directory that you created.
2. Add a rule in the `rules` file for each group of systems on which you want to install the Solaris software.

A rule within a `rules` file must adhere to the following syntax:

```
!<rule_keyword> <rule_value> <&&> !<rule_keyword> <rule_value>
... <begin> <profile>  <finish>
```

The following list explains each element of the `rules` file syntax:

- The exclamation point (!) is a symbol that is used before a keyword to indicate negation.
- `rule_keyword:` A predefined lexical unit or a word that describes a general system attribute, such as host name (hostname) or memory size (memsize). `rule_keyword` is used with the rule value to match a system with the same attribute to a profile.
- `rule_value:` A value that provides the specific system attribute for the corresponding `rule_keyword`.
- `&&:` A symbol (a logical AND) you must use to join rule keyword and rule value pairs in the same rule. During a custom JumpStart installation, a system must match every pair in the rule before the rule matches.
- `begin:` The name of an optional Bourne shell script that can be executed before the installation begins. If no `begin` script exists, you must type a minus sign (−) in this field. All `begin` scripts must be located in the JumpStart directory.

Use a `begin` script to perform one of the following tasks:

- Create derived profiles
- Back up files before upgrading

Important information about `begin` scripts:

- Do not specify something in the script that would prevent the mounting of file systems during an initial or upgrade installation. If the JumpStart program cannot mount the file systems, then an error occurs and installation fails.

- During the installation, output from the `begin` script is deposited in `/tmp/begin.log`. After the installation is completed, the log file is redirected to `/var/sadm/system/logs/begin.log`.
- Ensure that `root` owns the `begin` script and that the permissions are set to 644.
- You can use custom JumpStart environment variables in your `begin` scripts. For a list of environment variables, see `http://docs.sun.com/app/docs/doc/819-2396/6n4mi6eth?a=view`.
- Save `begin` scripts in the JumpStart directory.

The name of a text file that defines how the Solaris software is to be installed on the system when a system matches the rule is the profile. The information in a profile consists of profile keywords and their corresponding profile values. All profiles must be located in the JumpStart directory. You can create different profiles for every rule or the same profile can be used in more than one rule.

A profile consists of one or more profile keywords and their values. Each profile keyword is a command that controls one aspect of how the JumpStart program is to install the Solaris software on a system. For example, the following profile keyword and value specify that the JumpStart program should install the system as a server:

```
system_type server
```

1.3.2.4 Syntax of Profiles

A profile *must* contain the following:

- The `install_type` profile keyword as the first entry
- One keyword per line
- The `root_device` keyword if the systems that are being upgraded by the profile contain more than one root (`/`) file system that can be upgraded

A profile *can* contain the following:

- Commented text.
  Any text that is included after the # symbol on a line is treated by the JumpStart program as commented text. If a line begins with the # symbol, the entire line is treated as a comment.
- One or more blank lines.

1.3.2.5 Creating a Profile

To create a profile, do the following:

1. Use a text editor to create a text file. Any name can be used as the filename for a profile file. Sample profile files will be available in the JumpStart directory that you created.

2. Add profile keywords and values to the profile.
   Profile keywords and their values are case sensitive.

3. Save the profile in the JumpStart directory.

4. Ensure that `root` owns the profile and that the permissions are set to 644.

5. The user can test the profile before using it.

1.3.2.6 Profile Examples

The following two examples show how to use different profile keywords and profile values to control how the Solaris software is installed on a system.

Adding or Deleting Packages   The following listing shows a profile that deletes a package:

```
# profile keywords      profile values
# ----------------      --------------
  install_type          initial_install
  system_type           standalone
  partitioning          default
  filesys               any 512 swap    # specify size of /swap
  cluster               SUNWCprog
  package               SUNWman delete
  cluster               SUNWCacc
```

The variable names in the profile have the following meanings:

- `install_type`: The `install_type` keyword is required in every profile.
- `system_type`: The `system_type` keyword indicates that the system is to be installed as a standalone system.
- `partitioning`: The file system slices are determined by the software to be installed with the value `default`. The size of `swap` is set to 512 MB and is installed on any disk, value `any`.
- `cluster`: The Developer Solaris Software Group, `SUNWCprog`, is installed on the system.

- `package`: If the standard man pages are mounted from the file server, `s_ref`, on the network, the man page packages are not to be installed on the system. The packages that contain the System Accounting utilities are selected to be installed on the system.

Using the `fdisk` Keyword (for an x86 system)   The following listing shows a profile that uses the fdisk keyword:

```
# profile keywords       profile values
# ----------------       ------------------
  install_type           initial_install
  system_type            standalone
  fdisk                  c0t0d0 0x04 delete
  fdisk                  c0t0d0 solaris maxfree
  cluster                SUNWCall
  cluster                SUNWCacc delete
```

The variable names in the profile have the following meanings:

- `fdisk`: All `fdisk` partitions of type DOSOS16 (04 hexadecimal) are deleted from the `c0t0d0` disk.
- `fdisk`: A Solaris `fdisk` partition is created on the largest contiguous free space on the `c0t0d0` disk.
- `cluster`: The Entire Distribution Software Group, `SUNWCall`, is installed on the system.
- `cluster`: The system accounting utilities, `SUNWCacc`, are not to be installed on the system.

1.3.2.7 Testing a Profile

After you create a profile, use the `pfinstall(1M)` command to test the profile. Test the profile before using it to install or upgrade a system. Testing a profile is especially useful when it is being used for an upgrade with reallocation of disk space.

By looking at the output that is generated by `pfinstall`, one can quickly determine if a profile works as intended. For example, use the profile to determine if a system has enough disk space to upgrade to a new release of the Solaris software before performing an upgrade on that system.

1.3.2.8 Profile Test Examples

The following example shows how to use `pfinstall` to test a profile that is named `basic_prof`. The profile is tested against the disk configuration on a system on which the Solaris Express 5/07 software is installed. The `basic_prof` profile is located in the `/JumpStart` directory, and the path to the Solaris Operating System DVD image is specified because removable media services are being used.

```
# cd /JumpStart
# /usr/sbin/install.d/pfinstall -D -c /media/cdrom/pathname basic_prof
```

1.3.2.9 Validating the `rules` File

Before using a profile and `rules` file, the `check` script must be used to validate that the files are set up correctly. If all `rules` and profiles are correctly set up, the `rules.ok` file is created, which is required by the custom JumpStart installation software to match a system to a profile.

The following steps describe what the `check` script does.

1. The `rules` file is checked for syntax.

   `check` verifies that the rule keywords are legitimate and that the *begin*, *class*, and *finish* fields are specified for each rule. The *begin* and *finish* fields can consist of a minus sign (–) instead of a file name.

2. If no errors are found in the `rules` file, then each profile that is specified in the rules is checked for syntax.

3. If no errors are found, then `check` creates the `rules.ok` file from the `rules` file, removes all comments and blank lines, retains all rules, and adds the following comment line at the end:

   ```
   # version=2 checksum=num
   ```

Follow these steps to validate a `rules` file:

1. Ensure that the `check` script is located in the JumpStart directory.

   Note that the `check` script is in the `Solaris_10/Misc/JumpStart_sample` directory on the Solaris Operating System DVD or on the Solaris Software - 1 CD.

2. Change the directory to the JumpStart directory.

3. Run the `check` script to validate the `rules` file:

   ```
   # ./check -p <path> -r <file_name>
   ```

   The `-p <path>` parameter validates the `rules` file by using the `check` script from the Solaris software image instead of the `check` script from the system you are using. *path* is the Solaris Install Image on a local disk or a mounted Solaris Operating System DVD/CD.

Use this option to run the most recent version of `check` if your system is running a previous version of Solaris.

The `-r <file_name>` paremeter specifies a `rules` file other than the one that is named `rules`. Using this option, you can test the validity of a rule before you integrate the rule into the `rules` file.

As the `check` script runs, the script reports the checking of the validity of the `rules` file and each profile.

If no errors are encountered, then the script displays the following o/p:

```
The custom JumpStart configuration is ok
```

4. Ensure that `root` owns the `rules.ok` file and that the permissions are set to 644.

The *finish* script is an optional Bourne shell script that can be executed after the installation is completed. If no finish script exists, then you must type a minus sign (–) in this field. All finish scripts must be located in the JumpStart directory. A finish script performs tasks after the Solaris software is installed on a system, but before the system reboots. You can use finish scripts only when using custom JumpStart to install Solaris.

Tasks that can be performed with a `finish` script include the following:

- Adding files
- Adding individual packages or patches in addition to the ones that are installed in a particular software group
- Customizing the root environment
- Setting the system's root password
- Installing additional software

1.3.2.10 Important Information about Finish Scripts

- The Solaris installation program mounts the system's file systems on `/a`. The file systems remain mounted on `/a` until the system reboots. A finish script can be used to add, change, or remove files from the newly installed file system hierarchy by modifying the file systems that are respective to `/a`.
  - During the installation, output from the finish script is deposited in `/tmp/finish.log`. After the installation is completed, the log file is redirected to `/var/sadm/system/logs/finish.log`.
- Ensure that root owns the finish script and that the permissions are set to 644.

- Custom JumpStart environment variables can be used in finish scripts.
- Save finish scripts in the JumpStart directory.

1.3.2.11 Example of Adding Packages or Patches with a Finish Script

A finish script can be used to automatically add packages or patches after the Solaris software is installed on a system. Note that, when using the pkgadd(1M) or patchadd(1M) commands in finish scripts, use the -R option (alternate root) to specify /a as the alternate root.

1.3.3 Performing a Custom JumpStart Installation

This section describes how to perform a custom JumpStart installation on a SPARC based or an x86 based system. There are some subtle differences between the SPARC and x86 systems with regard to the steps to be followed during installation. So, we are providing all the steps for both the architectures separately. You should follow the procedures based on the architecture on which the installation is done.

During a custom JumpStart installation, the JumpStart program attempts to match the system that is being installed to the rules in the rules.ok file. The JumpStart program reads the rules from the first rule through the last. A match occurs when the system that is being installed matches all the system attributes that are defined in a rule. When a system matches a rule, the JumpStart program stops reading the rules.ok file and begins to install the system based on the matched rule's profile.

1.3.3.1 SPARC: Performing an Installation or Upgrade With the Custom JumpStart Program

To perform an installation or upgrade with the custom JumpStart program when the system is part of a network, follow these steps.

1. Ensure that an Ethernet connector or similar network adapter is attached to your system.

2. If the system is connected through a tip(1) line, ensure that the console window display is at least 80 columns wide and 24 rows long. For more information on tip lines, refer to refer to the tip(1) man page.

   To find out the current dimensions of the tip window, use the stty(1) command. For more information on the stty(1) command refer to the stty(1) man page.

3. When using the system's DVD-ROM or CD-ROM drive to install the Solaris software, insert the Solaris Operating System for SPARC Platforms DVD or the Solaris Software for SPARC Platforms - 1 CD in the drive.

4. When using a profile diskette, insert the profile diskette in the system's diskette drive.

5. Boot the system.

To perform an installation or upgrade with the custom JumpStart program on a new system that is out of the box, follow these steps.

1. Turn on the system.

2. To install or upgrade an existing system, shut down the system. At the `ok` prompt, type the appropriate options for the `boot` command. The syntax of the `boot` command is the following.

   ok **boot** [*cd-dvd*|**net**] - **install** [**url**|**ask**] *options*

   For example, by typing the following command, the OS is installed over the network by using a JumpStart profile.

```
ok boot net - install
http://131.141.2.32/JumpStart/config.tar
```

If the system is not preconfigured by using information in the `sysidcfg` file, then when prompted, answer the questions about system configuration. Follow the instructions on the screen to install the software.

When the JumpStart program finishes installing the Solaris software, the system reboots automatically.

After the installation is finished, installation logs are saved in the following directories:

```
/var/sadm/system/logs
/var/sadm/install/logs
```

1.3.3.2 x86: Performing an Installation or Upgrade With the Custom JumpStart Program

Use this procedure to install the Solaris OS for an x86 based system with the GRUB menu. If the system is part of a network, then ensure that an Ethernet connector or similar network adapter is attached to your system. To install a system that is connected through a `tip(1)` line, ensure that your window display is at least 80 columns wide and 24 rows long.

To determine the current dimensions of your `tip` window, use the `stty(1)` command.

1. When using a profile diskette, insert the profile diskette in the system's diskette drive.

2. Decide how to boot the system.

   - To boot from the Solaris Operating System DVD or the Solaris Software - 1 CD, insert the disk. Your system's BIOS must support booting from a DVD or CD.

   - To boot from the network, use Preboot Execution Environment (PXE) network boot. The system must support PXE. Enable the system to use PXE by using the system's BIOS setup tool or the network adapter's configuration setup tool.

   - For booting from a DVD or CD, you have the option to change the boot setting in your system's BIOS and set to boot from DVD or CD media. See your hardware documentation for instructions.

3. If the system is off, then turn the system on. If the system is on, then reboot the system.

   The GRUB menu is displayed. This menu provides a list of boot entries.

```
GNU GRUB version 0.95 (631K lower / 2095488K upper memory)
+----------------------------------------------------------------------+
|Solaris 10 10/08 image_directory                                      |
|Solaris 10 5/08 Serial Console tty                                    |
|Solaris 10 5/08 Serial Console ttyb (for 1x50, v60x and v65)          |
+----------------------------------------------------------------------+
Use the ^ and v keys to select which entry is highlighted. Press
enter to boot the selected OS, 'e' to edit the commands before
booting, or 'c' for a command-line.
```

The *image_directory* is the name of the directory where the installation image is located. The path to the JumpStart files was defined with the `add_install_client` command and the `-c` option.

Note

Instead of booting from the GRUB entry now, one can edit the boot entry. After editing the GRUB entry, then perform the JumpStart installation.

4. At the prompt, perform one of the following instructions:

```
Select the type of installation you want to perform:

            1 Solaris Interactive
            2 Custom JumpStart
            3 Solaris Interactive Text (Desktop session)
            4 Solaris Interactive Text (Console session)
            5 Apply driver updates
            6 Single User Shell
         Enter the number of your choice.
         Please make a selection (1-6).
```

5. To select the custom JumpStart method, type 2 and press Enter.

The JumpStart installation begins.

When the JumpStart program finishes installing the Solaris software, the system reboots automatically. Also, the GRUB menu.lst file is automatically updated. The instance of Solaris that you have installed appears in the next use of the GRUB menu.

After the installation is finished, installation logs are saved in a file. You can find the installation logs in the following directories:

- /var/sadm/system/logs
- /var/sadm/install/logs

1.4 Upgrading a Solaris System

As mentioned earlier in this chapter, there are three methods for upgrading the Solaris OS: standard installation, custom JumpStart, and Solaris Live Upgrade. For a UFS file system, you can upgrade a system by using any of these different upgrade methods. For a ZFS root pool, you must use Solaris Live Upgrade. ZFS will be the subject of the Live Upgrade section that follows.

Backing up your existing file systems before you upgrade to the Solaris OS is highly recommended. If you copy file systems to removable media, such as tape, you can safeguard against data loss, damage, or corruption.

- For detailed instructions on backing up your system, refer to the Solaris 10 version of the *System Administration Guide: Devices and Files Systems* at http://docs.sun.com.

- To back up your system when non-global zones are installed, see the Solaris 10 version of the *System Administration Guide: Solaris Containers-Resource Management and Solaris Zones* at http://docs.sun.com.

In previous releases, the restart mechanism enabled you to continue an upgrade after a loss of power or other similar problem. Starting with the Solaris 10 10/08 release, the restart mechanism is unreliable. If you have a problem, then your upgrade might not restart.

You cannot upgrade your system to a software group that is not installed on the system. For example, if you previously installed the End User Solaris Software Group on your system, then you cannot use the upgrade option to upgrade to the Developer Solaris Software Group. However, during the upgrade you can add software to the system that is not part of the currently installed software group.

1.5 Solaris Live Upgrade

Solaris Live Upgrade provides a method of upgrading a system while the system continues to operate. While your current boot environment is running, you can duplicate the boot environment and then upgrade the duplicate. Or, instead of upgrading, you can install a Solaris Flash archive on a boot environment. The original system configuration remains fully functional and unaffected by the upgrade or installation of an archive. When you are ready, you can activate the new boot environment by rebooting the system. If a failure occurs, you can quickly revert to the original boot environment with a simple reboot. This switch eliminates the normal downtime of the test and evaluation process.

Solaris Live Upgrade enables you to duplicate a boot environment without affecting the currently running system. You can then do the following:

- Upgrade a system.
- Change the current boot environment's disk configuration to different file system types, sizes, and layouts on the new boot environment.
- Maintain numerous boot environments with different images. For example, you can create one boot environment that contains current patches and create another boot environment that contains an Update release.

In this chapter, we will focus on upgrading by creating ZFS root file systems from an existing ZFS root pool. The ability to boot from a ZFS root pool was introduced in the Solaris 10 10/08 update.

When creating a new boot environment within the same ZFS root pool, the `lucreate` command creates a snapshot from the source boot environment and then a clone is made from the snapshot. The creation of the snapshot and clone is almost instantaneous and the disk space used is minimal. The amount of space ultimately required depends on how many files are replaced as part of the upgrade process. The snapshot is read-only, but the clone is a read-write copy of the snapshot. Any changes made to the clone boot environment are not reflected in either the snapshot or the source boot environment from which the snapshot was made.

The following example shows the `lucreate` command creating a new boot environment in the same root pool. The `lucreate` command names the currently running boot environment with the `-c zfsBE` option, and the `-n new-zfsBE` command creates the new boot environment. The `zfs list` command shows the ZFS datasets with the new boot environment and snapshot.

```
# lucreate -c zfsBE -n new-zfsBE
# zfs list
AME                            USED   AVAIL  REFER   MOUNTPOINT
rpool                          9.29G  57.6G    20K   /rpool
rpool/ROOT                     5.38G  57.6G    18K   /rpool/ROOT
rpool/ROOT/zfsBE               5.38G  57.6G   551M
rpool/ROOT/zfsBE@new-zfsBE     66.5K      -   551M   -
rpool/ROOT/new-zfsBE           5.38G  57.6G   551M
/tmp/.alt.luupdall.110034
rpool/dump                     1.95G      -  1.95G   -
rpool/swap                     1.95G      -  1.95G   -
```

After you have created a boot environment, you can perform an upgrade on the boot environment. The upgrade does not affect any files in the active boot environment. When you are ready, you activate the new boot environment, which then becomes the current boot environment.

References

As promised, this section contains an installation planning checklist (see Table 1.3). You can find an abundance of further information—reference, procedures, and examples—in the Solaris 10 documentation at `http://docs.sun.com`. For instance, the Solaris Flash archive feature mentioned previously is not covered in this book, but you can find all you need to know about it at `http://docs.sun.com`.

Table 1.3 Solaris Install – Initial Install Checklist

Question Asked		Description	Answer
Network connection		Is the system connected to a network?	Networked/ Non-networked
DHCP		Do you want to use Dynamic Host Configuration Protocol (DHCP) to configure network interfaces?	Yes/No
If "No" is selected for DHCP, then static address is to be provided.	IP Address	Supply the IP address for the system.	
	Subnet	If you are not using DHCP, is the system part of a subnet? If yes, what is the netmask of the subnet?	255.255.255.0
	IPv6	Do you want to enable IPv6 on this machine?	Yes/No
Host Name		Host name that you choose for the system. In case of DHCP, this question is not asked.	
Kerberos		Do you want to configure Kerberos security on this machine? If yes, supply the following information: 0Default Realm: 1Administration Server: 2First KDC: 3(Optional) Additional KDCs 4The Kerberos service is a client-server architecture that provides secure transactions over networks.	Yes/No
Name Service		Which name service should this system use? A naming service stores information such as userid, password, groupid, etc., in a central place, which enables users, machines, and applications to communicate across the network.	NIS+/NIS/DNS/ LDAP/None
NIS+ or NIS		Do you want to specify a name server or let the installation program find one? If you want to specify a name server, provide the following information.	Specify One/Find One
		Server's host name:	
		Server's IP Address:	

Table 1.3 Solaris Install – Initial Install Checklist (*continued*)

Question Asked	Description	Answer
DNS	The domain name system (DNS) is the name service that the Internet provides for TCP/IP networks. DNS provides host names to the IP address service translation. Provide IP addresses for the DNS server. You must enter at least one IP address (up to three addresses are allowed) and search domains.	
	Server's IP Address:	
	List of search domains:	
LDAP	Lightweight Directory Access Protocol (LDAP) defines a relatively simple protocol for updating and searching directories that are running over TCP/IP. Provide the following information about your LDAP profile.	
	Profile Name:	
	Profile Server:	
	If you specify a proxy credential level in your LDAP profile, provide this information also.	
	Proxy-bind distinguished name:	
	Proxy-bind password:	
Default Route	Do you want to specify a default route IP address or let the Solaris installation program find one? The default route provides a bridge that forwards traffic between two physical networks. When the system is rebooted, the specified IP address becomes the default route. Solaris installer can detect the default route, if the system is on a subnet that has a router that advertises itself by using the ICMP router discovery protocol. You can choose None if you do not have a router or do not want the software to detect an IP address at this time. The software automatically tries to detect an IP address on reboot.	Detect one/ Specify one/None

continues

Table 1.3 Solaris Install – Initial Install Checklist (*continued*)

Question Asked	Description	Answer
Time Zone	How do you want to specify your default time zone?	Geographic region Offset from GMT Time zone file
Root Password	Provide the root password for the system.	
Locales	For which geographic regions do you want to install support?	
SPARC: Power Management (only available on SPARC systems that support Power Management)	Do you want to use Power Management? Note that, if your system has Energy Star version 3 or later, you are not prompted for this information.	Yes/No
Automatic reboot	Reboot automatically after software installation?	Yes/No
CD/DVD ejection	Eject CD/DVD automatically after software installation?	Yes/No
Default or Custom Install	Do you want to customize the installation or go ahead with default installation? Select Default installation to format the entire hard disk and install a preselected set of software. Select Custom installation to modify the hard disk layout and select the software that you want to install. Note: This option is not available in text installer.	Default installation/ Custom installation
Software Group	Which Solaris Software Group do you want to install?	0Entire Plus OEM 1Entire 2Developer 3End User 4Core 5Reduced Networking

Table 1.3 Solaris Install – Initial Install Checklist (*continued*)

Question Asked	Description	Answer
Custom Package Selection	Do you want to add or remove software packages from the Solaris Software Group that you install? Note that, if you want select packages to add or remove, you will need to know about software dependencies and how Solaris software is packaged.	
Select Disks	On which disks do you want to install the Solaris software?	
x86: `fdisk` partitioning	Do you want to create, delete, or modify a Solaris `fdisk` partition? Each disk that is selected for file system layout must have a Solaris `fdisk` partition.	
	Select Disks for `fdisk` Partition Customization?	Yes/No
	Customize `fdisk` partitions?	Yes/No
Preserve Data	Do you want to preserve any data that exists on the disks where you are installing the Solaris software?	Yes/No
File Systems Auto-layout	Do you want the installation program to automatically lay out file systems on your disks? If no, you must provide file system configuration information.	Yes/No
Mount Remote File Systems	Do you want to install software located on another file system? If yes, provide the following information about the remote file system.	Yes/No
	Server:	
	IP Address:	
	Remote File System:	
	Local Mount Point:	

2

Boot, Service Management, and Shutdown

This chapter describes how the Solaris 10 operating system boots and explains options users and administrators have for changing the boot process. The chapter also describes the two methods of shutting down a Solaris 10 system. In addition, it describes the Service Management Facility (SMF) utility for managing system services. Some of the information in this chapter describes Solaris boot processes that apply to both the x86 and SPARC platform, but the chapter focuses primarily on booting the x86 platform.

2.1 Boot

Like most contemporary operating systems, Solaris initialization begins with the bootloader, continues with the kernel, and finishes with user-mode programs.

2.1.1 The Bootloader

On x86 platforms, the Solaris 10 OS is designed to be loaded by GNU Grand Unified Bootloader (GRUB). By default, the bootloader displays a boot menu with two entries:

```
Solaris 10 10/08 s10x_u6wos_07b X86
Solaris failsafe
```

When a Solaris boot entry is chosen, GRUB loads the kernel specified by the entry into memory and transfers control to it. The entry also directs GRUB to load a *boot archive* with copies of the kernel modules and configuration files essential for startup. See the boot(1M) manual page for more about the boot archive. The failsafe entry facilitates troubleshooting and recovery.

Note that the GRUB that is supplied with Solaris contains extensions to GNU GRUB required to load the Solaris OS.

2.1.2 The Kernel

The kernel starts by initializing the hardware, clearing the console, and printing a banner:

```
SunOS Release 5.10 Version Generic_137138-06 64-bit
Copyright 1983-2008 Sun Microsystems, Inc.  All rights reserved.
Use is subject to license terms.
```

After hardware initialization, the kernel mounts the root file system and executes user-mode programs.

2.1.3 User-Mode Programs

As with all UNIX operating systems, most Solaris functionality is driven by user-mode programs. The kernel starts them by executing the /sbin/init file in the first process, which always has process ID ("pid") 1.

Like other UNIX operating systems, init reads the /etc/inittab configuration file and executes programs according to it. Unlike most UNIX operating systems, the default inittab does not instruct init to execute init scripts in the /etc/rc*.d directories. Instead, the processes that implement most system-delivered functionality on Solaris are started by the service management facility or SMF. Accordingly, the Solaris init contains special-purpose functionality to start and restart (as necessary) the daemons that implement SMF. In turn, the facility is responsible for executing the init scripts. SMF is described in more detail in the next section.

Users accustomed to the Solaris 9 operating system will notice that the Solaris 10 operating system displays much less information on the console during boot. This is because SMF now starts service daemons with standard output directed to log files in /var/svc/log, rather than the console.

Near the end of startup, SMF will execute the `ttymon` program on the console device at the direction of the `console-login` SMF service:

```
examplehost login:
```

If the `SUNWdtlog` package was installed, SMF will also start an X server on the console device and the `dtlogin` greeter on the display as part of the `cde-login` SMF service as shown in Figure 2.1.

Figure 2.1 SMF Login

2.1.4 GRUB Extensions

The GRUB installed by Solaris differs from standard GNU GRUB in a few ways:

- It can read Solaris UFS file systems (which differ from BSD UFS file systems).
- It recognizes the `kernel$` and `module$` commands (since 10/08 release).

- It can read Solaris ZFS pools, and recognizes the `bootfs` command (since 10/08 release).

- It recognizes the `findroot` command (since 10/08 release).

As a result, versions of GRUB not delivered with Solaris will generally not be able to boot a Solaris system image.

2.1.5 Modifying Boot Behavior

The Solaris kernel can accept a string of boot arguments from the bootloader. Recognized arguments are listed in the `kernel`(1M) manual page. Commonly used arguments are shown in Table 2.1.

Table 2.1 Boot Arguments

Argument	Description
`-k`	Start the kernel debugger, `kmdb`, as soon as possible. See the `kmdb`(1M) manual page and later in this chapter.
`-s`	Single-user mode. Start only basic services and present an `sulogin` prompt.
`-v`	Be verbose by printing extra information on the console.
`-m verbose`	Instruct the SMF daemons to be verbose.

The boot arguments for a single boot sequence can be set from the GRUB menu. Select an entry and press the e key. GRUB will display the entry editing screen, as shown in Figure 2.2.

Figure 2.3 shows the GRUB edit menu. In this menu, you can modify the kernel behavior for a specified boot entry. This menu is accessed at boot time, by typing e to interrupt the boot process, then with the boot entry selected, typing e again to enter the edit menu for the selected entry.

Select the line beginning with `kernel` and press the e key.

After the path for `unix`, add the boot arguments. Press `enter` to commit the change and b to boot the temporarily modified entry.

Boot arguments for a single boot can also be set on the `reboot` command line. See the `reboot`(1M) manual page.

Boot arguments can be installed permanently by modifying `menu.1st` file. Use `bootadm list-menu` to locate the file in the file system.

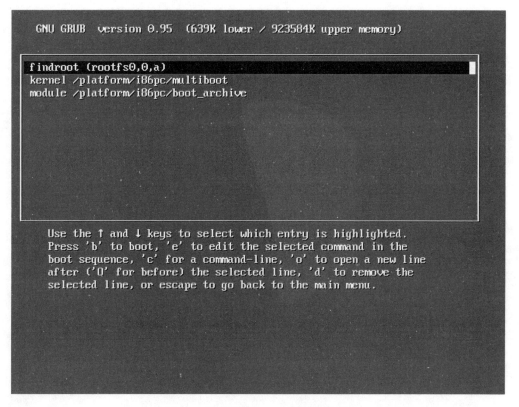

Figure 2.2 Editing a GRUB Entry

2.1.6 Run Levels

The Solaris OS defines eight *run levels*. Each run level is associated with particular system behaviors (see Table 2.2).

By default, Solaris boots into run level 3. This is taken from the `initdefault` entry of the `/etc/inittab` configuration file (see `inittab(4)`). It can be changed to a single boot sequence by specifying `-s` in the boot arguments (refer to Table 2.2).

To change the run level while the operating system is running, use the `init` command. See its manual page for a detailed description of run levels.

2.1.7 Troubleshooting

If you encounter problems during the boot process, check the tools and solutions described here for a remedy.

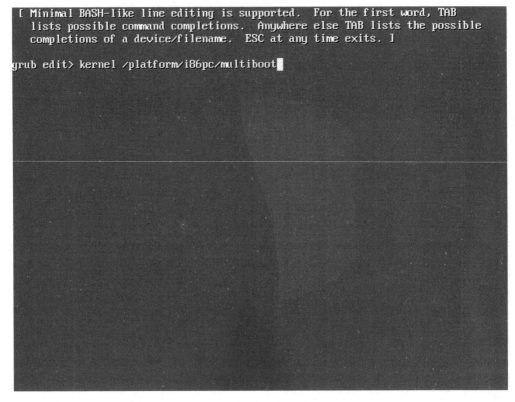

Figure 2.3 Editing the GRUB Menu at Boot Time

Table 2.2 Run Levels and Corresponding System Behaviors

Run Level	Behavior
S	Single-user mode. No login services running except for `sulogin` on the console.
0	The operating system is shut down and the computer is running its firmware.
1	Like S, except applications which deliver into `/etc/rc1.d` are also started.
2	Multi-user mode. Local login services running. Some applications—usually local—may be running.
3	Multi-user server mode. All configured services and applications running, including remote login and network-visible applications.
4	Alternative multi-user server mode. Third-party applications may behave differently than under run level 3.
5	Powered off.
6	Reboot.

2.1.7.1 Milestone none

If a problem prevents user programs from starting normally, the Solaris 10 OS can be instructed to start as few programs as possible during boot by specifying `-m  milestone=none` in the boot arguments. Once logged in, `svcadm milestone all` can be used to instruct SMF to continue initialization as usual.

2.1.7.2 Using the kmdb Command

If a problem prevents the kernel from starting normally, then it can be started with the assembly-level kernel debugger, `kmdb`. When the `-k` option is specified in the boot arguments, the kernel loads `kmdb` as soon as possible. If the kernel panics, `kmdb` will stop the kernel and present a debugging prompt on the console. If the `-d` option is also specified, `kmdb` will stop the kernel and present a debugging prompt as soon as it finishes loading. For more information, see the `kmdb`(1) manual page.

2.1.7.3 Failsafe boot

The second GRUB menu entry installed by default is labeled "failsafe". Selecting it will start the same kernel, but with the failsafe boot archive. It contains copies of the kernel modules and configuration files as delivered by the installer, without any user modifications. By default it also launches an interactive program that facilitates updating the normal boot archive for instances of the Solaris OS found on the disk.

2.2 Service Management Facility

The service management facility provides means for computer administrators to observe and control software services. Each service is modeled as an *instance* of an SMF *service*, which allows for a single service implementation to be executed multiple times simultaneously, as many are capable of doing.

Services and service instances are named by character strings. For example, the service implemented by `cron`(1M) is named `system/cron`, and Solaris includes an instance of it named `default`. Tools usually refer to service instances with fault management resource identifiers, or FMRIs, which combine the service name and the instance name. The FMRI of the default instance of `cron` is `svc:/system/cron:default`. The service instances known to SMF can be listed with the `svcs -a` command. For convenience, most SMF tools accept abbreviations for service FMRIs – see `svcadm`(1M)'s manual page.

Service implementations are controlled by the SMF *service manager*, `svc.startd`(1M). The current status and other information for service instances are printed by the svcs command. The -1 (ell) option produces long output, like the following:

```
examplehost$ svcs -l cron
fmri         svc:/system/cron:default
name         clock daemon (cron)
enabled      true
state        online
next_state   none
state_time   Mon Mar 16 18:25:34 2009
logfile      /var/svc/log/system-cron:default.log
restarter    svc:/system/svc/restarter:default
contract_id  66
dependency   require_all/none svc:/system/filesystem/local (online)
dependency   require_all/none svc:/milestone/name-services (online)
```

The first line, labeled fmri, contains the full FMRI of the service instance. The name line provides a short description. The remaining output is explained later.

2.2.1 enabled

The service manager considers each service instance to be *enabled* or *disabled*. When enabled, the service manager will attempt to start a service instance's implementation and restart it as necessary; when disabled, the facility will try to stop the implementation if it has been started. Whether a service is enabled can be changed with svcadm's enable and disable subcommands.

2.2.2 state, next_state, and state_time

To decide whether a service implementation should be started, the service manager always considers each service instance to be in one of six states.

disabled	The service implementation has not been started, or has been stopped.
offline	The service is not running, but will be started when its dependencies are met.
online	The service has started successfully.
degraded	The service is running, but at reduced functionality or performance.
maintenance	An operation failed and administrative intervention is required.
uninitialized	The service's restarter has not taken control of the service (restarters are explained later in this chapter).

While a service is in a stable state, the `next_state` field is `none`. While an operation to change the state of a service is incomplete, `next_state` will contain the target state. For example, before a service implementation is started the service manager sets the `next_state` to `online`, and if the operation succeeds, the service manager changes `state` and `next_state` to `online` and `none`, respectively.

The `state_time` line lists the time the `state` or `next_state` fields were updated. This time is not necessarily the last time the service instance changed states since SMF allows transitions to the same state.

2.2.3 `logfile`

The service manager logs some information about service events to a separate file for each service instance. This field gives the name of that file.

2.2.3.1 `restarter` and `contract_id`

The service's restarter interacts with the service's implementation, and the contract ID identifies the processes that implement the service. Details of both are explained in Section 2.2.5, "How SMF Interacts with Service Implementations."

2.2.4 `dependency`

These lines list the dependencies of the service instance. SMF dependencies represent dependencies of the service implementation on other services. The service manager uses dependencies to determine when to start, and sometimes when to stop, service instances.

Each dependency has a grouping and a set of FMRIs. The grouping dictates when a dependency should be considered satisfied. SMF recognizes four dependency groupings.

`require_all`	All services indicated by the FMRIs must be in the `online` or `degraded` states to satisfy the dependency.
`require_any`	At least one cited service must be `online` or `degraded` to satisfy the dependency.
`optional_all`	The dependency is considered satisfied when all cited services are `online`, `degraded`, `disabled`, in the `maintenance` state, or are `offline` and will eventually come `online` without administrative intervention. Services that don't exist are ignored.
`exclude_all`	All cited services must be `disabled` or in the `maintenance` state to satisfy the dependency.

When a service is enabled, the service manager will not start it until all of its dependencies are satisfied. Until then, the service will remain in the `offline` state.

The service manager can also stop services according to dependencies. This behavior is governed by the `restart_on` value of the dependency, which may take one of four values.

`none`	Do not stop the service if the dependency service is stopped.
`error`	Stop the service if the dependency is stopped due to a software or hardware error.
`restart`	Stop the service if the dependency is stopped for any reason.
`refresh`	Stop the service if the dependency is stopped or its configuration is changed (refreshed).

2.2.5 How SMF Interacts with Service Implementations

SMF manages most services through daemons, though it manages some with what is called "transient service." In cases where neither daemons nor transient service is appropriate, SMF allows for alternative service starters.

2.2.5.1 Services Implemented by Daemons

SMF starts a service implemented by daemons by executing its *start method*. The start method is a program specified by the service author; its path and arguments are stored in the SCF data for the service. (SCF is described in the next section.) If the method exits with status 0, the service manager infers that the service has started successfully (the daemons were started in the background and are ready to provide service) and transitions its state to `online`. If the method exits with status 1, the service manager concludes that the service failed and re-executes the method. If the method fails three times consecutively, then the service manager gives up, transitions the service to the `maintenance` state, and appends a note to the service's SMF log file in `/var/svc/log`. In all cases, the method is started with its standard output redirected to the service's SMF log file. The service daemon will inherit this unless the author wrote the start method to do otherwise.

After starting a service implemented by a daemon, the service manager will monitor its processes. If all processes exit, then the service manager will infer that the service has failed and will attempt to restart it by re-executing the start method. If this happens more than ten times in ten seconds, then the service manager will give up and transition the service to the `maintenance` state. Processes are monitored through a *process contract* with the kernel. Contracts are a new kernel abstraction documented in contract(4); process-type contracts are documented in process(4). Services treated by the service manager in this way are referred to as *contract services.*

To stop a contract service, the service manager executes the *stop method* specified by the service author. Stop methods exit with status 0 to signal that the service has been stopped successfully, in which case the service manager will transition the service to the disabled state. However, the facility uses process contracts to ensure that a contract service has been fully stopped. If a service's stop method exits with status 0 but processes remain in the contract, then svc.startd will send SIGKILL signals to the processes once each second until they have exited. Each time, svc.startd records a note in the service's /var/svc/log file.

The processes associated with a contract service can be listed with the svcs -p command. To examine the contract itself, obtain its ID number from the svcs -v command or the contract_id line of the output of svcs -l and pass it to the ctstat(1) command.

2.2.5.2 Services Not Implemented by Daemons

Some services are not implemented by daemons. For example, the file system services (e.g., svc:/system/filesystem/minimal:default) represent behavior implemented by the kernel. Instead of representing whether the behavior is available or not, the file system services represent whether parts of the file system namespace that are allowed to be separate file systems (/var, /var/adm, /tmp) have been mounted and are available. Ensuring this is the case does require programs to be executed (e.g., mount(1M)), but the service should still be considered online once those programs have exited successfully.

For such services, svc.startd provides the *transient service* model. After the start method exits with status 0, the service is transitioned to online and any processes it may have started in the background are not monitored.

2.2.5.3 Alternative Service Models

If a service author requires SMF to interact with his service in still a different way, then the facility allows him to provide or specify an alternative *service restarter.* When an author specifies a service restarter for a service, the facility *delegates* interaction with the service to the restarter, which must itself be an SMF service.

Solaris 10 includes a single alternative restarter: inetd(1M). inetd defers execution of a service's daemon until a request has been received by a network device. Before then, inetd reports services delegated to it to be online to signify readiness, even though no daemons may have been started. Operations specific to inetd-supervised services can be requested with the inetadm(1M) command.

The restarter for a service is listed by the svcs -l command. Services governed by the models provided directly by the service manager are listed with the special FMRI of svc:/system/svc/restarter:default as their restarter.

Since restarters usually require distinct SCF configuration for the services they control, the facility does not provide a way for an administrator to change the restarter specified for a service.

2.2.6 The Service Configuration Facility

The enabled status, dependencies, method specifications, and other information for each service instance are stored in a specialized database introduced with SMF called the service configuration facility. SCF is implemented by the libscf(3LIB) library and svc.configd(1M) daemon, and svccfg(1M) provides the most direct access to SCF for command line users.

In addition to SMF-specific configuration, the libscf(3LIB) interfaces are documented so that services can store service-specific configuration in SCF as well.

2.2.7 Health and Troubleshooting

Standard records of enabled status and states for each service permit an easy check for malfunctioning services. The svcs -x command, without arguments, identifies services that are enabled but not in the online state and attempts to diagnose why they are not running. When all enabled services are online, svcs -x exits without printing anything.

When a service managed by SMF is enabled but not running, investigation should start by retrieving the service manager's state for the service, usually with the svcs command:

```
examplehost$ svcs cron
STATE          STIME    FMRI
online         Mar_16   svc:/system/cron:default
```

If the state is maintenance, then the service manager's most recent attempt to start (or stop) the service failed. The svcs -x command may explain precisely why the service was placed in that state. The SMF log file for the service in /var/svc/log should also provide more information. Note that many services still maintain their own log files in service-specific locations.

When the problem with a service in the maintenance state is resolved, the svcadm clear command should be executed for the service. The service manager will re-evaluate the service's dependencies and start it, if appropriate.

If a service isn't running because it is in the offline state, SMF considers its dependencies to be unsatisfied. svcs -l will display the dependencies and their states, but if one of them is also offline, then following the chain can be tedious. svcs -x, when invoked for an offline service, will automatically follow dependency links to find the root cause of the problem, even if it is multiple links away.

2.2.8 Service Manifests

To deliver an SMF service, the author must deliver a *service manifest* file into a subdirectory of `/var/svc/manifest`. These files conform to the XML file format standard and describe the SCF data SMF requires to start and interact with the service. On each boot, the service manifests in `/var/svc/manifest` are loaded into the SCF database by the special `svc:/system/manifest-import:default` service.

Service manifests can also be imported directly into the SCF repository with the `svccfg import` command. It allows new SMF services to be created, including SMF services to control services that were not adapted to SMF by their authors.

2.2.9 Backup and Restore of SCF Data

SMF provides three methods for backing up SCF data.

2.2.9.1 Automatic

During each boot, SMF automatically stores a backup of persistent SCF data in a file whose path begins with `/etc/svc/repository-boot-`. Furthermore, whenever SMF notices that a file in a subdirectory of `/var/svc/manifest` has changed, the facility creates another backup of persistent SCF data after it has been updated according to the new files; the names of these backups begin with `/etc/svc/repository-manifest_import-`. In both cases, only the four most recent backups are retained and older copies are deleted. Two symbolic links, `repository-boot` and `repository-manifest_import`, are updated to refer to the latest copy of the respective backup type.

The SCF database may be restored by copying one of these files to `/etc/svc/repository.db`. However, this must not be done while the `svc.configd` daemon is executing.

2.2.9.2 Repository-wide

All persistent SCF data may be extracted with the `svccfg archive` command. It can be restored with the `svccfg restore` command.

2.2.9.3 Service-specific

The SCF data associated with the instances of a particular service may be extracted with the `svccfg extract` command. Note that the command only accepts service FMRIs and not instance FMRIs. To restore the service instances for such a file, delete the service with `svccfg delete` and import the file with `svccfg import`.

2.3 Shutdown

Solaris provides two main mechanisms to shut down the operating system. They differ in how applications are stopped.

2.3.1 Application-Specific Shutdown

With appropriate arguments, the shutdown(1M) and init(1M) commands begin operating system shutdown by instructing SMF to stop all services. The facility complies by shutting down services in reverse-dependency order, so that each service is stopped before the services it depends on are stopped since Solaris 10 11/06 release. Upon completion, the kernel flushes the file system buffers and powers off the computer, unless directed otherwise by the arguments.

As in Solaris 9, the kill init scripts (/etc/init.d/K*) for the appropriate runlevel are run at the beginning of shutdown. This is in parallel with SMF's shutdown sequence.

If an SMF service takes longer to stop than the service's author specified, SMF will complain and start killing the service's processes once every second until they have exited.

2.3.2 Application-Independent Shutdown

The reboot(1M), halt(1M), and poweroff(1M) commands skip both the SMF shutdown sequence explained previously and the init scripts and instead stop applications by sending a SIGTERM signal to all processes. After a 5 second wait, any remaining processes are sent a SIGKILL signal before the kernel flushes the file system buffers and stops. Since these commands don't invoke the stop procedures provided by application authors, this method has a chance of stopping applications before they have written all of their data to nonvolatile storage.

3

Software Management: Packages

This chapter describes packages and package tools and includes step-by-step procedures for installing and removing packages.

3.1 Managing Software Packages

Software management involves installing or removing software products. Sun and its third-party independent software vendors (ISVs) deliver software as a collection of one or more packages. The following sections describe packages and provide step-by-step procedures for adding and removing packages.

Patches are generally delivered as a set of sparse packages. Sparse packages are a minimalist version of a regular package. See Chapter 4, "Software Management: Patches," for information about how to apply patches and patching best practices.

3.2 What Is a Package?

The Solaris Operating System (Solaris OS) is delivered and installed with SVR4 packages. A *package* is a collection of files and directories in a defined format. This format conforms to the application binary interface (ABI), which is a supplement to the System V Interface Definition. The Solaris OS provides a set of utilities that interpret this format and provide the means to install a package, to remove a package, and to verify a package installation.

3.2.1 SVR4 Package Content

A package consists of the following:

- **Package objects**—These are the files to be installed.
- **Control files**—These files determine the way the application needs to be installed. These files are divided into information files and installation scripts.

The structure of a package consists of the following:

- Required components:
  - **Package objects**—Executable or data files, directories, named pipes, links, and devices.
  - **pkginfo file**—A required package information file defining parameter values such as the package abbreviation, full package name, and package architecture.
  - **pkgmap file**—A required package information file that lists the components of the package with the location, attributes, and file type for each component.

- Optional components:
  - **compver file**—Defines previous versions of the package that are compatible with this version.
  - **depend file**—Indicates other packages that this package depends upon.
  - **space file**—Defines disk space requirements for the target environment.
  - **copyright file**—Defines the text for a copyright notice displayed at the time of package installation.

- Optional installation scripts—These scripts perform customized actions during the installation of the package. Different installation scripts include:
  - **request scripts**—Request input from the administrator who is installing the package.
  - **checkinstall scripts**—Perform special file system verification.
  - **procedure scripts**—Define actions that occur at particular points during package installation and removal. There are four procedure scripts that you can create with these predefined names: `preinstall`, `postinstall`, `preremove`, and `postremove`.
  - **class action scripts**—Define a set of actions to be performed on a group of objects.

3.2.2 Package Naming Conventions

Sun packages always begin with the prefix SUNW, as in SUNWaccr, SUNWadmap, and SUNWcsu. Third-party packages usually begin with a prefix that corresponds to the company's stock symbol.

3.3 Tools for Managing Software Packages

You can use either a graphical user interface (GUI) or command line tools to install or remove packages. See Table 3.1 for a list of these tools.

For more information about these tools, see *System Administration Guide: Basic Administration* or the specific man pages listed in the table. For the guide and man pages, see http://docs.sun.com.

Table 3.1 Tools or Commands for Managing Software Packages

Tool or Command	Description	Man Page	Installed by Default?
installer	Starts the Solaris installation GUI so that you can add software from the Solaris media. The installer must be available either locally or remotely. Also, this GUI can determine what software is already installed on a system.	installer (1M)	This tool must be installed from the installation CD or DVD.
prodreg (GUI)	Starts an installer so that you can add, remove, or display software product information. Use the Solaris Product Registry to remove or display information about software products that were originally installed by using the Solaris installation GUI or the Solaris pkgadd command.	prodreg (1M)	This tool is installed by default.
Solaris Product Registry prodreg Viewer command-line interface (CLI)	Use the prodreg command to remove or display information about software products that were originally installed by using the Solaris installation GUI or the Solaris pkgadd command.	prodreg (1M)	This tool is installed by default.

continues

Table 3.1 Tools or Commands for Managing Software Packages (*continued*)

Tool or Command	Description	Man Page	Installed by Default?
pkgadd	Installs a signed or unsigned software package. A signed package includes a digital signature. A package with a valid digital signature ensures that the package has not been modified since the signature was applied to the package. Using signed packages is a secure method of downloading or installing packages, because the digital signature can be verified before the package is installed on your system.	pkgadd (1M)	This tool is installed by default.
pkgadm	Maintains the keys and certificates used to manage signed packages and signed patches.	pkgadm (1M)	This tool is installed by default.
pkgchk	Checks the installation of a software package.	pkgchk (1M)	This tool is installed by default.
pkginfo	Displays software package information.	pkginfo (1)	This tool is installed by default.
pkgparam	Displays software package parameter values.	pkgparam (1)	This tool is installed by default.
pkgrm	Removes a software package.	pkgrm (1M)	This tool is installed by default.
pkgtrans	Translates an installable package from one format to another format. The -g option instructs the pkgtrans command to generate and store a signature in the resulting data stream.	pkgtrans (1)	This tool is installed by default.

3.4 Installing or Removing a Software Package with the pkgadd or pkgrm Command

All the software management tools that are listed in the preceding table are used to install, remove, or query information about installed software. Both the Solaris Product Registry prodreg viewer and the Solaris installation GUI access installation data that is stored in the Solaris Product Registry. The package tools, such as the pkgadd and pkgrm commands, also access or modify installation data.

When you add a package, the `pkgadd` command uncompresses and copies files from the installation media to a system's local disk. When you remove a package, the `pkgrm` command deletes all files associated with that package, unless those files are also shared with other packages.

Package files are delivered in package format and are unusable as they are delivered. The `pkgadd` command interprets the software package's control files, and then uncompresses and installs the product files onto the system's local disk.

Although the `pkgadd` and `pkgrm` commands log their output to a log file, they also keep track of packages that are installed or removed. The `pkgadd` and `pkgrm` commands store information about packages that have been installed or removed in a software product database. By updating this database, the `pkgadd` and `pkgrm` commands keep a record of all software products installed on the system.

3.5 Using Package Commands to Manage Software Packages

The following procedures explain how to install and remove packages with the `pkgadd` command.

3.5.1 How to Install Packages with the `pkgadd` Command

This procedure provides the steps to install one or more packages.

1. Become superuser or assume an equivalent role.
2. Remove any already installed packages with the same names as the packages you are adding.

   This step ensures that the system keeps a proper record of software that has been added and removed.

   # **pkgrm** *pkgid* ...

   pkgid identifies the name of one or more packages, separated by spaces, to be removed.

   > **Caution**
   >
   > If the *pkgid* is omitted, the `pkgrm` command removes all available packages.

3. Install a software package to the system. The syntax for the `pkgadd` command is as follows:

   # **pkgadd -a** *admin-file* **-d** *device-name pkgid* ...

The following list provides explanations of each argument available for
pkgadd.

- **a** *admin-file*

  (Optional) Specifies an administration file that the pkgadd command
  should check during the installation. For details about using an administration file, see *System Administration Guide: Basic Administration*, which
  is available on http://docs.sun.com.

- **-d** *device-name*

  Specifies the absolute path to the software packages. *device-name* can be the
  path to a device, a directory, or a spool directory. If you do not specify the path
  where the package resides, the pkgadd command checks the default spool
  directory (/var/spool/pkg). If the package is not there, the package installation fails.

- *pkgid*

  (Optional) Represents the name of one or more packages, separated by
  spaces, to be installed. If omitted, the pkgadd command installs all available packages from the specified device, directory, or spool directory.

If the pkgadd command encounters a problem during installation of the package, then it displays a message related to the problem, followed by this prompt:

  ```
  Do you want to continue with this installation?
  ```

Chose one of the following responses:

  - If you want to continue the installation, type yes.
  - If more than one package has been specified and you want to stop the
    installation of the package being installed, type no.

    The pkgadd command continues to install the other packages.

  - If you want to stop the entire installation, type quit.

4. Verify that the package has been installed successfully.

   ```
   # pkgchk -v pkgid
   ```

   If no errors occur, a list of installed files is returned. Otherwise, the pkgchk
   command reports the error.

The following example shows how to install the SUNWpl5u package from a
mounted Solaris 10 DVD or CD. The example also shows how to verify that the
package files were installed properly.

The path on the DVD or CD `Product` directory varies depending on your release:

- For SPARC based media, the "s0" directory does not exist starting with the Solaris 10 10/08 release.
- For x86 based media, there is no "s0" directory in the Solaris 10 releases.

Example 3.1 Installing a Software Package From a Mounted CD

```
# pkgadd -d /cdrom/cdrom0/s0/Solaris_10/Product SUNWpl5u
    .
    .
    .
Installation of <SUNWpl5u> was successful.
# pkgchk  -v SUNWpl5u
/usr
/usr/bin
/usr/bin/perl
/usr/perl5
/usr/perl5/5.8.4
  .
  .
  .
```

If the packages you want to install are available from a remote system, then you can manually mount the directory that contains the packages, which are in package format, and install the packages on the local system.

The following example shows how to install a software package from a remote system. In this example, assume that the remote system named package-server has software packages in the /latest-packages directory. The mount command mounts the packages locally on /mnt. The pkgadd command installs the SUNWpl5u package.

Example 3.2 Installing a Software Package From a Remote Package Server

```
# mount -F nfs -o ro package-server:/latest-packages /mnt
# pkgadd -d /mnt SUNWpl5u
  .
  .
  .
Installation of <SUNWpl5u> was successful
```

If the automounter is running at your site, then you do not need to manually mount the remote package server. Instead, use the automounter path, in this case, /net/package-server/latest-packages, as the argument to the -d option.

```
# pkgadd -d /net/package-server/latest-packages SUNWpl5u
  .
  .
  .
Installation of <SUNWpl5u> was successful.
```

3.5.2 Adding Frequently Installed Packages to a Spool Directory

For convenience, you can copy frequently installed packages to a spool directory. If you copy packages to the default spool directory, /var/spool/pkg, then you do not need to specify the source location of the package when you use the pkgadd command. The source location of the package is specified in the -d *device-name* option. The pkgadd command, by default, checks the /var/spool/pkg directory for any packages that are specified on the command line. Note that copying packages to a spool directory is not the same as installing the packages on a system.

3.5.2.1 How to Copy Software Packages to a Spool Directory with the pkgadd Command

This procedure copies packages to a spool directory. The packages are then available for use when you install the packages elsewhere with the pkgadd command.

1. Become superuser or assume an equivalent role.
2. Remove any already spooled packages with the same names as the packages you are adding.

   # **pkgrm** *pkgid* ...

   pkgid identifies the name of one or more packages, separated by spaces, to be removed.

   > **Caution**
   >
   > If the *pkgid* option is omitted, then the pkgrm command removes all available packages.

3. Copy a software package to a spool directory.

   # **pkgadd -d** *device-name* **-s** *spooldir pkgid* ...

   The following list provides explanations of each argument used with the pkgadd command.

   - **-d** *device-name*

     Specifies the absolute path to the software packages. The device-name can be the path to a device, a directory, or a spool directory.

- **-s** *spooldir*

  Specifies the name of the spool directory where the package will be spooled. You must specify a *spooldir*.

- *pkgid*

  (Optional) The name of one or more packages, separated by spaces, to be added to the spool directory. If omitted, the pkgadd command copies all available packages to the spool directory.

4. Verify that the package has been copied successfully to the spool directory.

   $ **pkginfo -d** *spooldir* **| grep** *pkgid*

   If *pkgid* was copied correctly, the pkginfo command returns a line of information about the *pkgid*. Otherwise, the pkginfo command returns the system prompt.

The following example shows how to copy the SUNWman package from a mounted SPARC based Solaris 10 DVD or CD to the default spool directory (/var/spool/pkg).

The path on the DVD or CD Product directory varies depending on your release and platform:

- For SPARC based media, the "s0" directory does not exist starting with the Solaris 10 10/08 release.
- For x86 based media, there is no "s0" directory in the Solaris 10 releases.

Example 3.3 Setting Up a Spool Directory From a Mounted CD

```
# pkgadd -d /cdrom/cdrom0/s0/Solaris_10/Product -s /var/spool/pkg SUNWman
Transferring <SUNWman> package instance
```

If packages you want to copy are available from a remote system, then you can manually mount the directory that contains the packages, which are in package format, and copy them to a local spool directory.

The following example shows the commands for this scenario. In this example, assume that the remote system named package-server has software packages in the /latest-packages directory. The mount command mounts the package directory locally on /mnt. The pkgadd command copies the SUNWpl5p package from /mnt to the default spool directory (/var/spool/pkg).

Example 3.4 Setting Up a Spool Directory From a Remote Software Package Server

```
# mount -F nfs -o ro package-server:/latest-packages /mnt
# pkgadd -d /mnt -s /var/spool/pkg SUNWpl5p
Transferring <SUNWpl5p> package instance
```

If the automounter is running at your site, then you do not have to manually mount the remote package server. Instead, use the automounter path–which in this case is `/net/package-server/latest-packages`–as the argument to the `-d` option.

```
# pkgadd -d /net/package-server/latest-packages -s /var/spool/pkg SUNWp15p
Transferring <SUNWp15p> package instance
```

The following example shows how to install the SUNWp15p package from the default spool directory. When no options are used, the `pkgadd` command searches the `/var/spool/pkg` directory for the named packages.

Example 3.5 Installing a Software Package From the Default Spool Directory

```
# pkgadd SUNWp15p
    .
    .
    .
Installation of <SUNWp15p> was successful.
```

3.5.3 Removing Software Packages

To remove a software package, use the associated tool that you used to install a software package. For example, if you used the Solaris installation GUI to install the software, use the Solaris installation GUI to remove software.

> **Caution**
>
> Do not use the `rm` command to remove software packages. Doing so will result in inaccuracies in the database that keeps track of all installed packages on the system.

3.5.3.1 How to Remove Software Packages with the `pkgrm` Command

This procedure provides the steps to remove packages with the `pkgrm` command.

1. Become superuser or assume an equivalent role.
2. Remove an installed package.

    ```
    # pkgrm pkgid ...
    ```

pkgid identifies the name of one or more packages, separated by spaces, to be removed.

Caution

If the *pkgid* option is omitted, the pkgrm command removes all available packages.

This example shows how to remove a package.

Example 3.6 Removing a Software Package

```
# pkgrm SUNWctu

The following package is currently installed:
   SUNWctu          Netra ct usr/platform links (64-bit)
                    (sparc.sun4u) 11.9.0,REV=2001.07.24.15.53

Do you want to remove this package? y

## Removing installed package instance <SUNWctu>
## Verifying package dependencies.
## Removing pathnames in class <none>
## Processing package information.

  .
  .
  .
```

This example shows how to remove a spooled package.

For convenience, you can copy frequently installed packages to a spool directory. In this example, the -s option specifies the name of the spool directory where the package is spooled.

Example 3.7 Removing a Spooled Software Package

```
# pkgrm -s /export/pkg SUNWaudh
The following package is currently spooled:
   SUNWaudh          Audio Header Files
                     (sparc) 11.10.0,REV=2003.08.08.00.03

Do you want to remove this package? y

Removing spooled package instance <SUNWaudh>
```

4

Software Management: Patches

This chapter describes patches, provides best practices, and includes step-by-step procedures for applying patches.

4.1 Managing Software with Patches

Software management involves installing or removing software products. Sun and its third-party independent software vendors (ISVs) deliver software as a collection of one or more packages. Patches are generally delivered as a set of *sparse packages*. Sparse packages are a minimalist version of a regular package. A sparse package delivers only the files being updated.

The following sections describe patches and provide step-by-step procedures for applying patches. Also, a best practices section provides planning information for proactive and reactive patching.

4.2 What Is a Patch?

A *patch* adds, updates, or deletes one or more files on your system by updating the installed packages. A patch consists of the following:

- Sparse packages that are a minimalist version of a regular package. A sparse package delivers only the files being updated.

- Class action scripts that define a set of actions to be executed during the installation or removal of a package or patch.
- Other scripts such as the following:
  - Postinstallation and preinstallation scripts.
  - Scripts that undo a patch when the `patchrm` command is used. These scripts are copied onto the system's patch undo area.
  - Prepatch, prebackout, and postpatch scripts, depending on the patch being installed. The postbackout and prebackout scripts are copied into the `/var/sadm/patch/patch-id` directory and are run by the `patchrm` command.

For more detailed information, see Section 4.7, "Patch README Special Instructions."

4.2.1 Patch Content

In past Solaris releases, patches delivered bug fixes only. Over time, patches have evolved and now have many other uses. For the Solaris 10 Operating System (OS), patches are used to deliver the following:

- Bug fixes.
- New functionality—Bug fixes can sometimes deliver significant functionality, such as ZFS file systems or GRUB, the open source boot loader that is the default boot loader in the Solaris OS.

  Some features require the installation of new packages, but any change to existing code is always delivered in a patch.
  - If a new package is required, then the new features are typically available only by installing or upgrading to a Solaris 10 release that contains the new packages.
  - If the change is to existing code, then the change is always delivered in a patch. Because new functionality such as new features in ZFS and GRUB is delivered entirely by patches, the patches enable businesses to take advantage of the new functionality without having to upgrade to a newer release of the Solaris OS. Therefore, Sun ships some new functionality in standard patches.
- New hardware support—Sun also ships new hardware support in patches for similar reasons that Sun ships new functionality: the need to get support for hardware to market quickly and yet maintain a stable release model going forward.
- Performance enhancements or enhancements to existing utilities.

4.2.2 Patch Numbering

Patches are identified by unique patch IDs. A *patch ID* is an alphanumeric string that consists of a patch base code and a number that represents the patch revision number joined with a hyphen. The following example shows the patch ID for the Solaris 10 OS, 10th revision:

- SPARC: 119254-10
- x86: 119255–10

Patches are cumulative. Later revisions contain all of the functionality delivered in previous revisions. For example, patch 123456-02 contains all the functionality of patch 123456-01 plus the new bug fixes or features that have been added in Revision 02. The changes are described in the patch README file.

4.3 Patch Management Best Practices

This section provides guidelines for creating a patch management strategy for any organization. These strategies are only guidelines because every organization is different in both environment and business objectives. Some organizations have specific guidelines on change management that must be adhered to when developing a patch management strategy. Customers can contact Sun Services to help develop an appropriate patch management strategy for their specific circumstances.

This section also provides useful information and tips that are appropriate for a given strategy, the tools most appropriate for each strategy, and where to locate the patches or patch clusters to apply.

Your strategy should be reviewed periodically because the environment and business objectives change over time, because new tools and practices evolve, and because operating systems evolve. All of these changes require modifications to your existing patch management strategy.

The four basic strategies outlined in this section are the following:

- Proactive patch management
- Reactive patch management
- Security patch management
- Proactive patch management when installing a new system

> **Note**
>
> Before adding any patches, make sure you apply the latest revision of the patch utilities. The latest patch for the patch utilities must be applied to the live system in all cases. This chapter assumes that the latest patch for the patch utilities has been applied before any other patching is done.

4.3.1 Proactive Patch Management Strategy

The main goal of proactive patch management is problem prevention, especially preventing unplanned downtime. Often, problems have already been identified and patches have been released. The issue for proactive patching is identifying important patches and applying those patches in a safe and reliable manner.

For proactive patching, the system is already functioning normally. Because any change implies risk and risk implies downtime, why patch a system that is functioning normally? Although a system is functioning normally, an underlying issue could cause a problem. Underlying issues could be the following:

- Memory corruption that has not yet caused a problem.
- Data corruption that is silent until that data is read back in.
- Latent security issues.

    Most security issues are latent issues that exist but are not yet causing security breaches. These issues require proactive action to prevent security breaches.

- Panics due to code paths that have not been exercised before.

Use proactive patching as the strategy of choice, where applicable. Proactive patching is recommended for the following reasons:

- It reduces unplanned downtime.
- It prevents systems from experiencing known issues.
- It provides the capability to plan ahead and do appropriate testing before deployment.
- Planned downtime for maintenance is usually much less expensive than unplanned downtime for addressing issues reactively.

4.3.1.1 Core Solaris Tools for Patching

Solaris Live Upgrade is the recommended tool for patching proactively. The `patchadd` command can be used in situations where Solaris Live Upgrade is not appropriate.

Note

To track issues relevant to proactive patching, register to receive Sun Alerts. For the registration procedure, see Section 4.3.3.1, "How to Register for Sun Alerts." For a procedure to access patches, see Section 4.3.5.1, "How to Access Patches."

4.3.1.2 Benefits of Solaris Live Upgrade

The information in this section describes how to use the Solaris Live Upgrade and core patch utilities to patch a system. Sun also has a range of higher-level patch automation tools. See Section 4.5, "Patch Automation Tools," for more information.

To proactively apply patches, use Solaris Live Upgrade. Solaris Live Upgrade consists of a set of tools that enable you to create an alternate boot environment that is a copy of the current boot environment. You can then patch the newly created boot environment while the system is running. After the copy is patched, the new boot environment can be booted.

Note

A boot environment is a collection of mandatory file systems (disk slices and mount points) that are critical to the operation of the Solaris OS. These disk slices might be on the same disk or distributed across multiple disks. The active boot environment is the one that is currently booted. Only one active boot environment can be booted. An inactive boot environment is not currently booted, but can be in a state of waiting for activation on the next reboot.

The benefits of using Solaris Live Upgrade are the following:

- Decreased downtime—The only downtime that is needed is the time to boot between the currently running boot environment and the newly patched boot environment. Patching is not done on the currently running boot environment so that the system can continue to be in production until the timing is suitable to boot to the newly patched boot environment.
- Fallback to the original boot environment—If a problem occurs, you can reboot to the original boot environment. The patches do not need to be removed by using the `patchrm` command.

You can use Solaris Live Upgrade's `luupgrade` command to apply the Recommended Patch Cluster. In this example, you use the `luupgrade` command with the -t and -O options. The first -t option specifies to install a patch. The -O option with the second `-t` option instructs the `patchadd` command to skip patch dependency verification.

> **Example 4.1** Applying the Recommended Patch Cluster by Using the
> `luupgrade` Command

```
# cd 10_Recommended
# luupgrade -t -n be3 -O -t -s . ./patch_order
```

For a complete example of using Solaris Live Upgrade, see Section 4.4, "Example of Using Solaris Live Upgrade to Install Patches."

4.3.1.3 When to Use the `patchadd` Command Instead of Solaris Live Upgrade

If Solaris Live Upgrade is not applicable to the system being patched, then the `patchadd` command is used. After the appropriate patches are downloaded and all requirements are identified, then the patches can be applied by using the `patchadd` command. Table 4.1 provides a guide to when to use the `patchadd` command.

Table 4.1 When to Use the `patchadd` Command

Problem	Description
Limited disk resources	If disk resources are limited and you cannot set up an inactive boot environment, then you need to use the `patchadd` command. Also, if you are using Solaris Volume Manager for mirroring, then you might need to use the `patchadd` command. You need extra resources to set up a Solaris Volume Manager inactive boot environment.
Veritas Storage Foundation root disk	If you are using Veritas Storage Foundation to encapsulate the root disk, then you can use Solaris Live Upgrade to create a new boot environment. However, Solaris Live Upgrade does not support Veritas encapsulated root (/) file systems very well. The root (/) file system can be a Veritas Volume Manager volume (VxVM). If VxVM volumes are configured on your current system, then you can use the `lucreate` command to create a new boot environment. When the data is copied to the new boot environment, the Veritas file system configuration is lost and a UFS file system is created on the new boot environment.

Table 4.1 When to Use the `patchadd` Command (*continued*)

Problem	Description
Recommended Patch Cluster installation	If you want to install the Recommended Patch Cluster with the `cluster_install` script, then you do not have to use Solaris Live Upgrade or the `patchadd` command. The Recommended Patch Cluster can be installed by using the `cluster_install` script that comes with the Cluster. The `cluster_install` script invokes the `patchadd` command to apply the patches to the live boot environment in the installation order specified in the `patch_order` file.

If additional patches are to be applied to a Solaris 10 system by using the `patchadd` command, then the `-a` and `-M` options can be useful for identifying any missing requirements and identifying a valid installation order for the patches. While this method of applying patches has the major disadvantage of requiring you to patch the live system, which increases both downtime and risk, you can reduce the risk by using the `-a` option to inspect the patches before applying them against the actual system.

Note the following limitations to the `patchadd -M` option:

- This option is only available starting with the Solaris 10 03/05 release.
- You cannot apply patches using `-M` without the `-a` option, due to several problems in the current implementation.

In the following example, the `-a` option instructs the `-M` option to perform a dry run, so that no software is installed and no changes are made to the system. The output from the command is verbose but consists of an ordered list of patches that can be installed. Also, the dry run clearly identifies any patches that cannot be installed due to dependencies that must be satisfied first.

Example 4.2 Using the `patchadd` Command with the `-a` Option for a Dry Run

```
# patchadd -a -M patches-directory
```

After identifying the complete list of patches, you can install the patches one by one by using the `patchadd` command without the `-M` option.

In the following example of using `patchadd` in a loop, the `patch_order_file` is the ordered list from the `-M` and `-a` options. The `-q` option instructs the

-M option to run in "quiet" mode. Also, this option outputs headings for the install-able patches, which are called **Approved patches.**

Example 4.3 Applying the Patches by Using the patchadd Command

```
# patchadd -q -a -M . |grep "Approved patches:" |sort -u \
|sed -e "s/Approved patches://g" > patch_order_file 2>&1
# Cat patch_order_file
120900-03 121333-04 119254-50
#for i in 'cat patch_order-file'
do
          patchadd $i
done
```

4.3.1.4 Proactive Patching on Systems with Non-Global Zones Installed

Solaris Live Upgrade is the recommended tool for patching systems with non-global zones. The patchadd command can be used in situations where Solaris Live Upgrade is not applicable.

The Solaris Zones partitioning technology is used to virtualize operating system services and provide an isolated and secure environment for running applications. A non-global zone is a virtualized operating system environment created within a single instance of the Solaris OS. When you create a non-global zone, you produce an application execution environment in which processes are isolated from the rest of the system. This isolation prevents processes that are running in one non-global zone from monitoring or affecting processes that are running in other non-global zones. Even a process running with superuser privileges cannot view or affect activity in other zones. A non-global zone also provides an abstract layer that separates applications from the physical attributes of the system on which they are deployed. Examples of these attributes include physical device paths. For more information about non-global zones, see *System Administration Guide: Solaris Containers-Resource Management and Solaris Zones* available at http://docs.sun.com.

4.3.1.5 Using Solaris Live Upgrade When Non-Global Zones Are Installed

On systems with non-global zones installed, patching can be done by using Solaris Live Upgrade.

Note the following limitations for Solaris Live Upgrade:

- If you are running the Solaris 10 8/07 release or a later release, then Solaris Live Upgrade can be used to apply patches.
- If you are running a Solaris 10 release prior to the Solaris 10 8/07 release, then you must ensure that you have the software and bug fixes to run Solaris Live Upgrade.

- You cannot use the `luupgrade` command with the `-t` option to apply a list of patches using an order file because this option uses the `patchadd -M` option internally. Due to current issues with the `patchadd -M` option, this option can lead to unrecoverable errors.

To ensure that you have the software and bug fixes needed because you are running a Solaris 10 release prior to the 8/07 release, follow these steps:

1. Add the Solaris Live Upgrade packages from the Solaris 10 8/07 release to the live system.
2. Apply the list of required patches. If these patches are not installed, then Solaris Live Upgrade fails. These patches are needed to add the current bug fixes and the latest functionality for Solaris Live Upgrade. These patches are available on the SunSolve Web site in the info document "Solaris Live Upgrade Software: Minimum Patch Requirements." Search on SunSolve for info document 206844 at `http://sunsolve.sun.com`. This document lists the required patches and provides the process needed to update Solaris Live Upgrade so that a system with a release prior to the Solaris 10 05/08 release can use the software.

The Solaris 10 Live Upgrade Patch Bundle provides a quick way to install all the required patches to use Solaris Live Upgrade on systems that have non-global zones installed. This Patch Bundle provides non-global zones support for systems running a release prior to the Solaris 10 5/08 release.

> **Note**
>
> Starting with the Solaris 10 8/07 release, full support for installing non-global zones became available, including the capability to use Solaris Live Upgrade to upgrade or patch a system with non-global zones installed. However, due to problems, the required patches are needed to use Solaris Live Upgrade with non-global zones in the Solaris 10 8/07 release.

The list of required patches for a system with non-global zones is quite large. The patches must be applied to the live running environment. However, after these patches are applied, Solaris Live Upgrade can be used to patch going forward with all the benefits that Solaris Live Upgrade provides.

4.3.1.6 Using the `patchadd` Command When Non-Global Zones are Installed

If Solaris Live Upgrade is not an acceptable option, then use the same method outlined in Section 4.3.1.1, "Core Solaris Tools for Patching." You identify all the patches required and use the `patchadd` command with the `-a` and `-M` options to identify any missing requirements. The `-a` option performs a dry run and no patches are installed.

Pay attention to the `patchadd` `-a` and `-M` output. In particular, ensure that all non-global zones have passed the dependency tests. The `-a` option can help identify the following issues with non-global zones:

- Zones that cannot be booted
- Patches that did not meet all the required dependencies for a non-global zone

If the `-a` option identifies any issues, then those issues must be rectified before patching can begin.

Apply patches individually by using the `patchadd` command. To facilitate applying multiple patches, you can use `patchadd` `-a` `-M` *patch-dir* to produce an ordered list of patches that can be installed individually.

Due to current issues with `patchadd` `-M` option, do not run `-M` *patch-dir* without the `-a` option. The `-M` option can lead to unrecoverable errors.

If you are using the `patchadd` command, then run the following command first. This command verifies that all zones can be booted and that the specified patch is applicable in all zones.

Example 4.4 How to Identify Problems Before Applying Patches

```
# patchadd -a patch-id verify
```

4.3.2 Reactive Patch Management Strategy

Reactive patching occurs in response to an issue that is currently affecting the running system and which requires immediate relief. The most common response to fixing the system can often lead to worse problems. Usually, the fix is to apply the latest patch or patches. These patches could be the latest Recommended Patch Cluster or one or more patches that seem to be appropriate. This strategy might work if the root cause of the undiagnosed issue had been determined and if a patch has been issued to fix the issue. However, if this approach does not fix the problem, then the problem can be worse than it was before you applied the patch.

There are two reasons why this approach is fundamentally flawed:

- If the problem seems to go away, then you do not know whether the patch or patches actually fixed the underlying problem. The patches might have changed the system in such a way as to obscure the problem for now and the problem could recur later.

- Applying patches in a reactive patching session introduces an element of risk. When you are in a reactive patching situation, you must try to minimize risk (change) at all costs. In proactive patching, you can and should have tested the change you are applying. In a reactive situation, if you apply many changes and those changes do not fix the underlying issue or if they do fix the underlying issue, then you now have a system issue that still needs the root cause identified. Identifying the root cause involves a lot more risk. Furthermore, the changes that you applied might have negative consequences elsewhere on the system, which could lead to more reactive patching.

Therefore, if you experience a problem that is affecting the system, then you should spend time investigating the root cause of the problem. If a fix can be identified from such an investigation and that fix involves applying one or more patches, then the change is minimized to just the patch or set of patches required to fix the problem.

Depending on the severity of the problem, the patch or patches that fix the problem would be installed at one of the following times:

- Immediately
- At the next regular maintenance window, if the problem is not critical or a workaround exists
- During an emergency maintenance window that is brought forward to facilitate applying the fix

4.3.2.1 Tools for Analyzing Problems and Identifying Patches

Identifying patches that are applicable in a reactive patching situation can often be complex. If you have a support contract, then use the official Sun Support channels. To begin, you should do some analysis. Some tools that are useful in starting this analysis might include the following:

- The `truss` command with the options such as `-fae`
- The `dtrace` command (dynamic tracing framework) that permits you to concisely answer questions about the behavior of the operating system and user programs
- Various system analysis tools, such as `kstat`, `iostat`, `netstat`, `prstat`, `sar`, `vmstat`, and even `mdb`

When you are providing data to Sun engineers, use the Sun Explorer logs. These logs provide a good foundation to start an analysis of the system.

No standard tool for analyzing a problem can be recommended because each problem involves different choices. Using debug-level logging and examining various log files might also provide insight into the problem. Also, a proper recording system that records changes to the system should be considered. A record of recent system configuration changes can be investigated as possible root causes.

4.3.2.2 Tools for Applying Patches for Reactive Patching

The tool you use for reactive patching depends on the situation as follows:

- If a fix has been identified and a patch has been downloaded, then use Solaris Live Upgrade to apply patches. Solaris Live Upgrade is covered in more detail in Section 4.3.1.1, "Core Solaris Tools for Patching."

- If you need to apply the patch or patches immediately or the issue impacts Solaris Live Upgrade, then you should first run the `patchadd` command with the `-a` option. The `-a` option performs a dry run and does not modify the system. Prior to actually installing the patch or patches, inspect the output from the dry run for issues.

- If more than one patch is being installed, then you can use the `patchadd` command with the `-a` and `-M` options. These options perform a dry run and produce an ordered list of patches that can be installed. After determining that no issues exist, the patches should be installed individually by using the `patchadd` command.

- If the system has non-global zones installed, then you should apply all patches individually by using Solaris Live Upgrade with the `luupgrade` command. Or, you can use the `patchadd` command. Never use the `-M` option to the `patchadd` command with non-global zones. Also, never apply a list of patches using an order file with the `luupgrade` command with the `-t` option. The `-t` option uses the `patchadd  -M` option in the underlying software. There are problems with the `-M` option.

In addition to using the core Solaris Live Upgrade and patch utilities to patch a system, Sun also has a range of higher-level patch automation tools. For more information, see Section 4.5, "Patch Automation Tools."

4.3.3 Security Patch Management Strategy

Security patch management requires a separate strategy from proactive and reactive patching. For security patching, you are required to be proactive, but a sense of urgency prevails. Relevant security fixes might need to be installed proactively before the next scheduled maintenance window.

4.3.3.1 How to Register for Sun Alerts

To be prepared for security issues, register to receive Sun Alerts. When you register for Sun alerts, you also receive Security Alerts.

In addition, a security Web site contains more information about security and you can report issues there. On the SunSolve home page, see "Sun Security Coordination Team." On this page, you will find other resources such as the security blog.

1. Log in to the SunSolve Web site at `http://sunsolve.sun.com`.
2. Accept the license agreement.
3. Find the "Sun Alerts" section.
4. Click Subscribe to Sun Alerts.
5. Choose the newsletters and reports that you want to receive.

The Sun Alert Weekly Summary Report provides a summary of new Sun Alert Notifications about hardware and software issues. This report is updated weekly.

4.3.3.2 Tools for Applying Security Patches

The same rules for proactively or reactively applying patches also apply to applying security patches. If possible, use Solaris Live Upgrade. If Solaris Live Upgrade is not appropriate, then use the `patchadd` command. For more information, see Section 4.3.1.1, "Core Solaris Tools for Patching."

In addition to using Solaris Live Upgrade and the patch utilities to patch a system, Sun also has a range of higher-level patch automation tools. For more information, see Section 4.5, "Patch Automation Tools."

4.3.4 Proactive Patching When Installing a New System

The best time to proactively patch a system is during installation. Patching during installation ensures that, when the system boots, the system has the latest patches installed. Patching avoids any known issues that are outstanding. Also, if testing has been scheduled into the provisioning plan, then you can test the configuration in advance. In addition, you can create a baseline for all installations. Patching during installation requires that you use the JumpStart installation program.

The JumpStart installation program is a command-line interface that enables you to automatically install or upgrade several systems based on profiles that you create. The profiles define specific software installation requirements. You can also incorporate shell scripts to include preinstallation and postinstallation tasks. You choose which profile and scripts to use for installation or upgrade. Also, you can use a `sysidcfg` file to specify configuration information so that the custom JumpStart installation is completely hands off. *Solaris 10 Installation Guide: Custom Jump-Start and Advanced Installations* is available at `http://docs.sun.com`. You can find profile examples in the "Preparing Custom JumpStart Installations (Tasks)" chapter of the installation guide. Also, finish scripts can apply patches. See the examples in the chapter "Creating Finish Scripts" of the aforementioned *Solaris 10 Installation Guide*.

A JumpStart profile is a text file that defines how to install the Solaris software on a system. A profile defines elements of the installation; for example, the software group to install. Every rule specifies a profile that defines how a system is to be installed. You can create different profiles for every rule or the same profile can be used in more than one rule. Here is an example profile that performs an upgrade and installs patches.

In this example of a JumpStart profile, a system is upgraded and patched at the same time.

Example 4.5 Upgrading and Installing Patches with a JumpStart Profile

```
# profile keywords          profile values
# ----------------          ------------------
  install_type              upgrade
  root_device               c0t3d0s2
  backup_media              remote_filesystem timber:/export/scratch
  package                   SUNWbcp delete
  package                   SUNWxwman add
  cluster                   SUNWCacc add
  patch                     patch_list \
                            nfs://patch_master/Solaris_10/patches \
                            retry 5
  locale                    de
```

The following describes the keywords and values from this example:

- `install_type`
  The profile upgrades a system by reallocating disk space. In this example, disk space must be reallocated because some file systems on the system do not have enough space for the upgrade.

- `root_device`
  The root file system on `c0t3d0s2` is upgraded.

- `backup_media`
  A remote system that is named `timber` is used to back up data during the disk space reallocation.

- `package`
  The binary compatibility package, `SUNWbcp`, is not installed on the system after the upgrade.

- `package`

  The code ensures that the X Window System man pages are installed if they are not already installed on the system. All packages already on the system are automatically upgraded.

- `cluster`

  The system accounting utilities, `SUNWCacc`, are installed on the system.

- `patch`

  A list of patches are installed with the upgrade. The patch list is located on an NFS server named `patch_master` under the directories `Solaris_10/patches`. In the case of a mount failure, the NFS mount is tried five times.

- `locale`

  The German localization packages are installed on the system.

The following patch keyword example applies an individual patch. The patch keyword installs the single patch 119254-50 from the network where the Recommended Patch Cluster is located.

Example 4.6 JumpStart Profile for Applying an Individual Patch

```
patch 119254-50 nfs://server-name/export/images/SPARC/10_Recommended
```

In this example, the patch keyword applies the Recommended Patch Cluster from the network where the Cluster is located. The retry n keyword is an optional keyword. The n refers to the maximum number of times the installation process attempts to mount the directory.

Example 4.7 JumpStart Profile for Applying the Recommended Patch Cluster

```
patch patch_order nfs://server-name/export/10_Recommended retry 5
```

4.3.5 Identifying Patches for Proactive Patching and Accessing Patches

To track issues relevant to proactive patching, register to receive Sun Alerts. See Section 4.3.3.1, "How to Register for Sun Alerts." Alternatively, you can install the most recent Recommended Patch Cluster, which contains Sun Alerts. The Recommended Patch Cluster can be downloaded from the SunSolve Patch Access page. See Section 4.3.5.1, "How to Access Patches."

Individual patches can be downloaded from the Patches and Updates page on the Web site.

Note

Both the Recommended Patch Cluster and Sun Alert Patch Cluster contain only core Solaris OS patches. They do not contain patches for Sun Java Enterprise System, Sun Cluster software, Sun Studio software, or Sun N1 software. They do not contain other non-Solaris OS patches that address security, data corruption, or system availability issues.

4.3.5.1 How to Access Patches

Some patches are free, while other patches require a support contract.

- Patches that address security issues and patches that provide new hardware drivers are free.
- You must have a valid support contract to access most other Solaris patches, including the Solaris patch clusters, such as the Recommended Patch Cluster or the Sun Alert Patch Cluster. The following support contracts entitle customers to access all patches plus a wide range of additional support services:

  – Support contracts for Solaris OS only: Solaris Subscriptions
  – Support contracts for your entire system: Sun Spectrum Service Plans

For the Solaris 10 OS, patches for the patch utility patches use the following patch IDs:

- SPARC: 119254-xx
- x86: 119255-xx

To install the patches, follow these steps:

1. Log in to the SunSolve Web site at `http://sunsolve.sun.com`.
2. Accept the license agreement.
3. Find the section "Latest Patch Update."
   This section provides a complete list of prerequisite patches for each OS version that should be installed before other patches are applied.
4. Click the "Patches and Updates" section.
5. In the "Product Patches" section, select the OS for your platform (either SPARC or x86).
6. Download the patch.

7. Read the Special Install Instructions for all patches prior to installing them.

    Special Install Instructions can be updated after the patch has been released to the SunSolve Web site. These instructions clarify issues surrounding the particular patch installation or to notify users of newly identified issues.

4.4 Example of Using Solaris Live Upgrade to Install Patches

This section provides an example procedure for patching a system with a basic configuration. This procedure provides commands based on the Solaris 10 8/07 release. If you are using Solaris Live Upgrade from another release, then you might need slightly different procedures. For detailed planning information or procedures for more complex upgrading procedures, such as for upgrading when Solaris Zones are installed or upgrading with a mirrored root (/) file system, see *Solaris 10 Installation Guide: Solaris Live Upgrade and Upgrade Planning* available at `http://docs.sun.com`. This guide is available for each Solaris 10 release.

4.4.1 Overview of Patching with Solaris Live Upgrade

As Figure 4.1 shows, the Solaris Live Upgrade process involves the following steps.

1. Creating a new boot environment by using the `lucreate` command.
2. Applying patches to the new boot environment by using the `luupgrade` command.
3. Activating the new boot environment by using the `luactivate` command.
4. Falling back to the original boot environment if needed by using the `luactivate` command.
5. Removing an inactive boot environment by using the `ludelete` command. You can remove a boot environment after the running boot environment is stable.

Solaris Live Upgrade Patching Process.

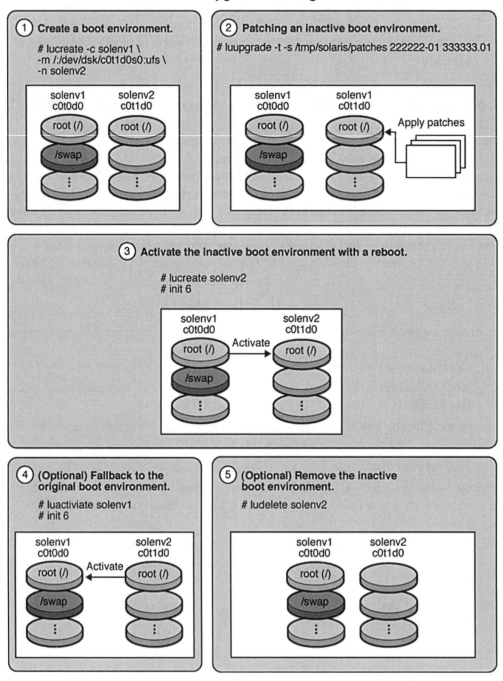

Figure 4.1 Solaris Live Upgrade Patching Process

4.4.2 Planning for Using Solaris Live Upgrade

Table 4.2 describes the requirements and limitations for patching with Solaris Live Upgrade. Table 4.3 describes limitations for activating a boot environment.

Table 4.2 Solaris Live Upgrade Planning and Limitations

Planning issue	Description
Disk space requirements	Using Solaris Live Upgrade involves having two boot environments on your system. Therefore, a prerequisite is to have enough disk space for both the original and new boot environments. You need either an extra disk or one disk large enough to contain both boot environments.
Supported releases	Sun supports and tests an upgrade from any release to a subsequent release that is no more than two releases ahead. For example, if you are running the Solaris 7 release, then you can upgrade to any Solaris 8 or Solaris 9 release, but not to a Solaris 10 release. If you are running the Solaris 7 release, then you would need to upgrade to the Solaris 8 release before using Solaris Live Upgrade.
	Any Solaris release includes all the releases within that release. For example, you could upgrade from the Solaris 9 release, to the Solaris 10 3/05 release or the Solaris 10 1/06 release.
	You need to upgrade to the latest version of the Solaris Live Upgrade software prior to patching the system, regardless of the version of the Solaris OS running on the system. You need the packages for the latest features and bug fixes.
Dependency order of patches	The `patchadd` command in the Solaris 10 release correctly orders patches for you, but the Solaris 9 and earlier releases require patches to be in dependency order. When using the `luupgrade` command to apply patches, apply the patches in dependency order, regardless of the Solaris release you are using. Sun uses dependency order as part of the standard testing of the `luupgrade` command and you can be assured that this order was tested.
Patch log evaluation	Patching can generate a number of errors. You should examine the patch log to determine whether any patch failures impact you.
	Sometimes a log indicates that a patch has failed to install, but this is not a problem. For example, if a patch delivers bug fixes for package A and your system does not have package A, then the patch fails to install. The installation log should be checked to ensure all messages are as expected.

continues

Table 4.2 Solaris Live Upgrade Planning and Limitations (*continued*)

Planning issue	Description
Support for third-party patches	You might not be able to apply third-party patches with Solaris Live Upgrade. All Sun patches conform to the requirement that preinstallation and postinstallation scripts never modify the running system when the target is an inactive boot environment. Furthermore, testing the application of Recommended Patches with Solaris Live Upgrade is part of Sun's standard test procedures. However, Sun cannot guarantee that all third-party patches are equally well behaved. When you intend to patch an inactive boot environment, you might need to verify that a third-party patch does not contain a script that attempts to modify the currently running environment.

When you activate a boot environment by using the `luactivate` command, the boot environment must meet the conditions described in the Table 4.3.

Table 4.3 Limitations for Activating a Boot Environment

Description	For More Information
The boot environment must have a status of **complete.**	Use the `lustatus` command to display information about each boot environment. `# lustatus BE-name` The BE-name variable specifies the inactive boot environment. If BE-name is omitted, `lustatus` displays the status of all boot environments in the system.
If the boot environment is not the current boot environment, then you cannot mount the partitions of that boot environment by using the `luumount` or `mount` commands.	See the `lumount`(1M) or `mount`(1M) man page at `http://docs.sun.com`.
The boot environment that you want to activate cannot be involved in a comparison operation.	To compare boot environments, you use the `lucompare` command. The `lucompare` command generates a comparison of boot environments that includes the contents of non-global zones.
If you want to reconfigure swap, do so prior to booting the inactive boot environment. By default, all boot environments share the same swap devices.	By not specifying swap with the `lucreate` command with the `-m` option, your current and new boot environment share the same swap slices. If you want to reconfigure the new boot environment's swap, use the `-m` option to add or remove swap slices in the new boot environment.

Table 4.3 Limitations for Activating a Boot Environment (*continued*)

Description	For More Information
x86 only: Activating the boot environment	If you have an x86 based system, you can activate a boot environment by using the GRUB menu instead of the `luactivate` command. Note the following exceptions: ■ If a boot environment was created with the *Solaris 8, 9, or 10 3/05 release*, then the boot environment must always be activated with the `luactivate` command. These older boot environments do not display in the GRUB menu. ■ The first time you activate a boot environment, you must use the `luactivate` command. The next time you boot, that boot environment's name is displayed in the GRUB main menu. You can thereafter switch to this boot environment by selecting the appropriate entry in the GRUB menu.

4.4.3 How to Apply a Patch When Using Solaris Live Upgrade for the Solaris 10 8/07 Release

Before installing or running Solaris Live Upgrade, you must install the patches in SunSolve info doc 206844.

These patches ensure that you have all the latest bug fixes and new features in the release. Ensure that you install all the patches that are relevant to your system before proceeding.

1. Become superuser or assume an equivalent role.

2. If you are storing the patches on a local disk, create a directory such as `/var/tmp/lupatches`.

3. From the SunSolve Web site, follow the instructions in info doc 206844 to remove and add Solaris Live Upgrade packages. The Web site is located at `http://sunsolve.sun.com`.

The following summarizes the info doc steps for removing and adding the packages:

1. Remove existing Solaris Live Upgrade packages.
   The three Solaris Live Upgrade packages SUNWluu, SUNWlur, and SUNWlucfg comprise the software needed to upgrade by using Solaris Live

Upgrade. These packages include existing software, new features, and bug fixes. If you do not remove the existing packages and install the new packages on your system before using Solaris Live Upgrade, upgrading to the target release fails. The SUMWlucfg package is new *starting with the Solaris 10 8/07 release*. If you are using Solaris Live Upgrade packages from a release previous to Solaris 10 8/07, then you do not need to remove this package.

```
# pkgrm SUNWlucfg SUNWluu SUNWlur
```

2. Install the new Solaris Live Upgrade packages.

    You can install the packages by using the `liveupgrade20` command that is on the installation DVD or CD. The `liveupgrade20` command requires Java software. If your system does not have Java software installed, then you need to use the `pkgadd` command to install the packages. See the SunSolve info doc for more information.

3. Choose to run the installer from DVD or CD media.

    a. If you are using the Solaris Operating System DVD, then change directories and run the installer:

        Change directories:

        ```
        /cdrom/cdrom0/Solaris_10/Tools/Installers
        ```

        Note

        For SPARC based systems, the path to the installer is different for releases previous to the Solaris 10 10/08 release:

        ```
        # cd /cdrom/cdrom0/s0/Solaris_10/Tools/Installers
        ```

        Run the installer:

        ```
        # ./liveupgrade20 -noconsole - nodisplay
        ```

        The `-noconsole` and `-nodisplay` options prevent the character user interface (CUI) from displaying. The Solaris Live Upgrade CUI is no longer supported.

    b. If you are using the Solaris Software-2 CD, run the installer without changing the path:

        ```
        % ./installer
        ```

4. Verify that the packages have been installed successfully.

    ```
    # pkgchk -v SUNWlucfg SUNWlur SUNWluu
    ```

5. Obtain the list of patches.

6. Change to the patch directory.

   # **cd /var/tmp/lupatches**

7. Install the patches.

   # **patchadd -M /var/tmp/lupatches** *patch-id patch-id*

   patch-id is the patch number or numbers. Separate multiple patch names with a space.

   > **Note**
   >
   > The patches need to be applied in the order specified in info doc 206844.

8. Reboot the system if necessary. Certain patches require a reboot to be effective.

   # **init 6**

   x86 only
   Rebooting the system is required. Otherwise, Solaris Live Upgrade fails.

9. Create the new boot environment.

   # **lucreate [-c *BE-name*] -m *mountpoint:device:fs-options* \
   [-m ...] -n *BE-name***

   Explanation of the lucreate options follows:

   - *-c BE-name*
     (Optional) Assigns the name *BE-name* to the active boot environment. This option is not required and is used only when the first boot environment is created. If you run lucreate for the first time and you omit the -c option, then the software creates a default name for you.

   - **-m** *mountpoint:device:fs-options* **[-m ...]**
     Specifies the file systems' configuration of the new boot environment in the vfstab file. The file systems that are specified as arguments to -m can be on the same disk or they can be spread across multiple disks. Use this option as many times as needed to create the number of file systems that is needed.

     — *mountpoint* can be any valid mount point or - (hyphen), indicating a swap partition.

     — *device* field is the name of the disk device.

     — *fs-options* field is ufs, which indicates a UFS file system.

- **-n** *BE-name*

  The name of the boot environment to be created. *BE-name* must be unique on the system.

In the following example, a new boot environment named `solaris2` is created. The root (/) file system is placed on `c0t1d0s4`.

```
# lucreate -n solaris2 -m /:/dev/dsk/c0t1d0s4:ufs
```

This command generates output similar to the following. The time to complete varies depending on the system.

```
Discovering physical storage devices.
Discovering logical storage devices.
Cross referencing storage devices with boot environment configurations.
Determining types of file systems supported.
Validating file system requests.
The device name <c0t1d0s4> expands to device path </dev/dsk/c0t1d0s4>.
Preparing logical storage devices.
Preparing physical storage devices.
Configuring physical storage devices.
Configuring logical storage devices.
Analyzing system configuration.
No name for current boot environment.
Current boot environment is named <solaris1>.
Creating initial configuration for primary boot environment <solaris1>.
The device </dev/dsk/c0t1d0s4> is not a root device for any boot environment.
PBE configuration successful: PBE name <solaris1> PBE Boot Device </dev/dsk/c0t1d0s4>
Comparing source boot environment <solaris1> file systems with the
file system(s) you specified for the new boot environment.
Determining which file systems should be in the new boot environment.
Updating boot environment description database on all BEs.
Searching /dev for possible boot environment filesystem devices.
Updating system configuration files.
The device </dev/dsk/c0t1d0s4> is not a root device for any boot environment.
Creating configuration for boot environment <solaris2>.
Source boot environment is <solaris1>.
Creating boot environment <solaris2>.
Creating file systems on boot environment <solaris2>.
Creating <ufs> file system for </> on </dev/dsk/c0t1d0s4>.
Mounting file systems for boot environment <solaris2>.
Calculating required sizes of file systems for boot environment <solaris2>.
Populating file systems on boot environment <solaris2>.
Checking selection integrity.
Integrity check OK.
Populating contents of mount point </>.
Copying.
Creating shared file system mount points.
Creating compare databases for boot environment <solaris2>.
Creating compare database for file system </>.
Updating compare databases on boot environment <solaris2>.
Making boot environment <solaris2> bootable.
Population of boot environment <solaris2> successful.
Creation of boot environment <solaris2> successful.
```

10. (Optional) Verify that the boot environment is bootable.

    The `lustatus` command reports if the boot environment creation is complete and if the boot environment is bootable.

```
# lustatus BE-name
boot environment Is        Active  Active   Can    Copy
name             Complete  Now     OnReboot Delete Status
-------------------------------------------------------
solaris1         yes       yes     yes      no     -
solaris2         yes       no      no       yes    -
```

11. Apply patches to the boot environment.

    The patches you apply can come from several sources. The following example provides steps for installing patches from the SunSolve database. However, the procedure can be used for any patch or patch bundle, such as patches from custom patch bundles, Sun Update Connection enterprise patches, the Enterprise Installation Services CD, or security patches.

    a. From the SunSolve Web site, obtain the list of patches at `http://sunsolve.sun.com`.

    b. Create a directory such as `/var/tmp/lupatches`.

    c. Download the patches to that directory.

    d. Change to the patch directory.
       # **cd /var/tmp/lupatches**

    e. Apply the patches.

    The `luupgrade` command syntax follows:

    # **luupgrade -n** BE-name **-t -s** path-to-patches patch-name

    The options for the `luupgrade` command are explained in the following list:

    – **-n** BE-name
      Specifies the name of the boot environment where the patch is to be added.

    – **-t**
      Indicates to add patches to the boot environment.

    – **-s** path-to-patches
      Specifies the path to the directory that contains the patches to be added.

    – **patch-name**
      Specifies the name of the patch or patches to be added. Separate multiple patch names with a space.

    In the following examples, the patches are applied to the solaris2 boot environment. The patches can be stored on a local disk or on a server.

This example shows the installation of patches stored in a directory on the local disk:

```
# luupgrade -n solaris2 -t -s /tmp/solaris/patches 222222-01 333333-01
```

This example shows the installation of patches stored on a server:

```
# luupgrade -n solaris2 -t -s
/net/server/export/solaris/patch-dir/patches 222222-01 333333-01
```

Note

The Solaris 10 `patchadd` command correctly orders patches for you, but Solaris 9 and earlier releases require patches to be in dependency order. When using the `luupgrade` command to apply patches, apply the patches in dependency order, regardless of the Solaris release you are using. Sun uses dependency order as part of the standard testing of the `luupgrade` command, and you can be assured that this order was tested.

12. Examine the patch log file to make sure no patch failures occurred.

13. Activate the new boot environment.

    ```
    # luactivate BE-name
    ```

    BE-name specifies the name of the boot environment that is to be activated.

    See the following documents for more information about activating a boot environment:

    – For an x86 based system, the `luactivate` command is required when you boot a boot environment for the first time. Subsequent activations can be made by selecting the boot environment from the GRUB menu. For step-by-step instructions, see *Solaris 10 8/07 Installation Guide: Solaris Live Upgrade and Upgrade Planning*. Specifically, see the chapter "Activating a Boot Environment With the GRUB Menu." The book is available at `http://docs.sun.com`.

    – To successfully activate a boot environment, that boot environment must meet several conditions. For more information, see Table 4.3.

14. Reboot the system.

```
# init 6
```

> **Caution**
>
> Use only the init or shutdown command to reboot. If you use the reboot, halt, or uadmin command, then the system does not switch boot environments. The most recently active boot environment is booted again.

The boot environments have switched and the new boot environment is now the active boot environment.

15. (Optional) Fall back to a different boot environment.

a. (Optional) Verify that the boot environment is bootable.

The lustatus command reports if the boot environment creation is complete and if the boot environment is bootable.

```
# lustatus BE-name
boot environmentIsActiveActiveCanCopy
name          CompleteNowOnRebootDeleteStatus
-----------------------------------------------------------
solaris1      yesyesyesno-
solaris2      yesnonoyes-
```

b. Activate the solaris1 boot environment.

The following procedures work if the boot environment is bootable. If the new boot environment is not viable or you want to switch to another boot environment, see *Solaris 10 Installation Guide: Solaris Live Upgrade and Upgrade Planning*. Specifically, see the chapter "Failure Recovery," which is available at http://docs.sun.com.

- For SPARC based systems activate the boot environment and reboot:

```
# /sbin/luactivate solaris1
# init 6
```

- For x86 based systems, reboot and choose the solaris1 boot environment from the GRUB menu.

```
GNU GRUB version 0.95 (616K lower / 4127168K upper memory)
+------------------------------------------------+
|solaris1
|solaris1 failsafe
|Solaris2
|solaris2 failsafe
+------------------------------------------------+
Use the ^ and v keys to select which entry is highlighted. Press enter to boot the
selected OS, 'e' to edit the commands before booting, or 'c' for a command-line.
# init 6
```

4.5 Patch Automation Tools

In addition to using Solaris Live Upgrade and the patch utilities to patch a system, a range of higher-level patch automation tools is available. See Table 4.4 for descriptions of patch automation tools.

Table 4.4 Patch Automation Tools Description

Tool	Description
Sun xVM Ops Center	Sun's premier patch management tool. Sun xVM Ops Center provides patch management to enterprise customers for systems running the Solaris 8, 9, and 10 releases or the Linux operating systems. Sun xVM Ops Center also provides OS and firmware provisioning, inventory, registration, and system management. See the Center's Web site at `http://www.sun.com/software/products/xvmopscenter/index.jsp`. Sun xVM Ops Center provides the following tools for managing your systems: ▪ **Optimize your maintenance window**—Use Sun xVM Ops Center's automation to check for dependencies, schedule update jobs, and stage your updates. You can also create patch policies to define which updates are applied. ▪ **Improve security and availability**—Make these improvements by keeping your Solaris and Linux systems updated with the latest patches. The Sun xVM Ops Center knowledge base captures all new patches, packages, Sun freeware, and RPMs. Sun develops and tests all dependencies and then publishes updated dependency rules to its clients.

Table 4.4 Patch Automation Tools Description (*continued*)

Tool	Description
	▪ **Register multiple systems**—Register your hardware and software, or gear, at the same time with the new, quick, and easy registration client in Sun xVM Ops Center.
	▪ **Manage and organize your registered Sun asset inventory**—Control your inventory by using the gear feature in Sun xVM Ops Center. Update your Solaris, Red Hat, and SuSE operating systems from a single console.
Patch Check Advanced (PCA):	A popular third-party tool developed by Martin Paul. PCA generates lists of installed and missing patches for Solaris systems and optionally downloads patches. PCA resolves dependencies between patches and installs them in the correct order. The tool is a good solution for customers interested in an easy-to-use patch automation tool.
	To try PCA, run these commands on any Solaris system:
	1. `$ wget http://www.par.univie.ac.at/solaris/pca/pca`
	2. `$ chmod +x pca`
	3. `$ ./pca`
`smpatch` command and Update Manager GUI	Both the `smpatch` command and Update Manager GUI are tools that are included in the Solaris OS.
	▪ `smpatch` is a command-line tool. This command enables you to analyze and update the Solaris OS with current patches.
	▪ The Update Manager GUI is based on the `smpatch` command. You can check which patches or updates are available or you can easily select the patches to install. To display the GUI, run update manager.
	For both of these tools, support from Sun is the following:
	▪ For customers with a valid support contract, all patches are available.
	▪ For customers without a valid support contract, only security and driver patches are available.

continues

Table 4.4 Patch Automation Tools Description (*continued*)

Tool	Description
Enterprise Installation Standards (EIS)	Enterprise Installation Standards (EIS) originated from Sun field personnel's goal of developing best practices for installation standards for systems installed at customer sites.
	EIS has traditionally been available only through Sun field personnel but is now available directly to customers from xVM OPs Center as baselines. Baselines provide a good option for customers who want to patch to a defined and tested patch baseline.
	The EIS set of patches is based on the Recommended Patch Cluster with additional patches included by the field engineers. These additional patches include products or patches to address issues that do not meet the criteria for inclusion in the Recommended Patch Cluster. The EIS patch baseline covers the Solaris OS and other products such as Sun Cluster, Sun VTS, System Service Processor (SSP), System Management Services (SMS), Sun StorEdge QFS, and Sun StorEdge SAM-FS. The baseline also includes patches that provide firmware updates.
	The EIS patch baseline is tested by QA prior to release. The images installed on servers by Sun's manufacturers are also based on the EIS patch baseline. Additional testing by Sun's manufacturers as well as feedback from the EIS user community raises confidence in the EIS patch baseline content. Because many system installations worldwide use the EIS methodology, any inherent problems quickly appear and can be addressed. If problems arise with the EIS patch baseline, recommendations are communicated to the EIS community. Sun field engineers consider installing the EIS set of patches on a new system a best practice. This set can also be used to patch existing systems to the same patch level.

4.6 Overview of Patch Types

Table 4.5 describes the specific types of patches that you can apply.

Table 4.5 Description of Patch Types

Patch type	Description
Kernel patch (formerly known as Kernel Update [KU] patch)	A generally available standard patch. This patch is important because of the scope of change affecting a system. A Kernel patch changes the Solaris kernel and related core Solaris functionality. A reboot is required to activate the new kernel version.

Table 4.5 Description of Patch Types (*continued*)

Patch type	Description
Deferred-Activation patches	Starting with patch 119254-42 and 119255-42, the patch installation utilities–`patchadd` and `patchrm`–have been modified to change the way that certain patches delivering features are handled. This modification affects the installation of these patches on any Solaris 10 release. These "deferred-activation" patches better handle the large scope of change delivered in feature patches.
	A limited number of patches are designated as a deferred-activation patch. Typically a deferred-activation patch is a kernel patch associated with a Solaris 10 release after the Solaris 10 3/05 release, such as the Solaris 10 8/07 release. Patches are designated a deferred-activation patch if the variable SUNW_PATCH_SAFE_MODE is set in the `pkginfo` file. Patches not designated as deferred-activation patches continue to install as before. For example, previously released patches, such as kernel patches 118833-36 (SPARC) and 118855-36 (x86), do not use the deferred-activation patching utilities to install.
	Previously, complex patch scripting was required for these kernel patches. The scripting was required to avoid issues during the patch installation process on an active partition because of inconsistencies between the objects the patch delivers and the running system (active partition). Now, deferred-activation patching uses the loopback file system (`lofs`) to ensure the stability of the running system. When a patch is applied to the running system, the `lofs` preserves stability during the patching process. These large kernel patches have always required a reboot, but now the required reboot activates the changes made by the `lofs`. The patch README provides instructions on which patches require a reboot.
Temporary patch (T-patch)	A patch that has been built and submitted for release but has not completed the full test and verification process.
	Before being officially released, Solaris patches are structurally audited, functionally verified, and subjected to a system test process. Testing occurs when patches are in the "T-patch" state. After successfully completing the test process, the patches are officially released. For an overview of Sun's patch test coverage, see the SunSolve Web site at `http://sunsolve.sun.com`. Find the "Patches and Updates" section and then the "Patch Documents and Articles" section. The text coverage is in the section "Testing Overview."
	A T-patch might be made available to a customer involved in an active escalation to verify that the patch fixes the customer's problem. This type of patch is identified by a leading "T" in the patch ID, for example, T108528-14. The words "Preliminary Patch - Not Yet Released" appear on the first line of the patch README file. After the patch has been tested and verified, the T-patch designation is removed and the patch is released.

continues

Table 4.5 Description of Patch Types (*continued*)

Patch type	Description
	Note: If you have a T-patch installed and then find that the patch is released at the same revision, there is no need to remove the T-patch and then install the released version. The released version and the T-patch are the same, except for the `README` file.
Security T-patches	The "Security T-Patches" section of the SunSolve site provides early access to patches that address security issues.
	These patches are still in the T-patch stage, which means they have not completed the verification and patch testing process. The installation of Security T-patches is at the user's discretion and risk. Information about the issues addressed by Security T-patches and possible workarounds is available through the Free Security Sun Alert data collection.
	On the SunSolve Web site, find the "Security Resources" section. See the "Security T-Patches and ISRs" or "Sun Security Coordination Team" sections.
Rejuvenated patch	Patches that become overly large or complex sometimes follow a process of **rejuvenation**. The rejuvenation process provides patches that incrementally install complex new functionality in relative safety. When a patch becomes a rejuvenated patch, no more revisions of the patch are created. Instead, further changes to the rejuvenated patch are delivered in a series of new patch IDs. These new patches depend upon and require the rejuvenated patch. If one of the new patches becomes complex over time, then that patch could become a rejuvenated patch. For example, the Kernel patch is rejuvenated when needed.
	The advantage of this process is that although a customer must install the complex patch once, future patches are much simpler to install.
	For more details, see the "Patch Rejuvenation" article on the SunSolve Web site at `http://sunsolve.sun.com`. Click on the "Patches and Updates" section, then see the "Documents Relating to Updating/Patching" section.
Point patch	A custom patch. This patch is provided to a customer as a response to a specific problem encountered by that customer. Point patches are only appropriate for the customers for whom the patches have been delivered. These patches are typically created for one customer because the majority of customers would consider the "fix" worse than the issue the fix is addressing. These patches are created on a branch of the Solaris source code base and are not folded back into the main source base.
	Access to a point patch is restricted and should only be installed after consultation with Sun support personnel.

Table 4.5 Description of Patch Types (*continued*)

Patch type	Description
Restricted patch (R-patch)	A rare patch that has a special lock characteristic. An R-patch locks the package modified. This lock prevents subsequent modification of the package by other patches.
	R-patches are used in circumstances similar to point patches. Like a point patch, an R-patch is only appropriate for the customer for whom the patches have been delivered. These patches are created on a branch of the Solaris source code base and are not folded back into the main source base.
	Before the "official" standard patch can be applied, an R-patch must be manually removed.
Interim Diagnostic Relief (IDR)	An IDR provides software to help diagnose a customer issue or provides preliminary, temporary relief for an issue. An IDR is provided in a patch format similar to an R-patch. However, because an IDR does not provide a final fix to the issue, an IDR is not a substitute for an actual patch. The official patch or patches should replace the IDR as soon as is practical.
	For more details, see the "Interim Relief/Diagnostics" article on the SunSolve Web site at `http://sunsolve.sun.com`. Click the "Patches and Updates" section and then see the "Documents Relating to Updating/Patching" section.
Interim Security Relief (ISR)	A patch that fixes a public security issue. This patch is a type of IDR. An ISR is an early stage fix that provides protection to a security vulnerability that is publicly known. An ISR has not completed the review, verification, and testing processes. The installation of an ISR is at the user's discretion and risk. An ISR is available on the "Security T-Patch" download section on SunSolve at `http://sunsolve.sun.com`. Information about the issues addressed by an ISR and possible workarounds is available through the Free Security Sun Alert data collection. On the SunSolve site, in the "Security Resources" section, see the "Sun Security Coordination Team" section.
Nonstandard patch	A patch that cannot be installed by using the `patchadd` command. A nonstandard patch is not delivered in package format. This patch must be installed according to the Special Install Instructions specified in the patch's `README` file. A nonstandard patch typically delivers firmware or application software fixes.

continues

Table 4.5 Description of Patch Types (*continued*)

Patch type	Description
Withdrawn patch	If a released patch is found to cause serious issues, then the patch is removed from the SunSolve Web site.
	▪ The patch is no longer available for download.
	▪ The README file remains on the SunSolve Web site. The README file is changed to state that the patch is withdrawn and a brief statement is added about the problem and why the patch was removed.
	▪ The patch is logged for a year in the list of withdrawn patches. On the SunSolve Web site, click the "Patches and Updates" section, then see the "Patch Reports" section for the "Withdrawn Patch Report."
	▪ A Sun Alert is released to notify customers about the withdrawn patch. The Sun Alert specifies any actions that should be taken by customers who have the withdrawn patch installed on their system. The Sun Alert appears in the list of recently published Sun Alerts.
Interactive patches	A patch that requires user interaction in order to be installed. The patch must be installed according to the Special Install Instructions specified in the patch's README file.
Update releases and script patches	Sun periodically releases updates to the current version of the Solaris distribution. These releases are sometimes known as an **Update** release. An Update release is a complete distribution and is named with a date designation; for example, Solaris 10 6/06 release.
	An Update release consists of all the packages in the original release, such as Solaris 10 3/05, with all accumulated patches pre-applied and includes any new features that are qualified for inclusion.
	The process of pre-applying patches involves some patches that do not get released. Therefore, a system with an Update release installed appears to have some patches applied that cannot be found on the SunSolve Web site. These patches are called **script patches**. Script patches do not deliver bug fixes or new features, but they deliver fixes that are a result of issues with the creation of the image. As a result, script patches are not made available for customers because they are not required outside of creating the Update release.
Genesis patch	A rare patch that installs a new package.
	Generally, new packages are only available as part of a new release of a product. Patches only change the content of packages already installed on a system. However, in rare cases, new packages can be installed on a system by applying a genesis patch. For example, patch 122640-05 is a genesis patch that delivers and installs ZFS packages. This patch contains new ZFS packages that are installed on systems with older Solaris 10 releases that do not contain the new ZFS functionality.

4.7 Patch README Special Instructions

Patches have associated metadata that describes their attributes. Metadata includes special handling requirements such as "reboot after installation" or "single-user mode installation required." These attributes are translated into text in the README file, which should be read.

The Solaris patch utilities also utilize the metadata contained in the pkginfo and pkgmap files.

4.7.1 When to Patch in Single-User Mode

You can avoid booting to single-user mode by using Solaris Live Upgrade. You can also avoid system downtime. Solaris Live Upgrade enables patches to be installed while your system is in production. You create a copy of the currently running system and patch the copy. Then, you simply reboot into the patched environment at a convenient time. You can fall back to the original boot environment, if needed.

If you cannot use Solaris Live Upgrade, then the patch README file specifies which patches should be installed in single-user mode. Although the patch tools do not force you to use single-user mode, the instructions in the patch's README file should be followed. Patching in single-user mode helps ensure that the system is quiesced. Minimizing activity on the system is important. Some patches update components on the system that are commonly used. Using single-user mode preserves the stability of the system and reduces the chances of these components being used while they are being updated.

Using single-user mode is critical for system patches like the kernel patch. If you apply a Kernel patch in multiuser mode, then you significantly increase your risk of the system experiencing an inconsistent state.

The patch properties apply to both installing and removing patches. If single-user mode was required for applying the patch, then you should also use single-user mode for removing a patch. Changes being made to the system are equally significant, irrespective of the direction in which they're being made, for example, installing instead of removing.

You can safely boot into single-user mode by changing the run level with the init command.

- Using the init s command does not quiesce the system enough for patches that specify single-user mode installation, but this command can be safely used.
- Using the init 0 command and then booting to single-user mode provides a more quiesced system because fewer daemons are running. However, this command requires a reboot.

4.7.2 When to Reboot After Applying or Removing a Patch

If a patch requires a reboot, then you cannot avoid the reboot. Sooner or later, you must reboot to enable the changes that the patch introduced. However, you can choose a strategy to defer the reboot until a more convenient time.

- One method is to use Solaris Live Upgrade, which enables patches to be installed while your system is running. You can avoid single-user mode and use multiuser mode. Then, you simply reboot into the patched environment at a more convenient time.

> **Note**
>
> Solaris Live Upgrade does not support Veritas encapsulated root (/) file systems very well. The root (/) file system can be a Veritas Volume Manager volume (VxVM). If VxVM volumes are configured on your current system, you can use the `lucreate` command to create a new boot environment. When the data is copied to the new boot environment, the Veritas file system configuration is lost and a UFS file system is created on the new boot environment.

- Another approach with similar benefits to Solaris Live Upgrade is to use RAID-1 volumes (disk mirroring) with Solaris Volume Manager. For example, you can split the mirror, mount the inactive root (/) file system mirror, and apply the patches to the copy by using the `patchadd -R` command. The `-R` option enables you to specify an alternate root (/) file system location. The `-R` option is usually intended for use with diskless clients, but the option can also be used to delay the reboot.

The README file for some patches specifies that a reboot is required after the patch has been installed or removed. This request for a reboot might contain two reboot instructions:

- The first instruction is to "reboot after" patching to see the fix. This instruction has no time constraints because this is just a reminder that some of the changes are not activated until a reboot occurs.
- The second instruction is to "reboot immediately" after patching.

    If you are patching an active boot environment, then a reboot is needed to activate certain objects that have been patched, like the kernel. After installation to an active boot environment, some patches specify in their README file that a reboot or reconfiguration reboot (`reboot -- -r`) is required.

    Some of these patches specify that a reboot must occur immediately after the patch is installed on an active boot environment. The reboot is required because the active boot environment is in an inconsistent state if the target system is running a kernel at a patch level below 120012-14. When the reboot is performed, the system is stabilized.

For example, a patch could deliver new kernel binaries and a new library. After the new kernel binaries are installed on the active boot environment, the kernel binaries are still inactive because they will not be loaded until the system is rebooted. The new library might contain interface or behavior changes that depend on the new kernel. However, the new library could be linked and invoked at any point after the library is installed in the file system. This can result in an inconsistent system state, which could potentially lead to serious problems.

Generally, you can complete patching operations before initiating the reboot, but normal operations should not be resumed until the reboot is performed. Some patches, such as 118855-36, require a reboot when they are applied to an active boot environment before further patches can be applied. The instruction is specified in the "Special Install Instructions" section of the patch's README file. As an added safety mechanism, such patches typically contain code to prevent further patching until the reboot is performed.

Kernel patch 120012-14 is the first patch to utilize the *deferred-activation patching* functionality. Deferred-activation patching was introduced in the Solaris 10 08/07 release to ensure system consistency during patching of an active boot environment. Such patches set the SAFEMODE parameter in their pkginfo file or files. Deferred-activation patching utilizes loopback mounts (lofs) to mask the patched objects until a reboot is performed. Deferred-activation patching is designed to enable subsequent patches to be applied before the reboot is initiated. If any subsequent patch directly or indirectly requires a patch installed in deferred-activation patching mode, the patch will also be automatically installed in deferred-activation patching mode by the patchadd command. Objects updated by using deferred-activation patching will be activated upon reboot of the system.

4.7.3 Patch Metadata for Non-Global Zones

Patches contain Solaris Zones specific metadata to ensure the correct patching of a Zones environment. Detailed information can be found in the following references available at http://docs.sun.com:

- See the patchadd command -G option.

- See *System Administration Guide: Solaris Containers-Resource Management and Solaris Zones*. Specifically, see the chapter "About Packages and Patches on a Solaris System With Zones Installed (Overview)."

4.8 Patch Dependencies (Interrelationships)

The functionality delivered in a patch, consisting of either bug fixes or new features, might have interrelationships with the functionality delivered in other patches.

These interrelationships are determined by three fields in the package's `pkginfo` file:

- The SUNW_REQUIRES field identifies patch dependencies. These prerequisite patches must be installed before the patch can be installed.
- The SUNW_OBSOLETES field identifies patches whose contents have been accumulated into this patch. This new patch obsoletes the original patches.
- The SUNW_INCOMPAT field identifies patches that are incompatible with this patch. Therefore, this patch cannot be installed on the same system.

These fields are used by the `patchadd` and `patchrm` commands to automatically ensure the consistency of the target system that is being patched. These fields are included in the patch `README` file.

4.8.1 SUNW_REQUIRES Field for Patch Dependencies

The SUNW_REQUIRES field identifies patch dependencies. The functionality delivered in a patch might have a code dependency on the changes or functionality that is delivered in other patches. Therefore, one patch requires one or more other patches to function correctly. If a patch depends on one or more patches, then the patch specifies the required patches in the SUNW_REQUIRES field in the `pkginfo` file in the patch's packages. This information is also reflected in the `README` file. Such prerequisite patches must be installed before this patch can be installed.

The dependency requirement can only work one way. If Patch A requires Patch B, Patch B cannot require Patch A. Because patches are cumulative, if Patch A-01 requires Patch B-01, any revision of Patch B greater than or equal to -01 also satisfies the requirement.

If other types of dependencies exist, then they are specified in the patch's `README` file and can include the following:

- Conditional dependencies indicate a hard-coded patch dependency that occurs only under specific conditions, for example, only if CDE 1.3 is installed on the target system.
- Soft dependencies indicate that other patches are required to completely deliver a particular bug fix or feature, but the system remains in a consistent state without the other patches.

4.8.2 SUNW_OBSOLETES Field for Patch Accumulation and Obsolescence

The SUNW_OBSOLETES field identifies patch accumulation and obsolescence. Sometimes, bug fixes or new features cause two or more existing patches to become closely intertwined. For example, a bidirectional, hard-coded dependency might exist between two patches. In such cases, it might be necessary to accumulate the functionality of two or more patches into one patch, thereby rendering the other patch or patches obsolete. The patch into which the other patch's functionality is accumulated specifies the patch ID or IDs of the patch or patches that it has obsoleted. This information is in the SUNW_OBSOLETES field in the pkginfo files delivered in the patch's sparse packages. This declaration is called *explicit obsolescence*.

The patch accumulation can only work one way. That is, if Patch A accumulates Patch B, Patch A now contains all of Patch B's functionality. Patch B is now obsolete. No further revision of Patch B will be generated.

Due to the accumulation of patches, a later revision of a patch "implicitly" obsoletes earlier revisions of the same patch. Patches that are implicitly obsoleted are not flagged in the SUNW_OBSOLETES field. For example, Patch A-Revision xx does not need to explicitly obsolete Patch A-Revision x-1 with a SUNW_OBSOLETES entry in the pkginfo file.

> **Note**
>
> For Solaris 10 releases after August 2007, a patch might be released that contains no new changes. This patch might state that it obsoletes another patch that was released some months earlier. This is a consequence of the Solaris Update patch creation process. If you have the obsoleted patch installed, and the new patch does not list any new changes, you do not need to install this new patch.
>
> For example, the timezones patch 122032-05 was obsoleted by patch 125378-02. If you already have 122032-05 installed, there is no need to install 125378-02 because patch 125378-02 does not deliver any new changes.

4.8.3 SUNW_INCOMPAT Field for Incompatibility

Occasionally, two or more patches are incompatible with one another. Incompatibility is frequently defined in point patches and IDRs. Incompatibility is rarely defined in regular patches. An incompatibility is specified in the SUNW_INCOMPAT field in the pkginfo file in the sparse package of one or both of the patches.

Patch incompatibility is two way. If Patch A or Patch B specifies an incompatibility with the other patch, then only one of the patches can be installed on the target system. For example, if Patch A is already installed on the target system and Patch B is incompatible with it, the patch install utility `patchadd` will not allow Patch B to be installed. If Patch B must be installed, Patch A must first be removed.

Both patches or an incompatible pairing do not have to define the incompatibility. Typically, a point patch or an IDR defines an incompatibility because these types of patches are from nonstandard code branches.

5

Solaris File Systems

This chapter describes file systems, which are an essential component of the Solaris Operating System (Solaris OS) that is used to organize and store data. This chapter describes the file systems that are commonly used by Solaris systems and describes how they are managed and used. This chapter also includes numerous examples that show how to work with file systems on the Solaris OS.

5.1 Solaris File System Overview

A *file system* is a hierarchical structure of directories that is used to organize and store files and other directories. A *directory*, or *folder*, is a container in which to store files and other directories. A *file* is a discrete collection of data, which can be structured in numerous formats. Such formats include architecture-specific binary files, plain text files, application-specific data files, and so on.

The *root file system* contains all the parts of the Solaris OS that are required to run the operating system on the hardware. The root file system is available by default. To make other file systems available to the system, they must be *mounted*, which attaches the file system to a specified directory in the hierarchy. The point of attachment is called the *mount point*. The root file system is mounted on the / mount point.

The Solaris OS supports the following types of file systems.

- **Local file systems.** Such file systems enable you to locally store data on storage media such as fixed disks, CD-ROMs, memory sticks, and diskettes. The Solaris OS supports the following local file systems:
  - **UFS** and **ZFS**—The UNIX file system (UFS) and ZFS file system are typically used on fixed disks, but can be used by CD-ROMs, memory sticks, and diskettes.
  - **PCFS**—The PC file system (PCFS) enables direct access to files on DOS formatted disks from within the Solaris OS. This file system is often used by diskettes.
  - **HSFS**—The High Sierra file system (HSFS) is a read-only variant of UFS that supports Rock Ridge extensions to ISO 9660. This format does not support hard links.
- **Distributed file systems.** These file systems enable you to access remote data that is stored on network servers as though the data is on the local system. The Solaris OS supports the Network File System (NFS), where a server exports the shared data and clients access the data over the network. NFS also uses the AUTOFS file system to automatically mount and unmount file systems.
- **Pseudo file systems.** Such file systems present virtual devices in a hierarchical manner that resembles a typical file system. A pseudo file system is also called a virtual file system. The Solaris OS supports several pseudo file systems, including the following:
  - **LOFS**—The loopback file system (LOFS) enables you to create a new virtual file system so that you can access files by using an alternative path name.
  - **TMPFS**—The temporary file system (TMPFS) uses swap space and main memory as a temporary backing store for file system reads and writes. This is the default file system that is used for the /tmp directory.

The remainder of this file system overview covers the general file system concepts such as mounting and unmounting file systems, using the /etc/vfstab file, determining a file system type, and monitoring file systems.

5.1.1 Mounting File Systems

A file system must be mounted on a mount point to be accessed. The root file system is mounted by default, so the files and directories that are stored in the root file system are always available. Even if a file system is mounted, files and directories in that file system can only be accessed based on ownership and permissions. For information about file system object permissions, see Chapter 11, "Solaris User Management."

The Solaris OS provides tools that enable you to manage file systems that are available on different kinds of storage media.

The following general guidelines might help you determine how to manage the mounting of file systems on your system.

- **Infrequently used local or remote file systems.** Do one of the following:
  - Use the mount command to manually mount the file system when needed.
  - Add an entry for the file system in the /etc/vfstab file that specifies that the file system should not be mounted at boot time. For more information about the /etc/vfstab file, see the vfstab(4) man page.

- **Frequently used local file systems.** Add an entry for the file system in the /etc/vfstab file that specifies that the file system should be mounted when the system is booted to the multiuser state.

- **Frequently used remote file systems.** Do one of the following:
  - Add an entry for the file system in the /etc/vfstab file that specifies that the file system should be mounted when the system is booted to the multiuser state.
  - Configure autofs, which automatically mounts the specified file system when accessed. When the file system is not accessed, autofs automatically unmounts it.

- **Local ZFS file systems.** Use the zfs mount command or set the mount-point property.

- **Removable media.** Attach the media to the system or insert the media into the drive and run the volcheck command.

Most file system types can be mounted and unmounted by using the mount and umount commands. Similarly, the mountall and umountall commands can be used to mount or unmount all of the file systems that are specified in the /etc/vfstab file.

The mount -v command shows information about the file systems that are currently mounted on the system. This information is retrieved from the /etc/mnttab file, which stores information about currently mounted file systems. The mount -v output describes the device or file system, the mount point, the file system type, the mount options, and the date and time at which the file system was mounted.

The following output shows UFS and NFS file systems, as well as several pseudo file systems. The root file system (/dev/dsk/c0t0d0s0) is a local UFS file system that is mounted at the / mount point, while the solarsystem:/export/home/terry and solarsystem:/export/tools file systems are remotely mounted at /home/terry and /share/tools on the local system. In addition, the mount -v output shows information about these pseudo file systems: devfs, dev, ctfs, proc, mntfs, objfs, fd, and tmpfs.

```
$ mount -v
/dev/dsk/c0t0d0s0 on / type ufs read/write/setuid/devices/intr/largefiles/logging/
xattr/onerror=panic/dev=2200000 on Mon Oct 20 11:25:08 2008
/devices on /devices type devfs read/write/setuid/devices/dev=55c0000 on Mon Oct 20
11:24:48 2008
/dev on /dev type dev read/write/setuid/devices/dev=5600000 on Mon Oct 20 11:24:48 2008
ctfs on /system/contract type ctfs read/write/setuid/devices/dev=5640001 on Mon Oct 20
11:24:48 2008
proc on /proc type proc read/write/setuid/devices/dev=5680000 on Mon Oct 20 11:24:48
2008
mnttab on /etc/mnttab type mntfs read/write/setuid/devices/dev=56c0001 on Mon Oct 20
11:24:48 2008
swap on /etc/svc/volatile type tmpfs read/write/setuid/devices/xattr/dev=5700001 on Mon
Oct 20 11:24:48 2008
objfs on /system/object type objfs read/write/setuid/devices/dev=5740001 on Mon Oct 20
11:24:48 2008
fd on /dev/fd type fd read/write/setuid/devices/dev=58c0001 on Mon Oct 20 11:25:09 2008
swap on /tmp type tmpfs read/write/setuid/devices/xattr/dev=5700002 on Mon Oct 20
11:25:14 2008
swap on /var/run type tmpfs read/write/setuid/devices/xattr/dev=5700003 on Mon Oct 20
11:25:14 2008
solarsystem:/export/home/terry on /home/terry type nfs remote/read/write/setuid/
devices/xattr/dev=5940004 on Mon Oct 20 13:55:06 2008
solarsystem:/export/tools on /share/tools type nfs remote/read/write/setuid/devices/
xattr/dev=5940006 on Mon Oct 20 13:55:08 2008
```

For more information about the mount command, see the mount(1M) man page and the man pages that are associated with particular file system types, such as mount_nfs(1M). Use the man command to access a man page. For example, to view the mount_nfs(1M) man page, type the following:

```
$ man mount_nfs
```

5.1.2 Unmounting File Systems

Unmounting a file system makes it unavailable and removes its entry from the /etc/mnttab file, which maintains information about currently mounted file systems and resources.

Some file system administration tasks cannot be performed on mounted file systems, such as when using the fsck command to check and repair a file system.

A file system cannot be unmounted if it is busy, which means that a program is accessing a directory or a file in that file system, or if the file system is being shared. You can make a file system available for unmounting by doing the following:

- Changing to a directory in a different file system
- Logging out of the system
- Using the `fuser` command to find and stop any processes that are accessing the file system
- Unsharing the file system
- Using the `umount -f` command to forcibly unmount a busy file system

  This practice is not recommended as it could cause a loss of data. The `-f` option is only available for UFS and NFS file systems.

The safest way to stop all processes that are accessing a file system before unmounting it is to use the `fuser` command to report on the processes that are accessing a particular file system. Once the processes are known, send a SIGKILL to each process.

The following example shows how an unmount of the `/export/home` file system failed because the file system is busy. The `fuser -c` command obtains the IDs of the processes that are accessing the file system. The `ps -ef` and `grep` commands enable you to identify the particular process. Next, use the `fuser -c -k` command to kill the running process. Finally, rerun the `umount` command to unmount the file system.

```
# umount /export/home
umount: /export/home busy
# fuser -c /export/home
/export/home:        9002o
# ps -ef | grep 9002
    root  9002  8979  0 20:06:17 pts/1     0:00 cat
# fuser -c -k /export/home
/export/home:        9002o
[1]+  Killed                  cat >/export/home/test
# umount /export/home
```

5.1.3 Using the `/etc/vfstab` File

To avoid having to manually mount file systems each time you want to access them, update the virtual file system table, `/etc/vfstab`. This file includes the list of file systems and information about how to mount them. You can use the `/etc/vfstab` file to do the following:

- Specify file systems to automatically mount when the system boots
- Mount file systems by specifying only the mount point name

An `/etc/vfstab` file is created based on your selections during installation.
You can edit the `/etc/vfstab` file on a system at any time. To add an entry, specify the following information:

- Device where the file system resides
- File system mount point
- File system type
- Whether to automatically mount the file system when the system boots
- Mount options

The following example `/etc/vfstab` file shows the file systems on a system
that has two disks, `c1t0d0` and `c1t1d0`. In this example, the UFS file system
entry for `/space` on the `/dev/dsk/c1t0d0s0` slice will be automatically mounted
on the `/space` mount point when the system boots.

```
# cat /etc/vfstab
#device           device             mount          FS      fsck    mount     mount
#to mount         to fsck            point          type    pass    at boot   options
#
fd        -       /dev/fd  fd        -       no      -
/proc     -       /proc    proc      -       no      -
/dev/dsk/c1t1d0s1         -          -       swap    -       no        -
/dev/dsk/c1t1d0s0         /dev/rdsk/c1t1d0s0         /       ufs     1       no        -
/dev/dsk/c1t0d0s0         /dev/rdsk/c1t0d0s0         /space  ufs     2       yes       -
swap      -       /tmp     tmpfs     -       yes     -
/devices          -          /devices          devfs   -       no        -
ctfs      -       /system/contract          ctfs    -       no        -
objfs     -       /system/object    objfs   -       no        -
```

5.1.4 Determining a File System Type

You can determine the type of a file system in one of the following ways:

- Using the `fstyp` command
- Viewing the FS type field in the `/etc/vfstab` file
- Viewing the contents of the `/etc/default/fs` file for local file systems
- Viewing the contents of the `/etc/dfs/fstypes` file for other file systems

If you have the raw device name of a disk slice that contains a file system, then
use the `fstyp` command to determine the file system's type.

You can also determine the file system type by looking at the output of the `mount  -v`
command or using the `grep` command to find the file system entry in one of the file

system tables. If the file system is mounted, search the `/etc/mnttab` file. If the file system is unmounted, search the `/etc/vfstab` file.

The following example determines the file system type for the `/space` file system by searching for its entry in the `/etc/vfstab` file. The fourth column of the file system entry indicates that the file system is of type `ufs`.

```
$ grep /space /etc/vfstab
/dev/dsk/c1t0d0s0       /dev/rdsk/c1t0d0s0       /space  ufs    2    yes    -
```

This example determines the file system type for currently mounted home directories by searching the `/etc/mnttab` file. Currently, only the home directory for user sandy is mounted and the third column indicates that the file system is of type `nfs`.

```
$ grep home /etc/mnttab
homeserver:/export/home/sandy  /home/sandy  nfs   xattr,dev=5940004  1224491106
```

5.1.5 Monitoring File Systems

The `fsstat` command, introduced in the Solaris 10 6/06 release, reports on file system operations for the specified mount point or file system type. The following example shows general UFS file system activity:

```
$ fsstat ufs
 new   name   name  attr  attr lookup rddir  read read  write write
 file remov  chng   get   set   ops   ops   ops bytes  ops bytes
24.6M 22.3M 2.08M  150G 13.2M  31.8G  311M 5.77G 7.50T 3.25G 6.07T ufs
```

5.2 UFS File Systems

The *UNIX File System* (UFS) is the default local disk-based file system used by the Solaris 10 Operating System.

In UFS, all information that pertains to a file is stored in a special file index node called the *inode*. The name of the file is not stored in the inode, but is stored in the directory itself. The file name information and hierarchy information that constitute the directory structure of UFS are stored in directories.

Each directory stores a list of file names and their corresponding inode numbers. The directory itself is stored in a file as a series of chunks, which are groups of the directory entries. Each directory contains two special files: dot (.) and dot-dot (. .).

The *dot file* is a link to the directory itself. The *dot-dot file* is a link to the parent directory.

Each UFS file system has a *superblock*, which specifies critical information about the disk geometry and layout of the file system. The superblock includes the location of each cylinder group and a list of available free blocks.

Each *cylinder group* has a backup copy of the file system's superblock to ensure the integrity of the file system should the superblock become corrupted. The cylinder group also has information about the in-use inodes, information about free fragments and blocks, and an array of inodes whose size varies according to the number of inodes in a cylinder group. The rest of the cylinder group is filled by the data blocks.

The next part of this section includes subsections that describe how to manage UFS file systems. The following subsections cover the following basic UFS management tasks:

- Creating a UFS file system
- Backing up and restoring file systems
- Using quotas to manage disk space

In addition to the basic tasks, the following subsections cover other UFS management tasks:

- Checking file system integrity
- Using access control lists
- Using UFS logging
- Using extended file attributes
- Using multiterabyte UFS file systems
- Creating UFS shapshots

For more information about the UFS file system, see *System Administration Guide: Devices and File Systems* on http://docs.sun.com.

5.2.1 Creating a UFS File System

Before you can create a UFS file system on a disk, the disk must be formatted and divided into slices. A *disk slice* is a physical subset of a disk that is composed of a single range of contiguous blocks. A slice can be used to hold a disk-based file system or as a raw device that provides, for example, swap space.

You need to create UFS file systems only occasionally, because the Solaris OS automatically creates them as part of the installation process. You need to create (or re-create) a UFS file system when you want to do the following:

- Add or replace disks
- Change the existing partitioning structure of a disk
- Fully restore a file system

The `newfs` command enables you to create a UFS file system by reading parameter defaults from the disk label, such as tracks per cylinder and sectors per track. You can also customize the file system by using the `newfs` command options. For more information, see the `newfs(1M)` man page.

Ensure that you have met the following prerequisites.

- The disk must be formatted and divided into slices.
- To recreate an existing UFS file system, unmount it first.
- Know the device name associated with the slice that will contain the file system.

> **Note**
>
> When you run the `newfs` command on a disk slice, the contents of that slice are erased. Hence, ensure that you specify the name of the slice on which you intend to create a new UFS file system.

The following example shows how to use the `newfs` command to create a UFS file system on the `/dev/rdsk/c0t1d0s7` disk slice.

```
# newfs /dev/rdsk/c0t1d0s7
/dev/rdsk/c0t1d0s7:  725760 sectors in 720 cylinders of 14 tracks, 72 sectors
        354.4MB in 45 cyl groups (16 c/g, 7.88MB/g, 3776 i/g)
super-block backups (for fsck -F ufs -o b=#) at:
 32, 16240, 32448, 48656, 64864, 81072, 97280, 113488, 129696, 145904, 162112,
 178320, 194528, 210736, 226944, 243152, 258080, 274288, 290496, 306704,
 322912, 339120, 355328, 371536, 387744, 403952, 420160, 436368, 452576,
 468784, 484992, 501200, 516128, 532336, 548544, 564752, 580960, 597168,
 613376, 629584, 645792, 662000, 678208, 694416, 710624
```

5.2.2 Backing Up and Restoring UFS File Systems

Backing up file systems means copying file systems to removable media such as tape to safeguard against loss, damage, or corruption. *Restoring* file systems means copying reasonably current backup files from removable media to a working directory.

The following example shows how to do a full backup of the UFS `/export/home/terry` home directory. The `ufsdump  0ucf  /dev/rmt/0` command performs a full backup (0) of the `/export/home/terry` directory to cartridge tape device `/dev/rmt/0` (`cf  /dev/rmt/0`) and updates the `/etc/dumpdates` file with the date of this backup (u). After the backup completes, the `ufsrestore` command reads the contents of the backup tape (`tf  /dev/rmt/0`):

```
# ufsdump 0ucf /dev/rmt/0 /export/home/terry
  DUMP: Date of this level 0 dump: Wed Mar 16 13:56:37 2009
  DUMP: Date of last level 0 dump: the epoch
  DUMP: Dumping /dev/rdsk/c0t0d0s7 (pluto:/export/home) to /dev/rmt/0.
  DUMP: Mapping (Pass I) [regular files]
  DUMP: Mapping (Pass II) [directories]
  DUMP: Writing 63 Kilobyte records
  DUMP: Estimated 105158 blocks (51.35MB).
  DUMP: Dumping (Pass III) [directories]
  DUMP: Dumping (Pass IV) [regular files]
  DUMP: 105082 blocks (51.31MB) on 1 volume at 5025 KB/sec
  DUMP: DUMP IS DONE
# ufsrestore tf /dev/rmt/0
       232        ./terry
       233        ./terry/filea
       234        ./terry/fileb
       235        ./terry/filec
       236        ./terry/letters
       237        ./terry/letters/letter1
       238        ./terry/letters/letter2
       239        ./terry/letters/letter3
       240        ./terry/reports
       241        ./terry/reports/reportA
       242        ./terry/reports/reportB
       243        ./terry/reports/reportC
```

5.2.3 Using Quotas to Manage Disk Space

Quotas enable system administrators to control the consumption of space in UFS file systems. Quotas limit the amount of disk space and the number of inodes, which roughly corresponds to the number of files, that individual users can acquire. For this reason, quotas are especially useful on the file systems that store home directories.

Quotas can be changed to adjust the amount of disk space or the number of inodes that users can consume. Additionally, quotas can be added or removed as system needs change. Quota commands enable administrators to display information about quotas on a file system, or search for users who have exceeded their quotas.

A system administrator can set file system quotas that use both hard limits and soft limits. The limits control the amount of disk space (in blocks) that a user can use and the number of inodes (files) that a user can create. A *hard limit* is an absolute limit that a user *cannot* exceed. When the hard limit is reached, a user cannot use more disk space or create more inodes until the user removes files and directories to create more space and make more inodes available.

A system administrator might set a *soft limit*, which the user can exceed while a soft limit timer runs. By default, the timer is set to seven days. The soft limit must be less than the hard limit. The timer begins to run when the user exceeds the soft limit. The timer stops running and is reset when the user goes below the soft limit. While the timer runs, the user is permitted to operate above the soft limit but still cannot exceed the hard limit. If the quota timer expires while the user is still above the soft limit, the soft limit becomes the hard limit.

Several commands are available for managing quotas on UFS file systems, such as the quota, edquota, quotaon, repquota, and quotacheck commands. For more information, see the quota(1M), edquota(1M), quotaon(1M), repquota(1M), and quotacheck(1M) man pages.

Setting up quotas involves these general steps:

- Ensure that quotas are enforced each time the system is rebooted by adding the rq mount option to each UFS file system entry in the /etc/vfstab file that will impose quotas.
- Create a quotas file in the top-level directory of the file system.
- Use the first quota as a prototype to configure other user quotas.
- Check the consistency of the proposed quotas with the current disk usage to ensure that there are no conflicts.
- Enable the quotas for one or more file systems.

This example shows how to configure quotas for user dana on the /export/home file system. First, add the rq mount option to the /export/home file system entry in the /etc/vfstab file to ensure that quotas are enforced after every system reboot.

```
# grep "\/export\/home" /etc/vfstab
/dev/dsk/c0t1d0s0   /dev/rdsk/c0t1d0s0   /export/home   ufs   1   no   rq
```

Next, create the /export/home/quotas file and ensure that the file is readable and writable by only superuser. Use the edquota command to specify quota information for the specified user, which is dana. The first time you specify quota limits for a file system, edquota shows you the default quota values, which specify no limits. The edquota line in the example shows the new disk space and inode limits.

The quota -v command verifies that the new quotas for user dana are valid. Enable quotas on the /export/home file system by running the quotaon -v /export/home command. The repquota -v /export/home command shows all quotas configured for the /export/home file system.

```
# touch quotas
# chmod 600 quotas
# edquota dana
fs /export/home blocks (soft = 100000, hard = 150000) inodes (soft = 1000, hard = 1500)
# quota -v dana
Disk quotas for dana (uid 1234):
Filesystem      usage  quota  limit    timeleft  files  quota  limit    timeleft
/export/home        0 100000 150000                  0   1000   1500
# quotaon -v /export/home
/export/home: quotas turned on
# repquota -v /export/home
/dev/dsk/c1t0d0s5 (/export/home):
                    Block limits                    File limits
User         used  soft   hard    timeleft  used  soft   hard    timeleft
dana      --     0 100000 150000                0   1000   1500
```

The edquota command can take a configured user quota to use as a prototype to create other user quotas. For example, the following command uses the dana quota as a prototype to create quotas for users terry and sandy.

edquota -p dana terry sandy

The quotacheck command is run automatically when a system is rebooted. If you are configuring quotas on a file system that has existing files, run the quotacheck command to synchronize the quota database with the files or inodes that already exist in the file system.

5.2.4 Checking File System Integrity

The UFS file system relies on an internal set of tables to keep track of used inodes and available blocks. When these internal tables are inconsistent with data on a disk, the file systems must be repaired. A file system can become inconsistent when the operating system abruptly terminates due to several reasons, including a power failure, improper shutdown procedure, or a software error in the kernel. Inconsistencies might also result from defective hardware or from problems with the disk or the disk controller firmware. Disk blocks can become damaged on a disk drive at any time.

File system inconsistencies, while serious, are uncommon. When a system is booted, a check for file system consistency is automatically performed by using the `fsck` command. Usually, this file system check repairs the encountered problems. The `fsck` command places files and directories that are allocated but unreferenced in the `lost+found` directory. The unreferenced files and directories use the inode number as the name. The `fsck` command creates the `lost+found` directory if it does not exist.

When run interactively, `fsck` reports each inconsistency found and fixes innocuous errors. However, for more serious errors, the command reports the inconsistency and prompts you to choose a response. You can run `fsck` with the `-y` or `-n` options, which specifies your response as yes or no, respectively. Note that some corrective actions might result in loss of data. The amount and severity of the data loss can be determined from the `fsck` diagnostic output.

The `fsck` command checks a file system in several passes. Each pass checks the file system for blocks and sizes, path names, connectivity, reference counts, and the map of free blocks. If needed, the free block map is rebuilt.

Before you run `fsck` on a local file system, unmount it to ensure that there is no activity on the file system.

This example shows the results of the `fsck` command run on the `/dev/rdsk/c0t0d0s7` disk device that contains the file system. As `fsck` runs, it outputs information about each phase of the check and the final line of the output describes the following:

- `files`—number of inodes in use

- `used`—number of fragments in use

- `free`—number of unused fragments

- `frags`—number of unused non-block fragments

- `blocks`—number of unused full blocks

- `fragmentation`—percentage of fragmentation, which is the number of free fragments times 100 divided by the total fragments in the file system

```
# fsck /dev/rdsk/c0t0d0s7
** /dev/rdsk/c0t0d0s7
** Last Mounted on /export/home
** Phase 1 - Check Blocks and Sizes
** Phase 2 - Check Pathnames
** Phase 3a - Check Connectivity
** Phase 3b - Verify Shadows/ACLs
** Phase 4 - Check Reference Counts
** Phase 5 - Check Cylinder Groups
2 files, 9 used, 2833540 free (20 frags, 354190 blocks, 0.0% fragmentation)
```

Sometimes a problem corrected during a later fsck pass can expose problems that are only detected by earlier passes. Therefore, run fsck until it no longer reports any problems to ensure that all errors have been found and repaired.

If the fsck command still cannot repair the file system, then you might use the ff, clri, and ncheck commands to investigate file system problems and correct them. If you cannot fully repair a file system but you can mount it read-only, then use the cp, tar, or cpio command to retrieve all or part of the data from the file system. If hardware disk errors are causing the problem, then you might need to reformat and repartition the disk before recreating the file system and restoring its data. Ensure that the device cables and connectors are functional before replacing the disk device because the same hardware error is usually issued by different commands.

The fsck command reports bad superblocks. Fortunately, copies of the superblock are stored within a file system, so the fsck command's automatic search for backup superblocks feature enables you to find a backup superblock. This search feature is new in the Solaris 10 6/06 release.

If a file system with a damaged superblock was created with newfs or mkfs customized parameters, such as ntrack or nsect, then using the automatically calculated superblock for the repair process could irreparably damage your file system. If all else fails and the superblock cannot be reconstructed, then use the fsck -o b command to replace the superblock with one of the copies.

For detailed information about the syntax that is used by these commands, see the clri(1M), ff(1M), fsck(1M), and ncheck(1M) man pages.

5.2.5 Using Access Control Lists

The traditional UNIX file system provides a simple file access control scheme that is based on users, groups, and others. Each file is assigned an owner and a group. Access permissions are specified for the file owner, group, and everyone else.

This scheme is flexible when file access permissions align with users and groups of users, but it does not provide any mechanism to assign access to lists of users that do not coincide with a UNIX group. For example, using the traditional file access control scheme to assign terry and sandy read access to file1 and to assign dana and terry read access to file2 is problematic. To access each file, terry would need to belong to two UNIX groups and use the chgrp command change from one group to the other.

Instead, you can use access control lists (ACLs) to specify lists of users that are assigned to a file with different permissions. An administrator can use the setfacl command to assign a list of UNIX user IDs and groups to a file. To view the ACLs associated with a file, use the getfacl command. The following example shows how to use the setfacl command to assign user dana read-write permissions for the memtool.c file. The getfacl memtool.c command shows file access information about the memtool.c file. The output shows the file owner (rmc) and group (staff), default mask and permissions for user, group, and other, and the access permissions for user dana. The plus sign (+) in the file permissions shown by the ls -l memtool.c command indicates that an ACL is assigned to the file.

```
# setfacl -m user:dana:rw- memtool.c
# getfacl memtool.c
# file: memtool.c
# owner: rmc
# group: staff
user::r--
user:dana:rw-           #effective:r--
group::r--              #effective:r--
mask:r--
other:r--
# ls -l memtool.c
-r--r--r--+  1 rmc      staff      638 Mar 30 11:32 memtool.c
```

ACLs provide a flexible mechanism to assign access rights to multiple users and groups for a file. When a file or directory is created in a directory that has default ACL entries, the newly created file has permissions that are generated according to the intersection of the default ACL entries and the permissions requested at file creation time. If the directory has default ACL entries, then the umask is not applied.

For information about the ls command and file permission modes, see the ls(1) and chmod(1) man pages. Also see the getfacl(1) and setfacl(1) man pages for information about viewing and assigning ACL entries. You can also view man pages by using the man command (see the man(1) man page). For example, run the following command to see the man page for the ls command:

$ **man ls**

5.2.6 Using UFS Logging

A file system must be able to deliver reliable storage to the hosted applications and in the event of a failure it must also be able to provide rapid recovery to a known state. Solaris file systems use logging (or journaling) to prevent the file system structure from becoming corrupted during a power outage or a system failure. A *journaling file system* logs changes to on-disk data in a separate sequential rolling log, which enables the file system to maintain a consistent picture of the file system state. In the event of a power outage or system crash, the state of the file system is known. Rather than using `fsck` to perform a lengthy scan of the entire file system, the file system log can be checked and the last few updates can be corrected as necessary.

UFS logging bundles the multiple metadata changes that comprise a complete UFS operation into a transaction. Sets of transactions are recorded in an on-disk log and then applied to the actual metadata of the UFS file system.

When restarted, the system discards any incomplete transactions and applies transactions for completed operations. The file system remains consistent because only completed transactions are ever applied. This consistency remains even when a system crashes, as a system crash might interrupt system calls and introduce inconsistencies into a UFS file system.

In addition to using the transaction log to maintain file system consistency, UFS logging introduces performance improvements over non-logging file systems. This improvement can occur because a file system with logging enabled converts multiple updates to the same data into single updates and thus reduces the number of required disk operations. By default, logging is enabled for all UFS file systems, except if logging is explicitly disabled or the file system does not have sufficient space for the log.

Ensure that you have sufficient disk space to meet general system needs, such as for users, for applications, and for UFS logging. If you do not have enough disk space for logging data, you might see a message similar to the following when you mount a file system:

```
# mount /dev/dsk/c0t4d0s0 /mnt
/mnt: No space left on device
Could not enable logging for /mnt on /dev/dsk/c0t4d0s0.
```

An empty UFS file system with logging enabled has some disk space consumed by the log. If you upgrade to the Solaris 10 OS from a previous Solaris release, then your UFS file systems have logging enabled, even if the logging option is not specified in the `/etc/vfstab` file. To disable logging, add the `nologging` option to the UFS file system entries in the `/etc/vfstab` file.

The UFS transaction log is allocated from free blocks on the file system, and uses approximately 1MB for each 1GB of file system, up to a maximum of 64MB. The log is continually flushed as it fills, and is flushed when the file system is unmounted or when any `lockfs` command is issued.

To enable UFS logging, specify the `logging` mount option in the `/etc/vfstab` file or when you manually mount the file system. You can enable logging on any UFS file system, including the root (/) file system. The `fsdb` command supports UFS logging debugging commands.

5.2.7 Using Extended File Attributes

The UFS, ZFS, NFS, and TMPFS file systems include extended file attributes, which enable you to associate metadata with files and directories in the file system. These attributes are logically represented as files within a hidden directory, called the extended attribute name space, that are associated with the target file.

The `runat` command enables you to add attributes and execute shell commands in the extended attribute directory. A file must have an attributes file before you can use the `runat` command to add attributes.

For information about the `runat` command, see the `runat(1)` man page.

The following example shows how to use the `runat` and `cp` commands to create the `attr.1` attribute file from the `/tmp/attrdata` source file to the attribute name space for `file1`. The second command uses the `runat` and `ls -l` commands to show the list of attributes on `file1`.

```
$ runat file1 cp /tmp/attrdata attr.1
$ runat file1 ls -l
```

Many Solaris file system commands have been modified to support file system attributes by providing an attribute-aware option. Use this option to query, copy, or find file attributes. For instance, the `ls` command uses the `-@` option to view extended file attributes. For more information, see the specific man page for each file system command.

5.2.8 Using Multiterabyte UFS File Systems

The Solaris 10 OS supports multiterabyte UFS file systems and file system commands. When creating a multiterabyte file system, the inode and fragment density are scaled assuming that each file is at least 1MB in size. By using the `newfs -T` command to create a UFS file system less than 1TB in size on a system running a 32-bit kernel, you can later expand this file system by using the `growfs` command when you boot the same system under a 64-bit kernel.

5.2.9 Creating UFS Snapshots

You can use the `fssnap` command to create a temporary, read-only snapshot of a mounted file system for backup operations.

The `fssnap` command creates a virtual device and a backing-store file. You can back up the virtual device, which looks and acts like a real device, with any of the existing Solaris backup commands. The backing-store file is a bitmap file that contains copies of pre-snapshot data that has been modified since the snapshot was taken.

Keep the following key points in mind when specifying backing-store files:

- The destination path of the backing-store files must have enough free space to hold the file system data. The size of the backing-store files vary with the amount of activity on the file system.
- The backing-store file location must be different from the file system that is being captured as a snapshot.
- The backing-store files can reside on any type of file system.
- Multiple backing-store files are created when you create a snapshot of a UFS file system that is larger than 512GB.
- Backing-store files are sparse files. The logical size of a sparse file, as reported by the ls command, is not the same as the amount of space that has been allocated to the sparse file, as reported by the du command.

The UFS snapshot feature provides additional availability and convenience for backing up a file system because the file system remains mounted and the system remains in multiuser mode during backups. You can use the tar or cpio command to back up a UFS snapshot to tape for more permanent storage. If you use the traditional methods, like the ufsdump command, to perform backups, the system should be in single-user mode to keep the file system inactive.

The following example shows how to use the fssnap command as superuser to create a snapshot of the file system for backup. First, ensure that the file system has enough space for the backing-store file by running the df -k command. Then, verify that a backing-store file, /usr-bsf, does not already exist. Use the fssnap -o command to create the UFS snapshot of the /usr file system and use the fssnap -i command to verify that that snapshot has been created. Next, mount the snapshot by using the mount command. When you are done with the snapshot, you can use the fssnap -d command to delete the snapshot.

```
# df -k .
# ls /usr-bsf
# fssnap -F ufs -o bs=/usr-bsf /usr
/dev/fssnap/0
# fssnap -i /usr
0      /usr
# mount -F ufs -o ro /dev/fssnap/0 /backups/home.bkup
# fssnap -d /usr
```

For detailed information about the syntax that is used by the fssnap command, see the fssnap(1M) man page.

5.3 ZFS File System Administration

The ZFS file system uses the concept of storage pools to manage physical storage. A *storage pool* describes the physical characteristics of the storage, such as device layout, data redundancy, and so on. The pool acts as an arbitrary data store from which datasets can be created. A *dataset* can be a clone, file system, snapshot, or volume. File systems are able to share space with all file systems in the pool. A ZFS file system can grow automatically within the space allocated to the storage pool. When new storage is added, all file systems within the pool can immediately use the additional space without having to perform additional configuration tasks.

ZFS uses a hierarchical file system layout, property inheritance, automanagement of mount points, and NFS share semantics to simplify file system management. You can easily set quotas or reservations, enable or disable compression, or manage mount points for numerous file systems with a single command. You can examine or repair devices without having to understand a separate set of volume manager commands. You can take an unlimited number of instantaneous snapshots of file systems, as well as back up and restore individual file systems.

In the ZFS management model, file systems are the central point of control. Managing a file system has very low overhead and is equivalent to managing a new directory. So, you can create a file system for each user, project, workspace, and so on to define fine-grained management points.

The next part of this section includes subsections that describe how to manage ZFS file systems. The following subsections cover the following basic ZFS management tasks:

- Using pools and file systems
- Backing up a ZFS file system

In addition to the basic tasks, the following subsections cover other ZFS management tasks:

- Using mirroring and striping
- Using RAID-Z
- Using copy-on-write and snapshots
- Using file compression
- Measuring performance
- Extending a pool
- Checking a pool
- Replacing a disk

For more information about the ZFS file system, see *ZFS Administration Guide* on `http://docs.sun.com`.

5.3.1 Using Pools and File Systems

ZFS combines storage devices, such as individual disks or LUNs presented from disk arrays, into pools of storage. File systems are created from the storage in the pool. A ZFS file system represents a set of characteristics for data, not for file storage. Therefore, ZFS storage is consumed when files are created, not when file systems are created.

The following example uses the `zpool` command to create a single pool, `testpool`, from a single disk, `c1t0d0s0`. The `zpool list` command shows information about the configured ZFS pools, in this example, only `testpool`.

```
# zpool create testpool /dev/dsk/c1t0d0s0
# zpool list
NAME       SIZE    USED  AVAIL    CAP  HEALTH  ALTROOT
testpool  10.9G    75K  10.9G     0%  ONLINE  -
```

Note

ZFS does not permit overlapping slices. So, if you use a disk that has a system slice layout, `zpool` will complain about slice 0 and 2 overlapping. Use the `-f` (force) option to override the check.

The following shows how to use the `zfs create` command to create some ZFS file systems (home, home/dana, home/sandy, and home/terry) from the pool, testpool:

```
# zfs create testpool/home
# zfs create testpool/home/dana
# zfs create testpool/home/sandy
# zfs create testpool/home/terry
# zfs list
NAME                   USED  AVAIL  REFER  MOUNTPOINT
testpool               174K  10.8G    19K  /testpool
testpool/home           75K  10.8G    21K  /testpool/home
testpool/home/sandy     18K  10.8G    18K  /testpool/home/sandy
testpool/home/terry     18K  10.8G    18K  /testpool/home/terry
testpool/home/dana      18K  10.8G    18K  /testpool/home/dana
```

The following example shows that space within the pool decreases after a 100MB file is created in `/testpool/home/dana`. 100MB are now used by the pool, /testpool, and the file system in which the file was created, /testpool/home/dana. Note that the other file systems in testpool do not show that space has been used. When space is used in any file system, the amount of space available to all file systems decreases. However, only the file system that has grown increases in size.

```
# dd if=/dev/zero of=/testpool/home/dana/testfile bs=64k count=1600
1600+0 records in
1600+0 records out
# zfs list
NAME                  USED  AVAIL  REFER  MOUNTPOINT
testpool              100M  10.7G    19K  /testpool
testpool/home         100M  10.7G    22K  /testpool/home
testpool/home/sandy    18K  10.7G    18K  /testpool/home/sandy
testpool/home/terry    18K  10.7G    18K  /testpool/home/terry
testpool/home/dana    100M  10.7G   100M  /testpool/home/dana
```

The zfs set command enables you to set property values on individual file systems. The properties and their valid values are described in the zfs(1M) man page. Note that the read-only options cannot be changed.

The following example shows how to use the zfs get all command to view the property values set on the testpool/home file system:

```
# zfs get all testpool/home
NAME      PROPERTY      VALUE                   SOURCE
testpool  type          filesystem              -
testpool  creation      Mon Oct 20 17:14 2008   -
testpool  used          100M                    -
testpool  available     10.7G                   -
testpool  referenced    22K                     -
testpool  compressratio 1.00x                   -
testpool  mounted       yes                     -
testpool  quota         none                    default
testpool  reservation   none                    default
testpool  recordsize    128K                    default
testpool  mountpoint    /testpool/home          default
testpool  sharenfs      off                     default
testpool  checksum      on                      default
testpool  compression   off                     default
testpool  atime         on                      default
testpool  devices       on                      default
testpool  exec          on                      default
testpool  setuid        on                      default
testpool  readonly      off                     default
testpool  zoned         off                     default
testpool  snapdir       hidden                  default
testpool  aclmode       groupmask               default
testpool  aclinherit    secure                  default
testpool  canmount      on                      default
testpool  shareiscsi    off                     default
testpool  xattr         on                      default
```

When a ZFS file system quota is used, the file system shows the quota sizing to the user. Setting a file system quota to a larger value causes the resulting file system to grow.

The following example shows how to set a 4GB quota on /testpool/home/sandy, which is reflected in the output of the zfs list command. The output from the df -h command also shows that the quota is set to 4GB as the value of the size field.

```
# zfs set quota=4gb testpool/home/sandy
# zfs list
NAME                    USED   AVAIL  REFER  MOUNTPOINT
testpool                100M   10.7G    19K  /testpool
testpool/home           100M   10.7G    22K  /testpool/home
testpool/home/sandy      18K   4.00G    18K  /testpool/home/sandy
testpool/home/terry      18K   10.7G    18K  /testpool/home/terry
testpool/home/dana      100M   10.7G   100M  /testpool/home/dana
# df -h /testpool/home/sandy
Filesystem            size   used  avail capacity  Mounted on
testpool/home/sandy   4.0G    18K   4.0G      1%   /testpool/home/sandy
```

5.3.2 Backing Up a ZFS File System

ZFS stores more than files. ZFS keeps track of pools, file systems, and their related properties. So, backing up only the files contained within a ZFS file system is insufficient to recover the complete ZFS configuration in the event of a catastrophic failure.

The zfs send command exports a file system to a byte stream, while the zfs receive command imports a file system from a byte stream. The following example shows how to use the zfs send and zfs receive commands to back up and restore a ZFS file system. The zfs snapshot command takes a snapshot of the testpool/testfs file system. The name of the snapshot is 20_Oct_8pm. Use the zfs list -t snapshot command to view the list of snapshots. The zfs send command creates the /tmp/testfs@8pm.send file, which is a copy of the /testpool/testfs file system and can be used to recover the file system. Next, use zfs destroy -r to recursively delete the file system, including any snapshots and clones. Finally, recreate the file system by using the zfs receive command and the snapshot file. Note that the recovery of the file system includes any snapshots that might exist.

```
# zfs snapshot testpool/testfs@20_Oct_8pm
# zfs list -t snapshot
NAME                         USED  AVAIL  REFER  MOUNTPOINT
testpool/testfs@20_Oct_8pm     0      -   102M  -
# zfs send -R testpool/testfs@20_Oct_8pm > /tmp/testfs@8pm.send
# zfs destroy -r testpool/testfs
# zfs receive testpool/testfs < /tmp/testfs@8pm.send
```

5.3.3 Using Mirroring and Striping

ZFS includes mirroring (RAID-1) and striping with parity (RAID-5) features in an easy-to-use interface. Both RAID-1 and RAID-5 include redundancy features that attempt to avoid data loss in the event of a disk failure. RAID-1 uses mirroring to accomplish this.

The following shows how to use the zpool attach command to attach a second disk, c1t0d0s1, to the existing non-mirrored pool, testpool. The zpool status command shows that both the original disk, c1t0d0s0, and the new disk, c1t0d0s1, are used for testpool.

```
# zpool attach testpool c1t0d0s0 c1t0d0s1
# zpool status
  pool: testpool
 state: ONLINE
 scrub: resilver completed after 0h0m with 0 errors on Mon Oct 20 17:41:20 2008
config:

        NAME           STATE     READ WRITE CKSUM
        testpool       ONLINE       0     0     0
          mirror       ONLINE       0     0     0
            c1t0d0s0   ONLINE       0     0     0
            c1t0d0s1   ONLINE       0     0     0

errors: No known data errors
```

The following example shows how to use the zpool add command to add two disks, c1t0d0s3 and c1t0d0s4, as a mirror to an existing pool, testpool. The zpool status command shows that the two new disks are part of testpool. This scenario represents a slight modification to RAID-1, called RAID 1+0, or RAID-10. In RAID-10, a number of disks are concatenated together, and a mirror is built of two sets of the concatenated disks.

```
# zpool add testpool mirror c1t0d0s3 c1t0d0s4
# zpool status
  pool: testpool
 state: ONLINE
 scrub: resilver completed after 0h0m with 0 errors on Mon Oct 20 17:41:20 2008
config:

        NAME           STATE     READ WRITE CKSUM
        testpool       ONLINE       0     0     0
          mirror       ONLINE       0     0     0
            c1t0d0s0   ONLINE       0     0     0
            c1t0d0s1   ONLINE       0     0     0
          mirror       ONLINE       0     0     0
            c1t0d0s3   ONLINE       0     0     0
            c1t0d0s4   ONLINE       0     0     0

errors: No known data errors
```

5.3.4 Using RAID-Z

ZFS also provides a RAID-5 like solution called RAID-Z, which avoids the silent corruption caused by the RAID-5 Write Hole. This problem might occur because RAID-5 does not atomically write an entire stripe to disk at the same time. Should a power failure occur and one of the disks becomes inconsistent with the other disks, the data that is necessary to rebuild the data is unavailable due to this inconsistency. RAID-Z avoids this problem by using dynamic stripe sizes, which means that all block writes are atomic operations.

Before you can create a RAID-Z pool, you must first delete and recreate an existing pool. The following example shows how to use the zfs create command to recreate a new RAID-Z pool made up of four disks. The resulting pool capacity is the same as a concatenation of three of the disks. In the event of a disk failure, the disk can be replaced and the pool will be automatically rebuilt from the remaining disks.

```
# zpool create testpool raidz c1t0d0s0 c1t0d0s1 c1t0d0s3 c1t0d0s4
# zpool status
  pool: testpool
 state: ONLINE
 scrub: none requested
config:

        NAME             STATE     READ WRITE CKSUM
        testpool         ONLINE       0     0     0
          raidz1         ONLINE       0     0     0
            c1t0d0s0     ONLINE       0     0     0
            c1t0d0s1     ONLINE       0     0     0
            c1t0d0s3     ONLINE       0     0     0
            c1t0d0s4     ONLINE       0     0     0

errors: No known data errors
```

5.3.5 Using Copy-on-Write and Snapshots

ZFS uses copy-on-write (COW) semantics, which means that every time data is written, the data is written to a new location on the device, instead of over-writing the existing data. In file systems such as UFS, a file is commonly written to the same data location as the file it replaced. In ZFS, an overwrite of a file occupies unused storage rather than overwriting the existing file. Since the original file still exists in storage, it is now possible to recover that file directly by the use of snapshots. A *snapshot* represents a point-in-time view of a file system, so any changes to the file system after that time are not reflected in the snapshot.

The following shows how to use the zfs create command to create a ZFS file system, testpool/testfs. The cp -r command copies the content from /etc to the new file system. The zfs snapshot command creates a snapshot called 20_Oct_6pm of the `testpool/testfs` file system. The `zfs   list` output includes the new `testpool/testfs@20_Oct_6pm` snapshot.

```
# zfs create testpool/testfs
# cp -r /etc/ /testpool/testfs
# zfs snapshot testpool/testfs@20_Oct_6pm
# zfs list
NAME                      USED   AVAIL   REFER   MOUNTPOINT
testpool                  102M   10.7G   407K    /testpool
testpool/testfs           102M   10.7G   102M    /testpool/testfs
testpool/testfs@20_Oct_6pm    0      -     102M    -
```

When a snapshot of this file system is made, the snapshot is available at the root of the file system in the `.zfs` directory. The following example shows that the `shadow` file in the `/testpool/testfs/etc` directory exists. When the file is removed, you can still access it from the snapshot directory. To restore the file to its original location, copy the file from the snapshot directory to the same location as the file you removed.

```
# ls -la /testpool/testfs/etc/shadow
-r--------   1 root      sys          405 Oct 16 18:00
/testpool/testfs/etc/shadow
# rm /testpool/testfs/etc/shadow
# ls -la /testpool/testfs/etc/shadow
/testpool/testfs/etc/shadow: No such file or directory
# ls -la /testpool/testfs/.zfs/snapshot/20_Oct_6pm/etc/shadow
-rw-r--r--   1 root      root         405 Oct 20 18:00
/testpool/testfs/.zfs/snapshot/20_Oct_6pm/etc/shadow
# cp /testpool/testfs/.zfs/snapshot/20_Oct_6pm/etc/shadow /testpool/testfs/etc/
# ls -la /testpool/testfs/etc/shadow
-rw-r--r--   1 root      root         405 Oct 20 18:11
/testpool/testfs/etc/shadow
```

Note

A snapshot does take up space and the files that are unique to the snapshot continue to consume disk space in the parent file system until the snapshot is deleted. To avoid running out of space in a pool that uses snapshots, consider the amount of space you might use for snapshots when you create the pool.

In addition to restoring files, you can use snapshots to roll back the primary file system to the specified snapshot. The following example shows how to use the `zfs rollback` command to revert the `testpool/testfs` file system to the contents of the `testpool/testfs@20_Oct_6pm` snapshot. Note that the file system must be unmounted for the snapshot rollback operation to occur.

```
# zfs rollback testpool/testfs@20_Oct_6pm
```

5.3.6 Using File Compression

ZFS supports transparent compression at the file system level. When compression is enabled, ZFS silently compresses the files within the file system. The following shows how to use the zfs set command to enable compression on the testpool/compress file system. The contents of the /etc directory are copied into /testpool/compress. The /testpool/testfs file system contains an uncompressed copy of /etc. The zfs list command shows that the storage used in /testpool/testfs is 102MB, while the storage used in the compressed file system is only 37.4MB. The zfs get compressratio command shows the compression ratio for the testpool/compress file system.

```
# zfs set compression=on testpool/compress
# cp -r /etc/ /testpool/compress
# zfs list
NAME                 USED  AVAIL  REFER  MOUNTPOINT
testpool             139M  10.6G   407K  /testpool
testpool/compress   37.4M  10.6G  37.4M  /testpool/compress
testpool/testfs      102M  10.6G   102M  /testpool/testfs
# zfs get compressratio testpool/compress
NAME                 PROPERTY      VALUE           SOURCE
testpool/compress    compressratio 2.71x           -
```

The following scenarios lend themselves to the use of transparent compression:

- **Storage of highly compressible files.** Often, storage of highly compressible files, such as text files, can be faster on a compressed file system than an uncompressed file system.

- **Low-utilization or archive file systems.** If the data is infrequently used, the time taken to uncompress files could easily offset the resulting storage needs of the data.

Note

Because the CPU is involved in file compression, enabling compression introduces additional CPU load on the server.

5.3.7 Measuring Performance

ZFS abstracts storage into pools and supports many file systems. As a result of this design, traditional methods for measuring performance do not quite work. ZFS has the zpool iostat and zpool status commands to track performance.

The following example shows the output of the zpool status command, which reports that the status of testpool is ONLINE with no data errors. In order to check I/O statistics, use the dd command to create a file, /testpool/testfs/file, and then run zpool iostat to report on the I/O statistics for testpool. The zpool iostat 5 5 command reports on the I/O statistics for testpool every five seconds for five iterations.

```
# zpool status
  pool: testpool
 state: ONLINE
 scrub: none requested
config:
        NAME          STATE     READ WRITE CKSUM
        testpool      ONLINE       0     0     0
          c1t0d0s0    ONLINE       0     0     0

errors: No known data errors
# dd if=/dev/zero of=/testpool/testfs/file bs=64k count=1600 &
# zpool iostat 5 5
               capacity     operations    bandwidth
pool        used  avail   read  write   read  write
----------  ----- -----  ----- -----  ----- -----
testpool    240M  10.7G      0      2  74.1K   131K

testpool    240M  10.7G      0      0      0      0
testpool    240M  10.7G      0      0      0      0
testpool    240M  10.7G      0    168      0  20.0M
testpool    240M  10.7G      0      0      0      0
```

5.3.8 Expanding a Pool

ZFS cannot currently expand a RAID-Z pool, as the data layout of the RAID-Z pool would need to be reconstructed. ZFS does enable you to easily expand a RAID-0 pool.

The following example shows how to use the zpool add command to add another disk to testpool. First, use the zpool status command to see that testpool has one disk, c1t0d0s0. Next, use the zpool add command to add the c1t0d0s1 disk to the pool. Finally, use zpool status to verify that testpool now has two disks, c1t0d0s0 and c1t0d0s1.

```
# zpool status
  pool: testpool
 state: ONLINE
 scrub: none requested
config:

        NAME          STATE     READ WRITE CKSUM
        testpool      ONLINE       0     0     0
          c1t0d0s0    ONLINE       0     0     0
errors: No known data errors
# zpool add testpool c1t0d0s1
# zpool status
  pool: testpool
 state: ONLINE
 scrub: none requested
config:
```

continues

```
        NAME          STATE     READ WRITE CKSUM
        testpool      ONLINE       0    0     0
          c1t0d0s0    ONLINE       0    0     0
          c1t0d0s1    ONLINE       0    0     0

errors: No known data errors
```

By adding another disk to the pool, you not only increase the resulting pool capacity, you also improve the throughput of the pool. The reason for this is that ZFS decouples file systems from storage. When using a concatenated pool, file operations are spread across all of the disks.

For example, if you create a file test.c, the resulting file storage is on one of the pool's disks. Should you create another file, test2.c, it is stored on one of the pool's disks, but probably not the same disk. Because the resulting storage is spread across all of the disks evenly, multiuser (or multithreaded) access is accelerated because all of the disks are in use rather than just a single disk. This storage scheme differs from older disk concatenation in which disk space was extended by stacking the disks one after the other. When the first disk was full, the second disk was used until full, and so on. In this situation, I/O performance was generally limited to a single disk's performance due to data locality.

5.3.9 Checking a Pool

ZFS uses block checksums to verify disk storage. ZFS is able to detect corruption and damage due to a system crash or media breakdown. The zpool scrub command checks a pool while that pool is in operation and reports on damaged files. The amount of time taken to check the pool depends on the amount of storage in use within the pool. Should an error occur, that error is reported in the check.

The following example shows how to use the zpool scrub command to start the check of testpool. While the check is running, the zpool status command shows the status of the pool as well as information about the pool scrub in progress.

```
# zpool scrub testpool
# zpool status
  pool: testpool
 state: ONLINE
status: One or more devices has experienced an error resulting in data
        corruption. Applications may be affected.
action: Restore the file in question if possible. Otherwise restore the
        entire pool from backup.
```

continues

```
      see: http://www.sun.com/msg/ZFS-8000-8A
    scrub: scrub in progress, 0.00% done, 111h54m to go
   config:
           NAME                STATE      READ  WRITE  CKSUM
           testpool            ONLINE        0      0      8
             c1t0d0s0          ONLINE        0      0      4
             c1t0d0s1          ONLINE        0      0      4
   errors: 4 data errors, use '-v' for a list
```

5.3.10 Replacing a Disk

When a failure occurs to a disk in a RAID pool, that disk must be replaced. The following example shows how to replace the disk. The following `zpool replace` command replaces disk `c1t0d0s1` with disk `c1t0d0s3`. The output of the `zpool status` command shows the disk replacement task is complete. After a mirror component is replaced, the data from the up-to-date mirror component is copied to the newly restored mirror component by means of the resilvering process. After the resilvering operation completes, the disk can be removed and replaced.

```
# zpool replace testpool c1t0d0s1 c1t0d0s3
# zpool status
   pool: testpool
  state: ONLINE
  scrub: resilver completed with 0 errors on Mon  Oct 20 18:46:35 2008
 config:
         NAME              STATE      READ WRITE CKSUM
         testpool          ONLINE        0     0     0
           mirror          ONLINE        0     0     0
             c1t0d0s0      ONLINE        0     0     0
             replacing     ONLINE        0     0     0
               c1t0d0s1    ONLINE        0     0     0
               c1t0d0s3    ONLINE        0     0     0
 errors: No known data errors
```

5.4 NFS File System Administration

The *Network File System* (NFS) is a distributed file system service that can be used to share files and directories with other systems on the network. From the user standpoint, remote resources that are shared by NFS appear as local files.

An *NFS server* shares files and directories with other systems on the network. These files and directories are sometimes called *resources*. The server keeps a list of currently shared resources and their access restrictions, such as read-write or read-only. When shared, a resource is available to be mounted by remote systems, which are called *NFS clients*.

The Solaris 10 OS supports the NFS Version 4 protocol (NFSv4), which provides file access, file locking, and mount capabilities that operate through firewalls. This NFSv4 implementation is fully integrated with Kerberos V5 to provide authentication, integrity, and privacy. NFSv4 also enables the negotiation of security flavors to be used between the client and the server on a per-file system basis.

By default, the Solaris 10 OS uses NFSv4. You can run other versions of NFS, as well. For information about selecting a different NFS version for the server or the client, see *System Administration Guide:Network Services* on http://docs.sun.com.

The next part of this section includes subsections that describe how to manage NFS file systems. The following subsections cover the following basic NFS management tasks:

- Finding available NFS file systems
- Mounting an NFS file system
- Unmounting an NFS file system
- Configuring automatic file system sharing
- Automounting file systems

For more information about NFS, see *System Administration Guide: Network Services* on http://docs.sun.com.

5.4.1 Finding Available NFS File Systems

The showmount command can be used to identify file systems on a known server that are shared by using the NFS service. The following example uses the showmount -e saturn command to list the file systems that are available for NFS mounts from the saturn server. The output shows the file system name and information about who can mount the file system.

```
# showmount -e saturn
export list for saturn:
/export/home        (everyone)
```

This example uses the showmount -a command to list all clients and the local directories that the clients have mounted from the neptune server:

```
# showmount -a neptune
lilac:/export/share/man
lilac:/usr/src
rose:/usr/src
tulip:/export/share/man
```

This example uses the `showmount -d` command to list the directories that have been mounted from the `neptune` server:

```
# showmount -d neptune
/export/share/man
/usr/src
```

5.4.2 Mounting an NFS File System

Mounting a file system manually provides a user temporary access to a file system. The following example shows how to create the `/testing` mount point and mount the file system. The `/mnt` directory is available for use as a temporary mount point. If `/mnt` is already being used, then use the `mkdir` command to create a mount point. The `mount` command mounts the `/export/packages` file system from the `pluto` server on the `/testing` mount point. When you no longer need the file system mounted, unmount it from the mount point by using the `umount` command.

```
# mkdir /testing
# mount -F nfs pluto:/export/packages /testing
# umount /testing
```

For detailed information about the syntax that is used by the `mount` and `umount` commands, see the `mount`(1M) and `umount`(1M) man pages.

5.4.3 Unmounting an NFS File System

Sometimes you need to unmount a file system prior to running certain programs or when you no longer need the file system to be accessible. The following example unmounts the file system from the `/usr/man` mount point.

```
# umount /usr/man
```

The following example shows that the `umount -a -V` command lists the commands to run if you want to unmount the currently mounted file systems:

```
# umount -a -V
umount /opt
umount /testing
umount /home
umount /net
```

For detailed information about the syntax that is used by the `umount` command, see the `umount`(1M) man page.

5.4.4 Configuring Automatic File System Sharing

An NFS server shares resources with other systems on the network by using the `share` command or by adding an entry to the `/etc/dfs/dfstab` file. When enabled, the NFS service automatically shares the resource entries in the `dfstab` file. The `dfstab` file also controls which clients can mount a file system. Configure automatic sharing if you need to share the same set of file systems on a regular basis, such as for home directories. Perform manual sharing when testing software or configurations or when troubleshooting problems.

The following example `dfstab` excerpt shows that three resources are shared. Two read-write resources are available for the `eng` client, `/sandbox` and `/usr/src`. The third resource is available to any client as a read-only mount, `/export/share/man`:

```
share   -F nfs   -o rw=eng   -d "sandbox"      /sandbox
share   -F nfs   -o rw=eng   -d "source tree"  /usr/src
share   -F nfs   -o ro   -d "man pages"  /export/share/man
```

The file systems are shared by restarting the system or by running the `shareall` command. After the resources are shared, running the `share` command lets you verify that the resources have been shared with the correct mount options.

```
# share
-  /sandbox       rw=eng   ""
-  /usr/src       rw=eng   ""
-  /export/share/man      ro    ""
```

5.4.5 Automounting File Systems

You can mount NFS file system resources by using a client-side service called automounting. *Automounting* enables a system to automatically mount and unmount NFS resources whenever they are accessed. The resource remains mounted as long as the directory is in use. If the resource is not accessed for a certain period of time, it is automatically unmounted.

Automounting provides the following features:

- Saves boot time by not mounting resources when the system boots
- Silently mounts and unmounts resources without the need for superuser privileges

- Reduces network traffic because NFS resources are mounted only when they are in use

This service is initialized by the `automount` utility, which runs automatically when a system is booted. The `automountd` daemon runs continuously and is responsible for the mounting and unmounting of NFS file systems on an as-needed basis. By default, the `/home` file system is mounted by the `automountd` daemon.

The automount service enables you to specify multiple servers to provide the same file system. This way, if one of these servers is down, another server can be used to share the resource. This client-side service uses the `automount` command, `autofs` file system, and `automountd` daemon to automatically mount the appropriate file system on demand.

The automount service, `svc:/system/filesystem/autofs`, reads the master map file, `auto_master`, to create the initial set of mounts at system startup time. These initial mounts are points under which file systems are mounted when access requests are received. After the initial mounts are made, the `automount` command is used to update `autofs` mounts, as necessary. After the file system is mounted, further accesses do not require any action until the file system is automatically unmounted.

The automount service uses a master map, direct maps, and indirect maps to perform automounting of file systems on demand.

5.4.5.1 Master Map

The *master map*, `auto_master`, determines the locations of all `autofs` mount points. The following example shows a sample `auto_master` file. The first field specifies the mount point for the automounted file systems. When `/-` is specified, a direct map is used and no particular mount point is associated with the map. The second field specifies the map to use to find mount information. The third field shows any mount options, as described in the `mount(1M)` man page.

```
# Master map for automounter
#
+auto_master
/net -hosts -nosuid,nobrowse
/home auto_home -nobrowse
/- auto_direct -ro
```

5.4.5.2 Direct Map

A *direct map* is an automount point. With a direct map, a direct association exists between a mount point on the client and a directory on the server. Direct maps have a full path name and indicate the relationship explicitly. The following example shows a typical direct map:

```
/usr/local -ro \
        /bin            ivy:/export/local/sun4 \
        /share          ivy:/export/local/share \
        /src            ivy:/export/local/src
/usr/man -ro            oak:/usr/man \
                        rose:/usr/man \
                        willow:/usr/man
/usr/games -ro          peach:/usr/games
/usr/spool/news -ro pine:/usr/spool/news \
                        willow:/var/spool/news
```

5.4.5.3 Indirect Map

An *indirect map* uses a substitution value of a key to establish the association between a mount point on the client and a directory on the server. Indirect maps are useful for accessing specific file systems, such as home directories. The auto_home map is an example of an indirect map. The following auto_master map entry specifies the name of the mount point, /home, the name of the indirect map that contains the entries to be mounted, auto_home, and any mount options, -nobrowse.

/home auto_home -nobrowse

The auto_home map might contain the following information about individual user's home directories:

```
terry pine:/export/home/terry
sandy apple:/export/home/sandy
dana -rw,nosuid peach:/export/home/dana
```

As an example, assume that the previous map is on host oak. Suppose that user dana's entry in the password database specifies the home directory as /home/dana. Whenever dana logs in to oak, the /export/home/dana directory that resides on peach is automatically mounted with the read-write and nosuid options set. The nosuid option means that setuid and setgid programs cannot be run. Anybody, including dana, can access this directory from any system that is configured with the master map that refers to the map in the previous example.

On a network that does not use a naming service, you must change all the relevant files (such as /etc/passwd) on all systems on the network to allow dana access to /home/dana. With NIS, make the changes to the NIS master server and propagate the relevant databases to the slave servers.

The following example shows how to configure /home to automount home directories that are stored on multiple file systems. First, you install home directory partitions under /export/home. If the file system has several partitions, then install the partitions under separate directories, such as /export/home1 and /export/home2. Then, use the Solaris Management Console tools to manage the auto_home map. For each user account, you add an entry such as the following:

```
dana        pluto:/export/home1/&
sandy       pluto:/export/home1/&
terry       saturn:/export/home2/&
```

The ampersand (&) character is substituted by the name in the first field, so the home directory for dana is pluto:/export/home1/dana.

With the auto_home map in place, users can refer to any home directory (including their own) with the path /home/*user*. *user* is their login name and the key in the map. This common view of all home directories is valuable when logging in to another user's computer. The automounter mounts your home directory for you. Similarly, if you run a remote windowing system client on another computer, the client program has the same view of the /home directory.

This common view also extends to the server. Using the previous example, if sandy logs in to the server pluto, the automounter provides direct access to the local disk by loopback-mounting /export/home1/sandy onto /home/sandy.

Users do not need to be aware of the real location of their home directories. If sandy needs more disk space and needs to have the home directory relocated to another server, a simple change is sufficient. You need only change sandy's entry in the auto_home map to reflect the new location. Other users can continue to use the /home/sandy path.

5.5 Removable Media

The Solaris OS includes removable-media services that enable regular users to access data that is stored on removable media. The Volume Management daemon, vold, manages removable media devices, such as CDs, DVDs, diskettes, USB, and FireWire. When you insert the media, vold automatically detects and mounts it.

Note that you might need to use the `volcheck` command to request that `vold` mount the media if you are using a legacy or non-USB diskette device. If the media is detected but is not mounted, then run the `volrmmount -i rmdisk0` command.

For more information about removable media, see *System Administration Guide: Devices and File Systems* on `http://docs.sun.com`.

Information stored on removable media can be accessed by the GNOME File Manager. You can access all removable media with different names. Table 5.1 describes the different media types that can be accessed with or without volume management.

Table 5.1 Removable Media Types

Media	Path	Volume management device alias name	Device name
First diskette drive	`/floppy`	`/vol/dev/aliases/` `floppy0`	`/dev/rdiskette` `/vol/dev/` `rdiskette0/`*volname*
First, second, third CD-ROM or DVD-ROM drives	`/cdrom0` `/cdrom1` `/cdrom2`	`/vol/dev/aliases/` `cdrom0` `/vol/dev/aliases/` `cdrom1` `/vol/dev/aliases/` `cdrom2`	`/vol/dev/rdsk/` `cntn`[`dn`]`/`*volname*
USB memory stick	`/rmdisk/` `noname`	`/vol/dev/aliases/` `rmdisk0`	`/vol/dev/dsk/`*cntndn*`/` *volname*`:c`

Most CDs and DVDs are formatted to the portable ISO 9660 standard, and can be mounted by volume management. However, CDs or DVDs that are formatted with UFS file systems are not portable between architectures, and can only be mounted on the architecture on which they were created.

The removable media is mounted a few seconds after insertion. The following examples show how to access information from a diskette (`floppy0`), USB memory stick (`rmdisk0`), and a DVD/CD (`cdrom0`), respectively. When the media is mounted, you can use other Solaris commands to access the data. For instance, the following `cp` command copies the `add_install_client` file from the CD to the current directory. After accessing the information from the device, use the `eject` command to remove the device or before removing the device.

```
$ ls /floppy
myfile
$ eject floppy0
$ ls /rmdisk
rmdisk0/        rmdisk1/
$ eject rmdisk0
$ ls /cdrom
cdrom0          sol_10_305_sparc
$ cp /cdrom/sol_10_305_sparc/s0/Solaris_10/Tools/add_install_client .
$ eject cdrom0
```

Occasionally, you might want to manage media without using removable media services. In such circumstances, use the mount command to manually mount the media. Ensure that the media is not being used. Remember that media is in use if a shell or an application is accessing any of its files or directories. If you are not sure whether you have found all users of a CD, then use the fuser command.

The following shows how to use the svcadm disable command to disable the removable media service as superuser:

svcadm disable volfs

5.5.1 Using the PCFS File System

PCFS is a file system type that enables direct access to files on DOS-formatted disks from within the Solaris OS. PCFS offers a convenient transportation vehicle for files between computers that run the Solaris OS and Windows or Linux. Once mounted, PCFS provides standard Solaris file operations that enable users to manage files and directories on a DOS-formatted disk. PCFS supports FAT12 (floppy), FAT16, and FAT32 file systems.

The following example shows how to use the mount -F pcfs command to mount PCFS file systems. The first example mounts the primary DOS partition from a SCSI disk (/dev/dsk/c1t0d0p0:c) on the /pcfs/c mount point. The second example mounts the first logical drive in the extended DOS partition (/dev/dsk/c1t0p0:d) from an IDE disk on the /pcfs/d mount point. The third example manually mounts the media in the first diskette drive (/dev/diskette) on the /pcfs/a mount point. The final example shows how to mount a PC Card memory device (/dev/dsk/c1t0d0s1) on the /pcfs mount point.

```
# mount -F pcfs /dev/dsk/c1t0d0p0:c /pcfs/c
# mount -F pcfs /dev/dsk/c1t0p0:d /pcfs/d
# mount -F pcfs /dev/diskette /pcfs/a
# mount -F pcfs /dev/dsk/c1t0d0s1 /pcfs
```

5.5.2 Using the HSFS File System

HSFS is a file system type that enables users to access files on High Sierra or ISO 9660 format CD-ROMs from within the Solaris OS. Once mounted, HSFS provides standard Solaris read-only file system operations that enable users to read and list files and directories.

The following example shows how to use the `mount -F hsfs` command to mount an HSFS file system from a CD (`/dev/dsk/c1t0d0s0`) on the `/mnt` mount point.

```
# mount -F hsfs /dev/dsk/c1t0d0s0 /mnt
```

5.6 Pseudo File System Administration

Pseudo file systems are file systems that look like regular file systems but represent virtual devices. Pseudo file systems present various abstractions as files in a file system. These are memory-based file systems that provide access to special kernel information and facilities.

This section describes swap space, the loopback file system, and the TMPFS file system, and provides examples of how they are used.

For more information about the pseudo file systems, see *System Administration Guide: Devices and File Systems* on `http://docs.sun.com`.

5.6.1 Using Swap Space

Solaris software uses some disk slices for temporary storage rather than for file systems. These slices are called swap slices. *Swap slices* are used as virtual memory storage areas when the system does not have enough physical memory to handle current processes. The virtual memory system maps physical copies of files on disk to virtual addresses in memory. Physical memory pages that contain the data for these mappings can be backed by regular files in the file system, or by swap space. If the memory is backed by swap space, then it is referred to as *anonymous memory,* because no identity is assigned to the disk space that is backing the memory.

A *dump device* is usually disk space that is reserved to store system crash dump information. By default, a system's dump device is configured to be a swap slice. If possible, you should configure an alternate disk partition as a *dedicated dump device* instead. Using a dedicated dump device provides increased reliability for crash dumps and faster reboot time after a system failure. You can configure a dedicated dump device by using the `dumpadm` command.

Initially, swap space is allocated as part of the Solaris installation process. The `/usr/sbin/swap` command is used to manage swap areas. The `-l` and `-s` options show information about swap resources.

The following example shows the output of the swap -l command, which identifies a system's swap areas. Activated swap devices or files are listed under the swapfile column.

```
# swap -l
swapfile             dev  swaplo blocks    free
/dev/dsk/c0t0d0s1  136,1       16 16415280 16415280
/dev/dsk/c0t0d0s2  136,2       16 37213184 37213184
```

The following example shows the output of the swap -s command, which enables you to monitor swap resources:

```
# swap -s
total: 5407640k bytes allocated + 451296k reserved = 5858936k used, 34198824k available
```

The used value plus the available value equals the total swap space on the system, which includes a portion of physical memory and swap devices (or files). Use the amount of available and used swap space shown by swap -s as a way to monitor swap space usage over time. If a system's performance is good, then use swap -s to determine how much swap space is available. When the performance of a system slows down, check the amount of available swap space to determine if it has decreased. Then you can identify what changes to the system might have caused swap space usage to increase.

As system configurations change and new software packages are installed, you might need to add more swap space. The easiest way to add more swap space is to use the mkfile and swap commands to designate a part of an existing UFS or NFS file system as a supplementary swap area. The following example shows how to create a 100MB swap file called /files/swapfile.

```
# mkdir /files
# mkfile 100m /files/swapfile
# swap -a /files/swapfile
# vi /etc/vfstab
(Add the following entry for the swap file):
/files/swapfile     -     -     swap    -     no    -
# swap -l
swapfile             dev  swaplo blocks    free
/dev/dsk/c0t0d0s1  136,1       16 16415280 16415280
/dev/dsk/c0t0d0s2  136,2       16 37213184 37213184
/files/swapfile      -         16 204784   204784
```

You can remove a swap file so that it is no longer available for swapping. The file itself is not deleted. Edit the /etc/vfstab file and delete the entry for the swap file. Recover the disk space so that you can use it for something else. If the swap space is a file, then remove it. Or, if the swap space is on a separate slice and you are sure you will not need it again, then make a new file system and mount the file system.

The following example shows how to remove an unneeded swap file and reclaim the space:

```
# swap -d /files/swapfile
# vi /etc/vfstab
(Remove the following entry for the swap file):
/files/swapfile    -     -     swap     -     no     -
# rm /files/swapfile
# swap -l
swapfile              dev  swaplo blocks    free
/dev/dsk/c0t0d0s1   136,1      16 16415280 16415280
/dev/dsk/c0t0d0s2   136,2      16 37213184 37213184
```

5.6.2 Using the TMPFS File System

A *temporary file system* (TMPFS) uses local memory for file system reads and writes, which is typically much faster than reads and writes in a UFS file system. TMPFS file systems can improve system performance by saving the cost of reading and writing temporary files to a local disk or across the network. Files in TMPFS file systems do not survive across reboots or unmounts.

If you create multiple TMPFS file systems, be aware that they all use the same system resources. Files that are created under one TMPFS file system use up space available for any other TMPFS file system, unless you limit TMPFS sizes by using the -o size option of the mount command.

The following example shows how to create, mount, and limit the size of the TMPFS file system, /export/reports, to 50MB.

```
# mkdir -m 777 /export/reports
# mount -F tmpfs -o size=50m swap /export/reports
# mount -v
```

The TMPFS file system is activated automatically in the Solaris environment by an entry in the /etc/vfstab file. The following example shows an entry in the /etc/vfstab file that mounts /export/test as a TMPFS file system at boot time. Because the size=*number* option is not specified, the size of the TMPFS file system on /export/test is limited only by the available system resources.

```
swap  -  /export/test  tmpfs  -  yes  -
```

5.6.3 Using the Loopback File System

A *loopback file system* (LOFS) is a virtual file system that provides an alternate path to an existing file system. When other file systems are mounted onto an LOFS file system, the original file system does not change.

> **Note**
>
> Be careful when creating LOFS file systems. Because LOFS file systems are virtual file systems, the potential for confusing both users and applications is enormous.

The following example shows how to create, mount, and test new software in the `/new/dist` directory as a loopback file system without actually having to install it:

```
# mkdir /tmp/newroot
# mount -F lofs /new/disk /tmp/newroot
# chroot /tmp/newroot ls -l
```

You can set up the system to automatically mount an LOFS file system at boot time by adding an entry to the end of the `/etc/vfstab` file. The following example shows an entry in the `/etc/vfstab` file that mounts an LOFS file system for the root (`/`) file system on `/tmp/newroot`:

```
/ - /tmp/newroot  lofs  -  yes  -
```

Ensure that the loopback entries are the last entries in the `/etc/vfstab` file. Otherwise, if the `/etc/vfstab` entry for a loopback file system precedes the file systems to be included in it, the loopback file system cannot be mounted.

References

man pages section 1M: System Administration Commands Part No: 816-6166. Sun Microsystems, Inc. 4150 Network Circle Santa Clara, CA 95054, USA. http://docs.sun.com/app/docs/doc/816-6166.

man pages section 1: User Commands Part No: 816-6165. Sun Microsystems, Inc. 4150 Network Circle Santa Clara, CA 95054, USA. http://docs.sun.com/app/docs/doc/816-6165.

System Administration Guide: Devices and File Systems Part No: 817-5093. Sun Microsystems, Inc. 4150 Network Circle Santa Clara, CA 95054, USA. http://docs.sun.com/app/docs/doc/817-5093.

ZFS Administration Guide Part No: 819-5461. Sun Microsystems, Inc. 4150 Network Circle Santa Clara, CA 95054, USA. http://docs.sun.com/app/docs/doc/819-5461.

System Administration Guide: Network Services Part No: 816-4555. Sun Microsystems, Inc. 4150 Network Circle Santa Clara, CA 95054, USA. http://docs.sun.com/app/docs/doc/816-4555.

Managing System Processes

This chapter discusses all the basic concepts for managing system processes in the Solaris Operating System. It covers:

- *Conditions of a process in Solaris*
- *Different states of a process*
- *Process context information*
- *Different commands and utilities present for monitoring and controlling the system processes in Solaris*
- *Process Manager utility for monitoring, controlling, and scheduling the system processes in Solaris*

6.1 Overview

The process is one of the fundamental abstractions of Unix. In Unix, every object is represented as either a file or a process. With the introduction of the /proc structure, there has been an effort to represent even processes as files.

A process is an instance of a running program or a program in execution. It can be any task that has an address space, executes its own piece of code, and has a unique process ID (PID). A process can create another process called a child process. Any process that creates the child process is called the parent process. This creation of new processes from existing parent processes is called forking (after the C function called `fork()`. Most processes in the system are created by fork system calls. The `fork` system call causes the current process to be split into two processes: a parent process and a child process. The child process continues to execute on the CPU until it completes. On completion, the child process returns to the system any resources that it used during its execution. While the child process is running, the parent process either waits for the child process to complete or continues to execute. If the parent process continues to execute, it periodically checks for the completion of the child process.

Running multiple processes has an impact on system performance because the processes consume system resources, such as memory and processor time, and some processes may even cause the system to hang. Managing processes becomes important in a multiuser environment such as Solaris. Managing processes involves monitoring the processes, finding the resource usage, finding the parent processes that have created child processes, assigning priority for processes, scheduling processes, and terminating processes.

From a system administrator perspective there are three broad categories of tasks associated with the management of the systems processes:

- Monitoring the processes
  - Viewing the PID, UID, and PPID
  - Viewing the priority of the process
  - Viewing the resource usage (in terms of memory and processor utilization)
  - Viewing the state of the process, etc.
- Controlling the processes
  - Using signals
  - Assigning the priority to the processes
- Scheduling the processes

Note

Throughout this chapter we use an imaginary process, namely `proc_exp`, having `1234` as its process id (PID), with the following command line:

```
# proc_exp arg1 arg2 arg3
```

where `arg1`, `arg2`, and `arg3` represent process arguments.

6.1.1 State of a Process

A process undergoes many changes during its lifetime. For example, if a parent process waits for the child process to complete execution, the parent process puts itself in sleep state. Such a change from one state to another state is known as context switching. During its lifetime a process can exist in any of these four states: *Ready* or *Runnable, Running, Sleep,* and *Zombie.* A runnable process is ready to execute whenever CPU time is available. It has acquired all the resources it needs and is just waiting for the CPU to become available. If the process is in the Run state, it means that the process is running on the CPU. In the Sleep state, the process waits for a child process to complete or waits for a resource to become available. Zombie is the phase in which the child process terminates, but its entry is not removed from the process table until the parent process acknowledges the death of the child process by executing `wait()` or `waitpid()` system call. In this case, the child process is said to be in a Zombie state. Zombie processes are also called as *defunct* processes.

6.1.2 Process Context

Solaris is a multitasking, multiprocessing operating system, in which a number of programs run at the same time. A program can be made up of many processes. A process is a part of a program running in its own address space. This means that many users can be active on the system at the same time, running many processes simultaneously. But only one process is active per processor at any given time while the other processes wait in a job queue. Because each process takes its turn running in very short time slices (much less than a second each), multitasking operating systems give the illusion that multiple processes are running at the same time.

Each time a process is removed from access to the processor, sufficient information on its current operating state must be stored such that when it is again scheduled to run on the processor it can resume its operation from an identical position. This operational state data is known as its *context* and the act of removing the process's thread of execution from the processor (and replacing it with another) is known as a process switch or *context switch*.

The *context* of a process includes the following operational state data:

- Register set image
    - Program counter: address of the next instruction
    - Stack pointer: address of the last element on the stack

- Processor status word: information about system state, with bits devoted to things like execution modes, interrupt priority levels, overflow bits, carry bits, etc.
- Memory management registers: Mapping of the address translation tables of the process
- Floating point unit registers
- User address space
  - Program text, data, user stack, shared memory regions, etc.
- Control information
  - u-area (user area), proc structure, kernel stack, address translation maps
- Credentials
  - User and group IDs (real and effective)
- Environment variables
  - Strings of the form variable = value

The **u area** includes the following:

- Process control block (PCB)
- Pointer to the proc structure
- Real/effective UID/GID
- Information regarding the current system call
- Signal handlers
- Memory management information (text, data, stack sizes)
- Table of open file descriptors
- Pointers to the current directory vnode and the controlling terminal vnode
- CPU usage statistics
- Resource limitations (disk quotas, etc.)

The **proc structure** includes the following:

- Identification: process ID and session ID
- Kernel address map location
- Current process state
- Pointers linking the process to a scheduler queue or sleep queue
- Pointers linking the process to lists of active, free, or zombie processes.
- Pointers keeping the structure in a hash queue based on PID

- Sleep channel (if the process is blocked)
- Scheduling priority
- Signal handling information
- Memory management information
- Flags
- Information on the relationship of this process and other processes

All of the information needed to keep track of a process when switching is kept in a data package called a *process control block (PCB)*. The process control block typically contains:

- Process ID (PID)
- Pointers to the locations in the program and its data where processing last occurred
- Register contents
- States of various flags and switches
- Memory information
- A list of files opened by the process
- The priority of the process
- The status of all I/O devices needed by the process

The new process is moved to the CPU by copying the PCB information into the appropriate locations (e.g., the program counter is loaded with the address of the next instruction to execute).

6.2 Monitoring the Processes

In Solaris, you can monitor processes that are currently executing on a system by using one of the commands listed in Table 6.1.

Table 6.1 Commands to Monitor the Processes

Command	Description
ps	Print status and information about active processes
pgrep	Find the process id (PID) of a process
prstat	View overall process statistics (similar to Linux top command)
preap	Reap zombie processes

continues

Table 6.1 Commands to Monitor the Processes (*continued*)

Command	Description
pstop	Temporarily freeze a process
prun	Continue a process that was stopped by pstop command
pwait	Wait for a process to finish
pwdx	List working directory for a process
pargs	Print the arguments and environment variables of a process
pfiles	Print the list of file descriptors associated with the process
pldd	List dynamic libraries associated with process (similar to ldd for executable)
ptree	Print a process ancestry tree
pstack	Get stack back trace of a process for debugging purposes
truss	Trace system calls and signals for a process
svcs	With the -p option, this command will list processes associated with each service instance. For more details, refer to Section 2.2, "Service Management Facility," in Chapter 2, "Boot, Service Management, and Shutdown."

Now let us examine each of the commands from Table 6.1 in more detail.

6.2.1 Process Status: ps

The ps command can be used to view the processes running on the system. Without options, ps prints information about processes that have the same effective user ID and the same controlling terminal as the invoker of ps command. The output contains only the process ID (PID), terminal identifier (TTY), cumulative execution time (TIME), and the command name (CMD). The output of the ps command is as shown below.

```
# ps
   PID TTY          TIME CMD
 27014 syscon       0:00 sh
 27151 syscon       0:00 ps
 27018 syscon       0:00 bash
```

You can print more detailed and comprehensive information about the running processes using different options available for the ps command, as described in Table 6.2.

Table 6.2 `ps` Command Options

Option	Description
-a	Lists information about all the most frequently requested processes. Processes not associated with a terminal will not be listed.
-e	Lists information about every process on the system.
-A	Lists information for all processes. Identical to the -e option.
-f	Lists full information for all processes.
-l	Generates a long listing.
-P	Prints the number of the processor to which the process is bound, if any, under an additional column header PSR. This is a useful option on systems that have multiple processors.
-u <username>	Lists only process data for a particular user. In the listing, the numerical user ID is printed unless you give -f option, which prints the login name.

Following is an example of using the `ps` command to list every process in the system:

```
# ps -ef
     UID   PID   PPID  C  STIME   TTY  TIME  CMD
    root     0      0  0  Apr 09  ?    1:15  sched
    root     1      0  0  Apr 09  ?    0:01  /sbin/init
    root     2      0  0  Apr 09  ?    0:00  pageout
    root     3      0  0  Apr 09  ?    7:06  fsflush
    root     7      1  0  Apr 09  ?    0:03  /lib/svc/bin/svc.startd
    root     9      1  0  Apr 09  ?    0:22  /lib/svc/bin/svc.configd
    root   505    504  0  Apr 09  ?    0:03  /usr/lib/autofs/automountd
  daemon   336      1  0  Apr 09  ?    0:00  /usr/lib/nfs/lockd
    root   151      1  0  Apr 09  ?    0:00  /usr/lib/picl/picld
    root   382      1  0  Apr 09  ?    0:02  /usr/lib/inet/inetd start
    root   170      1  0  Apr 09  ?    0:00  devfsadmd
  daemon   302      1  0  Apr 09  ?    0:00  /usr/bin/rpcbind
    root   311      1  0  Apr 09  ?    0:00  /usr/lib/netsvc/yp/ypbind
    root   144      1  0  Apr 09  ?    0:08  /usr/sbin/nscd
    root   616      1  0  Apr 09  ?    0:02  /usr/sfw/sbin/snmpd
    root   381      1  0  Apr 09  ?    0:00  /usr/sbin/cron
    root   313      1  0  Apr 09  ?    0:00  /usr/sbin/keyserv
  daemon   142      1  0  Apr 09  ?    0:00  /usr/lib/crypto/kcfd
  daemon   312      1  0  Apr 09  ?    0:00  /usr/lib/nfs/statd
    root   123      1  0  Apr 09  ?    0:00  /usr/lib/sysevent/syseventd
    root   159      1  0  Apr 09  ?    0:00  /usr/lib/power/powerd
    root   383    350  0  Apr 09  ?    0:00  /usr/lib/saf/ttymon
    root   350      7  0  Apr 09  ?    0:00  /usr/lib/saf/sac -t 300
```

Table 6.3 lists and describes the different process attribute fields displayed with the `ps` command.

Table 6.3 Process Attribute Fields

Field	Description
F	Flags associated with the process.
S	The state of the process. Refer to Table 6.4 for a complete list of the process states.
UID	The user ID of the process owner.
PID	The process ID of each process. This value should be unique. Generally, PIDs are allocated lowest to highest, but they wrap at some point.
PPID	The parent process ID. This identifies the parent process that started the process. Using the PPID enables you to trace the sequence of process creation that took place.
PRI	The priority of the process. Without `-c` option, higher numbers mean lower priority. With `-c` option, higher numbers mean higher priority.
NI	The nice value, used in priority computation. This is not printed when `-c` option is used. A process's nice number contributes to its scheduling priority. Making a process nicer means lowering its priority.
ADDR	The memory address of the process.
SZ	The SIZE field. This is the total number of pages in the process. Page size may vary on different hardware platforms. To display the page size on your system, issue the `/usr/bin/pagesize` command.
WCHAN	The address of an event for which the process is sleeping. If the address is `-`, then the process is running.
STIME	The starting time of the process (in hours, minutes, and seconds).
TTY	The terminal assigned to your process.
TIME	The cumulative CPU time used by the process in minutes and seconds.
CMD	The command (truncated) that generated the process.

Table 6.4 lists the codes used to show the various process states by the S field of the `ps` command.

Table 6.4 Process States

Code	Process state	Description
O	Running	The process is running on a CPU.
S	Sleeping	The process is waiting for an event to complete.
R	Runnable	The process is in the run queue.

Table 6.4 Process States (*continued*)

Code	Process state	Description
Z	Zombie	The process was terminated and the parent is not waiting.
T	Traced	The process was stopped by a signal because the parent is tracing it.
W	Waiting	The process is waiting for CPU usage to drop to the CPU-caps enforced limits.

6.2.2 Grepping for Process: `pgrep`

The `pgrep` command examines the active processes on the system and reports the process IDs of the processes whose attributes match the criteria specified on the command line. It can be used to replace the combination of the `ps` and `grep` commands to get the PID of a process based on some known process attributes. Following is an example of using the `pgrep` command. It also shows how the `pgrep` command can be used to replace the combination of the `ps` and `grep` commands:

```
# ps -e|grep sh
      3      ?        0:22    fsflush
   1238    pts/2     0:00    bash
    606      ?        0:00    sshd
   1234    pts/2     0:00    sh
   1274    pts/3     0:00    bash
   1270    pts/3     0:00    sh
#
# pgrep sh
3
1238
606
1234
1274
1270
```

6.2.3 Process Statistics Summary: `prstat`

The `prstat` command iteratively examines all active processes on the system and reports overall statistics on screen. The interesting thing about the `prstat` command is that information remains on the screen and gets updated periodically. By default, the `prstat` command updates the information screen every five seconds. However, the user can specify the sampling interval of choice on the command line. This command is similar to the `top` command in Linux. The syntax for the `prstat` command is as follows:

```
prstat [options] <count> <interval>
```

Table 6.5 describes some of the main options. Table 6.6 describes different arguments for the prstat command.

Table 6.5 Options for the prstat Command

Option	Description
-a	Displays separate reports about processes and users at the same time.
-c	Continuously prints new reports below previous reports instead of overwriting them.
-n <nproc>	Restricts the number of output lines. The <nproc> argument specifies how many lines of process or LWP (Light Weight Process or thread) statistics are reported.
-p <pidlist>	Reports only on processes that have a PID in the given list.
-s <key>	Sorts output lines by key in descending order. The four possible keys include: cpu time, size, rss, and pri. You can use only one key at a time.
-S <key>	Sorts output lines by key in ascending order.
-t	Reports total usage summary for each user.
-u <uidlist>	Reports only on processes that have an effective user ID (EUID) in the given list.
-U <uidlist>	Reports only on processes that have a real UID in the given list.

Table 6.6 Arguments for the prstat Command

Argument	Description
<count>	Specifies the number of times that the statistics are repeated. By default, prstat reports statistics until a termination signal is received.
<interval>	Specifies the sampling interval in seconds; the default interval is 5 seconds.

Following is an example of using prstat command with the sampling interval as one second:

```
# prstat 1
   PID  USERNAME SIZE  RSS    STATE PRI NICE TIME    CPU  PROCESS/NLWP
   796  noaccess 183M  100M   sleep 59  0    0:00:23 0.1% java/32
   1347 root     3440K 2888K  cpu5  59  0    0:00:00 0.0% prstat/1
   606  root     3520K 1280K  sleep 59  0    0:00:00 0.0% sshd/1
   567  root     2152K 1292K  sleep 59  0    0:00:00 0.0% snmpdx/1

(output edited for brevity)

   369  root     2040K 1164K  sleep 59  0    0:00:00 0.0% ttymon/1
   399  daemon   2448K 1272K  sleep 59  0    0:00:00 0.0% nfsmapid/6
   9    root     11M   9900K  sleep 59  0    0:00:05 0.0% svc.configd/14
   7    root     13M   11M    sleep 59  0    0:00:01 0.0% svc.startd/14
Total: 58 processes, 211 lwps, load averages: 0.00, 0.00, 0.00
```

Table 6.7 describes the column headings and their meanings in a `prstat` report.

Table 6.7 Column Headings for the `prstat` Command

Argument	Description
PID	The unique process identification number of the process
USERNAME	Login name or UID of the owner of the process
SIZE	The total virtual memory size of the process in kilobytes (K), megabytes (M), or gigabytes (G)
RSS	The resident set size of the process in kilobytes (K), megabytes (M), or gigabytes (G)
STATE	The state of the process: * cpu - The process is running on the CPU. * sleep - The process is waiting for an event to complete. * run - The process is in the run queue. * zombie- The process has terminated, and the parent is not waiting. * stop - The process is stopped.
PRI	The priority of the process
NICE	The value used in priority computation
TIME	The cumulative execution time for the process
CPU	The percentage of recent CPU time used by the process
PROCESS	The name of the process
NLWP	The number of lightweight processes (LWPs) or threads in the process

6.2.4 Reap a Zombie Process: `preap`

You can use the `preap` command to clean up a defunct or a zombie process. A zombie process has not yet had its exit status reaped, or claimed, by its parent. These processes are generally harmless, but can consume system resources if they are numerous. You need to specify the PID of the zombie process to be reaped with the `preap` command as shown below:

```
# ps -efl|grep Z
 F S UID  PID PPID C PRI NI  ADDR  SZ  WCHAN STIME TTY TIME CMD
 0 Z root 810 809  0 0   -   -     0   -       -   ?  0:00   <defunct>
 0 Z root 755 754  0 0   -   -     0   -       -   ?  0:00   <defunct>
 0 Z root 756 753  0 0   -   -     0   -       -   ?  0:00   <defunct>
#
# preap 810
810: exited with status 0
#
# ps -efl|grep Z
 F S UID  PID PPID C PRI NI  ADDR  SZ  WCHAN STIME TTY TIME CMD
 0 Z root 755 754  0 0   -   -     0   -       -   ?  0:00 <defunct>
 0 Z root 756 753  0 0   -   -     0   -       -   ?  0:00 <defunct>
```

In this example, the `preap` command successfully removed the zombie process with PID 810. Otherwise, the only way to remove them is to reboot the system.

6.2.5 Temporarily Stop a Process: `pstop`

A process can be temporarily suspended with the `pstop` command. You need to specify the PID of the process to be suspended as shown below:

```
# pstop 1234
```

6.2.6 Resuming a Suspended Process: `prun`

A temporarily suspended process can be resumed and made runnable with the `prun` command as shown below:

```
# prun 1234
```

6.2.7 Wait for Process Completion: `pwait`

The `pwait` command blocks and waits for termination of a process as shown below:

```
# pwait 1234
(sleep...)
```

6.2.8 Process Working Directory: `pwdx`

The current working directory of a process can be displayed using the `pwdx` command as shown below:

```
# pwd
/tmp/exp
# sleep 200
(sleep...)
# pgrep sleep
1408
# pwdx 1408
1408:    /tmp/exp
#
```

6.2.9 Process Arguments: `pargs`

The `pargs` command can be used to print the arguments and environment variables associated with a process. The `pargs` command solves a problem of the `ps` command being unable to display all the arguments that are passed to a process. The `ps` command, when used with `-f` option, prints the full command name and its arguments, up to a limit of 80 characters. If the limit is crossed then the command line is truncated.

With the `-e` option, `pargs` command can be used to display the environment variables that are associated with a process. Following is an example of using the `pargs` command:

```
# ps -ef|grep proc
    root  1234  1008   0 21:29:13 pts/9       0:00 /bin/sh ./proc_exp arg1 arg2 arg3
#
# pargs 1234
1234:   /bin/sh ./proc_exp arg1 arg2 arg3
argv[0]: /bin/sh
argv[1]: ./proc_exp
argv[2]: arg1
argv[3]: arg2
argv[4]: arg3
#
# pargs -e 1234
1234:   /bin/sh ./proc_exp arg1 arg2 arg3
envp[0]:  HZ=100
envp[1]:  TERM=vt100
envp[2]:  SHELL=/sbin/sh
envp[3]:  PATH=/usr/sbin:/usr/bin
envp[4]:  MAIL=/var/mail/root
envp[5]:  PWD=/
envp[6]:  TZ=Asia/Calcutta
envp[7]:  SHLVL=1
envp[8]:  HOME=/
envp[9]:  LOGNAME=root
envp[10]: _=./proc_exp
```

6.2.10 Process File Table: `pfiles`

A list of files open within a process can be displayed with the `pfiles` command as shown below:

```
# pfiles 1368
1368:   /usr/sbin/in.rlogind
  Current rlimit: 256 file descriptors
   0: S_IFCHR mode:0000 dev:285,0 ino:64224 uid:0 gid:0 rdev:0,0
      O_RDWR|O_NDELAY
   1: S_IFCHR mode:0000 dev:285,0 ino:64224 uid:0 gid:0 rdev:0,0
      O_RDWR|O_NDELAY
   2: S_IFCHR mode:0000 dev:285,0 ino:64224 uid:0 gid:0 rdev:0,0
      O_RDWR|O_NDELAY
   3: S_IFDOOR mode:0444 dev:288,0 ino:55 uid:0 gid:0 size:0
      O_RDONLY|O_LARGEFILE FD_CLOEXEC  door to nscd[156]
      /var/run/name_service_door
   4: S_IFCHR mode:0000 dev:279,0 ino:44078 uid:0 gid:0 rdev:23,4
      O_RDWR|O_NDELAY
      /devices/pseudo/clone@0:ptm
```

continues

```
  5:  S_IFCHR mode:0000 dev:279,0 ino:29885 uid:0 gid:0 rdev:4,5
      O_RDWR
      /devices/pseudo/clone@0:logindmux
  6:  S_IFCHR mode:0000 dev:279,0 ino:29884 uid:0 gid:0 rdev:4,6
      O_RDWR
      /devices/pseudo/clone@0:logindmux
```

This example lists the files open within the `in.rlogind` process, whose PID is 1368.

6.2.11 Process Libraries: `pldd`

A list of the libraries currently mapped into a process can be displayed with the `pldd` command. This is useful for verifying which version or path of a library is being dynamically linked into a process. Following is an example of using the `pldd` command:

```
# pldd 1368
1368:   /usr/sbin/in.rlogind
/lib/libc.so.1
/lib/libsocket.so.1
/lib/libnsl.so.1
/lib/libbsm.so.1
/lib/libmd.so.1
/lib/libsecdb.so.1
/lib/libcmd.so.1
```

6.2.12 Process Tree: `ptree`

When a Unix process forks or initiates a new process, the forking process is called a *parent process* and the forked process is called a *child process*. This parent-child relationship can be displayed with the `ptree` command. When the `ptree` command is executed for a PID, it prints the process ancestry tree, that is, all the parents and children for this process, with child processes indented from their respective parent processes as shown below:

```
# ptree 1733
397   /usr/lib/inet/inetd start
  1731  /usr/sbin/in.rlogind
    1733  -sh
      1737  bash
        1761  ptree 1733
```

6.2.13 Process Stack: `pstack`

The `pstack` command can be used to print the stack trace of a running process. In case of a multi-threaded process, the stack trace of all the threads within a process will be displayed by default as shown below:

```
# pstack 1234
1234    ./proc_exp arg1 arg2 arg3
---------------- lwp# 1 / thread# 1 ------------------
 fef74077 nanosleep (8047e10, 8047e18)
 080509e7 main     (4, 8047e60, 8047e74) + af
 080508a2 ???????? (4, 8047f10, 8047f1b, 8047f20, 8047f25, 0)
---------------- lwp# 2 / thread# 2 ------------------
 fef74077 nanosleep (feeaefb0, feeaefb8)
 08050af2 sub_b    (0) + 1a
 fef73a81 _thr_setup (feda0200) + 4e
 fef73d70 _lwp_start (feda0200, 0, 0, feeaeff8, fef73d70, feda0200)
---------------- lwp# 3 / thread# 3 ------------------
 fef74077 nanosleep (fed9efa8, fed9efb0)
 08050ac2 sub_a    (2) + ba
 fef73a81 _thr_setup (feda0a00) + 4e
 fef73d70 _lwp_start (feda0a00, 0, 0, fed9eff8, fef73d70, feda0a00)
---------------- lwp# 4 / thread# 4 ------------------
 fef74ad7 lwp_wait (5, fec9ff8c)
 fef70ce7 _thrp_join (5, fec9ffc4, fec9ffc0, 1) + 5a
 fef70e29 thr_join (5, fec9ffc4, fec9ffc0) + 20
 08050d0d sub_d    (2) + a5
 fef73a81 _thr_setup (feda1200) + 4e
 fef73d70 _lwp_start (feda1200, 0, 0, fec9fff8, fef73d70, feda1200)
---------------- lwp# 5 / thread# 5 ------------------
 fef74ad7 lwp_wait (3, feba0f94)
 fef70ce7 _thrp_join (3, feba0fcc, feba0fc8, 1) + 5a
 fef70e29 thr_join (3, feba0fcc, feba0fc8) + 20
 08050deb sub_e    (0) + 33
 fef73a81 _thr_setup (feda1a00) + 4e
 fef73d70 _lwp_start (feda1a00, 0, 0, feba0ff8, fef73d70, feda1a00)
```

The `pstack` command can be very helpful for debugging the process/thread hang issues. You can also print a specific thread's stack trace by supplying the thread-id (thread#) to the `pstack` command as shown below:

```
# pstack 1234/4
1234:   ./proc_exp arg1 arg2 arg3
---------------- lwp# 4 / thread# 4 ------------------
 fef74ad7 lwp_wait (5, fec9ff8c)
 fef70ce7 _thrp_join (5, fec9ffc4, fec9ffc0, 1) + 5a
 fef70e29 thr_join (5, fec9ffc4, fec9ffc0) + 20
 08050d0d sub_d    (2) + a5
 fef73a81 _thr_setup (feda1200) + 4e
 fef73d70 _lwp_start (feda1200, 0, 0, fec9fff8, fef73d70, feda1200)
```

6.2.14 Tracing Process: `truss`

One of the most useful commands, `truss`, can be used to trace the system calls
and signals made or received by a new or existing process. When used with `-d` flag,
`truss` command prints a time stamp on each line of the trace output as shown
below:

```
# truss -d date
Base time stamp:  1239816100.2290  [ Wed Apr 15 22:51:40 IST 2009 ]
 0.0000 execve("/usr/bin/date", 0x08047E78, 0x08047E80)  argc = 1
 0.0015 resolvepath("/usr/lib/ld.so.1", "/lib/ld.so.1", 1023) = 12
 0.0015 resolvepath("/usr/bin/date", "/usr/bin/date", 1023) = 13
 0.0016 sysconfig(_CONFIG_PAGESIZE)                      = 4096
 0.0016 xstat(2, "/usr/bin/date", 0x08047C58)            = 0
 0.0017 open("/var/ld/ld.config", O_RDONLY)              Err#2 ENOENT
 0.0017 mmap(0x00000000, 4096, PROT_READ|PROT_WRITE|PROT_EXEC, MAP_PRIVATE|MAP_ANON,
-1, 0) = 0xFEFF0000
 0.0018 xstat(2, "/lib/libc.so.1", 0x08047488)           = 0
 0.0018 resolvepath("/lib/libc.so.1", "/lib/libc.so.1", 1023) = 14
 0.0019 open("/lib/libc.so.1", O_RDONLY)                 = 3
 0.0020 mmap(0x00010000, 32768, PROT_READ|PROT_EXEC, MAP_PRIVATE|MAP_ALIGN, 3, 0) =
0xFEFB0000
 0.0020 mmap(0x00010000, 876544, PROT_NONE, MAP_PRIVATE|MAP_NORESERVE|MAP_ANON|MAP_
ALIGN, -1, 0) = 0xFEED0000
 0.0020 mmap(0xFEED0000, 772221, PROT_READ|PROT_EXEC, MAP_PRIVATE|MAP_FIXED|MAP_TEXT,
3, 0) = 0xFEED0000
 0.0021 mmap(0xFEF9D000, 27239, PROT_READ|PROT_WRITE, MAP_PRIVATE|MAP_FIXED|MAP_INIT-
DATA, 3, 774144) = 0xFEF9D000
 0.0021 mmap(0xFEFA4000, 5392, PROT_READ|PROT_WRITE, MAP_PRIVATE|MAP_FIXED|MAP_ANON,
-1, 0) = 0xFEFA4000
 0.0021 munmap(0xFEF8D000, 65536)                        = 0
 0.0023 memcntl(0xFEED0000, 123472, MC_ADVISE, MADV_WILLNEED, 0, 0) = 0
 0.0023 close(3)                                         = 0
 0.0025 mmap(0x00010000, 24576, PROT_READ|PROT_WRITE|PROT_EXEC, MAP_PRIVATE|MAP_
ANON|MAP_ALIGN, -1, 0) = 0xFEF90000
 0.0026 munmap(0xFEFB0000, 32768)                        = 0
 0.0027 getcontext(0x08047A10)
 0.0027 getrlimit(RLIMIT_STACK, 0x08047A08)              = 0
 0.0027 getpid()                                         = 2532 [2531]
 0.0027 lwp_private(0, 1, 0xFEF92A00)                    = 0x000001C3
 0.0028 setustack(0xFEF92A60)
 0.0028 sysi86(SI86FPSTART, 0xFEFA4BC0, 0x0000133F, 0x00001F80) = 0x00000001
 0.0029 brk(0x08062ED0)                                  = 0
 0.0029 brk(0x08064ED0)                                  = 0
 0.0030 time()                                           = 1239816100
 0.0030 brk(0x08064ED0)                                  = 0
 0.0031 brk(0x08066ED0)                                  = 0
 0.0031 open("/usr/share/lib/zoneinfo/Asia/Calcutta", O_RDONLY) = 3
 0.0032 fstat64(3, 0x08047CC0)                           = 0
 0.0032 read(3, " T Z i f\0\0\0\0\0\0\0\0".., 109)       = 109
 0.0032 close(3)                                         = 0
 0.0033 ioctl(1, TCGETA, 0x08047CE4)                     = 0
 0.0034 fstat64(1, 0x08047C50)                           = 0
Wed Apr 15 22:51:40 IST 2009
 0.0034 write(1, " W e d   A p r   1 5   2".., 29)       = 29
 0.0035 _exit(0)
```

The `truss` command is very helpful in debugging the process hang and the core dump issues. It can also be used to see which system process is taking more time and what parameters are passed for each system call.

You can use -p flag to specify the PID of the process to be traced as shown below:

```
# truss -p 1234
/4:     lwp_wait(5, 0xFEC8EF8C)             (sleeping...)
/3:     nanosleep(0xFED8DFA8, 0xFED8DFB0) (sleeping...)
/2:     nanosleep(0xFEEAEFB0, 0xFEEAEFB8) (sleeping...)
/5:     lwp_wait(3, 0xFEB8FF94)             (sleeping...)
/1:     nanosleep(0x08047E10, 0x08047E18) (sleeping...)
/2:     nanosleep(0xFEEAEFB0, 0xFEEAEFB8)               = 0
/1:     nanosleep(0x08047E10, 0x08047E18)               = 0
/1:     write(1, " M a i n   T h r e a d  ".., 23)      = 23
/1:     lwp_sigmask(SIG_SETMASK, 0xFFBFFEFF, 0x0000FFF7) = 0xFFBFFEFF [0x0000FFFF]
/1:     lwp_exit()
/2:     write(1, " B :   T h r e a d   e x".., 21)      = 21
/2:     lwp_sigmask(SIG_SETMASK, 0xFFBFFEFF, 0x0000FFF7) = 0xFFBFFEFF [0x0000FFFF]
/2:     lwp_exit()
/3:     nanosleep(0xFED8DFA8, 0xFED8DFB0)               = 0
/3:     lwp_sigmask(SIG_SETMASK, 0xFFBFFEFF, 0x0000FFF7) = 0xFFBFFEFF [0x0000FFFF]
/3:     lwp_exit()
/5:     lwp_wait(3, 0xFEB8FF94)                         = 0
/5:     write(1, " E :   A   t h r e a d  ".., 48)      = 48
/5:     write(1, " E :   J o i n   B   t h".., 17)      = 17
/5:     lwp_wait(2, 0xFEB8FF94)                         = 0
/5:     write(1, " E :   B   t h r e a d  ".., 48)      = 48
/5:     write(1, " E :   J o i n   C   t h".., 17)      = 17
/5:     lwp_wait(0, 0xFEB8FF94)                         = 0
/5:     write(1, " E :   C   t h r e a d  ".., 47)      = 47
/5:     nanosleep(0xFEB8FFA8, 0xFEB8FFB0) (sleeping...)
/5:     nanosleep(0xFEB8FFA8, 0xFEB8FFB0)               = 0
/5:     write(1, " E :   T h r e a d   e x".., 21)      = 21
/5:     lwp_sigmask(SIG_SETMASK, 0xFFBFFEFF, 0x0000FFF7) = 0xFFBFFEFF [0x0000FFFF]
/5:     lwp_exit()
...
```

You can use the -t flag to specify the list of specific system calls you are interested in tracing. In the following example the user is interested in tracing only `pread` and `pwrite` system calls for the process having a PID of 2614:

```
# truss -tpread,pwrite -p 2614
pread(6, "\0\0\0\0\0\0\0\0\0\0\0\0".., 262144, 0xC9EC3400) = 262144
pwrite(6, "\0\0\0\0\0\0\0\0\0\0\0\0".., 262144, 0xC9F03400) = 262144
pread(6, "\0\0\0\0\0\0\0\0\0\0\0\0".., 262144, 0xC9F03400) = 262144
pwrite(6, "\0\0\0\0\0\0\0\0\0\0\0\0".., 262144, 0xC9F43400) = 262144
pread(6, "\0\0\0\0\0\0\0\0\0\0\0\0".., 262144, 0xC9F43400) = 262144
pwrite(6, "\0\0\0\0\0\0\0\0\0\0\0\0".., 262144, 0xC9F83400) = 262144
```

continues

```
pread(6,  "\0\0\0\0\0\0\0\0\0\0\0\0".., 262144, 0xC9F83400) = 262144
pwrite(6, "\0\0\0\0\0\0\0\0\0\0\0\0".., 262144, 0xC9FC3400) = 262144
pread(6,  "\0\0\0\0\0\0\0\0\0\0\0\0".., 262144, 0xC9FC3400) = 262144
pwrite(6, "\0\0\0\0\0\0\0\0\0\0\0\0".., 262144, 0xCA003400) = 262144
pread(6,  "\0\0\0\0\0\0\0\0\0\0\0\0".., 262144, 0xCA003400) = 262144
pwrite(6, "\0\0\0\0\0\0\0\0\0\0\0\0".., 262144, 0xCA043400) = 262144
pread(6,  "\0\0\0\0\0\0\0\0\0\0\0\0".., 262144, 0xCA043400) = 262144
pwrite(6, "\0\0\0\0\0\0\0\0\0\0\0\0".., 262144, 0xCA083400) = 262144
pread(6,  "\0\0\0\0\0\0\0\0\0\0\0\0".., 262144, 0xCA083400) = 262144
pwrite(6, "\0\0\0\0\0\0\0\0\0\0\0\0".., 262144, 0xCA0C3400) = 262144
pread(6,  "\0\0\0\0\0\0\0\0\0\0\0\0".., 262144, 0xCA0C3400) = 262144
pwrite(6, "\0\0\0\0\0\0\0\0\0\0\0\0".., 262144, 0xCA103400) = 262144
pread(6,  "\0\0\0\0\0\0\0\0\0\0\0\0".., 262144, 0xCA103400) = 262144
pwrite(6, "\0\0\0\0\0\0\0\0\0\0\0\0".., 262144, 0xCA143400) = 262144
pread(6,  "\0\0\0\0\0\0\0\0\0\0\0\0".., 262144, 0xCA143400) = 262144
...
```

See the man pages for each of these commands for additional details.

6.3 Controlling the Processes

Controlling the processes in Solaris includes clearing hung processes, terminating unwanted or misbehaving processes, changing the execution priority of a process, suspending a process, resuming a suspended process, and so on. Following are the different ways the process can be controlled in Solaris.

6.3.1 The `nice` and `renice` Commands

If you wish to run a CPU intensive process, then you must know about the `nice` value of a process and the `nice` command. The `nice` value of a process represents the priority of the process. Every process has a `nice` value in the range from 0 to 39, with 39 being the nicest. The higher the `nice` value, the lower the priority. By default, user processes start with a `nice` value of 20. You can see the current `nice` value of a process in the **NI** column of `ps` command listing.

The `nice` command can be used to alter the default priority of a process at the start time. Following is an example of how to start a process with lower priority:

nice -n 5 proc_exp arg1 arg2 arg3

This command will start the process `proc_exp` with `nice` value 25, which will be higher than the `nice` value 20 of other running processes and hence `proc_exp` will have lower priority.

Following is an example to start a process with higher priority:

nice -n -5 proc_exp arg1 arg2 arg3

This command will start the process proc_exp with nice value 15, which will be less than the nice value 20 of other running processes and hence proc_exp will have higher priority.

The renice command can be used to alter the nice value of running processes. If proc_exp having PID 1234 was started with its default nice value of 20, the following command will lower the priority of this process by increasing its nice value to 25.

```
# renice -n 5 1234
```

or

```
# renice -n 5 -p 1234
```

The following command will increase the priority of proc_exp by decreasing its nice value to 15.

```
# renice -n -5 1234
```

or

```
# renice -n -5 -p 1234
```

For more information, see the nice(1M) and renice(1M) man pages.

6.3.2 Signals

Solaris supports the concept of signals, which are software interrupts. Signals can be used for communication between processes. Signals can be synchronously generated by an error in an application, such as SIGFPE and SIGSEGV, but most of the signals are asynchronous. A signal notifies the receiving process about an event. The following are the different ways to send a signal to a process:

- When a user presses terminal keys, the terminal will generate a signal; for example, when the user breaks a program by pressing the CTRL + C key pair.

- Hardware exceptions can also generate signals; for example, division by 0 generates SIGFPE (Floating Point Error) signal and invalid memory reference generates the SIGSEGV (Segmentation Violation) signal.

- The operating system kernel can generate a signal to inform processes when something happens. For example, SIGPIPE (Pipe Error) signal will be generated when a process writes to a pipe that has been closed by the reader.

- Processes can send the signal to other processes by using the kill(2) system call. Every process can send a signal in its privilege limitations. To send a signal, its real or effective user id has to be matched with the receiver process. Superuser can send signals without any restrictions.

There is also a Solaris command called kill that can be used to send signals from the command line. To send a signal, your real or effective user id has to be matched with that of the receiver process.

Every signal has a unique signal name and a corresponding signal number. For every possible signal, the system defines a default disposition, or action to take when it occurs. There are four possible default dispositions:

- Ignore: Ignores the signal; no action taken
- Exit: Forces the process to exit
- Core: Forces the process to exit, and creates a core file
- Stop: Stops the process (pause a process)

Programmers can code their applications to respond in customized ways to most signals. These custom pieces of code are called signal handlers. For more information on signal handlers, see the signal(3) man page.

Two signals are unable to be redefined by a signal handler. They are SIGKILL and SIGSTOP. SIGKILL always forces the process to terminate (Exit) and SIGSTOP always pauses a running process (Stop). These two signals cannot be caught by a signal handler.

Several other key points about signals are listed below:

- When a signal occurs, it is said that the signal is *generated*.
- When an action is taken for a signal, this means the signal is *delivered*.
- If a signal is between generation and delivery, this means the signal is *pending*, as clearly shown in Figure 6.1.
- It is possible to *block* a signal for a process. If the process does not ignore the blocked signal, then the signal will be pending.
- A blocked signal can be generated more than once before the process unblocks the signal. The kernel can deliver the signal once or more. If it delivers signals more than once, then the signal is *queued*. If the signals are delivered only once, then it is not queued. If multiple copies of a signal are delivered to a process while that signal is blocked, normally only a single copy of that signal will be delivered to the process when the signal becomes unblocked.

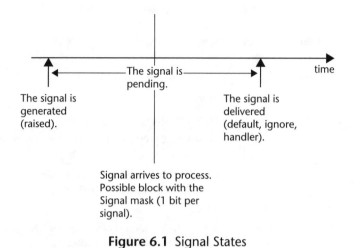

Figure 6.1 Signal States

- Each process has a signal mask. Signal masks define blocked signals for a process. It is just a bit array which includes one bit for each signal. If the bit is on, then that means the related signal will be blocked.

Note

The programmer can control (set or read) which signals are blocked (a blocked signal remains pending until the program unblocks that signal and the signal is delivered) with the `sigprocmask()` function. For more information, see the `sigprocmask` man page.

Table 6.8 provides the list of the most common signals an administrator is likely to use, along with a description and default action.

Table 6.8 Solaris Signals

Name	Number	Default Action	Description
SIGHUP	1	Exit	Hangup. Usually means that the controlling terminal has been disconnected.
SIGINT	2	Exit	Interrupt. User can generate this signal by pressing Ctrl+C.
SIGQUIT	3	Core	Quits the process. User can generate this signal by pressing Ctrl+\.
SIGILL	4	Core	Illegal instruction.

continues

Table 6.8 Solaris Signals (*continued*)

Name	Number	Default Action	Description
SIGTRAP	5	Core	Trace or breakpoint trap.
SIGABRT	6	Core	Abort.
SIGEMT	7	Core	Emulation trap.
SIGFPE	8	Core	Arithmetic exception. Informs the process of a floating point error like divide by zero.
SIGKILL	9	Exit	Kill. Forces the process to terminate. This is a sure kill. (Cannot be caught, blocked, or ignored).
SIGBUS	10	Core	Bus error.
SIGSEGV	11	Core	Segmentation fault. Usually generated when process tries to access an illegal address.
SIGSYS	12	Core	Bad system call. Usually generated when a bad argument is used in a system call.
SIGPIPE	13	Exit	Broken pipe. Generated when a process writes to a pipe that has been closed by the reader.
SIGALRM	14	Exit	Alarm clock. Generated by clock when alarm expires.
SIGTERM	15	Exit	Terminated. A gentle kill that gives the receiving process a chance to clean up.
SIGUSR1	16	Exit	User defined signal 1.
SIGUSR2	17	Exit	User defined signal 2.
SIGCHLD	18	Ignore	Child process status changed. For example, a child process has terminated or stopped.
SIGPWR	19	Ignore	Power fail or restart.
SIGWINCH	20	Ignore	Window size change.
SIGURG	21	Ignore	Urgent socket condition.
SIGPOLL	22	Exit	Pollable event occurred or Socket I/O possible.
SIGSTOP	23	Stop	Stop. Pauses a process. (Cannot be caught, blocked, or ignored).
SIGTSTP	24	Stop	Stop requested by user. User can generate this signal by pressing Ctrl+Z.
SIGCONT	25	Ignore	Continued. Stopped process has been continued.
SIGTTIN	26	Stop	Stopped—tty input.
SIGTTOU	27	Stop	Stopped—tty output.
SIGVTALRM	28	Exit	Virtual timer expired.
SIGPROF	29	Exit	Profiling timer expired.

Table 6.8 Solaris Signals (*continued*)

Name	Number	Default Action	Description
SIGXCPU	30	Core	CPU time limit exceeded.
SIGXFSZ	31	Core	File size limit exceeded.
SIGWAIT-ING	32	Ignore	Concurrency signal used by threads library.
SIGLWP	33	Ignore	Inter-LWP (Light Weight Processes) signal used by threads library.
SIGFREEZE	34	Ignore	Checkpoint suspend.
SIGTHAW	35	Ignore	Checkpoint resume.
SIGCANCEL	36	Ignore	Cancellation signal used by threads library.
SIGLOST	37	Ignore	Resource lost.
SIGRTMIN	38	Exit	Highest priority real time signal.
SIGRTMAX	45	Exit	Lowest priority real time signal.

Sometimes you might need to terminate or stop a process. For example, a process might be in an endless loop, it might be hung, or you might have started a long process that you want to stop before it has completed. You can send a signal to any such process by using the previously mentioned `kill` command, which has the following syntax:

```
kill [ - <signal>] <pid>
```

The `<pid>` is the process ID of the process for which the signal has to be sent, and `<signal>` is the signal number for any of the signal from Table 6.8. If you do not specify any value for `<signal>`, then by default, 15 (SIGTERM) is used as the signal number. If you use 9 (SIGKILL) for the `<signal>`, then the process terminates promptly.

However, be cautious when using signal number 9 to kill a process. It terminates the receiving process immediately. If the process is in middle of some critical operation, it might result in data corruption.

For example, if you kill a database process or an LDAP server process using signal number 9, then you might lose or corrupt data contained in the database. A good policy is to first always use the `kill` command without specifying any signal and wait for a few minutes to see whether the process terminates gently before you issue the `kill` command with -9 signal. Using the `kill` command without specifying the signal number sends SIGTERM (15) signal to the process with PID as

<pid> and thus the receiving process does the clean up job before terminating and does not result in data corruption.

As described earlier, the ps or pgrep command can be used to get the PID of any process in the system. In order to send SIGSTOP signal to process proc_exp, first you can determine the PID of proc_exp using the pgrep command as follows:

```
# pgrep proc_exp
1234
```

Now you can pass this PID to the kill command with signal number 23 (SIGSTOP) as follows:

```
# kill -23 1234
```

This will result in getting the process proc_exp paused.

There is another interesting Solaris command, pkill, which can be used to replace the pgrep and kill command combination. The pkill command works the same way as the kill command, but the only difference is, the pkill command accepts the process name as the last argument instead of PID. The syntax of the pkill command is as follows:

```
pkill [ - <signal>] <process name>
```

The <process name> is the name of the process (command name) to which the signal has to be sent. You can use a single pkill command to send SIGSTOP signal to process proc_exp as follows:

```
# pkill -23 proc_name
```

For more information, see the kill(1M) and pkill(1M) man pages.

6.4 Process Manager

Both Solaris desktop environments–CDE and JDS–provide a GUI based Process Manager utility that can be used for monitoring and controlling systems processes. The advantage of using this GUI based Processor Manager is that you can monitor and control system processes without any need to remember the complex commands and their syntax as discussed in this chapter so far. For example, instead of using the `ps` command with different options, you can invoke this Process Manager and it opens up showing all the system processes. You can sort the process list alphabetically, numerically, or based on any other field. You can use the filter text box to show only the processes that match the text typed in the filter box. You can search for a desired process by typing the relevant text in the find text box. You can terminate a process by highlighting it using the mouse pointer and then clicking kill.

In order to use the Process Manager utility, you need to log into the Desktop Environment of Solaris, either the Common Desktop Environment (CDE) or Java Desktop Environment (JDS). In CDE you can start the Processor manager by executing the `sdtprocess` command on the shell terminal, as shown below:

```
# sdtprocess &
```

or

```
# /usr/dt/bin/sdtprocess &
```

Alternatively, you can click Find Process on the Tools subpanel, as shown in Figure 6.2.

In JDS you can start the Process Manager either by executing the `sdtprocess` command or pressing Ctrl+Alt+Delete on the keyboard. The Process Manager window opens, as shown in Figure 6.3.

The Process Manager displays and provides access to processes that are running on a system. Table 6.9 describes the different fields displayed in the Process Manager window.

With the Process Manager, you can sort the processes on the system on the basis of any of the items in the given list. For example, if you click the CPU% column heading, the process list will be sorted and displayed on the basis of the CPU usage, as shown in Figure 6.4. The list updates every 30 seconds, but you can choose a value in the Sampling field of the Process manager to update the list as frequently as you like.

You can filter the processes that match the specified text. Type some text in the Filter text box in the Process Manager and press the Enter key. This displays the process entries that match the typed text. Figure 6.5 shows the processes containing `/usr/sbin` in their process entries.

Empty the Filter text box and press Enter to redisplay all the processes on the system.

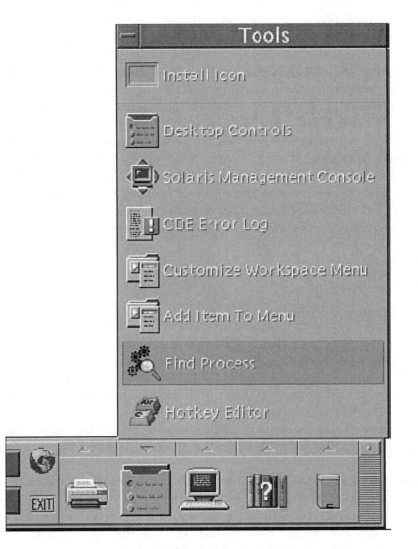

Figure 6.2 Tools Subpanel of CDE

Table 6.9 Fields in Process Manager Window

Column Heading	Description
ID	Process ID
Name	Name of the process
Owner	Login ID of the owner of the process
CPU%	Percentage of CPU time consumed

Table 6.9 Fields in Process Manager Window (*continued*)

Column Heading	Description
RAM	Physical memory or amount of RAM currently occupied by this process
Size	Total swap size in virtual memory
Started	Date when the process was started (or current time, if process was started today)
Parent	Parent process ID
Command	Actual Unix command (truncated) being executed

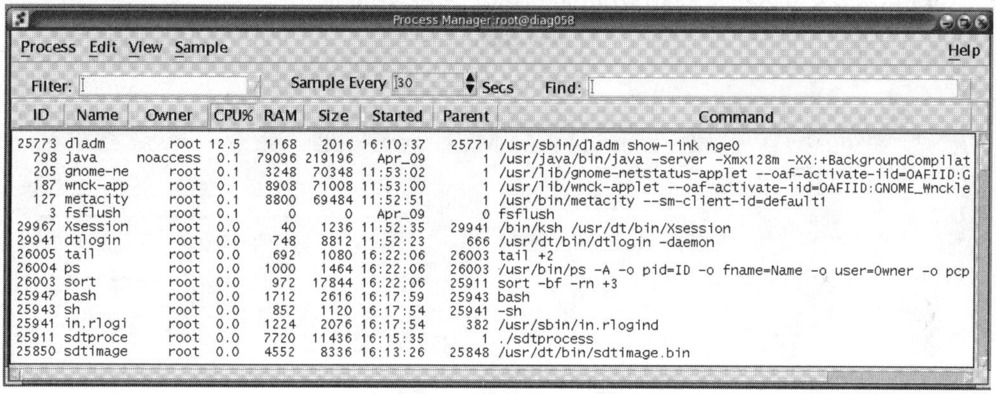

Figure 6.3 Process Manager Window

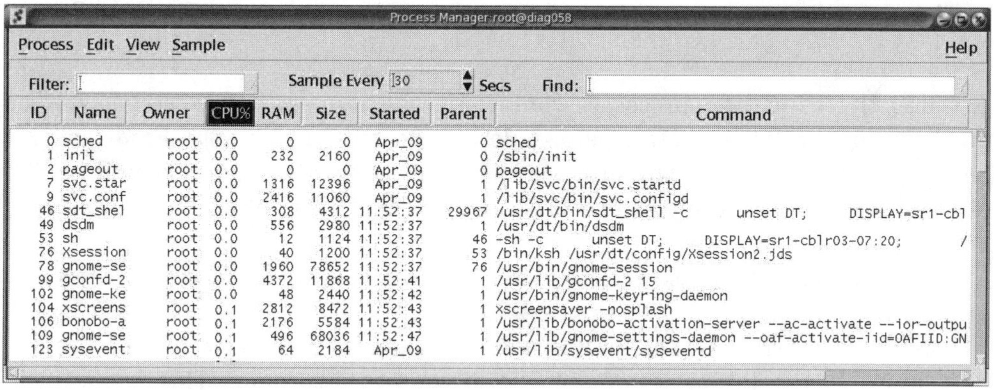

Figure 6.4 Process Manager Window Sorted by CPU%

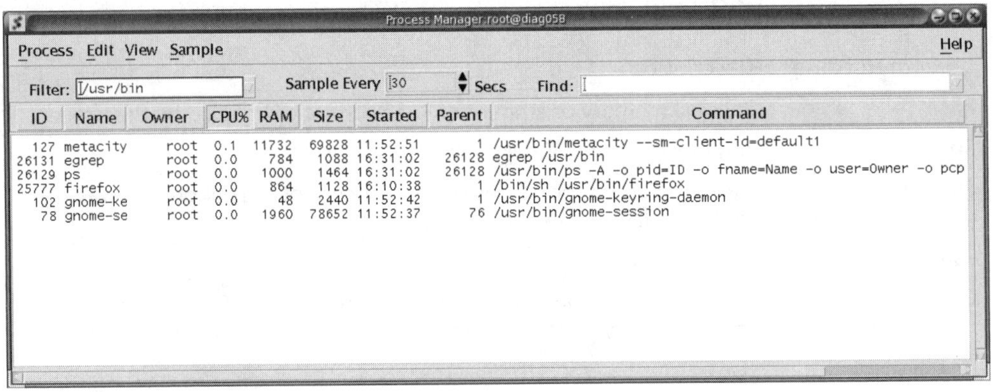

Figure 6.5 Process Manager Window after Specifying `/usr/bin` in the Filter Text Box

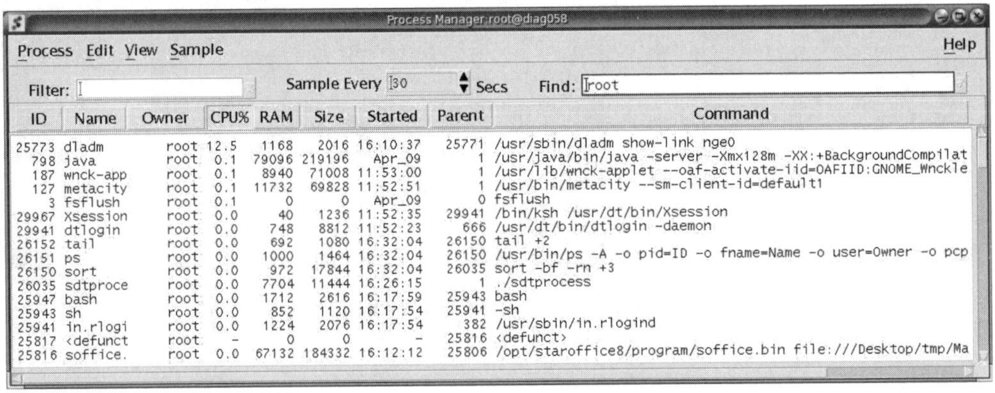

Figure 6.6 Process Manager Window after Specifying `root` in the Find Text Box

Using the **Find** box, processes containing the requested text string will be displayed in the Process Manager window. Type some text in the Find text box and press the Enter key. The processes containing the specified text will be displayed with the first occurrence of the specified text highlighted. This is shown in Figure 6.6.

Empty the Find text box and press Enter to redisplay all the processes on the system.

To kill a process, select or highlight the process from the listing and click the **Kill** option in the Process menu, shown at top of the window. This is shown in Figure 6.7. You also can use the Ctrl+C keyboard combination to kill the selected process or select the Kill option from the options that are available when you press the right mouse button. This will send SIGINT signal to the selected process.

Process Manager.root@diag058

Process	Edit	View	Sample						Help

Look up Owner...
Signal...
Debug...   Ctrl+G

Sample Every 30   ⬍ Secs   Find: [

	U%	RAM	Size	Started	Parent	Command
Trace System Calls...	1	79108	219196	Apr_09	1	/usr/java/bin/java -server -Xmx128m -XX:+BackgroundCompilat
	1	3248	70348	11:53:02	1	/usr/lib/gnome-netstatus-applet --oaf-activate-iid=OAFIID:G
Trace Children...	1	9480	71048	11:53:00	1	/usr/lib/wnck-applet --oaf-activate-iid=OAFIID:GNOME_Wnckle
	1	11636	75612	11:52:52	1	gnome-panel --sm-client-id default2
Show Stack... Ctrl+t	1	0	0	Apr_09	0	fsflush
Show Ancestry...	0	40	1236	11:52:35	29941	/bin/ksh /usr/dt/bin/Xsession
	0	748	8812	11:52:23	666	/usr/dt/bin/dtlogin -daemon
Kill Ctrl+C	0	692	1080	16:52:12	26497	tail +2
	0	1000	1464	16:52:12	26497	/usr/bin/ps -A -o pid=ID -o fname=Name -o user=Owner -o pcp
Exit	0	964	17844	16:52:12	26035	sort -bf -rn +3
	0	10236	69660	16:39:02	1	/usr/lib/nautilus-throbber --oaf-activate-iid=OAFIID:Nauti1
26035 sdtproce root 0.0		7944	11444	16:26:15	1	./sdtprocess
25943 sh root 0.0		860	1120	16:17:54	25941	-sh
25941 in.rlogi root 0.0		1224	2076	16:17:54	382	/usr/sbin/in.rlogind
25817 <defunct root -		0	0		25816	<defunct>
25816 soffice. root 0.0		67132	184332	16:12:12	25806	/opt/staroffice8/program/soffice.bin file:///Desktop/tmp/Ma

Figure 6.7 Process Manager Window with `kill` Selected

Process Manager.root@diag058

Process	Edit	View	Sample						Help

Look up Owner...
Signal...
Debug...   Ctrl+G

Sample Every 30   ⬍ Secs   Find: [

	U%	RAM	Size	Started	Parent	Command
Trace System Calls...	5	1168	2016	16:10:37	25771	/usr/sbin/dladm show-link nge0
	2	11740	69828	11:52:51	1	/usr/bin/metacity --sm-client-id=default1
Trace Children...	1	79096	219196	Apr_09	1	/usr/java/bin/java -server -Xmx128m -XX:+BackgroundCompilat
	1	3248	70348	11:53:02	1	/usr/lib/gnome-netstatus-applet --oaf-activate-iid=OAFIID:G
Show Stack... Ctrl+t	1	8984	71048	11:53:00	1	/usr/lib/wnck-applet --oaf-activate-iid=OAFIID:GNOME_Wnckle
	1	0	0	Apr_09	0	fsflush
Show Ancestry...	0	40	1236	11:52:35	29941	/bin/ksh /usr/dt/bin/Xsession
	0	748	8812	11:52:23	666	/usr/dt/bin/dtlogin -daemon
Kill Ctrl+C	0	692	1080	16:38:12	26326	tail +2
	0	1000	1464	16:38:12	26326	/usr/bin/ps -A -o pid=ID -o fname=Name -o user=Owner -o pcp
Exit	0	964	17844	16:38:12	26035	sort -bf -rn +3
26325 sdtimage root 0.0		4608	8336	16:37:47	26323	/usr/dt/bin/sdtimage.bin
26323 sdtimage root 0.0		900	1200	16:37:47	1	/bin/ksh ./sdtimage
26035 sdtproce root 0.0		7888	11444	16:26:15	1	./sdtprocess
25947 bash root 0.0		1712	2616	16:17:59	25943	bash
25943 sh root 0.0		852	1120	16:17:54	25941	-sh

Figure 6.8 Process Manager Window with Show Ancestry Selected

You can also send signals of your choice to a process, similar to the signals sent from the command line using the `kill` command. For example, to send signal 9 (sure kill) for killing a process, select or highlight the process from the listing. Click the Process menu from the toolbar at the top of the Process Manager window and then click the **Signal** option. This will display a Signal window where you can specify 9 in the Signal text box and press Enter to kill the process.

Another interesting feature of the Process Manager utility is the capability to display the ancestry of a process. When a Unix process initiates one or more processes, they are called child processes or children. Child and parent processes have the same user ID. To view a process along with all its child processes, highlight the process in the Process manager window. Click the Process menu from the toolbar at the top of the Process Manager window and then click the **Show Ancestry** option, as shown in Figure 6.8. The Process Manager will display another window containing the process tree for the specified process, as shown in Figure 6.9. Child processes are indented from the respective parent processes.

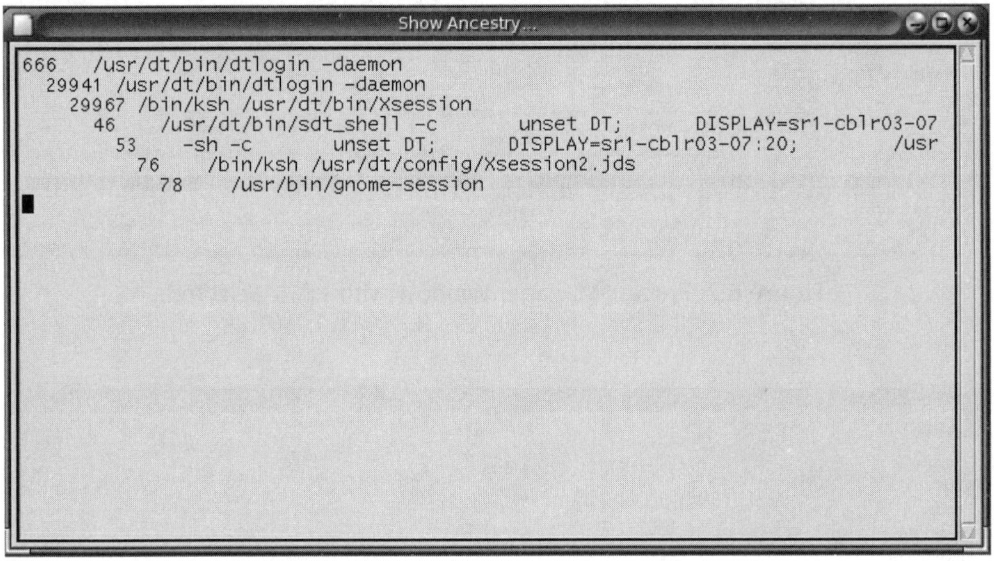

Figure 6.9 Show Ancestry Window

The command line equivalent to the Show Ancestry selection in the Process Manager is the `ptree` command, as described earlier in this chapter.

6.5 Scheduling Processes

From the user or system administrator's perspective, scheduling processes includes assigning priorities to the processes based on their importance and the need, executing a job at a time when the user will not be physically present at the system to manually start the job, distributing the job load over time, and executing a job repeatedly in a periodic fashion without manually having to start it each time.

Of the four tasks mentioned previously, the use of the `nice` and `renice` commands to assign priorities to the processes was described earlier in this chapter. Using these commands, you can increase the priority of a process that you want to complete faster. Similarly, if there is a long process taking most of the CPU time and it is not important to get this process done fast, you can use these commands to reduce its priority so that other process will get to run more.

For the other three tasks, use the `crontab` utility and the `at` command described below.

6.5.1 `cron` Utility

The `cron` utility is a general Unix utility named after Chronos (meaning "time"), the ancient Greek god of time. It allows tasks to be automatically run in the background at regular intervals by the `cron` daemon. These tasks are often termed as `cron` jobs in Solaris.

Note

A daemon is a software process that runs in the background continuously and provides the service to the client upon request. For example, `named` is a daemon. When requested, it will provide DNS service. Other examples are:

- `sendmail` (to send/route email)
- `Apache/httpd` (web server)
- `syslogd` (the system logging daemon, responsible for monitoring and logging system events or sending them to users on the system)
- `vold` (the volume manager, a neat little daemon that manages the system CD-ROM and floppy. When media is inserted into either the CD-ROM or the floppy drive, `vold` goes to work and mounts the media automatically.)

Most of the daemons like those above and including `cron` are started at system boot up time and they remain active in the background until the system is shut down.

Crontab (CRON TABle) is a file that contains commands, one per line, that are read and executed by the `cron` daemon at the specified times. Each line or entry has six fields separated by space characters. The beginning of each line contains five date and time fields that tell the `cron` daemon when to execute the command. The sixth field is the full `pathname` of the program you want to run. These fields are described in Table 6.10.

The first five fields can also use any one of the following formats:

- A comma separated list of integers, like 1,2,4 to match one of the listed values.
- A range of integers separated by a dash, like 3-5, to match the values within the range.

Table 6.10 The `crontab` File

Field	Description	Values
1	Minute	0 to 59. A * in this field means every minute.
2	Hour	0 to 23. A * in this field means every hour.
3	Day of month	1 to 31. A * in this field means every day of the month.
4	Month	1 to 12. A * in this field means every month.
5	Day of week	0 to 6 (0 = Sunday). A * in this field means every day of the week.
6	Command	Enter the command to be run.

Note

- Each command within a `crontab` file must be on a single line, even if it is very long.
- Lines starting with # (pound sign) are treated as comment lines and are ignored.

The following are some examples of entries in the `crontab` file.

Example 6.1: Reminder

```
0 18 1,15 * * echo "Update your virus definitions" > /dev/console
```
This entry displays a reminder in the user's console window at 5.00 p.m. on 1st and 15th of every month to update the virus definitions.

Example 6.2: Removal of Temporary Files

```
30      17     *     *     *              rm /home/user_x/tmp/*
```
This entry removes the temporary files from `/home/user_x/tmp` each day at 5:30 p.m.

The `crontab` files are found in the `/var/spool/cron/crontabs` directory. All the `crontab` files are named after the user they are created by or created for. For example, a `crontab` file named `root` is supplied during software installation. Its contents include the following command lines:

```
10 3 * * * /usr/sbin/logadm
15 3 * * 0 /usr/lib/fs/nfs/nfsfind
30 3 * * * [ -x /usr/lib/gss/gsscred_clean ] && /usr/lib/gss/gsscred_clean
#10 3 * * * /usr/lib/krb5/kprop_script ___slave_kdcs___
```

- The first command line instructs the system to run `logchecker` everyday at 3:10 a.m.
- The second command line orders the system to execute `nfsfind` on every Sunday at 3:15 a.m.
- The third command line runs each night at 3:30 a.m. and executes the `gsscred` command.
- The fourth command is commented out.

Other `crontab` files are named after the user accounts for which they are created, such as `puneet, scott, david,` or `vidya.` They also are located in the `/var/spool/cron/crontabs` directory.

When you create a `crontab` file, it is automatically placed in the `/var/spool/cron/crontabs` directory and given your user name. You can create or edit a `crontab` file for another user, or root, if you have superuser privileges.

6.5.1.1 Creating and Editing `crontab` Files

You can create a `crontab` file by using `crontab -e` command. This command invokes the text editor that has been set for your system environment. The default editor for your system environment is defined in the EDITOR environment variable. If this variable has not been set, the `crontab` command uses the default editor, `ed`, but you can choose an editor that you know well.

The following example shows how to determine if an editor has been defined, and how to set up `vi` as the default.

```
$ echo $EDITOR
$
$ EDITOR=vi
$ export EDITOR
```

If you are creating or editing a `crontab` file that belongs to `root` or another user, then you must become superuser or assume an equivalent role.

You do not need to become superuser to create or edit your own `crontab` file. The following are the steps to create a new or edit an existing `crontab` file:

1. Create a new `crontab` file, or edit an existing file.

   ```
   $ crontab -e [username]
   ```

The username specifies the name of the user's account for which you want to create or edit a crontab file. If you want to operate on your own crontab file then leave this option blank ($ crontab -e).

1. Add command lines to the crontab file.
   Follow the syntax described in Table 6.10.

3. Save the changes and exit the file. The crontab file will be placed in the /var/spool/cron/crontabs directory.

4. Verify your crontab file changes.

   ```
   # crontab -l [username]
   ```

   The contents of the crontab file for user <username> will be displayed.

   ```
   $ crontab -l
   ```

   The contents of your crontab file will be displayed.

6.5.1.2 Removing Existing crontab Files

You can use the crontab -r command to remove any existing crontab file. As noted previously, to remove a crontab file that belongs to root or another user, you must become superuser or assume an equivalent role.

```
# crontab -r [username]
```

This will remove the crontab file for user <username>, if any.

```
$ crontab -r
```

This will remove your existing crontab file, if any.

6.5.1.3 Controlling Access to crontab

You can control access to crontab by modifying two files in the /etc/cron.d directory: cron.deny and cron.allow. These files permit only specified users to perform crontab tasks such as creating, editing, displaying, and removing their own crontab files. The cron.deny and cron.allow files consist of a list of user names, one per line. These access control files work together in the following manner:

- If cron.allow exists, only the users listed in this file can create, edit, display, and remove crontab files.
- If cron.allow doesn't exist, all users may submit crontab files, except for users listed in cron.deny.
- If neither cron.allow nor cron.deny exists, superuser privileges are required to run crontab.

Superuser privileges are required to edit or create `cron.deny` and `cron.allow`.

During the Solaris software installation process, a default `/etc/cron.d/cron.deny` file is provided. It contains the following entries:

- daemon
- bin
- nuucp
- listen
- nobody
- noaccess

None of the users listed in the `cron.deny` file can access `crontab` commands. The system administrator can edit this file to add other users who are denied access to the `crontab` command. No default `cron.allow` file is supplied. This means that, after the Solaris software installation, all users (except the ones listed in the default `cron.deny` file) can access `crontab`. If you create a `cron.allow` file, the only users who can access `crontab` commands are those whose names are specified in this `cront.allow` file.

For more information, see the `crontab` man page.

6.5.2 The `at` Command

Unlike the `cron` utility, which allows you to schedule a repetitive task to take place at any desired regular interval, the `at` command lets you specify a one-time action to take place at some desired time. For example, you might use `crontab` to perform a backup each morning at 4 a.m. and use the `at` command to remind yourself of a meeting later in the day.

6.5.2.1 Creating an `at` Job

To submit an `at` job, type at and then specify an execution time and a program to run, as shown in the following example:

```
# at 09:20am today
at> who > /tmp/log
at> <Press Control-d>
job   912687240.a       at     Thu    Jun  30    09:20:00
```

When you submit an `at` job, it is assigned a job identification number (912687240 in the case just presented), which becomes its filename along with the `.a` extension. The file is stored in the `/var/spool/cron/atjobs` directory.

The `cron` daemon controls the scheduling of `at` files similar to the way it does for `crontab` jobs.

The command syntax for `at` is shown here:

```
at [-m] <time> <date>
```

The `at` command syntax is described in Table 6.11.

Table 6.11 `at` Command Syntax

Option	Description
-m	Sends you mail after the job is completed.
\<time\>	The hour when you want to schedule the job. Add `am` or `pm` if you do not specify the hours according to a 24-hour clock (`midnight`, `noon`, and `now` are acceptable keywords). Minutes are optional.
\<date\>	The first three or more letters of a month, a day of the week, or the keywords `today` or `tomorrow`.

By default, users can create, display, and remove their own `at` job files. To access `at` files that belong to `root` or other users, you must have superuser privileges.

Following is an example of creating an `at` job:

```
$ at -m 2130
at> rm /home/jonny/*.backup
at> <Press Control-D>

job 897355800.a at Thu Jun 30 21:30:00 2009
```

This shows the `at` job that user `jonny` created to remove his backup files at 9:30 p.m. He used the `-m` option so that he would receive an email message after the job is done.

6.5.2.2 Checking Jobs in Queue

To check your jobs that are waiting in the `at` queue, use the `atq` command. This command displays status information about the `at` jobs you created. You can also use the `atq` command to verify that you have created an `at` job. The `atq` command confirms that `at` jobs have been submitted to the queue, as shown in the following example:

```
$ atq

Rank       Execution Date        Owner      Job    Queue  Job Name
1st        Jun 30, 2009 09:20    root  912687240.a  a     stdin
2nd        Jun 30, 2009 21:30    jonny 897355800.a  a     stdin
```

Another way to check an `at` job is to issue the `at -1` command. This command shows the status information on all jobs submitted by a user, or for a particular job whose `id` is specified. The command syntax is as follows:

```
$ at -1 [job-id]
```

The `<job-id>` is the identification number of the job whose status you want to display. If no `<job-id>` is specified, then status information on all jobs submitted by this particular user is displayed.

Following is an example using `at -1` command:

```
$ at -1
897543900.a    Sat Jul 14 23:45:00 2004
897355800.a    Thu Jul 12 19:30:00 2004
897732000.a    Tue Jul 17 04:00:00 2004
```

6.5.2.3 Removing Existing `at` Jobs

You can use the `at -r` command to remove any existing `at` job. Once again, to remove an `at` job that belongs to `root` or another user you must become superuser or assume an equivalent role. You do not need to become superuser or assume an equivalent role to remove your own `at` job.

```
# at -r [job-id]
```

This will remove the job with identification number `job-id`.

Verify that the `at` job has been removed by using the "`at-1`" or `atq` command to display the jobs remaining in the `at` queue. The job whose identification number you specified should not appear.

In the following example, a user wants to remove an `at` job that was scheduled to execute at 4 a.m. on July 17th. First, the user displays the `at` queue to locate the job identification number. Next, the user removes this job from the `at` queue using the at -r command. Finally, the user verifies that this job has been removed from the queue using the at -l command:

```
$ at -l
897543900.a    Sat Jul 14 23:45:00 2003
897355800.a    Thu Jul 12 19:30:00 2003
897732000.a    Tue Jul 17 04:00:00 2003
$ at -r 897732000.a
$ at -l 897732000.a
at: 858142000.a: No such file or directory
```

6.5.2.4 Controlling Access to at

You can set up a file to control access to the at command, permitting only speci-fied users to create, remove, or display queue information about their at jobs. The file that controls access to at is /etc/cron.d/at.deny. It consists of a list of user names, one per line.

The users listed in this file cannot access at commands. The default at.deny file, created during the Solaris OS software installation, contains the following user names:

- daemon
- bin
- smtp
- nuucp
- listen
- nobody
- noaccess

With superuser privileges, you can edit this file to add other user names whose at access you want to restrict.

For more information, see the at(1) man page.

7

Fault Management

This chapter discusses the basic concepts and components of the Fault Management system in the Solaris 10 Operating System (Solaris 10 OS). It covers the following:

- *An overview of the Fault Manager*
- *How a user is notified of faults in the system*
- *Displaying and repairing faults*
- *Managing log files and Fault Manager modules*
- *Description of the on-disk files related to the Fault Manager*
- *Pointers to additional online resources*

7.1 Overview

The Solaris 10 Operating System (Solaris 10 OS) introduced an exciting new feature called *Predictive Self-Healing*. This feature provides fine-grained fault isolation and restart capability, where possible, for any hardware or software component that experiences a problem. The feature set is comprised of the Fault Manager and the Service Manager. The Service Manager Facility (SMF) is discussed in Chapter 2. This chapter discusses the Fault Manager.

Solaris Fault Management provides a new architecture for building resilient error handlers, structured error telemetry, automated diagnostic software, response agents, and structured messaging. Many parts of the Solaris software stack participate in Fault Management, including the CPU, memory and I/O subsystems, Solaris ZFS, an increasing set of device drivers, and other management stacks.

At a high level, the Fault Management stack is comprised of error detectors, diagnosis engines, and response agents (see Figure 7.1). *Error detectors*, as the name suggests, detect errors in the system and perform any immediate, required handling. The error detectors issue well-defined error reports, or *ereports*, to a diagnosis engine. A *diagnosis engine* interprets ereports and determines if a fault is present in the system. When such a determination is made, the diagnosis engine issues a *suspect list* that describes the field-replaceable unit (FRU) or set of FRUs that might be the cause of the problem. Suspect lists are interpreted by response agents. A *response agent* attempts to take some action based on the suspect list. Responses include logging messages, taking CPU strands offline, retiring memory pages, and retiring I/O devices.

The error detectors, diagnosis engines, and response agents are connected by the Fault Manager daemon (fmd), which acts as a multiplexor between the various components.

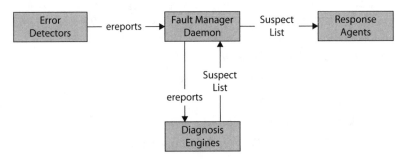

Figure 7.1 Fault Management

The Fault Manager daemon is itself a service under SMF control. The service is enabled by default and controlled just like any other SMF service, as the following example shows:

```
# svcs fmd
STATE          STIME    FMRI
online         11:25:44 svc:/system/fmd:default
# svcadm disable fmd
# svcs svc:/system/fmd:default
STATE          STIME    FMRI
disabled       15:27:45 svc:/system/fmd:default
# svcadm enable fmd
# svcs fmd
STATE          STIME    FMRI
online         15:27:51 svc:/system/fmd:default
```

7.2 Fault Notification

Often, the first interaction with the Fault Manager is a system message indicating that a fault has been diagnosed. Messages are sent to both the console and the `/var/adm/messages` file. All messages from the Fault Manager use the following format:

```
1   SUNW-MSG-ID: AMD-8000-AV, TYPE: Fault, VER: 1, SEVERITY: Major
2   EVENT-TIME: Tue May 13 15:00:02 PDT 2008
3   PLATFORM: Sun Ultra 20 Workstation, CSN: 0604FK401F, HOSTNAME: hexterra
4   SOURCE: eft, REV: 1.16
5   EVENT-ID: 04837324-f221-e7dc-f6fa-dc7d9420ea76
6   DESC: The number of errors associated with this CPU has exceeded
    acceptable levels.  Refer to http://sun.com/msg/AMD-8000-AV for more information.
7   AUTO-RESPONSE: An attempt will be made to remove this CPU from service.
8   IMPACT: Performance of this system may be affected.
9   REC-ACTION: Schedule a repair procedure to replace the affected CPU.
    Use fmdump -v -u <EVENT_ID> to identify the module.
```

Table 7.1 explains the information contained in Fault Notification messages.

Table 7.1 Fault Manager Messages

Line 1	The SUNW-MSG-ID, event TYPE, and SEVERITY are listed. The SUNW-MSG-ID is a code for the type of diagnosis. No two events share the same message ID. The TYPE is either Fault or Defect. A Fault generally indicates a physical problem with hardware, whereas a Defect indicates a problem with either software or firmware. The SEVERITY is Minor, Major, or Critical. Typically, Major and Critical events call for the immediate scheduling of maintenance, whereas Minor events could wait until the next normally scheduled maintenance.
Line 2	EVENT-TIME: Time of the diagnostic event.
Line 3	PLATFORM: Details about the platform that experienced the event.
Line 4	SOURCE: The Fault Management module that issued the diagnosis.
Line 5	EVENT-ID: The universally unique ID (UUID) associated with the event. The UUID is an input used with several Fault Management command-line utilities.
Line 6	DESC: A brief description of the nature of the event, including a pointer to a knowledge article on `http://sun.com/msg` that can contain additional information about this event.
Line 7	AUTO-RESPONSE: A brief description of any response actions the system will take to attempt to isolate the affected component. Note that the response action is an *attempt*. A response agent might not be able to isolate the affected component due to configuration or other constraints. For example, the system won't allow the last CPU in the system to be taken offline.
Line 8	IMPACT: A brief description of any impact the event has on the system.
Line 9	REC-ACTION: A listing of actions that a user or a service provider can take to address the fault and return the system to a healthy state.

> **Note**
>
> For historical and backwards compatibility reasons, the action to take often refers to the `fmdump` command. However, as of the Solaris 10 5/08 release, the preferred method to display fault information and determine the FRUs involved is the `fmadm   faulty` command. The `fmadm` command is discussed below.

When notified of a diagnosed fault, always consult the recommended knowledge article (Line 6) for additional details. The knowledge article might contain additional actions that a user or a service provider should take beyond those listed on Line 9.

Fault Manager fault events can also be plugged into a Simple Network Management Protocol (SNMP) monitoring system. One of the response agents is the `snmp-trapgen` module. This module requires the System Management Agent (SMA), which is part of the Solaris freeware packages. Configuration of traps is straightforward, with typical modifications to the `/etc/sma/snmp/snmp.conf` file. Fault Management also provides a Management Information Base (MIB) plug-in for use with SMA, which resides in `/usr/lib/fm/`isainfo -k`/libfmd_snmp.so.1`. It is beyond the scope of this chapter to describe in detail the setup and usage of Fault Management in an SNMP monitoring configuration. However, the topic has been discussed in several online sources[1].

7.3 Displaying Faults

The `fmadm faulty` command is used to display any faulty components in the system, as shown in the following example:

```
 1    # fmadm faulty
 2    --------------- ------------------------------------ -------------- ---------
 3    TIME            EVENT-ID                             MSG-ID         SEVERITY
 4    --------------- ------------------------------------ -------------- ---------
 5    May 13 15:00:02 04837324-f221-e7dc-f6fa-dc7d9420ea76 AMD-8000-AV    Major
 6
 7    Fault class : fault.cpu.amd.dcachedata
 8    Affects     : cpu:///cpuid=0
 9                        degraded but still in service
10    FRU         : "CPU 0" (hc://:product-id=Sun-Ultra-20-Workstation:
chassis-id=0604FK401F:server-id=hexterra/motherboard=0/chip=0)
11                        faulty
12
13    Description : The number of errors associated with this CPU has exceeded
14                  acceptable levels.  Refer to http://sun.com/msg/AMD-8000-AV for
15                  more information.
16
17    Response    : An attempt will be made to remove this CPU from service.
18
19    Impact      : Performance of this system may be affected.
20
21    Action      : Schedule a repair procedure to replace the affected CPU.   Use
22                  fmdump -v -u <EVENT_ID> to identify the module.
```

Of primary interest is Line 10, which shows the data for the impacted FRUs. The more human-readable location string is presented in quotation marks ("CPU 0" in the preceding example). The quoted value is intended to match the label on the physical hardware. The FRU is also represented in a Fault Management Resource Identifier (FMRI) format, which includes descriptive properties about the system containing the fault, such as its host name and chassis serial number. On platforms that support it, the part number and serial number of the FRU are also included in the FRU's FMRI.

The Affects lines (Lines 8 and 9) indicate the components that are impacted by the fault and their relative state. In this example, a single CPU strand is impacted. It is "degraded," which means it has *not* been taken offline by the system. In this example, this machine is a single CPU system and the last CPU cannot be taken offline for obvious reasons. Another reason that an attempt to offline a CPU might fail is if real-time threads are bound to the affected CPU.

If this were a multiprocessor system, then one could expect the affected CPU to be taken offline by the operating system, as shown in the following example:

```
# psrinfo
0        faulted   since 05/13/2008 12:55:26
1        on-line   since 05/12/2008 11:47:26
```

The faulted state indicates that the processor has been taken offline by a Fault Management response agent. The fmadm faulty command also combines some details from the console message into the output (Lines 13–22), notably, the severity and the action to take to address the fault.

As mentioned earlier, some console messages and knowledge articles might instruct the user to use the older fmdump -v -u *UUID* command to display fault information. While now less preferred, this command still operates, as shown in the following example:

```
1    # fmdump -v -u 04837324-f221-e7dc-f6fa-dc7d9420ea76
2    TIME                    UUID                                    SUNW-MSG-ID
3    May 13 15:00:02.2409 04837324-f221-e7dc-f6fa-dc7d9420ea76 AMD-8000-AV
4    100%  fault.cpu.amd.dcachedata
5
6    Problem in: hc://:product-id=Sun-Ultra-20-Workstation:
chassis-id=0604FK401F:server-id=hexterra/motherboard=0/chip=0/cpu=0
7        Affects: cpu:///cpuid=0
8            FRU: hc://:product-id=Sun-Ultra-20-Workstation:
chassis-id=0604FK401F:server-id=hexterra/motherboard=0/chip=0
9        Location: CPU 0
```

The information about the impacted FRUs is still present, although separated across two lines (Lines 8 and 9). The Location string presents the human-readable FRU string, and the FRU line presents the formal FMRI. Note that the severity, descriptive text, and action are not shown with the fmdump command.

7.4 Repairing Faults

Once Fault Management has faulted a component in your system, you will want to repair it. A repair can happen in one of two ways: implicitly or explicitly.

An *implicit repair* can occur when the faulty component is replaced, provided the component has serial number information that the Fault Manager can track. On many of Sun's SPARC based systems, serial number information is included in the FMRIs so that the Fault Manager can determine when components have been removed from operation, either through replacement or other means (e.g., Blacklisting). When such detections occur, the Fault Manager daemon will no longer display the affected resource in the fmadm faulty output. The resource is maintained in the daemon's internal resource cache until the fault event is 30 days old, at which point it is purged.

Implicit repairs do not apply to all systems and are unlikely to occur on generic x86 based hardware. Note that in the previous fault example, while there is a chassis-id in the FMRIs, no FRU serial number information is available. So the Fault Manager daemon would not be able to detect a FRU replacement, necessitating an explicit repair.

The fmadm repair command is used to explicitly mark a fault as repaired. It takes either a UUID or an FMRI as an argument. For example:

```
# fmadm repair 04837324-f221-e7dc-f6fa-dc7d9420ea76
fmadm: recorded repair to 04837324-f221-e7dc-f6fa-dc7d9420ea76
```

7.5 Managing Fault Management Log Files

The Fault Manager daemon (fmd) maintains two persistent log files of events: the error log and the fault log. The error log persistently records inbound telemetry information (ereports), and the fault log persistently records diagnosis and repair events. Both log files are in the Extended Accounting format associated with libexacct(3LIB). The log files reside in /var/fm/fmd.

These log files are viewed by using the fmdump command.

```
# fmdump -?
fmdump: illegal option -- ?
Usage: fmdump [-efvV] [-c class] [-R root] [-t time] [-T time] [-u uuid]
              [-n name[.name]*[=value]] [file]
       -c  select events that match the specified class
       -e  display error log content instead of fault log content
       -f  follow growth of log file by waiting for additional data
       -R  set root directory for pathname expansions
       -t  select events that occurred after the specified time
       -T  select events that occurred before the specified time
       -u  select events that match the specified uuid
       -n  select events containing named nvpair (with matching value)
       -v  set verbose mode: display additional event detail
       -V  set very verbose mode: display complete event contents
```

With no options, fmdump displays the contents of the fault log. The -e option instructs fmdump to examine the error log.

Various options provide more detailed and granular scrutiny of the log files. However, the commonly used options are -v for more verbose output and -u to list only those events associated with a UUID.

7.5.1 Automatic Log Rotation

Both the error and fault log files have historical recording, similar to the /var/adm/messages. By default, up to 10 historical error and fault log files are kept. With historical logging, the need for log rotation follows. The rotation of fmd log files is managed by the logadm command. By default, logadm is run from the root user's crontab each day at 03:10 a.m. The logadm.conf entries for fmd log files are as follows:

```
# grep /var/fm/fmd /etc/logadm.conf
/var/fm/fmd/errlog -M '/usr/sbin/fmadm -q rotate errlog && mv /var/fm/fmd/
errlog.0- $nfile' -N -s 2m
 /var/fm/fmd/fltlog -A 6m -M '/usr/sbin/fmadm -q rotate fltlog && mv /var/fm/fmd/
fltlog.0- $nfile' -N -s 10m
```

The errlog file is rotated when the active file grows larger than 2 MB. The fltlog log threshold for rotation is 10 MB. Also note the use of -A on the fltlog file, which means that fault log files older than 6 months are deleted, irrespective of size.

In addition, note that after the `fmadm rotate` command, an `mv` command renames the file to a final archived name. So, automatic rotation is a two-step process:

1. `fmadm rotate` creates a `"*log.0-"` file.
2. `logadm` renames the `"*log.0-"` file to `"*log.[0-9]"`.

The following example shows output indicating a system with automatically rotated error log files:

```
# cd /var/fm/fmd ; ls -l errlog*
-rw-r--r--   1 root     root      2014185 Jun 25 16:32 errlog
-rw-r--r--   1 root     root      2049327 Jun 10 16:30 errlog.0
-rw-r--r--   1 root     root      3123843 May 28 16:30 errlog.1
-rw-r--r--   1 root     root      2174873 May 19 16:30 errlog.2
-rw-r--r--   1 root     root      2049173 May  7 16:30 errlog.3
-rw-r--r--   1 root     root      2293094 Apr 22 16:30 errlog.4
-rw-r--r--   1 root     root      2583748 Apr  9 16:30 errlog.5
-rw-r--r--   1 root     root      2867374 Mar 10 16:30 errlog.6
-rw-r--r--   1 root     root      2187465 Feb  8 16:30 errlog.7
-rw-r--r--   1 root     root      2211937 Jan 25 16:30 errlog.8
-rw-r--r--   1 root     root      2328587 Jan  2 16:30 errlog.9
```

7.5.2 Manual Log Rotation

The Fault Manager daemon error and fault log files can also be rotated manually. The `logadm.conf` entries show that the `fmadm rotate` *logname* command is used for an on-demand log rotation, followed by some post processing. The following output shows what happens if just the `fmadm rotate` *logname* command is used:

```
# ls -l /var/fm/fmd
total 54
drwx------   3 root     sys          512 May 13 14:55 ckpt
-rw-r--r--   1 root     root       13049 May 13 15:00 errlog
-rw-r--r--   1 root     root       11013 May 13 15:01 fltlog
drwx------   2 root     sys          512 May 13 15:01 rsrc
drwx------   2 root     sys          512 May 13 02:04 xprt
# fmadm rotate errlog
fmadm: errlog has been rotated out and can now be archived
# fmadm rotate fltlog
fmadm: fltlog has been rotated out and can now be archived
# ls -l /var/fm/fmd
total 58
drwx------   3 root     sys          512 May 13 14:55 ckpt
-rw-r--r--   1 root     root         330 May 13 15:01 errlog
-rw-r--r--   1 root     root       13049 May 13 15:00 errlog.0-
-rw-r--r--   1 root     root         330 May 13 15:01 fltlog
-rw-r--r--   1 root     root       11013 May 13 15:01 fltlog.0-
drwx------   2 root     sys          512 May 13 15:01 rsrc
drwx------   2 root     sys          512 May 13 02:04 xprt
```

Note that manual rotation leaves a `"*log.0-"` file. When rotated automatically, `logadm` summarily renames this file to the next historical log file. Manual rotation executes the rotation steps only within `fmd`, which creates the `"*log.0-"` file. The result is that the next manual rotation will *overwrite* the previous `"*log.0-"` file. For example:

```
# ls -l /var/fm/fmd/errlog*
-rw-r--r--   1 root        root          330 May 18 11:01 errlog
-rw-r--r--   1 root        root        13049 May 13 15:00 errlog.0-
# fmadm rotate errlog
fmadm: errlog has been rotated out and can now be archived
# ls -l /var/fm/fmd/errlog*
-rw-r--r--   1 root        root          329 Jul 25 18:35 errlog
-rw-r--r--   1 root        root          330 May 18 11:01 errlog.0-
```

Note that `errlog.0-` has been overwritten. Any information in the log file from May 13 15:00 is gone. Recall that automatic log rotation is a two-step process. Using the `fmadm rotate` command directly only performs the first step.

A cleaner on-demand log rotation method is to use `logadm` to process the `logadm.conf` files, but to override the default rotation periods and sizes. This method has the advantage of ensuring that the historical log files are preserved. For example:

```
# ls -l errlog*
-rw-r--r--   1 root        root          330 May 13 15:01 errlog
-rw-r--r--   1 root        root        13049 May 13 15:00 errlog.0-
# logadm -p now -s 1b /var/fm/fmd/errlog
# ls -l errlog*
-rw-r--r--   1 root        root          330 Sep 11 10:17 errlog
-rw-r--r--   1 root        root          330 May 13 15:01 errlog.0

And similarly for the fault log:

# ls -l fltlog*
-rw-r--r--   1 root        root          330 May 13 15:01 fltlog
-rw-r--r--   1 root        root        11013 May 13 15:01 fltlog.0-
# logadm -p now -s 1b /var/fm/fmd/fltlog
# ls -l fltlog*
-rw-r--r--   1 root        root          330 Sep 11 10:22 fltlog
-rw-r--r--   1 root        root          330 May 13 15:01 fltlog.0
```

7.5.3 Log Rotation Failures

The rotation of a log file can fail. If a rotation request is made while an ereport is being written to the log file, then `fmd` will wait 200 milliseconds and then retry the rotation. If after 10 attempts the rotation is still not successful, fmd will abandon the operation and report the following error:

```
# fmadm rotate errlog
fmadm: failed to rotate errlog: log file is too busy to rotate (try again later)
```

Such a condition can persist if a steady stream of errors is occurring on a system, such as a "storm" of correctable errors. Even with rotation failures, ereports are still persistently logged to the errlog file.

7.5.4 Examining Historical Log Files

Once log files have been rotated, you can use the fmdump command with the -f *file* option to examine historical information. For example:

```
# fmdump -v -u 04837324-f221-e7dc-f6fa-dc7d9420ea76
TIME                 UUID                 SUNW-MSG-ID
fmdump: /var/fm/fmd/fltlog is empty

# fmdump -f "fltlog.0" -v -u 04837324-f221-e7dc-f6fa-dc7d9420ea76
TIME                 UUID                 SUNW-MSG-ID
May 13 15:00:02.2409 04837324-f221-e7dc-f6fa-dc7d9420ea76 AMD-8000-AV
   100%          fault.cpu.amd.dcachedata

            Problem in: hc://:product-id=Sun-Ultra-20-Workstation:
chassis- id=0604FK401F:server-id=hexterra/motherboard=0/chip=0/cpu=0
            Affects: cpu:///cpuid=0
                FRU: hc://:product-id=Sun-Ultra-20-Workstation:
chassis-id=0604FK401F:server-id=hexterra/motherboard=0/chip=0
            Location: CPU 0
```

The fmdump command displays any events in the fltlog.0 file associated with UUID 04837324-f221-e7dc-f6fa-dc7d9420ea76.

7.6 Managing fmd and fmd Modules

There are several command line utilities provided with Solaris Fault Management. Typical tasks include listing loaded modules and gathering statistics on those modules. In some cases, such as when troubleshooting, it may be necessary to load or unload modules or to tune a module via its configuration file.

7.6.1 Loading and Unloading Modules

Solaris Fault Management provides a framework in which various modules (diagnosis engines, response agents) plug into. The fmadm config command lists the currently loaded modules, with their versions, descriptions, and status. For example:

```
# fmadm config
MODULE                 VERSION STATUS   DESCRIPTION
cpumem-retire          1.1     active   CPU/Memory Retire Agent
disk-transport         1.0     active   Disk Transport Agent
eft                    1.16    active   eft diagnosis engine
fmd-self-diagnosis     1.0     active   Fault Manager Self-Diagnosis
io-retire              2.0     active   I/O Retire Agent
snmp-trapgen           1.0     active   SNMP Trap Generation Agent
sysevent-transport     1.0     active   SysEvent Transport Agent
syslog-msgs            1.0     active   Syslog Messaging Agent
zfs-diagnosis          1.0     active   ZFS Diagnosis Engine
zfs-retire             1.0     active   ZFS Retire Agent
```

The preceding list is typical for an x86 or x64 based system running the Solaris 10 5/08 release. Different versions of the Solaris OS, SPARC based systems, and so forth might have a differing set of modules. Modules range from platform specific, to machine architecture (i86pc, i86xpv, sun4u, sun4v) specific, to completely generic.

Table 7.2 describes the fmd modules.

Table 7.2 fmd Module Descriptions

Module	Description
cpumem-retire	Takes offline CPU strands and retires memory pages diagnosed as faulty
disk-transport	Preprocessor for disk errors
Eft	The Eversholt diagnosis engine, which runs a multitude of fault trees for various subsystems
fmd-self-diagnosis	Internal self-diagnosis module for fmd
io-retire	Retires or takes offline I/O devices diagnosed as faulty
snmp-trapgen	Issues a v1 or v2 SNMP trap per fault
sysevent-transport	Receives events on a sysevent channel
syslog-msgs	Logs events to the console and message log
zfs-diagnosis	Diagnosis engine for ZFS errors
zfs-retire	Retire agent for ZFS faults

On startup, by default, `fmd` searches for loadable modules in the following directories:

- `/usr/platform/`uname -i`/lib/fm/fmd/plugins`
- `/usr/platform/`uname -m`/lib/fm/fmd/plugins`
- `/usr/lib/fm/fmd/plugins`

If any modules have the same name, the first module encountered is loaded and subsequent modules are skipped. For example, the Solaris OS has a generic `io-retire` agent for taking offline faulted I/O devices. Suppose platform `SUNW,FOO` also delivers a module called `io-retire`. In the system, two `io-retire.so` files would exist:

- `/usr/lib/fm/fmd/plugins/io-retire.so`
- `/usr/platform/SUNW,FOO/lib/fm/fmd/plugins/io-retire.so`

On `SUNW,FOO`, `fmd` would load and use the platform-specific `io-retire` module. All other platforms would use the common `io-retire` module from `/usr/lib/fm`.

Modules can be loaded and unloaded while the `fmd` service remains active by using the `fmadm unload` *module-name* command, where *module-name* is the name reported by the `fmadm config` command. For example:

```
# fmadm unload snmp-trapgen
fmadm: module 'snmp-trapgen' unloaded from fault manager
# fmadm config
MODULE                VERSION STATUS  DESCRIPTION
cpumem-retire         1.1     active  CPU/Memory Retire Agent
disk-transport        1.0     active  Disk Transport Agent
eft                   1.16    active  eft diagnosis engine
fmd-self-diagnosis    1.0     active  Fault Manager Self-Diagnosis
io-retire             2.0     active  I/O Retire Agent
sysevent-transport    1.0     active  SysEvent Transport Agent
syslog-msgs           1.0     active  Syslog Messaging Agent
zfs-diagnosis         1.0     active  ZFS Diagnosis Engine
zfs-retire            1.0     active  ZFS Retire Agent
```

Loading a module works similarly, although an absolute path for the module must be specified. For example:

```
# fmadm load /usr/lib/fm/fmd/plugins/snmp-trapgen.so
fmadm: module '/usr/lib/fm/fmd/plugins/snmp-trapgen.so' loaded into fault manager
# fmadm config
MODULE                VERSION STATUS  DESCRIPTION
cpumem-retire         1.1     active  CPU/Memory Retire Agent
disk-transport        1.0     active  Disk Transport Agent
eft                   1.16    active  eft diagnosis engine
```

```
fmd-self-diagnosis      1.0      active  Fault Manager Self-Diagnosis
io-retire               2.0      active  I/O Retire Agent
snmp-trapgen            1.0      active  SNMP Trap Generation Agent
sysevent-transport      1.0      active  SysEvent Transport Agent
syslog-msgs             1.0      active  Syslog Messaging Agent
zfs-diagnosis           1.0      active  ZFS Diagnosis Engine
zfs-retire              1.0      active  ZFS Retire Agent
```

In normal operations, modules do *not* need to be loaded and unloaded. However, the functionality can be helpful in a debugging situation.

7.6.2 fmd Statistics

The Fault Manager daemon (fmd) and many of its modules track statistics. The fmstat command reports those statistics. Without options, fmstat gives a high-level overview of the events, processing times, and memory usage of the loaded modules. For example:

```
# fmstat
module              ev_recv ev_acpt wait  svc_t  %w  %b  open  solve  memsz  bufsz
cpumem-retire          1       0    0.0   403.5   0   0   0     0      419b   0
disk-transport         0       0    0.0   500.6   0   0   0     0      32b    0
eft                    0       0    0.0     4.8   0   0   0     0      1.4M   43b
fmd-self-diagnosis     0       0    0.0     4.7   0   0   0     0      0      0
io-retire              0       0    0.0     4.5   0   0   0     0      0      0
snmp-trapgen           0       0    0.0     4.5   0   0   0     0      32b    0
sysevent-transport     0       0    0.0  1444.4   0   0   0     0      0      0
syslog-msgs            0       0    0.0     4.5   0   0   0     0      0      0
zfs-diagnosis          0       0    0.0     4.7   0   0   0     0      0      0
zfs-retire             0       0    0.0     4.5   0   0   0     0      0      0
```

The fmstat(1M) man page describes each column in this output. Note that the open and solve columns apply only to Fault Management cases, which are only created and solved by diagnosis engines. These columns are immaterial for other modules, such as response agents.

Statistics on an individual module can also be displayed by using the -m *module* option. This syntax is commonly used with the -z option to suppress zero-valued statistics. For example:

```
# fmstat -z -m cpumem-retire
      NAME VALUE              DESCRIPTION
   cpu_flts 1                 cpu faults resolved
```

The command output shows that the `cpumem-retire` agent has successfully processed a request to take a CPU offline.

7.6.3 Configuration Files

Many `fmd` modules have a configuration file for tailoring the behavior of the module. While these files are not typically changed from what is delivered in the Solaris OS, it is helpful to know about them.

Configuration files have the same name as the module binary on disk, but with a `.conf` suffix. For example:

```
# cd /usr/lib/fm/fmd/plugins
# ls -l io-retire*
-rw-r--r--   1 root      bin          1150 Jul 10 17:57 io-retire.conf
-r-xr-xr-x   1 root      bin         44780 Jul 10 17:57 io-retire.so
```

A `.conf` file is read once when the module loads. Changes to the `.conf` file require an unload and reload of the associated module.

In Section 7.6, "Managing `fmd` and `fmd` Modules," the search path for `fmd` modules was outlined. The `.conf` file for a module is taken from the same directory as the module that is loaded. Using the same example from that section, assume there is an `io-retire` agent specific to the `SUNW,FOO` platform:

```
/usr/lib/fm/fmd/plugins/io-retire.so
/usr/lib/fm/fmd/plugins/io-retire.conf
/usr/platform/SUNW,FOO/lib/fm/fmd/plugins/io-retire.so
/usr/platform/SUNW,FOO/lib/fm/fmd/plugins/io-retire.conf
```

On `SUNW,FOO`, the agent in `/usr/platform/SUNW,FOO/lib/fm/fmd/plugins/` is loaded, and the `.conf` file in that same directory is used. The `.conf` file in `/usr/lib/fm/fmd/plugins` is ignored. On all other platforms, the agent and `.conf` file from `/usr/lib/fm/fmd/plugins` are used.

A real-world example of this scenario is the Fault Management Event Transport Module (ETM), which is used on `sun4v` class systems. On `sun4v` systems, this module subscribes to Fault Management events and transports them to a Service Processor. Different platforms have different error events and different fault diagnoses, so different `.conf` files are used in the respective `/usr/platform` directories to tailor the module's behavior[2].

`fmd` has its own `.conf` file as well: `/etc/fm/fmd.conf`. By default, `fmd` ships with no configuration file changes of any kind. Unless directed by your service team, it is not suggested to change the default settings.

As described in Section 7.4, "Repairing Faults," implicitly repaired faults expire after 30 days. The expiry duration is configurable in `fmd.conf`. To set the expiry to 14 days, you would specify the following:

```
setprop rsrc.age 14d
```

Another example is the retry semantics for log rotation:

```
setprop log.waitrotate 600ms
setprop log.tryrotate 20
```

This parameter instructs `fmd` to try up to 20 times to rotate a log file, waiting 600 milliseconds between attempts (instead of the defaults of 10 attempts with 200 milliseconds between attempts).

All of the `fmd.conf` tunable parameters are documented in the *Fault Management Daemon Programmer's Reference Manual*, which is available from the OpenSolaris Fault Management Community Web site at `http://opensolaris.org/os/community/fm`.

7.7 Fault Management Directories

The directories of interest for Solaris Fault Management are:

- Fault management libraries, dictionaries, CLIs (see Figure 7.2)
- Platform specific fault management content (see Figure 7.3)
- Architecture specific fault management content (see Figure 7.4)
- Log and core files (see Figure 7.5)

7.8 Solaris Fault Management Downloadable Resources

The OpenSolaris Fault Management community offers many downloadable document and utilities, many of which are completely applicable to Solaris 10.

7.8.1 Solaris FMA Demo Kit

The Solaris Fault Management Architecture (FMA) Demo Kit consists of a set of scripts that provides an automated harness for demonstrating the capability of the Solaris OS to handle and diagnose CPU, memory, and PCI I/O errors. The

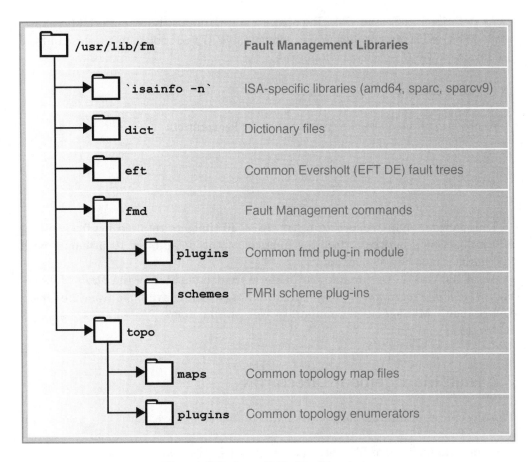

Figure 7.2 /usr/lib/fm Directory

Solaris FMA Demo Kit runs on stock Solaris systems, out-of-the-box. No custom error injection hardware or drivers is required. It is available at the following location:

- http://opensolaris.org/os/community/fm/demokit/

The example CPU fault in this book was generated by using the Solaris FMA Demo Kit.

7.8.2 Events Registry

The FMA Events Registry is the central repository for all Fault Management events (ereports, faults, defects, and so on) and the knowledge articles associated

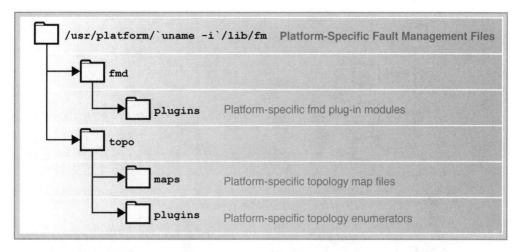

Figure 7.3 /usr/platform/'uname -i'/lib/fm Directory

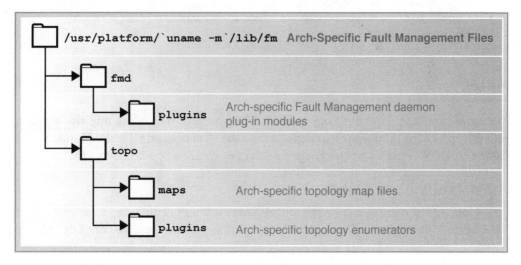

Figure 7.4 /usr/platform/'uname -m'/lib/fm Directory

with each fault message code. The registry can be downloaded from the Open Solaris Fault Management Community page. The registry also includes a set of scripts that can query the Events Registry for information about error and

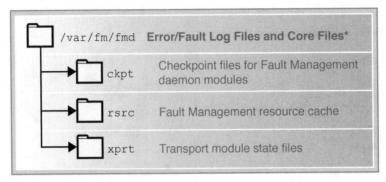

*If a bug in the Fault Manager daemon or one of its modules causes the daemon to dump core, the core file is stored in /var/fm/fmd.

Figure 7.5 `/var/fm/fmd` Directory

fault events. An example of the utilities, and one potential usage, is described in this blog:

- `http://blogs.sun.com/sdaven/entry/cruising_the_events_registry`

Notes

For more information about Solaris Fault Management, including additional documentation, blogs, and news articles, visit the OpenSolaris Fault Management Community Web site at `http://opensolaris.org/os/community/fm`.

1. FMA/MIB Online Sources,
   `http://blogs.sun.com/pmonday/entry/fun_with_the_fma`
   `http://blogs.sun.com/wesolows/entry/a_louder_voice_for_the`

2. The following is the search URL for `etm.conf` on the OpenSolaris site,
   `http://src.opensolaris.org/source/`
   `searchq=&defs=&refs=&path=etm.conf &hist=&project=%2Fonnv`

8

Managing Disks

This chapter discusses all of the basic concepts for managing disks in the Solaris Operating System (Solaris OS). It covers the following:

- *Definition of a device driver and other disk-related terminology and how devices (specifically, disks) are managed in the Solaris OS*
- *How EFI-labeled disks are different from VTOC-labeled disks, including details about the advantages and disadvantages of using EFI labels*
- *Details on the default contents of different slices on a disk*
- *How to use the* format *utility to identify disks connected to the system, format a disk, create slices, label a disk (EFI or VTOC), recover a corrupted disk label, and identify and repair the defective sectors on the disk.*
- *How to create an* fdisk *Solaris partition*
- *Description of some useful disk management commands*

8.1 Hard Disk Drive

To many people, a hard disk drive (commonly known just as hard disk) is a "black box" of sorts; that is, it is thought of as just a small device that somehow stores data. There is nothing wrong with this approach as long as all you care about is that it stores data. If you use your hard disk as more than just a place to "keep stuff," then you want to know more about your hard disk. It is hard to really administer or understand the factors that affect performance, reliability, and inter-facing without knowing how the drive works internally.

A hard disk uses round, flat disks called *platters*, coated on both sides with a spe-cial media material designed to store information in the form of magnetic patterns. The platters are mounted by cutting a hole in the center and stacking them onto a *spindle*. The platters rotate at high speed, driven by a special *spindle motor* con-nected to the spindle. Special electromagnetic read/write devices called heads are mounted onto sliders and used to either record information onto the disk or read information from it. The sliders are mounted onto *arms*, all of which are mechani-cally connected into a single assembly and positioned over the surface of the disk by a device called an *actuator*. A logic board called a *disk controller* controls the activ-ity of the other components and communicates with rest of the system.

Disk platters are either single-sided or double sided. Single sided platters store the data only on one side of the platter and hence have only one read/write head per platter. Double sided platters store the information on both the side of the plat-ter and hence have two read/write heads per platter. All modern hard disk drives contain double sided platters.

Figure 8.1 clearly shows the different components of the hard disk drive dis-cussed previously.

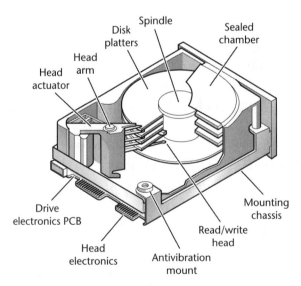

Figure 8.1 Hard Disk Drive Components

8.2 Disk Terminology

Before performing a disk management task, you should understand the following basic terms:

- **block**

    A sector or group of sectors that function as the smallest data unit permitted; since blocks are often defined as a single sector, the terms 'block' and 'sector' are sometimes used interchangeably. Usually, a disk block is 512 bytes.

- **cylinder**

    The collection of tracks present at the same concentric position on each disk platter on a disk. Figure 8.2 clearly shows the tracks, sectors, and cylinders.

- **device driver**

    A low-level program that functions as a communication interface between the kernel and a specific piece of hardware.

- **disk controller**

    A chip and its associated circuitry that controls the disk drive by translating the computer data and commands into low-level commands interpreted by the disk drive circuitry.

- **disk label**

    The first sector of a disk that is reserved for storing information about the disk's controller, geometry, and slices. Another term used for the disk label is VTOC (Volume Table of Contents) on a disk with a VTOC label.

- **sector**

    The smallest addressable unit on a disk platter. Usually, a sector holds 512 bytes. Sectors are grouped into logical blocks that function as the smallest data unit permitted.

- **track**

    A concentric ring on a disk platter that passes under a single stationary disk head as the disk platter rotates. A track consists of a series of sectors positioned end-to-end in a circular path. The number of sectors per track varies with the radius of a track on the platter. The outer tracks are larger and can hold more sectors than the inner tracks.

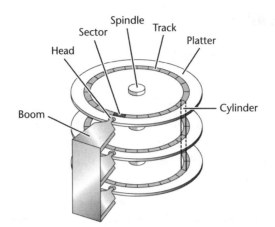

Figure 8.2 Hard Disk Tracks, Sectors, and Cylinders

8.3 Disk Device Naming Conventions

In the Solaris OS, each disk device is referenced in three ways:

- **Physical device name**—Represents the full device path name in the device information hierarchy. Physical device names uniquely identify the physical location of the hardware devices on the system. They are created when the device is first added to the system and are stored in the /devices directory.

- **Instance name**—Represents the kernel's abbreviated name for every possible device on the system. The mapping of this abbreviated name and its associated physical device name is maintained in the /etc/path_to_inst file. For example:

  - sd<n>
    where sd (scsi disk) is the disk name and n is the number, such as the instance name of sd0 for the first SCSI disk device

  - dad<n>
    where dad (direct access device) is the disk name and n is the number, such as the instance name of dad0 for the first IDE (Integrated Drive Electronics) disk device

- **Logical device name**—Logical device names are symbolic links to the physical device names that are stored in the /devices directory. Logical device names are used primarily to refer to a device when you are typing some disk or file system commands on the command line. Table 8.1 lists some of these commands and shows how they use logical device names. All logical device names are stored in the /dev directory. Logical device names contain the controller number, target number, disk number, and slice number (s0 to s7) or `fdisk` partition number (p0 to p4) and are represented as (c<n>t<n>d<n>[s<n>,p<n>]).

Note

IDE devices do not use a target number and are represented as (c<n>d<n>[s<n>,p<n>]).

Every disk device has an entry in both the /dev/dsk and /dev/rdsk (raw disk device) directories for the block and character disk devices, respectively. To display the entries in the /dev/dsk directory, type the following command:

```
# ls /dev/dsk

c0d0p0          c0d0s15          c1t0d0p3          c1t0d0s4

c0d0p1          c0d0s2           c1t0d0p4          c1t0d0s5

c0d0p2          c0d0s3           c1t0d0s0          c1t0d0s6

c0d0p3          c0d0s4           c1t0d0s1          c1t0d0s7

c0d0p4          c0d0s5           c1t0d0s10         c1t0d0s8

c0d0s0          c0d0s6           c1t0d0s11         c1t0d0s9

c0d0s1          c0d0s7           c1t0d0s12

c0d0s10         c0d0s8           c1t0d0s13

c0d0s11         c0d0s9           c1t0d0s14

c0d0s12         c1t0d0p0         c1t0d0s15

c0d0s13         c1t0d0p1         c1t0d0s2

c2d0s14         c1t0d0p2         c1t0d0s3
```

- **c0d0s0** through **c0d0s15**
  Identifies the device names for disk slices 0 through 15 for an IDE disk that is attached to Controller 0, on Disk Unit 0. This IDE disk is the master disk on the primary IDE bus.

  c0d0p0 represents the entire disk. c0d0p1 through c0d0p4 identify the four `fdisk` partitions on this disk.

- **c1t0d0s0** through **c1t0d0s15**
  Identifies the device names for disk slices 0 through 15 for a SCSI disk that is attached to Controller 1, at Target 0, on Disk Unit 0.

  c1t0d0p0 represents the entire disk. c1t0d0p1 through c1t0d0p4 identify the four `fdisk` partitions on this disk.

8.3.1 Specifying the Disk Subdirectory in Commands

Disk and file system commands require the use of either a raw (character) device interface or a block device interface. The distinction is made by how data is read from the device.

Raw device interfaces transfer only small amounts of data at a time. Block device interfaces include a buffer from which large blocks of data are read at once. Different commands require different interfaces:

- When a command requires the raw device interface, specify the /dev/rdsk subdirectory (the "r" signifies "raw").

- When a command requires the block device interface, specify the /dev/dsk subdirectory.

When you are unsure whether a command requires the use of /dev/dsk or /dev/rdsk, check the man page for that command. Table 8.1 shows which interface is required for some commonly used disk and file system commands.

Table 8.1 Device Interface Type Required by Some Frequently Used Commands

Command (with Man Page)	Reference Interface Type	Example of Use
df(1M)	Block	/dev/dsk/c0t3d0s6
fsck(1M)	Raw	-p /dev/rdsk/c0t0d0s0
mount(1M)	Block	/dev/dsk/c1t0d0s7 /export/home
newfs(1M)	Raw	/dev/rdsk/c0t0d1s1
prtvtoc(1M)	Raw	/dev/rdsk/c0t0d0s2

8.4 Overview of Disk Management

This section gives an overview of the different software concepts you need to be aware of while managing the disks connected to a system. It also gives a brief introduction to the Solaris format utility, which can be used to perform most of the disk management tasks.

8.4.1 Device Driver

A *device driver* is a low-level program that functions as a communication interface between the kernel and a specific piece of hardware. Before the Solaris OS can communicate with a device, the device must have a driver. When the system boots for the first time, the kernel calls all the device drivers in the system to determine which devices are available and to initialize those devices by creating the device files in the /devices directory and the logical links in the /dev directory. In addition, the kernel maintains the instance name for every possible device on the system. For example, sd0 and sd1 represent the instance names of two disk devices. The mapping of instance names is maintained in the /etc/path_to_inst file.

The *devfsadm* command manages the special device files in the /dev and /devices directories. By default, the *devfsadm* command attempts to load every driver in the system and attach them to all possible device instances. Then, the command creates the device files in the /devices directory and the logical links in the /dev directory. In addition to managing the /dev and /devices directories, this command maintains the *path_to_inst* instance database. For more information, see the *path_to_inst*(4) man page.

> **Note**
>
> If you remove a disk from a running system or make any configuration changes and you want that change to take affect without rebooting the system, then you can run the devfsadm command from command line.

8.4.2 Disk Labels (VTOC or EFI)

A special area of every disk is reserved for storing information about the disk's controller, geometry, and slices. This information is called the *disk label*. Another term that is used to describe the disk label is the VTOC (Volume Table of Contents) on a disk with a VTOC label. To "label" a disk means to write slice information onto the disk. You usually label a disk after you change its slices.

If you fail to label a disk after you create slices, the slices will be unavailable because the Solaris OS has no way of knowing about the slices.

The Solaris 10 OS supports the following two disk labels:

- SMI—The traditional VTOC label for disks that are less than 1TB in size.

- EFI—Provides support for disks that are larger than 1TB on systems that run a 64-bit Solaris kernel. The Extensible Firmware Interface (EFI) disk label is not available for disks connected to a system running a 32-bit Solaris kernel. A disk that is less than 1 TB (terabyte) in size can be labeled with an EFI label using format -e command.

The following are the advantages of using EFI labels as compared to SMI labels:

- Provides support for disks greater than 1TB in size.
- Provides usable slices 0–6, where slice 2 is just another slice.
- Partitions (or slices) cannot overlap with the primary or backup label or with any other partitions. The size of the EFI label is usually 34 sectors, so partitions start at sector 34. This feature means that no partition can start at sector zero (0).
- Information that was stored in the alternate cylinders area (the last two cylinders of the disk) in case of SMI is now stored in slice 8.
- No cylinder, head, or sector information is stored in the EFI label. Sizes are reported in blocks.
- If you use the `format` utility to change partition sizes, the unassigned partition tag is assigned to partitions with sizes equal to zero. By default, the `format` utility assigns the `usr` partition tag to any partition with a size greater than zero. You can use the Partition Change menu to reassign partition tags after the partitions are changed.
- Solaris ZFS uses EFI labels by default. For more information about ZFS, refer to Chapter 5, "Solaris File Systems."

The following are the disadvantages of using EFI labels as compared to VTOC labels:

- You cannot boot from a disk with an EFI disk label.
- The SCSI driver, `ssd` or `sd`, currently supports only up to 2 terabytes. If you need greater disk capacity than 2 terabytes, use a disk and storage management product such as Solaris Volume Manager to create a larger device. For more information about using Solaris Volume Manger, refer to *Solaris Volume Manger Administration Guide*.
- Layered software products intended for systems with EFI-labeled disks might be incapable of accessing a disk without an EFI disk label.
- You cannot use the `fdisk` command on a disk with an EFI label that is greater than 1 terabyte in size.
- A disk with an EFI label is not recognized on systems running previous Solaris releases.
- The EFI disk label is not supported on IDE disks.
- You cannot use the Solaris Management Console's Disk Manager tool to manage disks with EFI labels. Instead, use the `format` utility to partition disks

with EFI labels. Then, you can use the Solaris Management Console's Enhanced Storage tool to manage volumes and disk sets with EFI-labeled disks.

- The EFI specification prohibits overlapping slices. The entire disk is represented by c#t#d#.
- The EFI label provides information about disk or partition sizes in sectors and blocks, but not in cylinders and heads.
- The following `format` utility options are either not supported or not applicable on disks with EFI labels:
  - The Save option is not supported because disks with EFI labels do not need an entry in the `format.dat` file.
  - The Backup option is not applicable because the disk driver finds the primary label and writes it back to the disk.

8.4.3 Disk Slices

In the Solaris OS, files are *not* stored directly on the disk. Instead, files stored on a disk are contained in file systems. Each file system on a disk is assigned to a slice, which is a group of sectors that are reserved for use by that file system. Each disk slice appears to the operating system (and to the system administrator) as though it were a separate disk drive.

On x86 based systems, you can consider disk slices as subpartitions within the Solaris partition. Therefore, a slice is composed of a single range of contiguous blocks. The boundaries of a disk slice are defined when a disk is partitioned by using the Solaris `format` utility or the Solaris Management Console's Disks tool. The slice information for a particular disk can be viewed by using the `prtvtoc` command.

The following are important points to remember when you are managing disk slices:

- Each disk slice can hold only one file system.
- A file system cannot span multiple slices.
- For x86 based systems, a single disk can be divided into a maximum of four primary `fdisk` partitions. And only one of them can be a Solaris partition, meaning that only one partition can have the Solaris OS installed on it.

The slice configuration for VTOC-labeled disks and EFI-labeled disks differs. For VTOC-labeled disks, the Solaris `fdisk` partition is divided into 10 slices, numbered 0–9 (by using the `format` utility), where slice 2 represents the entire disk and cannot be changed.

For EFI-labeled disks, the disk is divided into 7 slices, numbered 0–6, where slice 2 is just another slice and can be used like any other slice to store a file system. Slice 8 is created by default and is used for alternate sectors. This slice should not be modified or deleted.

> **Note**
>
> For x86 based systems, VTOC-labeled disks have 16 slices. Slice 8 is used to hold boot code. Slice 9 is used for alternate sectors on some types of disks. Higher slices (10–15) are available for use, but not supported by the `format` utility at this time.

Disks on x86 based systems are divided into `fdisk` partitions. An `fdisk` partition is a section of the disk that is reserved for a particular operating system, such as the Solaris OS.

The Solaris OS places 10 slices, numbered 0–9, on a Solaris `fdisk` partition for VTOC-labeled disks and 7 slices, numbered 0–6, for EFI-labeled disks (see Table 8.2).

Table 8.2 Description of One Possible Slice Arrangement of the Solaris OS on a Root (System) Disk

Slice	File System	Comments
0	`root (/)`	Holds operating system files and directories.
		EFI—You cannot boot from a disk with an EFI label.
1	`swap`	Provides virtual memory or swap space.
2		**VTOC**—Refers to the entire disk, by convention.
		The size of this slice should not be changed.
		EFI—Optional slice that can be defined based on your site's needs.
3	`/export`	Optional slice that can be defined based on your site's needs. Can be used on a server to hold alternative versions of operating systems that are required by client systems.
4		Optional slice that can be defined based on your site's needs.
5	`/opt`	Optional slice that can be defined based on your site's needs.
		Can be used to hold application software that is added to a system. If a slice is not allocated for the `/opt` file system during installation, the `/opt` directory is placed on slice 0.
6	`/usr`	Holds OS commands (also known as *executables*). This slice also holds documentation, system programs (`init` and `syslogd`, for example), and library routines.

Table 8.2 Description of One Possible Slice Arrangement of the Solaris OS
on a Root (System) Disk (*continued*)

Slice	File System	Comments
7	/home or /export/ home	Holds files that are created by users.
8		**VTOC**—Contains information necessary to boot the Solaris OS from the disk. The slice resides at the beginning of the Solaris fdisk partition (although the slice number itself does not indicate this fact), and is known as the *boot slice*.
		EFI—A reserved slice created by default. This area is similar to the VTOC's alternate cylinders.
		Do *not* modify or delete this slice.
9		**VTOC**—Provides an area that is reserved for alternate disk blocks. Slice 9 is known as the *alternate sector slice*.
		EFI—Not applicable.

Caution

The disk label is stored in block 0 of each disk. So, third-party database applications that create raw data slices must not start at block 0. Otherwise, the disk label will be overwritten and the data on the disk will be inaccessible.

Do *not* use the following areas of the disk for raw data slices, which are sometimes created by third-party database applications:

- Block 0 where the disk label is stored
- Slice 2, which represents the entire disk with a VTOC label

---

8.4.4 Slice Arrangements on Multiple Disks

Although a single large disk can hold all slices and their corresponding file systems, two or more disks are often used to hold a system's slices and file systems.

Note

A slice cannot be split between two or more disks. However, multiple swap slices on separate disks are allowed because the Solaris OS can swap onto more than one swap device.

For example, a single disk might hold the root (/) file system, a swap slice, and the /usr file system, while another disk might hold another swap slice, /export/home file system and other file systems that contain user data.

In a multiple disk arrangement, the disk that contains the operating system and swap slice (that is, the disk that holds the root (/) and /usr file systems and the slice for swap space) is called the *system disk*. Other disks are called *secondary disks* or *non-system disks*.

When you arrange a system's file systems on multiple disks, one main advantage is that you can modify file systems and slices on the secondary disks without having to shut down the system or reload the operating system.

When you have more than one disk, you also increase input/output (I/O) volume. By distributing the disk load across multiple disks, you can avoid I/O bottlenecks.

8.4.5 Partition Table

An important part of the disk label is the *partition table*. The partition table identifies a disk's slices, the slice boundaries (in cylinders), and the total size of the slices. You can display a disk's partition table by using the format utility or the prtvtoc command described later in this chapter. Table 8.3 describes the fields in a partition table.

Table 8.3 Partition Table Fields

Term	Value	Description
Part	0–9 or 0–6	**VTOC**—Partitions or slices, numbered 0–9.
		EFI—Partitions or slices, numbered 0–6.
Tag	0=unassigned 1=boot 2=root 3=swap 4=usr 5=backup 6=stand 7=var 8=home 9=alternates 11=reserved	This value usually describes the file system that is mounted on the partition or how the slice (partition) is being used.
Flag	wm	The slice is writable and mountable.
	wu	The slice is writable and unmountable. This state is the default for the swap slice.
	rm	The slice is read-only and mountable.
	ru	The slice is read-only and unmountable.
Cylinders		**VTOC**—The starting and ending cylinder number for the slice.
		EFI—Not displayed on EFI-labeled disks.
Size		The slice size is specified in:
		▪ MB: megabytes
		▪ GB: gigabytes
		▪ B: blocks
		▪ C: cylinders

Table 8.3 Partition Table Fields (*continued*)

Term	Value	Description
Blocks		**VTOC**—The total number of cylinders and the total number of sectors per slice. **EFI**—Not displayed on EFI-labeled disks.
First Sector		**VTOC**—Not displayed on VTOC-labeled disks. **EFI**—The starting block number.
Last Sector		**VTOC**—Not displayed on VTOC-labeled disks. **EFI**—The ending block number.

The following is an example of a partition table for a VTOC-labeled disk, which is displayed by using the format utility:

```
Current partition table (original):
Total disk cylinders available: 24619 + 2 (reserved cylinders)

Part      Tag    Flag   Cylinders      Size          Blocks

0   unassigned   wm      1 -  1452    2.00GB   (1452/0/0)  4194828
1   unassigned   wm   1453 -  3630    3.00GB   (2178/0/0)  6292242
2       backup   wu      0 - 24618   33.91GB   (24619/0/0)71124291
3   unassigned   wm      0                0    (0/0/0)     0
4   unassigned   wm      0                0    (0/0/0)     0
5   unassigned   wm      0                0    (0/0/0)     0
6   unassigned   wm   3631 - 24618   28.91GB   (20988/0/0)60634332
7   unassigned   wm      0                0    (0/0/0)     0
8         boot   wu      0 -    0     1.41MB   (1/0/0)     2889
9   unassigned   wm      0                0    (0/0/0)     0
```

The following is an example of a partition table for an EFI-labeled disk, which is displayed by using the format utility:

```
Current partition table (original):

Part     Tag    Flag   First Sector  Size    Last Sector
0       root    wm          34      300.00GB  29145633
1        usr    wm      629145634   300.00GB  1258291233
2  unassigned   wm           0            0   0
3  unassigned   wm           0            0   0
4  unassigned   wm           0            0   0
5  unassigned   wm           0            0   0
6        usr    wm      1258291234  628.77GB  2576924637
8   reserved    wm      2576924638    8.00MB  2576941021
```

8.4.6 `format` Utility

Formatting prepares a storage medium, usually a disk, for reading and writing. When you format a disk, the operating system does the following:

- Erases all available information on the disk
- Tests the disk to make sure that all sectors are reliable
- Marks bad sectors (that is, those sectors that are scratched or otherwise damaged)
- Creates internal address tables that the operating system later uses to locate information

You must format a disk before you can use it. When you take an already formatted disk through the format process again, it is referred to, logically, as "reformatting." Formatting involves the following two separate processes:

- The disk media is prepared for use by writing the format information to the disk.
- An up-to-date list of disk defects is compiled based on a surface analysis.

Note

A small percentage of total disk space that is available for data is used to store defects and formatting information. This is why, after formatting, a new disk usually shows only 90–95 percent of the total capacity available for data. This percentage varies according to disk geometry, and decreases as the disk ages and develops more defects.

Formatting a disk might take anywhere from a few minutes to several hours depending on the type and size of the disk.

Caution

Formatting a disk is a destructive process, so make sure that any existing useful data on the disk is backed up before you start.

The Solaris OS provides a powerful disk administration tool, the `format` utility, to partition and maintain the disks connected to the system. This utility is used to perform the following tasks:

- Search your system for all attached disk drives and report the following information:
  - Target location
  - Disk geometry

- Whether the disk is formatted
- Whether the disk has a mounted partition and if so, which partition (slice) is mounted on which directory
- Retrieve the disk label and display the partition table
- Format disks
- Analyze disks for errors
- Repair defective sectors
- Partition disks
- Label disks

> **Note**
>
> You must be superuser (root user) to run the `format` utility. If you are not superuser but you try to use this utility, then the following error message is displayed:
>
> ```
> $ format
> Searching for disks...done
> No permission (or no disks found)!
> ```
>
> In most cases, disks are formatted by the manufacturer or reseller. So, they do not need to be reformatted when you install the drive. Also, you do not need to perform a surface analysis with the `format` utility when adding a disk drive to an existing system, unless you suspect that disk defects are causing problems. The main reason that you would use the `format` utility is to view or change the partitioning scheme on a disk.

8.4.7 `format` Menu and Command Descriptions

This section describes the `format` utility's menu and commands. The `format` main menu looks like the following:

```
FORMAT MENU:
             disk       - select a disk
             type       - select (define) a disk type
             partition  - select (define) a partition table
             current    - describe the current disk
             format     - format and analyze the disk
             fdisk      - run the fdisk program
             repair     - repair a defective sector
             label      - write label to the disk
             analyze    - surface analysis
             defect     - defect list management
             backup     - search for backup labels
             verify     - read and display labels
```

continues

```
                save        - save new disk/partition definitions
                inquiry     - show vendor, product and revision
                volname     - set 8.character volume name
                !<cmd>      - execute <cmd>, then return
        quit
        format>
```

Table 8.4 describes the `format` main menu options.

Table 8.4 Descriptions for `format` Main Menu Options

Option	Command or Menu?	Description
disk	Command	Lists all of the system's disk drives. Also enables you to choose the disk you want to use in subsequent operations. This disk is referred to as the *current disk*.
type	Command	Identifies the manufacturer and model of the current disk. Also displays a list of known drive types. Choose the Auto configure option for all SCSI-2 disk drives.
partition	Menu	Creates and modifies slices. For more information, see the Partition menu.
current	Command	Displays the following information about the current disk: ▪ Device name and device type ▪ Number of cylinders, alternate cylinders, heads, and sectors ▪ Physical device name
format	Command	Formats the current disk by using one of the following sources of information, in this order: 1. Information that is found in the `format.dat` file 2. Information from the automatic configuration process 3. Information that you type at the prompt if no `format.dat` entry exists This command does not apply to IDE disks. IDE disks are preformatted by the manufacturer.
`fdisk`	Menu	x86 platform only: Runs the `fdisk` program to create a Solaris `fdisk` partition.
repair	Command	Repairs a specific block on the current disk.
label	Command	Writes a new label to the current disk.
analyze	Menu	Does surface analysis by running read, write, and compare tests. For more information, see the Analyze menu.

Table 8.4 Descriptions for `format` Main Menu Options (*continued*)

Option	Command or Menu?	Description
defect	Menu	Retrieves and prints defect lists. For more information, see the Defect menu.
		This feature does not apply to IDE disks. IDE disks perform automatic defect management.
backup	Command	VTOC—Searches for backup labels.
		EFI—Not supported.
verify	Command	Displays the following information about the current disk:
		• Device name and device type
		• Number of cylinders, alternate cylinders, heads, and sectors
		• Partition table
save	Command	VTOC—Saves new disk and partition information.
		EFI—Not applicable.
inquiry	Command	Displays the vendor, product name, and revision level of the current drive (SCSI disks only).
volname	Command	Labels the disk with a new eight-character volume name.
quit	Command	Exits the `format` main menu.

8.4.8 Partition Menu

The Partition menu looks similar to the following:

```
format> partition
PARTITION MENU:
           0        - change '0' partition
           1        - change '1' partition
           2        - change '2' partition
           3        - change '3' partition
           4        - change '4' partition
           5        - change '5' partition
           6        - change '6' partition
           7        - change '7' partition
           select   - select a predefined table
           modify   - modify a predefined partition
                      table
           name     - name the current table
           print    - display the current table
           label    - write partition map and label to
                      the disk
           quit
partition>
```

Table 8.5 describes the Partition menu options.

Table 8.5 Descriptions for Partition Menu Options

Subcommand	Description
change 'n' partition	Enables you specify the following information for the new slice: ▪ Identification tag ▪ Permission flags ▪ Starting cylinder ▪ Size
select	Enables you to choose a predefined slice table.
modify	Enables you to change all the slices in the slice table. This command is preferred over the individual change "x" partition commands.
name	Enables you to specify a name for the current slice table.
quit	Exits the Partition menu.

8.4.9 x86: `fdisk` Menu

The `fdisk` menu appears on x86 based systems only and looks similar to the following:

```
format> fdisk
                        Total disk size is 1855 cylinders
                        Cylinder size is 553 (512 byte) blocks
=========  ======      =========  =====  =========  ======  ===

                                             Cylinders
        Partition  Status    Type          Start   End   Length   %
        =========  ======    =============  =====  ===  ======  ===


            1                 DOS-BIG         0     370    371   20

            2      Active     SOLARIS        370   1851   1482   80

        SELECT ONE OF THE FOLLOWING:
            1.   Create a partition
            2.   Change Active (Boot from) partition
            3.   Delete a partition
            4.   Exit (Update disk configuration and exit)
            5.   Cancel (Exit without updating disk configuration)
        Enter Selection:
```

Table 8.6 describes the `fdisk` menu options.

Table 8.6 x86: Descriptions for `fdisk` Menu Options

Menu option	Description
Create a partition	Creates an `fdisk` partition. You must create a separate partition for each operating system such as the Solaris OS or DOS.
	There is a maximum of four partitions per disk. You are prompted for the size of the `fdisk` partition as a percentage of the disk.
Change Active partition	Enables you to specify the partition to be used for booting. This menu option identifies where the first stage boot program looks for the second stage boot program.
Delete a partition	Deletes a previously created partition. This command destroys all the data in the partition.
Exit	Writes a new version of the partition table and exits the `fdisk` menu.
Cancel	Exits the `fdisk` menu without modifying the partition table.

8.4.10 Analyze Menu

The Analyze menu looks similar to the following:

```
format> analyze

          ANALYZE MENU:
               read      - read only test    (doesn't harm SunOS)
               refresh   - read then write   (doesn't harm data)
               test      - pattern testing   (doesn't harm data)
               write     - write then read     (corrupts data)
               compare   - write, read, compare (corrupts data)
               purge     - write, read, write   (corrupts data)
               verify    - write entire disk, then verify (corrupts data)
               print     - display data buffer
               setup     - set analysis parameters
               config    - show analysis parameters
               quit
analyze>
```

Table 8.7 describes the Analyze menu options.

Table 8.7 Descriptions for Analyze Menu Options

Subcommand	Description
read	Reads each sector on the current disk. Repairs defective blocks as a default.
refresh	Reads then writes data on the current disk without harming the data. Repairs defective blocks as a default.
test	Writes a set of patterns to the disk without harming the data. Repairs defective blocks as a default.
write	Writes a set of patterns to the disk and then reads the data on the disk. Destroys existing data on the disk. Repairs defective blocks as a default.
compare	Writes a set of patterns to the disk, reads the data, and then compares it to the data in the write buffer. Destroys existing data on the disk. Repairs defective blocks as a default.
purge	Removes all data from the disk so that the data cannot be retrieved by any means. Repairs defective blocks as a default.
verify	Writes unique data to each block on the entire disk in the first pass. Reads and verifies the data in the next pass. Destroys existing data on the disk. Repairs defective blocks as a default.
print	Displays the data in the read/write buffer.
setup	Enables you to specify the following surface analysis parameters. (Note that defaults are shown in bold.) Analyze entire disk? **yes** Starting block number: depends on drive Ending block number: depends on drive Loop continuously? **no** Number of passes: **2** Repair defective blocks? **yes** Stop after first error? **no** Use random bit patterns? **no** Number of blocks per transfer: **126** Verify media after formatting? **yes** Enable extended messages? **no** Restore defect list? **yes** Restore disk label? **yes**

Table 8.7 Descriptions for Analyze Menu Options (*continued*)

Subcommand	Description
config	Displays the current analysis parameters.
quit	Exits the Analyze menu.

8.4.11 Defect Menu

The Defect menu looks similar to the following:

```
format> defect

        DEFECT MENU:
                primary   - extract manufacturer's defect list
                grown     - extract manufacturer's and repaired defects lists
                both      - extract both primary and grown defects lists
                print     - display working list
                dump      - dump working list to file
                quit
        defect>
```

Table 8.8 describes the Defect menu options.

Table 8.8 Descriptions for Defect Menu Options

Subcommand	Description
primary	Reads the manufacturer's defect list from the disk drive and updates the in-memory defect list.
grown	Reads the grown defect list, which are defects that have been detected during analysis, and then updates the in-memory defect list.
both	Reads both the manufacturer's defect list and the grown defect list, and then updates the in-memory defect list.
print	Displays the in-memory defect list.
dump	Saves the in-memory defect list to a file.
quit	Exits the Defect menu.

8.5 Disk Management Procedures

This section describes the different disk management operations in detail.

8.5.1 How to Identify the Disks on a System

The `format` utility can be used to list all the disks connected to the system. The step-by-step procedure is given below:

1. Become superuser.
2. Identify the disks that are recognized on the system by using the `format` utility.

    `# format`

    The `format` utility displays a list of disks that it recognizes under AVAILABLE DISK SELECTIONS.

Example 8.1 Identifying the Disks on an x86 Based System

The following example shows how to identify the disks on an x86 based system.

```
# format
AVAILABLE DISK SELECTIONS:
    0. c0d0 <DEFAULT cyl 615 alt 2 hd 64 sec 63>
       /pci@0,0/pci-ide@7,1/ata@0/cmdk@0,0
    1. c0d1 <DEFAULT cyl 522 alt 2 hd 32 sec 63>
       /pci@0,0/pci-ide@7,1/ata@0/cmdk@1,0
    2. c1d0 <DEFAULT cyl 817 alt 2 hd 256 sec 63>
       /pci@0,0/pci-ide@7,1/ata@1/cmdk@0,0
Specify disk (enter its number):
```

The output shows that disk 0 is connected to the first PCI host adapter (pci-ide@7...), which is connected to the ATA interface (ata...).

8.5.2 How to Determine If a Disk Is Formatted

The `format` utility can be used to determine whether a disk is formatted. The step-by-step procedure is given below:

1. Become superuser.
2. Invoke the `format` utility.

    `# format`

    A numbered list of disks is displayed.

3. Type the number of the disk that you want to check.

    `Specify disk (enter its number):  disk-number`

4. Verify that the disk you specified is formatted by noting the following message:

    `[disk formatted]`

Example 8.2 Determining If a Disk Is Formatted

The following example shows that disk `c1t0d0` is formatted.
```
# format
    AVAILABLE DISK SELECTIONS:
       0. /dev/rdsk/c1t0d0s0 <SUN18G cyl 7506 alt 2 hd 19 sec 248>
                /sbus@2,0/QLGC,isp@2,10000/sd@0,0
       1. /dev/rdsk/c1t1d0s0 <SUN18G cyl 7506 alt 2 hd 19 sec 248>
                /sbus@2,0/QLGC,isp@2,10000/sd@1,0
       2. /dev/rdsk/c1t8d0s0 <SUN18G cyl 7506 alt 2 hd 19 sec 248>
                /sbus@2,0/QLGC,isp@2,10000/sd@8,0
       3. /dev/rdsk/c1t9d0s0 <SUN18G cyl 7506 alt 2 hd 19 sec 248>
                /sbus@2,0/QLGC,isp@2,10000/sd@9,0
    Specify disk (enter its number): 0
    selecting /dev/rdsk/c1t0d0s0
    [disk formatted]
```

8.5.3 How to Format a Disk

As already mentioned under the introduction of the `format` utility, in most cases, disks are already formatted by the manufacturer or reseller. So, they do not need to be reformatted when you install the drive. But if there is a need, the `format` utility can be used to format or reformat a disk. The step-by-step procedure is given below:

1. Become superuser.
2. Invoke the `format` utility.

   ```
   # format
   ```

   A numbered list of disks is displayed.

3. Type the number of the disk that you want to check.

   ```
   Specify disk (enter its number):  disk-number
   ```

   Caution

   Do not select the system disk. If you format your system disk, you delete the operating system and any data on this disk.

4. To begin formatting the disk, type `format` at the `format>` prompt. Confirm the command by typing `y` or `yes`.

```
format> format
Ready to format. Formatting cannot be interrupted and takes 23 minutes (estimated).
Continue? yes
```

5. Verify that the disk format was successful by noting the following messages:

```
Beginning format. The current time Tue ABC xx xx:xx:xxxxxx
Formatting...
done
Verifying media...
pass 0 - pattern = 0xc6dec6de 2035/12/18
pass 1 - pattern = 0x6db6db6d 2035/12/18
Total of 0 defective blocks repaired.
```

6. Exit the `format` utility.

   ```
   format> quit
   ```

Example 8.3 Formatting a Disk

The following example shows how to format the disk `c0t6d0`.

```
# format
Searching for disks...done


AVAILABLE DISK SELECTIONS:
       0. c0t0d0 <SUNW18G cyl 7506 alt 2 hd 19 sec 248
          /pci@1f,0/pci@1,1/scsi@2/sd@0,0
       1. c0t1d0 <FUJITSU  MAN3367M SUN36G  1804 43d671f>
          /pci@1f,0/pci@1,1/scsi@2/sd@1,0
       2. c0t2d0 <FUJITSU  MAN3367M SUN36G  1804 43d671f>
          /pci@1f,0/pci@1,1/scsi@2/sd@2,0
       3. c0t3d0 <FUJITSU  MAN3367M SUN36G  1804 43d671f>
          /pci@1f,0/pci@1,1/scsi@2/sd@3,0
       4. c0t4d0 <FUJITSU  MAN3367M SUN36G  1804 43d671f>
          /pci@1f,0/pci@1,1/scsi@2/sd@4,0
       5. c0t5d0 <FUJITSU  MAN3367M SUN36G  1804 43d671f>
          /pci@1f,0/pci@1,1/scsi@2/sd@5,0
       6. c0t6d0 <FUJITSU  MAN3367M SUN36G  1804 43d671f>
          /pci@1f,0/pci@1,1/scsi@2/sd@6,0
Specify disk (enter its number): 6
selecting c0t6d0
[disk formatted]
format> format
Ready to format.  Formatting cannot be interrupted
and takes 332 minutes (estimated). Continue? y
Beginning format. The current time is Wed Jan  7 16:16:05 2008

Formatting...
99% complete (00:00:21 remaining) done

Verifying media...
pass 0 - pattern = 0xc6dec6de 1132922

pass 1 - pattern = 0x6db6db6d 71132922

Total of 0 defective blocks repaired.
format> quit
```

8.5.4 How to Identify a Defective Sector by Performing a Surface Analysis

A hard disk contains millions of sectors. A bad sector is one that cannot be used to store data. If a sector goes bad, then the already-stored data in that sector is lost. A sector can go bad because of physical damages or scratches. Such sectors are also called *defective sectors*. During manufacturing of the disk, only some of the sectors go bad. In addition, some of the sectors normally go bad during the lifespan of the disk.

When a disk is formatted, all sectors of the disks are analyzed and the list of all the bad sectors is prepared, marking them unusable. Once marked as unusable during the disk operations, the Operating System does not access or store any data in bad sectors. The storage capacity of the disk decreases by the total size of the bad sectors.

The `format` utility can identify and mark the bad sectors on the disk and if possible repair them. The step-by-step procedure is given below:

1. Become superuser.

2. Unmount the file system on the slice that contains the defective sector or on which you want to perform the surface analysis.

   # **umount /dev/dsk/device-name**

   For more information, see the umount(1M) man page.

3. Invoke the `format` utility.

   # **format**

   A numbered list of disks is displayed.

4. Select the affected disk.

   Specify disk (enter its number): **disk-number**

5. Select the Analyze menu by typing analyze at the format> prompt.

   format> **analyze**

6. Set up the analysis parameters by typing setup at the analyze> prompt.

   Use the parameters shown here:

```
analyze> setup
Analyze entire disk [yes]? n
Enter starting block number [0, 0/0/0]: 12330
Enter ending block number [2052287, 2035/13/71]: 12360
```

continues

```
Loop continuously [no]? y
Repair defective blocks [yes]? n
Stop after first error [no]? n
Use random bit patterns [no]? n
Enter number of blocks per transfer [126, 0/1/54]: 1
Verify media after formatting [yes]? y
Enable extended messages [no]? n
Restore defect list [yes]? y
Create defect label [yes]? y
```

7. Find the defect by using the read command.

```
analyze> read
Ready to analyze (won't harm SunOS). This takes a long time,
but is interruptible with Control-C. Continue? y
pass 0
2035/12/1825/7/24
pass 1
Block 12354  (18/4/18), Corrected media error (hard data ecc)
25/7/24
^C
Total of 1 defective blocks repaired.
```

8.5.5 How to Repair a Defective Sector

Most disks keep aside some spare sectors that can be used to replace future references to bad sectors by performing repair operations. The format utility can be
used to repair a defective sector. The step-by-step procedure is given below:

1. Become superuser.

2. Invoke the format utility.

    # **format**

    A numbered list of disks is displayed.

3. Select the disk that contains the defective sector.

    Specify disk (enter its number): **disk-number**

4. Select the repair command by typing repair at the format> prompt.

    format> **repair**

5. Type the defective block number.

```
Enter absolute block number of defect: 12354
Ready to repair defect, continue? y
Repairing block 12354 (18/4/18)...ok.
format>
```

8.5.6 How to Display the Partition Table or Slice Information

You can use the `format` utility to check whether a disk has the appropriate disk slices. If you determine that a disk does not contain the slices you want to use, use the `format` utility to recreate them and label the disk.

1. Become superuser.

2. Invoke the `format` utility.

   ```
   # format
   ```

   A numbered list of disks is displayed.

3. Type the number of the disk for which you want to display slice information.

   ```
   Specify disk (enter its number): disk-number
   ```

4. Select the Partition menu by typing `partition` at the `format>` prompt.

   ```
   format> partition
   ```

5. Display the slice information for the selected disk.

   ```
   partition> print
   ```

6. Exit the `format` utility.

   ```
   partition> q
   format> q
   #
   ```

7. Verify the displayed slice information by identifying specific slice tags and slices. If the screen output shows that no slice sizes are assigned, the disk probably does not have slices.

Example 8.4 Displaying Disk Slice Information (VTOC)

The following example displays slice information for a disk with a VTOC label.

```
# format
Searching for disks...done
AVAILABLE DISK SELECTIONS:
       0. c0t0d0 <DEFAULT cyl 24611 alt 2 hd 27 sec 107>          /pci@0,0/
pci8086,2545@3/pci8086,1460@1d/pci8086,341a@7,1/sd@0,0
       1. c0t1d0 <DEFAULT cyl 24619 alt 2 hd 27 sec 107>                 /
pci@0,0/pci8086,2545@3/pci8086,1460@1d/pci8086,341a@7,1/sd@1,0
       Specify disk (enter its number): 1
       selecting c0t1d0
       [disk formatted]
```

continues

Example 8.4 Displaying Disk Slice Information (VTOC) *(continued)*

```
format> partition
partition> print
Current partition table (original):
Total disk cylinders available: 24619 + 2 (reserved cylinders)


Part      Tag    Flag   Cylinders     Size          Blocks

0    unassigned   wm      1 -  1452   2.00GB   (1452/0/0) 4194828
1    unassigned   wm   1453 -  3630   3.00GB   (2178/0/0) 6292242
2        backup   wu      0 - 24618  33.91GB   (24619/0/0)71124291
3    unassigned   wm      0               0    (0/0/0)      0
4    unassigned   wm      0               0    (0/0/0)      0
5    unassigned   wm      0               0    (0/0/0)      0
6    unassigned   wm   3631 - 24618  28.91GB   (20988/0/0)60634332
7    unassigned   wm      0               0    (0/0/0)      0
8          boot   wu      0 -    0    1.41MB   (1/0/0)     2889
9    unassigned   wm      0               0    (0/0/0)      0
partition> q
format> q
#
```

Example 8.5 Displaying Disk Slice Information (EFI)

The following example shows the slice information for a disk with an EFI label.

```
# format
    Searching for disks...done
    Specify disk (enter its number): 1
    selecting c1t1d0
    [disk formatted]
format> partition
partition> print
    Current partition table (original):

    Part      Tag    Flag   First Sector  Size    Last Sector
    0         root    wm         34      300.00GB   29145633
    1         usr     wm     629145634   300.00GB   1258291233
    2    unassigned   wm          0          0          0
    3    unassigned   wm          0          0          0
    4    unassigned   wm          0          0          0
    5    unassigned   wm          0          0          0
    6         usr     wm     1258291234  628.77GB   2576924637
    8    reserved     wm     2576924638   8.00MB    2576941021
    partition> q
    format> q
    #
```

8.5.7 Creating Disk Slices (Partitioning a Disk) and Labeling a Disk

The `format` utility is most often used by system administrators for partitioning disks. The steps involve the following:

- Determining which slices are needed

- Determining the size of each slice or partition
- Using the `format` utility to partition the disk, that is, to create the disk slices
- Labeling the disk with new partition information

Then, you can create the file system for each slice or partition.

The easiest way to partition a disk is to use the `format` utility's `modify` command from the Partition menu. The `modify` command enables you to create partitions by specifying the size of each partition without having to keep track of the starting cylinder boundaries. The `modify` command also keeps tracks of any disk space that remains in the "free hog" slice.

> **Note**
>
> When you use the `format` utility to change the size of one or more disk slices, you designate a temporary slice that will expand and shrink to accommodate the resizing operations. This temporary slice donates or "frees" space when you expand a slice and receives or "hogs" the discarded space when you shrink a slice. For this reason, this slice is sometimes called the *free hog slice*.
>
> The free hog slice exists only during installation or when you run the `format` utility. There is no permanent free hog slice during day-to-day operations.

The step-by-step procedure of partitioning and then labeling a disk using the `format` utility is given below:

1. Become superuser.

2. Invoke the `format` utility.

   ```
   # format
   ```

   A numbered list of disks is displayed.

3. Type the number of the disk that you want to repartition.

   ```
   Specify disk (enter its number): disk-number
   ```

4. Select the Partition menu by typing `partition` at the `format>` prompt.

   ```
   format> partition
   ```

5. Display the current partition (slice) table.

   ```
   partition> print
   ```

6. Start the modification process.

   ```
   partition> modify
   ```

7. Set the disk to all free hog.

   ```
   Choose base (enter number) [0]? 1
   ```

8. Create a new partition table by typing **yes** when prompted to continue.

   ```
   Do you wish to continue creating a new partition table based
   on above table[yes]? yes
   ```

9. Identify the free hog partition (slice) and the sizes of the slices when prompted.

   When adding a *system disk*, you must set up slices for the following:

   – root (slice 0) and swap (slice 1)

   – /usr (slice 6)

   After you identify the slices, the new partition table is displayed.

10. Make the displayed partition table the current partition table by typing **yes** when prompted.

    ```
    Okay to make this the current partition table[yes]? yes
    ```

    If you do not want the current partition table and you want to change it, type **no** and go to Step 6.

11. Name the partition table.

    ```
    Enter table name (remember quotes): "partition-name"
    ```

    where *partition-name* is the name for the new partition table.

12. Label the disk with the new partition table after you have finished allocating slices on the new disk.

    ```
    Ready to label disk, continue? Yes
    ```

13. Quit the Partition menu.

    ```
    partition> quit
    ```

14. Verify the new disk label.

    ```
    format> verify
    ```

15. Exit the format utility.

    ```
    format> quit
    ```

Example 8.6 Partitioning and Labeling a Disk

The following example shows how to partition a disk by using the `format` utility.

```
# format
  Searching for disks...done
AVAILABLE DISK SELECTIONS:
0. c0t0d0 <DEFAULT cyl 24611 alt 2 hd 27 sec 107>
          /pci@0,0/pci8086,2545@3/pci8086,1460@1d/pci8086,341a@7,1/sd@0,0
1. c0t1d0 <DEFAULT cyl 24619 alt 2 hd 27 sec 107>
          /pci@0,0/pci8086,2545@3/pci8086,1460@1d/pci8086,341a@7,1/sd@1,0
Specify disk (enter its number): 1
selecting c0t1d0
[disk formatted]
format> partition
partition> print
Current partition table (original):
Total disk cylinders available: 24619 + 2 (reserved cylinders)


Part      Tag    Flag   Cylinders        Size        Blocks

0    unassigned  wm       1 -  1452    2.00GB    (1452/0/0)   4194828
1    unassigned  wm    1453 -  3630     .00GB    (2178/0/0)   6292242
2        backup  wu       0 - 24618   33.91GB    (24619/0/0)  71124291
3    unassigned  wm       0                0    (0/0/0)       0
4    unassigned  wm       0                0    (0/0/0)       0
5    unassigned  wm       0                0    (0/0/0)       0
6    unassigned  wm    3631 - 24618   28.91GB    (20988/0/0)  60634332
7    unassigned  wm       0                0    (0/0/0)       0
8          boot  wu       0 -    0     1.41MB    (1/0/0)       2889
9    unassigned  wm       0                0    (0/0/0)       0


partition> modify
Select partitioning base:
0. Current partition table (original)
1. All Free Hog
Choose base (enter number) [0]? 1

Part      Tag    Flag   Cylinders        Size        Blocks

        0       root    wm       0          0 (0/0/0)        0
1       swap   wu       0                0 (0/0/0)       0
2       backup wu       0 - 24618   33.91GB    (24619/0/0)  71124291
3    unassigned wm       0          0  (0/0/0)       0
4    unassigned wm       0          0  (0/0/0)        0
5    unassigned wm       0          0  (0/0/0)       0
6        usr   wm   0          0 (0/0/0)        0
7    unassigned wm       0          0  (0/0/0)       0
8          boot wu       0 -    0     1.41MB    (1/0/0)       2889
9    alternates wm       0          0  (0/0/0)       0


    Do you wish to continue creating a new partition
    table based on above table[yes]? yes
    Free Hog partition[6]? 6
    Enter size of partition '0' [0b, 0c, 0.00mb, 0.00gb]: 6gb
    Enter size of partition '1' [0b, 0c, 0.00mb, 0.00gb]: 4gb
    Enter size of partition '3' [0b, 0c, 0.00mb, 0.00gb]:
    Enter size of partition '4' [0b, 0c, 0.00mb, 0.00gb]:
    Enter size of partition '5' [0b, 0c, 0.00mb, 0.00gb]: 1gb
    Enter size of partition '7' [0b, 0c, 0.00mb, 0.00gb]:
```

Example 8.6 Partitioning and Labeling a Disk (*continued*)

```
     Part         Tag   Flag   Cylinders    Size       Blocks

     0           root   wm     1 - 4356    6.00GB   (4356/0/0)    2584484
     1           swap   wu  4357 - 7260    4.00GB   (2904/0/0)    8389656
     2         backup   wu     0 - 24618  33.91GB   (24619/0/0)  71124291
     3     unassigned   wm     0                0   (0/0/0)       0
     4     unassigned   wm     0                0   (0/0/0)       0
     5     unassigned   wm  7261 - 7986    1.00GB   (726/0/0)     2097414
     6            usr   wm  7987 - 24618  22.91GB   (16632/0/0)   8049848
     7     unassigned   wm     0                0   (0/0/0)       0
     8           boot   wu     0 - 0       1.41MB   (1/0/0)       2889
     9     alternates   wm     0                0   (0/0/0)       0

           Okay to make this the current partition table[yes]? yes
           Enter table name (remember quotes): "new"
           Ready to label disk, continue? yes
           partition> print
           Current partition table (new):
           Total disk cylinders available: 24619 + 2 (reserved cylinders)

     Part         Tag   Flag   Cylinders    Size       Blocks

     0           root   wm     1 - 4356    6.00GB   (4356/0/0)    2584484
     1           swap   wu  4357 - 7260    4.00GB   (2904/0/0)    8389656
     2         backup   wu     0 - 24618  33.91GB   (24619/0/0)  71124291
     3     unassigned   wm     0                0   (0/0/0)       0
     4     unassigned   wm     0                0   (0/0/0)       0
     5     unassigned   wm  7261 - 7986    1.00GB   (726/0/0)     2097414
     6            usr   wm  7987 - 24618  22.91GB   (16632/0/0)   8049848
     7     unassigned   wm     0                0   (0/0/0)       0
     8           boot   wu     0 - 0       1.41MB   (1/0/0)       2889




           partition> q
           format> q
           #
```

8.5.8 Creating a File System On a Disk

After you create the disk slices and label the disk, you can create file systems on
the disk. The following example shows how to create a UFS file system on a disk
slice by using the newfs command:

```
# newfs /dev/rdsk/c0t1d0s5
```

where `/dev/rdsk/c0t1d0s5` is the raw device where the file system has to be created.

For more information about the different types of file systems and the `newfs` command, see Chapter 5, "Solaris File Systems," or the `newfs(1M)` man page.

Note

Once you create the file system, you can verify the file system by mounting it and determining if it is mounted properly.

```
# mount /dev/rdsk/c<n>t<n>d<n>s<n> /mnt
# ls /mnt
   lost+found
```

8.5.9 Additional Commands to Manage Disks

8.5.9.1 `prtvtoc` Command

The `prtvtoc` command can be used to print a disk label. In other words, the `prtvtoc` command enables the contents of the VTOC (volume table of contents) to be viewed. The command can be used only by superuser.

The following is an example of using the `prtvtoc` command to print the label of a VTOC-labeled disk.

```
# prtvtoc /dev/rdsk/c0t0d0s2
* /dev/rdsk/c0t0d0s2 partition map
*
* Dimensions:
*     512 bytes/sector
*      63 sectors/track
*     255 tracks/cylinder
*   16065 sectors/cylinder
*    4426 cylinders
*    4424 accessible cylinders
*
* Flags:
*    1: unmountable
*   10: read-only
*
*                    First     Sector    Last      Mount
* Partition  Tag  Flags  Sector    Count     Sector    Directory
      0        2    00   4225095 14683410  18908504   /
      1        3    01   16065    4209030   4225094
      2        5    00   0       71071560  71071559
      3        0    00   18908505 37479645 56388149   /Temp
      5        0    00   56388150 14683410 71071559
      8        1    01   0        16065     16064
```

The following is an example of using the `prtvtoc` command to print the label of an EFI-labeled disk.

```
# prtvtoc /dev/rdsk/c2t1d0s1
* /dev/rdsk/c2t1d0s1 partition map
*
* Dimensions:
* 512 bytes/sector
* 8385121 sectors
* 8385054 accessible sectors
*
* Flags:
* 1: unmountable
* 10: read-only
*
*                          First    Sector   Last    Mount
* Partition  Tag  Flags    Sector   Count    Sector  Directory
      0        2    01      34       41006    41039
      1        2    00      41040    8327663  8368702  /mnt
      8       11    00      8368703  16384    8385086
```

For more information about the `prtvtoc` command, see the `prtvtoc(1M)` man page.

8.5.9.2 `fmthard` Command

Though the `format` utility can be used to manually lay out the slices on a disk and save the label to disk, when you perform administrative tasks such as creating disk mirrors, it can be useful to copy the label of an existing disk to another disk. Also, sometimes you might want to use the same partitioning scheme for multiple disks connected to your system. These tasks can be performed by using the `fmthard` command.

The following example shows how to print the disk label of disk `c0t1d0s2` by using the `fmthard` command.

```
# fmthard -i -n "" /dev/rdsk/c0t1d0s2
* /dev/rdsk/c0t1d0s2 default partition map
*
* Dimensions:
*      512 bytes/sector
*      107 sectors/track
*       27 tracks/cylinder
*    24621 cylinders
*    24619 accessible cylinders
*
```

```
* Flags:
*    1:   unmountable
*   10:   read-only
*
* Partition     Tag      Flag        First Sector     Sector Count
    0            2        00          2889             24955182
    1            3        01          24958071         4194828
    2            5        00          0                71101179
    3            0        00          29152899         20974140
    4            0        00          50127039         20974140
    8            1        01          0                2889
```

The following example shows how to use the `fmthard` command to save the disk label of disk c0t1d0s2 into the /tmp/dl0 file.

```
# fmthard -i -n "" /dev/rdsk/c0t1d0s2 > /tmp/dl0
# cat /tmp/dl0

* /dev/rdsk/c0t0d0s2 default partition map
*
* Dimensions:
*      512 bytes/sector
*      107 sectors/track
*       27 tracks/cylinder
*    24621 cylinders
*    24619 accessible cylinders
*
* Flags:
*    1:   unmountable
*   10:   read-only
*
* Partition     Tag      Flag        First Sector     Sector Count
    0            2        00          2889             24955182
    1            3        01          24958071         4194828
    2            5        00          0                71101179
    3            0        00          29152899         20974140
    4            0        00          50127039         20974140
    8            1        01          0                2889
```

The following example shows how to use the `fmthard` command to copy the label of disk c0t0d0s2 to another disk, c0t1d0s2.

```
# fmthard -i -n "" /dev/rdsk/c0t0d0s2 > /tmp/dl0
# fmthard -s /tmp/dl0 -n "" /dev/rdsk/c0t1d0s2
```

Alternatively, using pipes, you can use the following single command, instead of the preceding two commands:

```
# fmthard -i -n "" /dev/rdsk/c0t0d0s2|fmthard -s - /dev/rdsk/
c0t1d0s2
```

Also, you can use the `prtvtoc` command to obtain the existing disk's label and then copy the label to another disk by using the `fmthard` command, as follows:

```
# prtvtoc /dev/rdsk/c0t0d0s2 | fmthard -s - /dev/rdsk/c0t1d0s2
```

Note

You can label multiple disks simultaneously by providing the raw device names of multiple disks to the `fmthard` command.

For more information about the `fmthard` command, see the `fmthard(1M)` man page.

8.5.9.3 `fsck` Command

The `fsck` command is a UNIX utility for checking and repairing file system inconsistencies in UFS file systems. A file system can become inconsistent due to several reasons. The most common is abnormal shutdown due to hardware failure or power failure or from switching off the system without following the proper shutdown procedure. Due to these reasons, the file system's superblock is not updated and has mismatched information related to system data blocks, free blocks, and inodes.

The `fsck` command operates in two modes: interactive and noninteractive, as follows:

- In interactive mode, `fsck` examines the file system and stops at each error it finds, gives the problem description, and asks for a user response. Usually, the question is whether to correct the problem or continue without making any changes to the file system.

- In noninteractive mode, `fsck` tries to repair all the problems it finds in a file system without stopping for a user response. This mode is useful when a file system has many inconsistencies. However, the disadvantage is that some useful files that `fsck` detects as corrupted are removed.

If a file system has problems at boot time, the noninteractive mode of `fsck` is run, and all errors that are considered safe to correct are corrected. However, if the file system still has problems, then the system boots in single-user mode, asking the user to manually run `fsck` to correct the problems.

Note

The `fsck` command does not repair a mounted file system. If it is run on a mounted file system, sometimes it can result in data loss or file system corruption.

For more information about the `fsck` command, see the `fsck(1M)` man page.

8.5.9.4 du Command

"du" stands for disk usage. This command is used to show the amount of disk space consumed by one or more directories (or directory trees). This command is very useful for determining which subdirectory has the most files and is consuming the most space. The following are some examples of using the `du` command.

The following example shows the disk usage of the current working directory (.) and its subdirectories in blocks:

du

```
# du
40      ./temp
40      ./logs
40      ./good
160     .
#
```

The following example shows the disk usage of the current working directory (.) and its subdirectories in 1024-byte units (kilobytes):

du -k

```
# du -k
20      ./temp
20      ./logs
20      ./good
80      .
#
```

The following example shows the disk usage of the /home/sun subdirectory in blocks:

```
# du /home/sun
40       /home/sun/temp
40       /home/sun/logs
40       /home/sun/good
160      /home/sun
#
```

The following example shows only a summary of the disk usage of the /home/sun subdirectory (in kilobytes):

```
# du -ks /home/sun
80       /home/sun
#
```

The following example shows a summary of the disk usage of each subdirectory (and its files) of /home/sun (in kilobytes):

```
# du -ks /home/sun/*
16       /home/sun/abc.c
20       /home/sun/good
20       /home/sun/logs
20       /home/sun/temp
#
```

For more information about the du command, see the du(1) man page.

9

Managing Devices

The information in this chapter is useful both for managing devices on your own laptop and for managing devices on a network of x86 based systems. This chapter helps answer questions such as: Why do I have no network connectivity? Why do I have no audio? This chapter also explains how to easily deploy the same new driver to a large number of systems.

This chapter presents techniques to discover physical devices on a Solaris system and to determine whether a driver module exists for each device. This chapter explains how to install a driver and determine whether a driver is working properly. This chapter also explains how to create a functional system if a driver does not exist. Lastly, this chapter provides command summaries for adding, removing, and updating drivers on the system and for deploying new drivers in network installation and boot images, as well as on installation media.

9.1 Solaris Device Driver Introduction

The first boot of the Solaris OS after an installation or upgrade forces the system to reexamine the devices on the system and attach the correct drivers. The Solaris OS examines the hardware system buses for devices and specific identification numbers. For example, most modern computer motherboards provide a switched bus interconnect that supports PCI/PCI Express peripherals. Devices that connect to the PCI/PCI Express bus[1, 2] are often found inserted into slots that follow a fairly strict standard. This standard enables the Solaris OS and other operating systems to query the bus for device information. Each PCI device contains configuration information located in its firmware. When powered and probed, the device reports a specific vendor ID, device ID, and device class, often expressed in hexadecimal format. The Solaris OS and most other modern operating systems contain a table that maps device IDs and classes to specific device driver modules. When a driver is found that matches a particular device, the kernel loads the driver module and initializes that device.

9.2 Analyzing Lack of Device Support

After you have successfully installed the Solaris OS, you might find that one of your devices does not respond or behave as expected. One possible cause is that the system does not recognize your device. Another possibility is that you need an updated or different driver for the device. Perhaps the driver exists, but the system does not know which driver module to load and initialize.

9.2.1 Device Does Not Work

The first step in diagnosing a device problem is to check the mechanical fitness of the device. Is the device properly installed? Is the peripheral card correctly seated in its slot? Does the device have correct power and cabling? Has the device been shown to work correctly on another system? Is the device specified for this system?

If the Solaris Fault Management system detects a problem with a device, messages about the problem can be displayed by using the `fmdump` command. Messages are also traditionally written to the console and to the `/var/adm/messages` file. Fault management messages give a brief recommended action to take and point you to more information at `http://www.sun.com/msg/`. If the Fault Management system takes a device offline, the message "(retired)" is displayed in the `prtconf` output. For more information, see Chapter 7, "Fault Management."

If the device seems to be installed correctly and you have no error reports in `/var/adm/messages`, then you need to determine whether the system has a driver for that device and whether the driver is attached to the device.

9.2.2 Obtaining Information About Devices

To determine whether a device driver is available, you need specific vendor and device identifier information about the device. The Solaris OS provides both a graphical user interface (GUI) and a command line interface (CLI) for obtaining this information.

For PCI devices, the industry has standardized on vendor ID and device ID declarations that are reported when firmware is queried. A good source of information on known vendor devices and their IDs and descriptions can be found in the `pci.ids` file at the PCI ID Repository Web site.[3] With the vendor name and model name of your device, you can find the vendor ID and device ID on this site.

9.2.2.1 Using the Graphical User Interface

The easiest way to display information about the hardware devices on your system and whether Solaris drivers are available for them is to use the graphical Sun Device Detection Tool. You can run the Sun Device Detection Tool from `http://www.sun.com/bigadmin/hcl/hcts/device_detect.jsp` without installing anything on your system. You do not even need to be running the Solaris OS to use this tool.

The OpenSolaris OS comes with a version of this tool called Device Driver Utility in Applications > System Tools. The Device Driver Utility can be invoked from the OpenSolaris Live CD. In this way, you can obtain information about OpenSolaris support for your devices before you install the system.

An example of the Sun Device Detection Tool is shown in Figure 9.1.

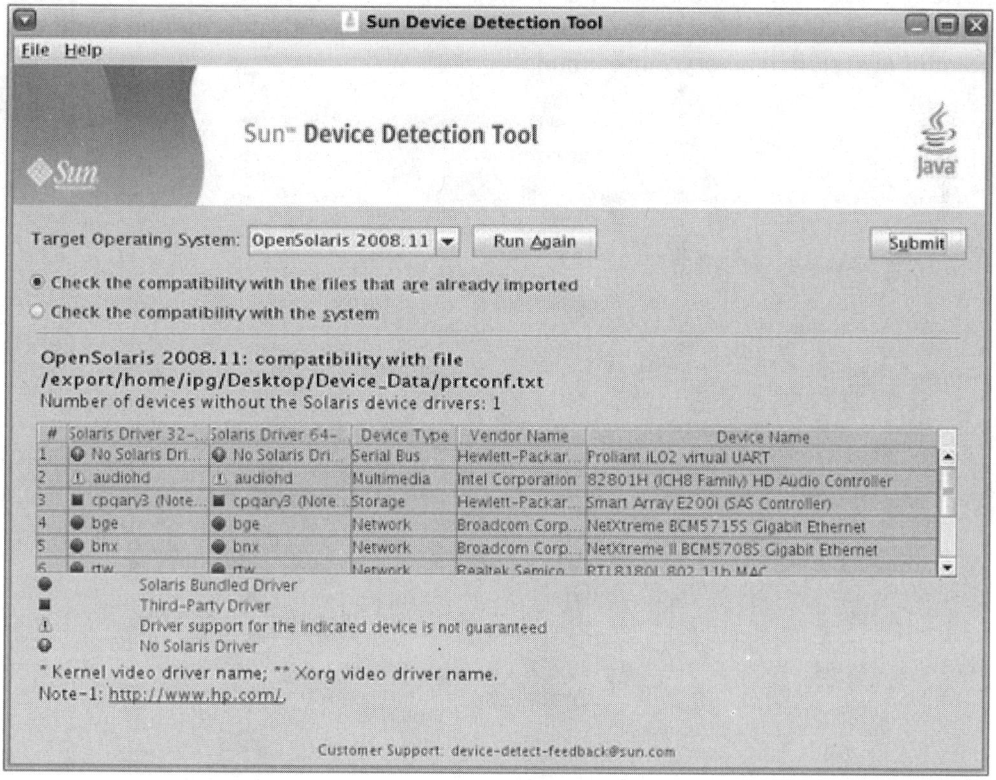

Figure 9.1 Sun Device Detection Tool

To display detailed information about a device such as the PCI vendor ID and device ID, hover your mouse pointer over a table row in the Sun Device Detection Tool, or click your right mouse button on a table row in the Device Driver Utility. If a suitable driver is not already installed on your system, this tool provides information about Sun and third-party drivers that are available for the device. If the device has no Solaris driver or the intended driver is malfunctioning on your system, the tool shows a warning icon.

For each device that is reported to have a driver problem, use the detailed information from the tool to note the driver name, PCI vendor ID, and device ID. This information is needed to determine whether the device has a driver.

9.2.2.2 Using the Command Line Interface

The Solaris OS also provides commands with text output about the devices on your system.

The Print System Configuration Command   The prtconf command shows what devices are known to the system. Executed with no options, the default output of prtconf provides a basic view of the device tree, along with information about the amount of system memory. For example:

```
System Configuration:  Sun Microsystems  i86pc
Memory size: 2040 Megabytes
System Peripherals (Software Nodes):

i86pc
    scsi_vhci, instance #0
    isa, instance #0
        motherboard (driver not attached)
        fdc, instance #0
            fd, instance #0
        lp, instance #0
        i8042, instance #0
            keyboard, instance #0
            mouse, instance #0
        asy, instance #0
        motherboard (driver not attached)
        pit_beep, instance #0
    pci, instance #0
        pci1019,2624, instance #0
        display, instance #0
        pci1019,2950, instance #0
        pci8086,27d0, instance #0
        pci8086,27d6, instance #1
            pci1019,8136, instance #0
        pci1019,2624, instance #0
        pci1019,2624, instance #1
        pci1019,2624, instance #2
        pci1019,2624, instance #3
        pci1019,2624, instance #0
        pci8086,244e, instance #0
```

```
    pci1019,2624 (driver not attached)
    pci-ide, instance #0
        ide, instance #0
            sd, instance #0
        ide (driver not attached)
    pci-ide, instance #1
        ide, instance #2
            cmdk, instance #0
        ide (driver not attached)
    pci1019,2624 (driver not attached)
iscsi, instance #0
pseudo, instance #0
options, instance #0
agpgart, instance #0
xsvc, instance #0
used-resources (driver not attached)
cpus, instance #0
    cpu (driver not attached)
```

The "(driver not attached)" message indicates that the device is currently not in use. A driver is loaded into memory when a device that the driver manages is accessed. A driver might be unloaded from memory when the device is not being used.

The -D flag (prtconf -D) gives the same output in addition to the name of the driver that is being used to manage the device. The -p and -v flags (prtconf -pv) provide more output, including the pci-config space information on all the devices. For example:

```
[...]
            Node 0x000018
                assigned-addresses:
81020010.00000000.0000e800.00000000.00000100.83020018.00000000.febff000.00000000.
00001000
                reg:
00020000.00000000.00000000.00000000.00000000.01020010.00000000.00000000.00000000.
00000100.03020018.00000000.00000000.00000000.00001000
                compatible: 'pciex10ec,8136.1019.8136.1' + 'pciex10ec,8136.1019.8136' +
'pciex10ec,8136.1' + 'pciex10ec,8136' + 'pciexclass,020000' + 'pciexclass,0200' +
'pci10ec,8136.1019.8136.1' + 'pci10ec,8136.1019.8136' + 'pci1019,8136' +
'pci10ec,8136.1' + 'pci10ec,8136' + 'pciclass,020000' + 'pciclass,0200'
                model: 'Ethernet controller'
                power-consumption: 00000001.00000001
                devsel-speed: 00000000
                interrupts: 00000001
                subsystem-vendor-id: 00001019
                subsystem-id: 00008136
                unit-address: '0'
                class-code: 00020000
                revision-id: 00000001
                vendor-id: 000010ec
                device-id: 00008136
                pcie-capid-pointer: 00000060
                pcie-capid-reg: 00000001
                name: 'pci1019,8136'
```

continues

```
      Node 0x00000a
         assigned-addresses:  8100e820.00000000.0000d880.00000000.00000020
         reg:
0000e800.00000000.00000000.00000000.00000000.0100e820.00000000.00000000.00000000.
00000020
         compatible: 'pci8086,27c8.1019.2624.1' + 'pci8086,27c8.1019.2624' +
'pci1019,2624' + 'pci8086,27c8.1' + 'pci8086,27c8' + 'pciclass,0c0300' +
'pciclass,0c03'
         model:  'Universal Serial Bus UHCI compliant'
         power-consumption:  00000001.00000001
         fast-back-to-back:
         devsel-speed:  00000001
         interrupts:  00000001
         max-latency:  00000000
         min-grant:  00000000
         subsystem-vendor-id:  00001019
         subsystem-id:  00002624
         unit-address:  '1d'
         class-code:  000c0300
         revision-id:  00000001
         vendor-id:  00008086
         device-id:  000027c8
         name:  'pci1019,2624'
[...]
```

The output of `prtconf`, while quite detailed, is not the most easily understood view of the system devices. The advantage of using `prtconf` is that it can be run by any user.

The Scan PCI Buses Command   An alternative utility for displaying device information is the `scanpci` command. The `scanpci` command is in `/usr/X11/bin/scanpci` and is only available on systems that use Xorg. The `scanpci` command is available on x86 based systems that are running at least the Solaris 10 release, but this command might not be available on SPARC based systems. Also, this command must be run by superuser.

The `scanpci` command provides a concise list of device IDs and descriptions, if known. Without any options, the `scanpci` command provides output similar to the following:

```
pci bus 0x0000 cardnum 0x00 function 0x00: vendor 0x8086 device 0x2770
 Intel Corporation 82945G/GZ/P/PL Memory Controller Hub

pci bus 0x0000 cardnum 0x02 function 0x00: vendor 0x8086 device 0x2772
 Intel Corporation 82945G/GZ Integrated Graphics Controller

pci bus 0x0000 cardnum 0x1b function 0x00: vendor 0x8086 device 0x27d8
 Intel Corporation 82801G (ICH7 Family) High Definition Audio Controller

pci bus 0x0000 cardnum 0x1c function 0x00: vendor 0x8086 device 0x27d0
 Intel Corporation 82801G (ICH7 Family) PCI Express Port 1

pci bus 0x0000 cardnum 0x1c function 0x03: vendor 0x8086 device 0x27d6
 Intel Corporation 82801G (ICH7 Family) PCI Express Port 4
```

```
pci bus 0x0000 cardnum 0x1d function 0x00: vendor 0x8086 device 0x27c8
  Intel Corporation 82801G (ICH7 Family) USB UHCI Controller #1

pci bus 0x0000 cardnum 0x1d function 0x01: vendor 0x8086 device 0x27c9
  Intel Corporation 82801G (ICH7 Family) USB UHCI Controller #2

pci bus 0x0000 cardnum 0x1d function 0x02: vendor 0x8086 device 0x27ca
  Intel Corporation 82801G (ICH7 Family) USB UHCI Controller #3

pci bus 0x0000 cardnum 0x1d function 0x03: vendor 0x8086 device 0x27cb
  Intel Corporation 82801G (ICH7 Family) USB UHCI Controller #4

pci bus 0x0000 cardnum 0x1d function 0x07: vendor 0x8086 device 0x27cc
  Intel Corporation 82801G (ICH7 Family) USB2 EHCI Controller

pci bus 0x0000 cardnum 0x1e function 0x00: vendor 0x8086 device 0x244e
  Intel Corporation 82801 PCI Bridge
pci bus 0x0000 cardnum 0x1f function 0x00: vendor 0x8086 device 0x27b8
  Intel Corporation 82801GB/GR (ICH7 Family) LPC Interface Bridge

pci bus 0x0000 cardnum 0x1f function 0x01: vendor 0x8086 device 0x27df
  Intel Corporation 82801G (ICH7 Family) IDE Controller

pci bus 0x0000 cardnum 0x1f function 0x02: vendor 0x8086 device 0x27c0
  Intel Corporation 82801GB/GR/GH (ICH7 Family) SATA IDE Controller

pci bus 0x0000 cardnum 0x1f function 0x03: vendor 0x8086 device 0x27da
  Intel Corporation 82801G (ICH7 Family) SMBus Controller

pci bus 0x0002 cardnum 0x00 function 0x00: vendor 0x10ec device 0x8136
  Realtek Semiconductor Co., Ltd. RTL8101E PCI Express Fast Ethernet controller
```

Use the -v flag (`scanpci -v`) to obtain more details on a specific class of device.

Man Page Information About Devices   The Device and Network Interfaces man pages (section 7) provide descriptions of drivers and interfaces available on your system. Most Solaris leaf-node drivers include a man page in section (7D). For example, to obtain information about the Solaris driver for the popular Intel Pro/ 1000 Gigabit Ethernet card, you would type the following man command in a terminal window:

```
% man e1000g
```

9.2.3 Obtaining Information About Drivers

The device information tools might give you the name of the driver that manages that device. If you need to replace a driver, you need more information about driver modules.

9.2.3.1 Solaris Kernel Modules

The Solaris kernel is a C program. A *device driver* is a *kernel module* that provides the kernel and applications access to some device functionality. The Solaris OS also supports pseudo-device types that provide software-only services to the kernel. Examples of pseudo devices include a software random-number generator or a fortune cookie message generator.

Device drivers must adhere to a mature and strict set of interfaces known in the Solaris OS as the device driver interfaces/driver-kernel interfaces (DDI/DKI). Adherence to these standards means that in most cases, an old driver will continue to work on a newer Solaris system. These DDI/DKI implementations are actually callbacks to functions that the kernel expects to find during driver load and initialization. When a user or system command requests a specific device service, the kernel executes the function calls implemented in that driver.

The Solaris OS supports loadable kernel modules. Loadable kernel modules are loaded at boot time or by request, and are unloaded by request. If no known device exists for a particular module, then that module is not loaded and has no effect on the kernel. If a device is known, then the module loads and runs within the kernel.

If poorly written, kernel module code can destabilize the entire system and threaten essential security. Kernel code must always be placed under higher scrutiny in code reviews and quality assurance testing so as not to disrupt the system. A poorly written application running on top of the Solaris OS might use too many resources but is unlikely to do more damage than dump a core file if it crashes. Other applications run by other users should continue to run. In contrast, if the kernel crashes, then the entire system panics, taking down all the applications with it.

Figure 9.2 shows how a device driver interacts with the rest of the system.

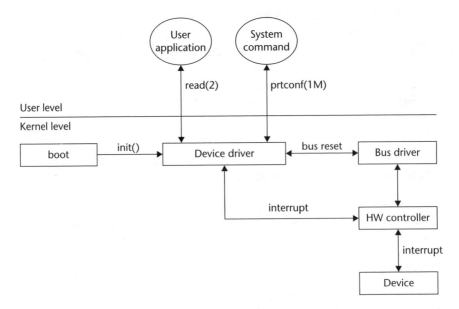

Figure 9.2 Functional Diagram of System and Application Interaction with Solaris Kernel Modules

9.2.3.2 Where Driver Modules Are Located

Most kernel modules for leaf node devices can be found in the `/kernel/drv/`
`$arch` directory where `$arch` is `sparcv9` for 64-bit SPARC binaries, `$arch` is
`amd64` for x64 modules, and `$arch` is blank for 32-bit x86 modules. Other system
directories might also contain drivers, but those directories are usually reserved
for Solaris-specific nexus and pseudo drivers. Base locations for drivers are shown
in the following list. The listed directories are for 32-bit x86 systems. For other
architectures, append `$arch` to the directory name.

- `/kernel/drv` (default location for most leaf-node drivers)
- `/kernel/misc`
- `/usr/kernel/drv`
- `/usr/kernel/misc`
- `/platform/i86pc/kernel/drv`
- `/platform/i86pc/kernel/misc`

9.2.3.3 Solaris Device Tree

If a kernel module manages and registers other devices, then that kernel module
usually controls some central hub or nexus on the hardware. These modules are
called *nexus drivers* and are already implemented in the Solaris OS. The actual
modules that attach to and enable a specific hardware controller such as a network
interface controller (NIC) or host bus adapter (HBA) are known as *leaf-node* drivers. The nexus and leaf-node drivers are arranged to form a device tree. Figure 9.3
shows a representation of a Solaris device tree.

The following explains how applications interact with kernel modules to use a
device. The Solaris OS uses a device file system known as `devfs`. The Solaris
`devfs` is comprised of two parts: a logical device tree that lists virtual names for
common devices and a physical device tree that contains the path to physically
mapped buses and attached devices. The logical device tree is located in the `/dev`
directory off of the root (/) file system. Almost all the drivers in the `/dev`
directory are links to the `/devices` directory. The `/dev` directory is UNIX
standard. The `/devices` directory is specific to the Solaris OS. The `/devices`
directory shows relationships among devices. In the `/devices` directory, a directory represents a nexus device.

The physical devices can have long, cryptic path names. The physical devices are
found in a special, noneditable directory in `/devices`. For example, the logical

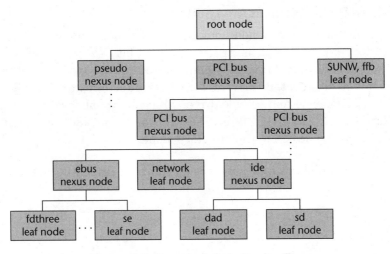

Figure 9.3 Sample Solaris Device Tree

device /dev/audio might point to ./sound/0, and a full listing of /dev/sound/0 might look like the following:

```
% ls -l /dev/sound/0
lrwxrwxrwx 1 root myuser 49 Sep 5 15:54 0 -> ../../devices/pci@0,
0/pci1019,2950@1b:sound,audio
```

In this example, the kernel and running applications access the audio device through this exposed special node file handle with a long path name, which is actually in /devices.

The /devices file system cannot be altered by using any usual file system commands. Instead, the Solaris OS controls this file system exclusively. Nodes are created in devfs primarily when a driver module attaches to a device during initialization. Prior to the Solaris 10 OS, /devices was an on-disk file system composed of subdirectories and files. Beginning with the Solaris 10 OS, /devices is a virtual file system that creates these subdirectories and special files on demand. For more information about the device-file system, see the devfs(7FS) man page.

The /dev namespace supports multiple file system instances as needed. A global instance of the /dev file system is created automatically when the system is booted. Subsequent /dev instances are created and mounted when needed, such as when devices are added to a non-global zone. When a non-global zone is shut down, the available /dev instance is unmounted and unavailable.

9.2.3.4 Module Major and Minor Numbers

A *device number* identifies a particular device and minor node or instance in the Solaris device tree. If you list fully the physical device path of the audio device discussed in the preceding section, you see output like the following:

```
% ls -l /devices/pci@0,0/pci1019,2950@1b:sound,audio
crw------- 1 myuser myuser 78, 0 Apr 8 2008 /devices/pci@0,0/
pci1019,2950@1b:sound,audio
```

This listing shows two numbers of a special node file: 78 and 0. The 78 is the *major number* and represents the index of the kernel module as loaded into the system. A mapping table for known devices is listed in the /etc/name_to_major file. You might see an entry such as the following in this file:

```
audiovia823x 78
```

In the Solaris OS, the major number is chosen for you when you install the driver so that it will not conflict with any other major number. The kernel uses the major number to associate the I/O request with the correct driver code. The kernel uses this association to decide which driver to execute when the user reads or writes to the device file.

The 0 in the file listing represents the *instance number* or node. As is usual in UNIX and the C language, indexes increment starting with 0.

9.2.3.5 Device Names

This section explains the meaning of each part of a complex device name in the /dev and /devices directories. The following example shows the name of a disk slice:

```
/dev/dsk/c0t0d0s7 -> ../../devices/pci@1c,600000/scsi@2/sd@0,0:h
```

The following explains each part of the name of the file in the /dev directory. Device names in this directory are managed by the devfsadmd daemon.

- c0—Controller 0.
- t0—Target 0. On SCSI controllers, this value is the disk number.
- d0—SCSI LUN. This value indicates a virtual partitioning of a target or single physical device.
- s7—Slice 7 on the target 0 disk.

The following explains each part of the name of the file in the /devices directory. Names in this directory show the physical structure and the real device names. Note that some of the components of the device name in the /devices directory are subdirectories.

- pci@1c,600000—PCI bus at address 1c,600000. This address is meaningful only to the parent device.
- scsi@2—SCSI controller at address 2 on the PCI bus at address 1c,600000. This name corresponds to the c0 in /dev/dsk/c0t0d0s7.
- sd@0,0—SCSI disk at address 0,0 on the SCSI controller at address 2. This name represents target 0, LUN 0 and corresponds to the t0d0 in /dev/dsk/c0t0d0s7. The sd name and driver can also apply to IDE CD-ROM devices.
- sd@0,0:h—Minor node h on the SCSI disk at address 0,0. This name corresponds to the s7 in /dev/dsk/c0t0d0s7.

9.2.3.6 Obtaining Driver Version Information

Prior to testing a new driver binary, information about a current running version might be important. Embedded within most driver binaries is information about the version. Most drivers provide a non-null string that is read and recorded when the kernel loads the module. Users can retrieve that information by running the modinfo command to look for that module. For example, if you have a running NIC that loads the e1000g module, you would run the following command:

```
# modinfo | grep e1000g
286 fffffffff86ec000  32f48  53   1  e1000g (Intel PRO/1000 Ethernet 5.2.11)
```

The output provides information about the module such as the major number, the kernel address where the module has been loaded, the size of the module, and the module name. The most useful piece of information for you is probably the text string of the version, which is 5.2.11 in this example.

The modinfo command only reports on modules that are loaded. If a module is not loaded, you can manually load the module and then use the modinfo command. If your system supports both 64-bit and 32-bit modes, be sure to load the driver module that is the same bit width as the current running kernel. Use the isainfo command to determine the bit width of the current kernel. The `isainfo` command prints the names of the native instruction sets for applications supported by the current version of the operating system. For example:

```
# isainfo -v
64-bit amd64 applications
        ssse3 cx16 mon sse3 sse2 sse fxsr mmx cmov amd_sysc cx8 tsc fpu
32-bit i386 applications
        ssse3 ahf cx16 mon sse3 sse2 sse fxsr mmx cmov sep cx8 tsc fpu
```

The `isainfo` command with the `-k` option prints the name of the instruction set used by the operating system kernel components such as device drivers. The following output shows that this kernel is running in 64-bit mode:

```
# isainfo -kv
64-bit amd64 kernel modules
```

To manually load a kernel module, use the `modload` command. The 64-bit version of the driver module is in `/kernel/drv/amd64`. Use the following commands to query the module:

```
# modload /kernel/drv/amd64/e1000g
# modinfo | grep e1000g
```

If the driver module implementation presents a blank string for the `modinfo` command, you might still be able to extract the information you want by using the `strings` command. For example:

```
# strings /kernel/drv/amd64/e1000g | grep -i ver
e1000_polarity_reversal_workaround_82543
e1000g_get_driver_control
e1000g_set_driver_params
version
AutoNegAdvertised
ESB2 receiver disabled
Recv_Oversize
Tx Pkt Over Size
Driver Ver. 5.2.11
```

The last line in this example shows that the driver binary has an embedded text string that declares that it is version 5.2.11, which confirms the `modinfo` information.

9.2.4 Does the Device Have a Driver?

After performing the queries described in the preceding section, you know which device is not working as well as the vendor ID, device ID, and device class of the device. These values are provided in hexadecimal format. You can use these values to search for a supported driver.

For example, the sample `scanpci` output shown when discussing the "Scan PCI Buses Command" earlier in this chapter shows that the system has an ICH7 family chipset and a Realtek RTL8101E Ethernet controller. The network controller has a vendor ID of `0x10ec` and a device ID of `0x8136`. You can use this device ID number to check whether the `/etc/driver_aliases` file shows that this driver is available.

The `/etc/driver_aliases` file shows which devices are bound to which drivers. Each line in the `/etc/driver_aliases` file shows a driver name followed by a device name. You can search this file to determine which driver is managing your device. If a driver is not listed in this file, then the Solaris OS does not load or attach to that driver.

Entries in the `/etc/driver_aliases` file are plain text, and they concatenate the vendor ID and device ID into a single string with a comma separator and no spaces. The hexadecimal prefix `0x` is omitted, and each device ID is also trimmed of any preceding zeros. The entire group is preceded with a `pci` or `pciex`.

The `/etc/driver_aliases` file does have an entry that matches the Realtek RTL8101E Ethernet controller, as the following shows:

```
rge "pci10ec,8136"
```

This line indicates that the Solaris driver that supports this device is `rge`.

9.2.4.1 Does the Device Have a Class Driver?

Another example is the High Definition Audio Controller, with vendor and device IDs `pci8086,27d8`. You probably will not find explicit support for this device in `/etc/driver_aliases`. For many devices that follow an architectural standard such as IDE/ATAPI (Integrated Drive Electronics/Advanced Technology Attachment Packet Interface) devices, serial UART (Universal Asynchronous Receiver-Transmitter) devices, USB, or High Definition Audio, the Solaris OS provides a single *class driver* that is designed to work with most, if not all, devices that adhere to that particular device standard. To determine the class of a particular device, look for information such as the following in the verbose `scanpci` output (`/usr/X11/bin/scanpci -v`):

```
pci bus 0x0000 cardnum 0x1b function 0x00: vendor 0x8086 device 0x27d8
 Intel Corporation 82801G (ICH7 Family) High Definition Audio Controller
 CardVendor 0x1019 card 0x2950 (Elitegroup Comp Systems, Card unknown)
  STATUS    0x0010  COMMAND 0x0046
  CLASS     0x04 0x03 0x00  REVISION 0x01
  BIST      0x00  HEADER 0x00  LATENCY 0x00  CACHE 0x08
  BASE0     0x00000000fea38004  addr 0x00000000fea38000  MEM 64BIT
  MAX_LAT   0x00  MIN_GNT 0x00  INT_PIN 0x01  INT_LINE 0x0a
  BYTE_0    0x03  BYTE_1  0x00  BYTE_2  0x00  BYTE_3  0x03
```

Under the CLASS line in this example, the first two octets are 0x04 and 0x03. Combined, and omitting the hexadecimal prefixes, they identify the device class of 0403. The /etc/driver_aliases file shows the following mapping for a driver for this entry:

```
audiohd "pciclass,0403"
```

This mapping tells you that this class of device is supported by the audiohd driver module in the Solaris OS. If for some reason, the scanpci command does not work or you do not have root access, the prtconf -pv command works similarly and shows the same device as a mixed-mode device with a device class of 00040300. Note that the middle two octets for prtconf output are used in the mapping of the device class to the driver module.

9.2.4.2 Does the Device Have a Third-Party Driver?

If no Solaris driver exists for your device, check for a third-party driver. If you are using the OpenSolaris OS, use the Device Driver Utility in Applications > System Tools. For Solaris 10 releases, access the Sun Device Detection Tool from http://www.sun.com/bigadmin/hcl/hcts/device_detect.jsp. See Section 9.2.2, "Obtaining Information About Devices," earlier in this chapter.

The OpenSolaris open-source project site (http://www.opensolaris.org) might have an early access driver that enables your device.

9.2.4.3 Could a Similar Device Be Used?

If using different hardware is a possibility, check the Solaris Hardware Compatibility List (HCL) at http://www.sun.com/bigadmin/hcl/ for a device that has equivalent functionality and is supported in the Solaris OS. If your system is x86 based, check the Solaris for x86 Device Support database at http://www.sun.com/bigadmin/hcl/devicelist/.

9.2.5 Current Driver Does Not Work

You might have a driver that seems to be the correct driver for your device, but the device still does not work. Often, a newer revision of hardware seems to be recognized but does not function correctly. For example, this problem can happen with High Definition Audio controllers where the manufacturer uses a nonstandard or noncompliant codec or flashes incorrect audio capabilities into the controller that do not match the codec capabilities. In these cases, the driver might attach and then fail. If the device does not respond, then you can obtain more information by checking the /var/adm/messages file for entries related to audiohd. A quick way to check after a reboot is to run the following command:

```
# dmesg | grep audiohd
```

Any errors that are reported provide a good starting point to research on the Web whether other people have encountered a similar problem.

If the logs on your system have reset or overflowed with too much output for other reasons, you might still be able to retrieve error output from previous system message logs by running the following command:

```
# grep audiohd /var/log/messages*
```

Finally, you can go to http://bugreport.sun.com/bugreport/ and submit a request for enhancement (RFE) for a driver to support your device.

9.2.6 Can a Driver for a Similar Device Work?

A Solaris driver for a similar device might work for your device if your device belongs to the same chip family as the device that is supported by the candidate driver. This might be the case for on-board soldered devices. For example, a chipset vendor might license the same hardware core of a peripheral that is sold as a retail add-on card, but due to form factor differences, the manufacturer assigns a different device ID. The Solaris OS does not load this driver because the device ID and device class of the device do not match any existing device driver.

With the vendor name (which is the concatenation of the vendor ID and device ID into a single string with a comma separator and no spaces) and PCI ID of your device, search the Solaris Hardware Compatibility Lists (http://www.sun.com/bigadmin/hcl/) or the Solaris for x86 Device Support list (http://www.sun.com/bigadmin/hcl/devicelist/) for a similar device.

To test whether a driver for a similar device works, you can add a new entry to the /etc/driver_aliases file. Normally, editing the /etc/driver_aliases file is strongly discouraged. You could cause your system to panic if you make a mistake. With caution, complete the following steps.

1. Save a copy of your `/etc/driver_aliases` file.

2. As superuser, create a new entry in the `/etc/driver_aliases` file using the device ID for your device. The `/etc/driver_aliases` file is in the following format:
   `driver "pcivendor-id,device-id"`

3. Use the `update_drv` command to update the driver configuration.
   # **/usr/sbin/update_drv** `driver-name`

4. Use the `devfsadm` command to rebuild the `/dev` device tree.
   # **/usr/sbin/devfsadm -i** `driver-name`

5. Reboot the system.

The driver loads the next time you access your device. To load the driver explicitly, use the `modload` command.

If the driver attaches to the device, check whether the device functions correctly. If the driver does not attach to the device, inspect the `/var/adm/messages` output for any reboot messages and error output for that driver module.

9.3 Installing and Updating Drivers

Driver modules for the Solaris OS can come in a several forms: SVR4 package, Image Packaging System (IPS) package, Install Time Update (ITU) package, binary object, or open source.

If you have only source code for your driver module, you need to have a build environment and header files installed on your system to build the driver.

9.3.1 Backing Up Current Functioning Driver Binaries

Before installing a new kernel module, back up any existing modules of the same name. Copy the specific modules from the `/kernel/drv` and `/kernel/drv/$arch` directories to a new location. Then, you can recover these files later if the new modules do not work as expected. For example, if you plan to install a new version of the `e1000g` driver on an x64 platform, you could use the following command to save your current `e1000g` modules:

```
# cd /; tar cvf e1000g-backup.tar /kernel/drv/e1000g \
/kernel/drv/e1000g.conf /kernel/drv/amd64/e1000g
```

9.3.2 Package Installations

SVR4 packages can be installed on either Solaris or OpenSolaris systems. To install SVR4 packages, use the following `pkgadd` command as superuser:

```
# pkgadd package-name
```

IPS packages can only be installed on OpenSolaris systems. To install an IPS package, use the Package Manager tool on your OpenSolaris system.

ITU packages are a special form of packaging that works with the Solaris installer. This form of packaging is very convenient when you need to install storage drivers for new HBAs because in order to persist the Solaris OS onto storage, you need a driver at installation time to actually access the storage.

Ideally, a driver package or patch package removes the old driver, installs the new driver, registers the new driver with the kernel, and attempts to attach and configure any devices. If a new driver installation from a package does not work as expected, check the system hardware and the `driver_aliases` list. You might need to add device support to the new driver as described previously.

9.3.3 Install Time Updates

One form of driver package, the ITU package, is specifically designed to provide driver access during installation. These special packages are designed to be copied to removable media (diskettes, CD-ROM disks, and USB jump drives) and inserted at the beginning of Solaris installation to update the operating system installation image with some new functionality.

This functionality is necessary for some new storage host bus adapters (HBAs), for example. If all the disks are physically attached to a new HBA that the Solaris installation image does not support, then you cannot install the Solaris OS. The solution to this problem is an ITU. Sun provides tools in `/usr/bin` such as `itu`, `pkg2du`, `mkcd`, and `updatemedia` to help developers produce ITUs.

If you install the Solaris OS from DVD or CD media or by using a Preboot Execution Environment (PXE) boot, and you have an ITU, you need to take action just after the GRUB boot selection and the kernel boot. A text console window should appear that has options such as the following:

```
Select the type of installation you want to perform:
    1 Solaris Interactive
    2 Custom JumpStart
    3 Solaris Interactive Text (Desktop session)
    4 Solaris Interactive Text (Console session)
    5 Perform an Install Time Update (ITU)
    6 Exit to Shell
```

```
Enter the number of your choice followed by the <ENTER> key.
Alternatively, enter custom boot arguments directly.

If you wait 30 seconds without typing anything,
an interactive installation will be started.
```

To perform an ITU, choose option 5 and follow the directions to insert the media.

9.3.4 Manual Driver Binary Installation

To install a binary object, copy the binary to the correct driver module directory. Before installing a driver, review the sections in this chapter about obtaining information about devices and drivers. You need to know where device files and drivers are located and how to compare driver module versions.

9.3.4.1 Installing the Driver Binary

If the new driver or driver update that you want to install is a binary rather than a package, copy the appropriate files into the correct /kernel/drv and /kernel/drv/$arch directories. For example, for an x86 based system capable of running in both 64-bit and 32-bit mode, copy the x64 binary into /kernel/drv/amd64/ and the 32-bit x86 binary into /kernel/drv. If you have an archive file with subdirectories ./debug32, ./debug64, ./obj32, and ./obj64, the drivers to test are in the ./obj32 and ./obj64 directories. Make sure that you are superuser when you copy the kernel modules. For example:

```
# cd [my-unpacked-driver-dir]
# cp obj32/mydriver /kernel/drv/
# cp obj64/mydriver /kernel/drv/amd64/
# cp mydriver.conf  /kernel/drv/
```

If the driver binaries are delivered in a way such that you cannot tell what type of binary they are, run the UNIX file command on the file to determine what it is. For example:

```
# file mydriver
mydriver:   ELF 32-bit LSB relocatable 80386 Version 1
```

This output indicates that *mydriver* is a 32-bit x86 binary.

9.3.4.2 Avoiding Recurring Panic

If you have any doubts about whether the driver is well tested, copy the driver to the /tmp directory, and link to the /kernel/drv directory. Some kernel module errors can cause the system to panic. The Solaris OS automatically reboots itself after a panic. The Solaris OS loads any drivers it can during boot. If your new driver has an error that panics the system when you load the driver, then the system will panic again when it tries to reboot after the panic. The system will continue the cycle of panic, reboot, and panic as it attempts to reload the faulty driver every time it reboots after panic. The Solaris OS removes all files from the /tmp directory every time the system reboots. Copy the new driver to the /tmp directory to avoid recurring panic and reboot if the driver has a fatal error. For example:

```
# cp mydriver /tmp
# ln -s /tmp/mydriver /kernel/drv/amd64/mydriver
```

Remember to move the driver to the /kernel/drv directory when you are satisfied that the driver is working correctly.

9.3.4.3 Avoiding a Hard Hang

Another good precaution is to enable the Deadman feature to avoid a hard hang. If your system is in a hard hang, then you cannot break into the debugger. If you enable the Deadman feature, the system panics instead of hanging indefinitely. You can then use the kmdb kernel debugger to analyze your problem or to back out the driver you just installed.

The Deadman feature checks every second whether the system clock is updating. If the system clock is not updating, then the system is in an indefinite hang. If the system clock has not been updated for 50 seconds, the Deadman feature induces a panic and puts you in the debugger.

Take the following steps to enable the Deadman feature.

1. Make sure that you are capturing crash images with dumpadm.

2. Set the snooping variable in the /etc/system file.
   set snooping=1

3. Reboot the system so that the /etc/system file is read again, and the snooping setting takes effect.

Note that any zones on your system inherit the Deadman setting as well.

If your system hangs while the Deadman feature is enabled, you see output similar to the following on your console:

```
panic[cpu1]/thread=30018dd6cc0: deadman: timed out after 9 seconds of clock inactivity

panic: entering debugger (continue to save dump)
```

Inside the debugger, use the `::cpuinfo` command to investigate why the clock interrupt was unable to fire and advance the system time.

9.3.4.4 Registering the New Driver

At this point, you need to indicate to the system that a new driver exists and to register the new driver to a particular hardware vendor and device ID. Use the `prtconf` and `/usr/X11/bin/scanpci` commands to obtain the hardware device ID. Then, use the `add_drv` command as shown in the following example to add the driver module and register it with the running system:

```
# add_drv -i '"pci108e,4df8"' mydriver
```

This command should return no value or message. A message usually indicates a problem with the driver attaching to the device.

Some types of drivers have a dependency on some other framework module. Drivers that commonly have such a dependency are hardware RAID storage HBAs. Most such peripherals are designed to look and interact like SCSI controllers. Therefore, these peripherals depend upon the built-in `scsi` framework. When you install these types of drivers manually, be sure to use the `-c` *class-name* option with the `add_drv` command, where *class-name* is the class name of a particular Solaris framework. For storage HBAs, you probably need to use `add_drv -c scsi`. This command causes the system to also update the `/etc/driver_classes` file and to load the dependent class modules. Without the addition of a class name, the operating system does not know how to load or map a dependent module when the primary HBA driver is loaded. Then, if a dependency exists on a SCSI module, that module is not loaded and the HBA appears to function incorrectly or not function at all.

9.3.4.5 Loading and Testing the New Driver

If you received no message from the add_drv command, then the device should now be recognized by the system. You can test the device and driver by using the following commands:

```
# modload /kernel/drv/amd64/mydriver
# devfsadm -C -i mydriver
```

If this driver replaced a driver with the same name, then you might need to reboot the system to unload the old driver out of the kernel. This is especially true if the device was in use when you installed the new driver. To force the Solaris OS to rediscover devices, create an empty file named reconfigure in the root (/) file system, and reboot.

```
# touch /reconfigure; reboot
```

9.3.4.6 Adding Device Support to an Existing Driver

Sometimes, the driver already exists and attaches to a known list of devices. You might want to continue to support those devices while adding support for more devices with a modified binary. To add device support to an existing driver, copy the binaries as described in "Installing the Driver Binary," but do not use the add_drv or update_drv commands. Instead, edit the /etc/driver_aliases file as described previously to add any new device entries and driver module names. Then, create the empty reconfigure file in the root (/) file system and reboot. In some cases, the system might continue to cache an entry for an old device in /etc/path_to_inst, even after you pull the card from the system and perform a reconfiguration reboot. If that happens, run devfsadm with the -C flag to clean up the files. If an unwanted entry still is not removed, edit the /etc/path_to_inst file and delete the entries that are no longer on the system. Then, perform a reconfiguration reboot.

9.3.5 Adding a Device Driver to a Net Installation Image

You might want to have a system installation image that includes your new driver so that you can easily install the modified system on many machines without reinstalling the new driver. For example, you might want to install on platforms that have new storage and new network cards that require a driver that is not included in the original installation image. You can create your own installation image and deliver that image over the network to any machine, or you can create your own DVD or CD installation image.

If you plan to deploy the Solaris OS over the network, the first step to create your own custom installation image for x86 platforms is to implement a Preboot Execution Environment (PXE) boot JumpStart installation that boots clients using DHCP. See the following sections for instructions.

This installation has two objectives:

- To install the driver into the Solaris miniroot image that is used during installation boot
- To install a copy of the driver onto the system where the installation will occur

9.3.5.1 Network PXE Boot Installation

Perhaps the fastest and most convenient way to install the Solaris OS is over the network from a Solaris JumpStart server. The process for SPARC based systems is the following.

1. Configure the netinstall client to boot over the network.
2. Just after powering up the client, use BOOTP to broadcast for network information.
3. The BOOTP server replies with network, bootstrap, and installation information.
4. The client configures its network and retrieves bootstrap and installation files.

Many x86 based systems come enabled with Intel's PXE firmware that extends the PC BIOS with a similar capability to perform network bootstraps and installations. The process for PCs is essentially identical, except that PXE boot leverages DHCP to retrieve network, bootstrap, and installation information in steps 2 and 3. Solaris JumpStart servers can also boot x86 systems with the addition of DHCP server support for the PXE boot clients. All the required server software components already come bundled into the Solaris OS. All that's needed is configuration.

9.3.5.2 Setting Up a JumpStart PXE Boot Server

The Solaris installation media usually includes a utility to install the basic Jump-Start server. Inserting optical media into a running Solaris system usually prompts the volume manager to mount the media at /cdrom.

1. Change to the following directory:

    `# cd /cdrom/sol_10_106_x86/Solaris_10/Tools`

    You should see the JumpStart installation script `setup_install_server`.

2. Specify the command and a target installation directory:

    `# ./setup_install_server /export/install`

    Change the target directory, `/export/install`, to another location as
    needed. Running this command requires about three gigabytes or more of
    disk space on the slice that holds the target directory. The command might
    take an hour or more as all the components are copied to the target directory
    from optical media. The time depends on the speed of the optical drive and of
    the main system.

    If you only have a CD-ROM drive and no support for DVDs, then you must
    install from multiple disks. The initial installation is the same for the first
    CD as for the DVD.

    a. After the initial `setup_install_server`, exit the current directory back
        to the root directory.

    b. Eject the first CD from the File Manager window and insert additional
        CDs. On each CD, change directories to the `/cdrom/sol_10_106_*/`
        `Solaris10/Tools/` directory. Then, run the `add_to_install_server`
        command with the same target directory you started with.

3. When the install server setup completes, export the installation file system to
    the network. To do so, edit the `/etc/dfs/dfstab` file, and insert the follow-
    ing line:

    `share -F nfs -o ro,anon=0 -d "jumpstart dir" /export/install`

4. Edit `/export/install` to wherever you unpacked the install server.

5. After saving and exiting the editor, enable or restart the NFS server by
    running the following command:

    `# svcadm enable svc:/network/nfs/server ; shareall`

6. For completeness, you can create a directory. For example:

    `# mkdir /export/install/jumpstart`

7. Copy the `jumpstart_sample` files to the directory you created in the
    previous step:

```
# cp -r /export/install/Solaris_10/Misc/jumpstart_sample/* \
/export/install/jumpstart
```

9.3.5.3 Setting Up a DHCP Server for PXE Boot

The previous section covered most of the tasks required to transfer JumpStart installation packages to the server, and to make these packages accessible over the network through NFS. However, before an x86 boot client can access those packages, it must boot over the network and obtain initial network and boot files to begin the installation. For most network installation environments, the same JumpStart host also runs DHCP and PXE boot server processes for the boot clients.

When a PXE boot client starts, it broadcasts for network information and boot files. The network information is provided through DHCP. Then, the Solaris network boot program (nbp) and other initialization files such as the Solaris x86.miniroot file are transferred using TFTP (trivial file transfer protocol). Finally, once the Solaris installer has started, the JumpStart installation packages are transferred through NFS.

Configuring the Solaris DHCP requires the following.

- Configuring the DHCP server to recognize and respond to the PXE boot client.
- Creating all PXE boot directories. You will need to copy or link appropriate files that will be required by the client during bootup.

If a DHCP server is already configured, you can unconfigure it by using the dhcpconfig command with the unconfigure flag. For example:

```
# dhcpconfig -Ux
```

The server you configure here will answer promiscuously for all PXE boot requests for the Solaris OS on x86 platforms and works well on an isolated subnet where it is the only installation service. However, if this DHCP service must coexist with other services, or if it requires specific configurations, then customizations are available to respond to requests only from specific MAC addresses or for specific networks. For more information, see "DHCP" in *System Administration Guide: IP Services.*[4]

The following is a script that simplifies most generic DHCP configurations for PXE:

```
#!/bin/sh
dhcpconfig -D -r SUNWbinfiles -p /var/dhcp
dhcpconfig -N network -m netmask -t routerip
dhtadm -A -s SrootOpt -d 'Vendor=SUNW.i86pc,1,ASCII,1,0'
dhtadm -A -s SrootIP4 -d 'Vendor=SUNW.i86pc,2,IP,1,1'
```

continues

```
dhtadm -A -s SrootNM -d 'Vendor=SUNW.i86pc,3,ASCII,1,0'
dhtadm -A -s SrootPTH -d 'Vendor=SUNW.i86pc,4,ASCII,1,0'
dhtadm -A -s SswapIP4 -d 'Vendor=SUNW.i86pc,5,IP,1,0'
dhtadm -A -s SswapPTH -d 'Vendor=SUNW.i86pc,6,ASCII,1,0'
dhtadm -A -s SbootFIL -d 'Vendor=SUNW.i86pc,7,ASCII,1,0'
dhtadm -A -s Stz -d 'Vendor=SUNW.i86pc,8,ASCII,1,0'
dhtadm -A -s SbootRS -d 'Vendor=SUNW.i86pc,9,NUMBER,2,1'
dhtadm -A -s SinstIP4 -d 'Vendor=SUNW.i86pc,10,IP,1,1'
dhtadm -A -s SinstNM -d 'Vendor=SUNW.i86pc,11,ASCII,1,0'
dhtadm -A -s SinstPTH -d 'Vendor=SUNW.i86pc,12,ASCII,1,0'
dhtadm -A -s SsysidCF -d 'Vendor=SUNW.i86pc,13,ASCII,1,0'
dhtadm -A -s SjumpsCF -d 'Vendor=SUNW.i86pc,14,ASCII,1,0'
dhtadm -A -s Sterm -d 'Vendor=SUNW.i86pc,15,ASCII,1,0'
dhtadm -A -s SbootURI -d 'Vendor=SUNW.i86pc,16,ASCII,1,0'
dhtadm -A -m PXEClient:Arch:00000:UNDI:002001 -d
':BootFile="nbp.SUNW.i86pc":BootSrvA=serverip:'
dhtadm -A -m SUNW.i86pc -d \
    ':SinstNM="server":SinstIP4=serverip:\
SinstPTH="/export/install":SrootNM="server":\
SrootIP4=serverip:\
SrootPTH="/export/install/Solaris_10/Tools/Boot":\
SjumpsCF="server:/export/install/jumpstart":\
SsysidCF="server:/export/install/jumpstart":'
```

In the third line of the script above *network* should be replaced with the network address for your subnet (for example, 192.168.100.0). The *netmask* is your netmask (for example, 255.255.255.0), and the *routerip* is the IP address of your router (for example, 192.168.100.1). On the last line of the script, replace *server* with the host name of the install server. This server name is the same name that you specified in the dhtadm line: SinstNM="*server*". Finally, replace *serverip* with the IP address of the install server. Cut and paste the script into a file, and run the script as superuser.

Edit the /etc/hosts file and add one or more client entries with an IP address. For two clients, do the following:

```
192.168.100.101 pxeclient1
192.168.100.102 pxeclient2
```

Next, add those entries to the DHCP server client table by using the pntadm command. For example:

```
# pntadm -A 192.168.100.101 -m server -h pxeclient1 network
# pntadm -A 192.168.100.102 -m server -h pxeclient2 network
```

The *server* and *network* arguments have the same meaning as for the server and network macros specified by the last line of the PXE configuration script.

Send a HUP signal to the in.dhcp process by issuing the following command:

```
#  pkill -HUP in.dhcpd
```

This signal forces the DHCP server to reread its configuration files. This should take care of the first step of DHCP server configuration.

To configure the boot files for TFTP, the Solaris OS provides a command to simplify the creation and copying of all the files to the /tftpboot directory. Run the following command from the /export/install/images/Solaris_10/Tools directory:

```
#  ./add_install_client -d SUNW.i86pc i86pc
```

You can now test your x86 client and boot PXE on the Solaris OS.

9.3.5.4 Adding a Driver

Once you have a functional network installation server, you need to customize the initial boot image that comes over the network. This image is called the *miniroot*. On x86 based systems, the miniroot can be unpacked, modified, and repacked to enable the installation bootstrapping to start, recognize the new device, and config-ure it. For example, using the root_archive command on the JumpStart server, you can run the following commands:

```
# cd /path-to-jumpstart-install/boot
# /boot/solaris/bin/root_archive unpack ./x86.miniroot ./unpacked
```

These commands copy the driver binaries to the /path_to_jumpstart_ install/boot/unpacked directory. Then, just as you would manually add a driver module to a running system, you copy the binaries to the ./unpacked direc-tory's ./kernel/drv directory. You then add required mapping information into the miniroot driver_aliases file and other files by using the add_drv command with the -b flag to specify the alternate boot directory to target. For example:

```
# add_drv -b full-path-to-unpacked -n -v -m '* 0600 root sys' -i
"device-ids" mydrivername
```

The *full-path-to-unpacked* path is likely to be *path-to-jumpstart/* boot/unpacked. The device IDs (*device-ids*) are the same format as in Section 9.3.4, "Manual Driver Binary Installation." For example:

```
'"pci108e,4df8" "pci108e,4014" "pci108e,401f"'
```

Once the unpacked miniroot has the driver installed, you can repack it, again using the `root_archive` command. However, first save a copy of the old miniroot. For example, you might want to run the following commands:

```
# cd /path_to_jumpstart_install/boot/
# cp ./x86,miniroot ./x86.miniroot.orig
# /boot/solaris/bin/root_archive pack ./x86.miniroot ./unpacked
```

9.3.6 Adding a Device Driver to a CD/DVD Installation Image

To add a device driver to a CD/DVD installation image, copy and modify an existing image and then create a new ISO.

1. Copy the contents of an existing install CD/DVD to a file system where you can modify those contents. The following example shows one way to perform this copy if you have Solaris 10 installation media:

    ```
    # cd /cdrom/sol_10_106/x86; find . -depth -print|cpio -vpdm targetdir
    ```

    The x86 miniroot should be in *targetdir*/boot/x86.miniroot.

2. Repeat the same unpacking and repacking procedures as shown in the previous section.

3. Use the following `mkisofs` command to create a new CD/DVD ISO image:

    ```
    # mkisofs -o outfilename.iso -b boot/grub/stage2_eltorito \
    -c .catalog -no-emul-boot -boot-load-size 4 \
    -boot-info-table -relaxed-filenames -N -L -l -r -J \
    -d -D -V volname targetdir
    ```

    In the Solaris OS, the `mkisofs` command is available only when you specify an Entire install so that you obtain the `SUNWwebminu` package.

4. Burn the ISO images by using either the `cdrw` or `cdrecord` command, as follows:

    ```
    # cdrw -i outfilename.iso
    ```

The `cdrecord` example uses the `--scanbus` option first to scan the system for available DVD burners, as follows:

```
# cdrecord -scanbus
Cdrecord-ProDVD-ProBD-Clone 2.01.01a38 (i386-pc-solaris2.11)
Copyright (C)
1995-2008 Jorg Schilling
Warning: Using USCSI interface.
Using libscg version 'schily-0.9'.
Scsibus0:
    0,0,0     0) 'HL-DT-ST' 'DVD-RAM GSA-H55N' '1.03'
Removable CD-ROM
    0,1,0     1) *
    0,2,0     2) *
    0,3,0     3) *
# cdrecord -v dev=2,1,0 -eject outfilename.iso
```

If you only have software ISO images, you do not need to burn CD/DVD blank media. The Solaris OS enables you to mount ISO images using the loopback mount file systems. If you know the absolute path to the ISO image, you can use the following command to mount the ISO image as an ISO or HSFS (ISO High Sierra File System):

```
# /usr/sbin/lofiadm -a iso-absolute-imagepath
```

This command returns the loopback path where the image is available. This path is usually `/dev/lofi/1` if you have no other loopback mounted file systems in use. Use the following command to mount an ISO image:

```
# mount -F hsfs /dev/lofi/1 /mnt
```

9.3.7 Swapping Disks

One way to prepare for a possible disk failure is to maintain standby disks that are preformatted with the operating system already installed. The operating system is usually an archive copy of a reference system that is copied onto a spare hard drive. If your system has a disk failure, you can replace the disk drive and have the system running again in minutes. To use this method, all important data must be stored remotely.

9.3.7.1 Duplicating a Reference Platform

The Solaris OS supports flash archive, or `flar`, images for creating an installable image that duplicates a reference platform. To use this method, the target host system must remain identical to the reference system. You cannot replace your system with a flash archive under the following conditions:

- If critical peripherals are located in different slots on the two systems and therefore enumerate differently during system boot

- If the two systems have had different BIOS updates, which change the device tree

The Solaris OS rediscovers devices when the system boots. One problem with a running reference system is that the Solaris OS keeps binary archives and records of the previous boot to optimize bootstrapping times. If device mapping and device trees become unsynchronized, the system probably cannot boot and might cycle through partial reboots repeatedly until interrupted. In such cases, you need to rebuild the device tree for that disk image.

9.3.7.2 Rebuilding the Device Tree

A solution to the problem of swapping in a disk with a stale device tree is to boot using the Solaris Failsafe option and confirm that you want to mount the main disk under /a. Then rebuild and reconfigure the device tree and boot device properly on the main disk slice.

1. To rebuild the device tree, first execute the following commands to obtain some information about the system:

```
# mv /a/dev /a/dev.orig
# mv /a/devices /a/devices.orig
# mv /a/etc/path_to_inst /a/etc/path_to_inst.orig
# touch /a/etc/path_to_inst
# mkdir /dev
# chown root:sys /dev
# cd /; tar cvf - devices | (cd /a; tar xfp -)
# devfsadm -C -r /a
```

These commands move the existing device tree information to the boot slice mounted under /a. Then these commands copy the existing dynamically created device tree from the failsafe boot to /a.

2. Reconfigure the system to specify the location of the default physical boot device to the booting kernel.

   The location of the physical boot device is specified in the /boot/solaris/bootenv.rc file. The entry in the bootenv.rc file refers to a physical device that points to a path in the /devices directory. To determine the physical path, do a full listing on the logical path in /dev.

a. To find the logical path, run the `df` command and look for `/a`. The output shows an entry similar to the following:

```
# df -k
Filesystem          kbytes     used      avail    capacity  Mounted on
/dev/dsk/c1d0s0  15496821  10691245  4650608  70%       /a
```

b. Do a full listing on `/dev/dsk/c1d0s0`, which looks similar to the following:

```
# ls -l /dev/dsk/c1d0s0
lrwxrwxrwx   1 root       root        51 Apr  8  2008 /dev/dsk/c1d0s0 ->
../../devices/pci@0,0/pci-ide@1f,2/ide@0/cmdk@0,0:a
```

This output indicates that the physical path to the boot device is `/devices/pci@0,0/pci-ide@1f,2/ide@0/cmdk@0,0:a`.

c. Use this information to edit the `/a/boot/solaris/bootenv.rc` file to correct the entry for `bootpath`. Do not include the `/devices` prefix in the path. Enclose the path in single straight quotation marks, as the following shows:

```
# TERM=ansi; export TERM
# vi /a/boot/solaris/bootenv.rc
...
setprop bootpath '/pci@0,0/pci-ide@1f,2/ide@0/cmdk@0,0:a'
...
:wq
```

3. Update the boot archive on `/a`, as follows:

   # bootadm update-archive -v -R /a

4. Perform a reconfiguration reboot, as follows:

```
# touch /a/reconfigure
# cd /; sync; sync; sync; umount /a
# reboot
```

The system now boots normally. You might receive a few warning messages the first time the system boots because the system will again attempt to configure the hardware paths and device tree when it finds an empty /etc/path_to_inst file.

9.4 When Drivers Hang or Panic the System

Driver modules are part of the kernel, and errors in kernel modules can have much worse effects than errors in user applications. Driver developers have the responsibility to make sure the driver meets high quality standards. Following are some techniques to use if a driver causes your system to crash, hang, or panic.

During the Solaris boot process, the boot firmware or BIOS on the system is in control. The objective is to load the kernel, execute it, and then hand over control to that kernel, which then bootstraps itself by loading system-configuration information and driver modules. Long before the system completes its boot process and displays a login window, a bad driver could cause the kernel to crash. The system might halt and not boot. Or, the system might be up and running with processes executing, and then crash and cause the kernel to panic.

The Solaris OS provides tools that enable you to see what is happening during the boot process and to diagnose the problem. By default, the Solaris OS records runtime crash dumps, which can provide information about the call stack at the time of the crash.

9.4.1 Device Driver Causes the System to Hang

If the Solaris OS is hanging or crashing during boot, the problem might be in a kernel module. By default, the Solaris boot process is fairly terse, and you receive little output about how the boot process proceeds. To obtain more information, turn on verbose output by specifying the -v flag at the boot PROM for SPARC based systems or through the GRUB menu for x86 based systems. Note that previous versions of Solaris booting might require different flags such as -m verbose or -V.

For SPARC based systems, type the following at the ok prompt:

```
ok> boot -v
```

For x86 based systems, at the GRUB menu, use the up arrow and down arrow keys to select the GRUB option for the Solaris version you want to run, and then type e to edit that entry. Then, use the arrow keys to go to the kernel line, and type e again. Typing e puts you into edit mode so that you can edit the kernel line to insert a -v flag. Insert the -v flag *after* the main kernel path, but *before* any options to be passed to the booted kernel, such as after a -B flag. For example, the kernel line might look like the following:

```
kernel$ /platform/i86pc/kernel/$ISADIR/unix -v -B
\ prop1=val1,prop2=val2,...
```

Press the Enter key, and then type b to boot your edited entry.

Verbose booting displays many lines of output as the kernel boots and loads modules. If a hang occurs after a load line, the output stops. For example:

```
...
8042 device: mouse is /isa/i8042@1,60/mouse@1
ehci0 is /pci@0,0/pci8086,464c@1d,7
uhci0 is /pci@0,0/pci8086,464c@1d
uhci1 is /pci@0,0/pci8086,464c@1d,1
uhci2 is /pci@0,0/pci8086,464c@1d,2
pseudo-device: stmf_sbd0
stmf_sbd0 is /pseudo/stmf_sbd@0
audiohd0 is /pci@0,0/pci8086,d603@1b
sdhost0 is /isa/i8042@1,60/mouse@1
```

In this example, the sdhost driver (instance 0) is a laptop SD card reader, and it might be causing the hang. (See the sdhost(7D) man page.) You can disable this driver at the boot command line for the SPARC boot PROM and at the GRUB command line. To disable a driver, insert disable-*drivername*=true after a -B flag, where *drivername* is replaced by the name of the module you want to disable. For example, at the GRUB command line, type the following command:

```
kernel$ /platform/i86pc/kernel/$ISADIR/unix -v -B
disable-sdhost=true
```

Press the Enter key, and then type b to boot. If the boot succeeds, then you have identified the problem driver. You can disable this driver permanently by appending the following line to the /etc/system file:

```
exclude sdhost
```

During initial boot, once the kernel is loaded and executed, the system first reads the /etc/system file for any boot-time directives.

Another way to disable a driver as a boot option is to create a GRUB boot entry in the /boot/grub/menu.lst file for the Solaris OS (or in the /rpool/boot/

`grub/menu.lst` file for the OpenSolaris OS) that contains the `-B disable-`*drivername*`=true` option. This GRUB menu option enables you to boot with the particular driver disabled or without the driver disabled. Note that once a driver is disabled, you cannot load another module with that name into the kernel during runtime. To test an update of that driver, you must reboot.

If the changes to `/etc/system` cause the system to stop booting, then you need to back out those changes. One way to back out those changes on an x86 platform is to boot failsafe at the GRUB command line. Then, mount the disk, edit the `/a/etc/system` file, save, exit, and reboot normally. If you do not have a GRUB option to boot failsafe, then you can use the `-a` option to boot interactively. This method works on both the GRUB command line for x86 and x64 based systems and at the Open Boot PROM on SPARC based systems. At the GRUB command line, type the following:

```
kernel$ /platform/i86pc/kernel/$ISADIR/unix -a
```

For Open Boot PROM, type the following:

```
ok> boot -a
```

As the system boots, the kernel pauses and interactively asks questions at each major step, including when individual modules are loaded and when `/etc/system` directives are performed. At the appropriate point during booting, you can bypass directives that might be causing the system to hang.

9.4.2 Device Driver Causes the System to Panic

A driver module might load and attach successfully to a device, but then crash the system at a later time when the kernel attempts to use the device. When the Solaris OS crashes, the default behavior is to attempt to create a crash log in `/var/crash/`*hostname*. You also see two related files: `unix.`*#* and `vmcore.`*#*, where *#* is the crash dump number.

You can obtain a quick stack trace of what the kernel was doing when it panicked. Run the `$C` MDB command after starting MDB to load the crash dump. For example:

```
# cd /var/crash/myhost
# mdb unix.0 vmcore.0
> $C
ffffff000499b790 vpanic()
ffffff000499b7d0 0xffffffffffac8959940()
ffffff000499b820 segmap_unlock+0xf1()
ffffff000499b8b0 segmap_fault+0x128()
ffffff000499bf10 mydriver_uvec_enter+3e()
ffffff000499c490 mydriver_req_scsi_psthru+a4()
ffffff000499c780 mydriver_intr+0x124()
```

After the vpanic() call shown in this output, you can see that the kernel panics after *mydriver* enters an interrupt service routine and then causes the system to crash.

If a particular driver continues to cause system failure at the same place, you can use the rem_drv command to remove the driver, or you can disable or exclude that particular driver by adding an exclude directive to the /etc/system file as shown below and then rebooting.

```
exclude problem-driver
```

9.4.3 Device Driver Degrades System Performance

You might have a driver that runs but does not run well. Perhaps your driver has poor performance. Perhaps your driver uses too much CPU time because the driver throws too many system interrupts or because the algorithms are implemented inefficiently. If your driver leaks memory, over time the kernel will exhaust its memory resources and the entire system will hang or crash. Some devices might obtain resources in a way that prevents other kernel tasks from completing.

Various tools and techniques can help you isolate which kernel module is causing problems. The Solaris OS provides several performance monitoring tools. For example, vmstat and mpstat provide performance information about the kernel. If the CPU utilization, especially the system time taken, is unusually high, then the work performed by the kernel is unusually high. Unusually high amounts of work performed by the kernel might be a driver issue. A high intr field in mpstat output might indicate a device that throws an unusually high number of interrupts, causing the system to stop and service those interrupts and therefore consume more CPU resources.

If you suspect a particular driver is causing system-wide problems, you can exclude that driver during boot, either through the GRUB menu or by adding an exclude directive to the /etc/system file as shown below and then rebooting.

```
exclude problem-driver
```

If the problem disappears, look for an update for that driver that you can install.

Another way to diagnose problems in driver code is to print the time stamp when functions in a driver module are entered. You can output these time stamps with the following one-line Dynamic Tracing (DTrace) script:

```
# dtrace -F -m 'drivername{trace(timestamp);}'
```

The *drivername* variable is the name of the particular kernel module you want to monitor. This output can be considerable so you might want to run this command for only a brief period and dump data to a file in /tmp if the system has sufficient memory.

To view memory used by modules in the kernel, the Solaris OS provides a built-in kernel debugger feature that can output module statistics such as how much memory has been allocated by each module. This kernel feature requires more memory statistics gathering than what is done by default. To enable more detailed memory statistics gathering, append the following line to the /etc/system file, and reboot:

set kmem_flags=0xf

After the system has rebooted, log in as superuser and type the following command:

```
# mdb -k
> ::kmausers
```

This command provides a snapshot of the running kernel, including what kernel memory pages are allocated and what function allocated them. Names of functions that are called by a particular driver module have a unique prefix that identifies them with that driver module. It is not unusual for a driver to allocate 10 to 20 megabytes of memory for cache or buffering. This is common, for example, on 1 Gigabit Ethernet and 10 Gigabit Ethernet network cards or fast storage HBAs. However, when the amount of kernel memory allocated exceeds several hundred megabytes and continues to grow, the kernel might run out of memory.

9.5 Driver Administration Commands and Files

This section lists important commands and files that are referenced in this chapter.

9.5.1 Driver Administration Command Summary

The following commands are useful for managing drivers. Most of these commands are described in this chapter. Use the man command to get more information. Man page section numbers are shown for reference.

- add_drv(1M)—Updates the /etc/driver_aliases and /etc/driver_classes files, as necessary, and registers a new driver with the kernel for use
- add_to_install_server(1M)—Merges other Solaris installation media with an existing image on a Net Install Server
- cdrw(1)—Reads and writes CDs

- cdrecord(1)—Creates CD/DVD/BD disks
- df(1M)—Displays the number of free disk blocks and free files
- devfsadm(1M)—Maintains the /dev namespace
- devfsadmd(1M)—Daemon started during system startup that handles both reconfiguration boot processing and updating /dev and /devices
- dhcpconfig(1M)—Configures DHCP service
- dmesg(1M)—Collects system diagnostic messages to form an error log
- dumpadm(1M)—Configures operating system crash dump
- file(1)—Displays the type of a file
- file(1B)—Determines the type of a file by examining its contents
- flar(1M)—Administers flash archives
- fmdump(1M)—Displays fault management log files
- isainfo(1)—Displays instruction set architecture information
- itu(1M)—Converts packages to Driver Update format and patches Solaris installation media for Install Time Update
- kmdb(1)—Starts the kernel debugger
- mdb(1)—Starts the modular debugger
- mkcd(1M)—Creates a bootable Solaris ISO image
- mkisofs(8)—Makes an ISO file system
- modinfo(1M)—Lists kernel modules loaded in the system and other module statistics like major number, size, module name, and revision, if provided in the driver
- modload(1M)—Loads a kernel module
- modunload(1M)—Attempts to unload a kernel module
- mpstat(1M)—Provides performance information about the kernel
- pkg2du(1M)—Converts driver packages to Driver Update format
- pkgadd(1M)—Transfers software packages to the system
- pntadm(1M)—Manages DHCP network tables
- prtconf(1M)—Enumerates devices recognized by the system
- rem_drv(1M)—Removes a device driver from the system
- root_archive(1M)—Manages bootable miniroot archives
- /usr/X11/bin/scanpci(1)—Optional command bundled with Xorg packages that provides easier-to-read enumeration of devices
- setup_install_server(1M)—Sets up an install server, sets up a WANboot install server, or sets up a boot server

- `strings(1)`—Finds printable strings in an object or binary file
- `update_drv(1M)`—Rereads the `.conf` file for a driver and reconfigures the driver with those parameters
- `updatemedia(1M)`—Modifies Solaris media with patches and packages
- `vmstat(1M)`—Provides performance information about the kernel

9.5.2 Driver Administration File Summary

The following files are used to manage drivers. Most of these files are described in this chapter. Use the `man` command to get more information. Man page section numbers are shown for reference.

- `devfs(7FS)`—Device file system
- `devices(4)`—Device configuration information
- `driver.conf(4)`—Driver configuration files
- `/etc/driver_aliases`—Shows which devices are bound to which drivers
- `/etc/driver_classes`—Driver class binding file
- `/etc/name_to_major`—Lists all devices and their major numbers
- `/etc/name_to_sysnum`—Maps system call number to system calls
- `/etc/path_to_inst(4)`—Device instance number file
- `/etc/system(4)`—System configuration information file
- `e1000g(7D)`—Intel PRO/1000 Gigabit family of network interface controllers
- `scsi(4)`—Configuration files for SCSI target drivers
- `sdhost(7D)`—Standard-compliant Secure Digital slot driver
- `/var/adm/messages`—Time-stamped system error and informational messages

Notes

1. Conventional PCI 3.0 & 2.3: An Evolution of the Conventional PCI Local Bus Specification, `http://www.pcisig.com/specifications/conventional/`
2. PCI Express: Performance Scalability for the Next Decade, `http://www.pcisig.com/specifications/pciexpress/`

3. The PCI ID Repository Web site, `http://pci-ids.ucw.cz/`. Searchable PCI vendor and device lists, `http://www.pcidatabase.com/`. Repository of vendor IDs, device IDs, subsystems, and device classes used in PCI devices, `http://pciids.sourceforge.net/`

4. *System Administration Guide: IP Services,* `http://docs.sun.com/app/docs/doc/819-3000`

Further Reading

Solaris™ Internals: Solaris 10 and OpenSolaris Kernel Architecture, Second Edition; Jim Mauro, Richard McDougall; Prentice Hall 2007; ISBN: 978-0-13-148209-8

Solaris™ Performance and Tools: DTrace and MDB Techniques for Solaris 10 and OpenSolaris; Richard McDougall, Jim Mauro, Brendan Gregg; Prentice Hall 2007; ISBN: 978-0-13-156819-8

Solaris Dynamic Tracing Guide, `http://wikis.sun.com/display/DTrace/Documentation`

Solaris Modular Debugger Guide, `http://docs.sun.com/doc/817-2543`

10

Solaris Networking

This chapter describes basic networking concepts and provides various procedures to help you configure systems to connect to the network.

10.1 Introduction to Network Configuration

This section introduces you to network configuration by describing the TCP/IP networking stack and the privileges required to configure it.

10.1.1 Overview of the TCP/IP Networking Stack

IP interfaces provide the connection between the system and the network. These IP interfaces are configured over data links, which in turn correspond to instances of network hardware devices or network interface cards (NICs) in the system. Certain systems can have NICs or network adapters already built in. However, you can install additional NICs. Each IP interface has an underlying data link. Each physical network device has a data link that is configured above it. The relationship is illustrated in Figure 10.1.

The figure is a partial representation of the networking stack based on the Open Systems Interconnection (OSI) model. Only three layers, hardware, link, and interface, are shown to illustrate the relationship among devices, links, and interfaces. The figure shows two NICs, ce and qfe, on the hardware layer. The device ce has a single device instance ce0, while qfe has multiple device instances, qfe0 to qfe3. The devices qfe0 through qfe2 are not used. Devices ce0 and qfe3 are

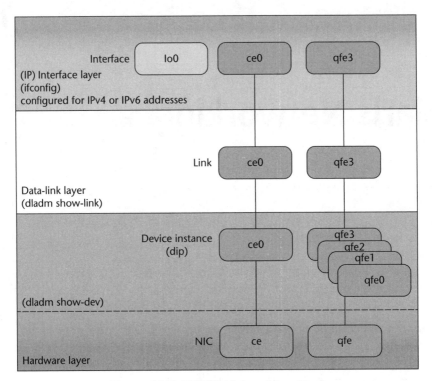

Figure 10.1 TCP/IP Networking Stack

used and have corresponding links ce0 and qfe3 on the data-link layer. In the figure, the IP interfaces are likewise named after their respective underlying hardware, ce0 and qfe3. These interfaces can be configured with IPv4 or IPv6 addresses to host both types of network traffic. Note also the presence of the loopback interface lo0 on the interface layer. This interface is used for localhost IP traffic, mainly socket-based inter-process communication (IPC).

The figure also shows that different administrative commands are used at each layer of the stack. For example, NICs in the system are listed by the dladm show-dev command. Information about links on the data-link layer is displayed by the dladm-show-link command. The ifconfig command shows the IP interface configuration on the interface layer.

When you configure the network, dladm and ifconfig are the most common commands that you use. You also add information to certain configuration files to create a persistent network configuration. The most common files are /etc/hostname.*interface*, where *interface* is the specific interface that is used on the system, and /etc/hosts. Other configuration files are used depending on the particular task you want to perform to set up your network. These files are further described in subsequent sections in this chapter.

> **Note**
>
> For more details about the different commands to configure the network, see the *man pages section 1: User Commands* (http://docs.sun.com/app/docs/doc/816-5165) and *man pages section 1M: System Administration Commands* (http://docs.sun.com/app/docs/doc/816-5166).

10.1.2 Configuring the Network as Superuser

You need to be superuser or root to configure the network. In the Solaris 10 OS, role-based access control (RBAC) is used to obtain proper privileges to perform specific actions without needing to become superuser. In RBAC, specific privileges are assigned to specific roles which, in turn, are assigned to specific profiles. For example, the Primary Administrator role includes the Primary Administrator profile. For more information about roles and about creating and assigning the role to a user, refer to Chapter 11, "Solaris User Management."

10.2 Setting Up a Network

To help you become familiar with the procedures used to configure the network, this chapter uses a sample network setup of a company, XYZ, Inc. XYZ, Inc. has the network topology shown in Figure 10.2.

> **Note**
>
> For more information about network configuration, see *System Administration Guide: IP Services* (http://docs.sun.com/app/docs/doc/816-4554).

10.2.1 Components of the XYZ, Inc. Network

The components of the corporate network are as follows.

- XYZ, Inc.'s network is divided into two subnetworks. The subnetworks are assigned the following network segments: 192.168.5.0/26 and 192.168.5.64/26.
- The network will use naming services to facilitate the identification of systems. In Table 10.1, only those systems that are used in the procedures in

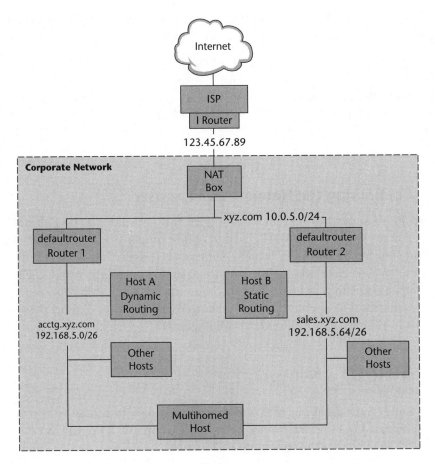

Figure 10.2 Local Network Topology of XYZ, Inc.

this chapter are listed. However, you should create a list of names for all the systems that are part of the network.

■ Network segments are also identified with domain names. The company's entire network is identified as xyz.com. The two subnetworks are called acctg.xyz.com (the accounting domain) and sales.xyz.com (the sales domain).

Table 10.1 shows the systems and their corresponding names and domains.

Table 10.1 Systems and System Names for XYZ, Inc.

System	Assigned Name	Domain
Network Address Translation (NAT) Box	Gobi	xyz.com
Router 1	Tigris	acctg.xyz.com (192.168.5.0/26 segment)
Router 2	Everest	sales.xyz.com (192.168.5.64/26 segment)
System (sample client host in the Sales domain that does not use static routing)	Kilimanjaro	sales.xyz.com
System (sample client host in the Accounting domain)	Mekong	acctg.xyz.com
Multihomed host	Amazon	acctg.xyz.com
Host B (sample client host in the Sales domain that is set up with static routing)	Denali	sales.xyz.com

- Gobi connects the `xyz.com` to the external network or the Internet. Gobi is called the network address translation (NAT) box because it is responsible for translating between addresses that are valid in the XYZ network and the addresses that are valid in the external network or the Internet.

- Tigris and Everest manage the routing information of all the systems in the network, for both their respective domains. These routers run routing protocols such as RIP (routing information protocol).

- Tigris will be configured to provide the dynamic host configuration protocol (DHCP) service for its clients in the accounting domain. Thus, the client hosts in its network do not need to be configured with static IP addresses.

- The sales domain that is served by Everest will be configured with static IP addresses. This configuration is therefore the opposite of the configuration in the accounting domain that uses DHCP.

- Client hosts of both domains have single configured interfaces.

- The multihomed host Amazon allows connections between the two domains. It will also be configured to provide naming services. In particular, XYZ, Inc. will use the network information service (NIS).

10.2.2 Configuring the Sales Domain

Setting up a network involves configuring a router and the other client hosts on the network. The router manages the routes that network traffic traverses to allow systems to communicate within the network and externally with other networks. After you configure the router, you configure the clients that will use the router's networking services.

In XYZ, Inc.'s network setup, the sales domain is serviced by Everest, its router. One of the client hosts in the sales domain, Denali, is also configured with static routing. Static routing will be explained later in this chapter.

In this section, two procedures are described.

- Section 10.2.2.1, "How to Configure the Router for the Sales Domain," describes how to configure the router to provide networking services.

- Section 10.2.2.2, "How to Configure Client Hosts in the Sales Domain," describes the steps to configure the client hosts in the domain. The sample system will be Kilimanjaro.

- In a later procedure, another client host, Denali, will be configured with static routing.

10.2.2.1 How to Configure the Router for the Sales Domain

Everest will serve as the router for the sales domain. The following steps guide you to configure the router to enable it to provide networking services.

1. As superuser or an administrator with the proper RBAC privileges on Everest, determine which interfaces are physically installed.

```
# dladm show-link
ce0      type: legacy       mtu:1500      device:ce0
bge0     type: non-vlan     mtu:1500      device:bge0
```

The command output reports two links that correspond to two devices or NICs installed on Everest: ce0 and bge0. You can also list the NICs in a system by using the command dladm show-dev.

Everest has two roles. It physically forwards traffic between systems on the sales domain and systems in the 10.0.5.0/24 network so that all the systems in both networks can communicate with each other. Everest also collects routing information such as routing protocols to both networks' systems. Thus it can share the information with other systems that run the same protocol or use the information to forward packets properly.

To perform these roles, the two interfaces must be configured appropriately.

2. Configure one interface with an IP address to connect to the main domain, xyz.com, which is on the 10.0.5.0 network.

   # **ifconfig ce0 plumb 10.0.5.20/24 up**

3. Configure another interface with an IP address to connect to the accounting domain, which is on the 192.168.5.64/26 network.

   # **ifconfig bge0 plumb 192.168.5.70/26 up**

   Note that the prefix length of the network is not on an 8-bit boundary. The first 26 bits of the address specify the network address. The remaining 6 bits identify the individual hosts in the subnetwork. The variable subnet masks are suitable in cases where large numbers of hosts are not needed on a network, such as in our example.

4. (Optional) To verify the results of the previous steps, use the ifconfig -a command.

   Check to see that the interfaces are flagged with the UP keyword and their specific IP addresses are properly assigned. After you have become accustomed to the ifconfig command to configure interfaces, you can skip this verification step.

```
# ifconfig -a
lo0: flags=1000849 <UP,LOOPBACK,RUNNING,MULTICAST,IPv4> mtu
8232 index 1
       inet 127.0.0.1 netmask ff000000
ce0: flags=1000843<UP,BROADCAST,RUNNING,MULTICAST,IPv4>mtu
1500 index 2
       inet 10.0.5.20 netmask ffffff00 broadcast
192.255.255.255
       ether 8:0:20:c1:1b:c6
bge0: flags=1000840<UP,BROADCAST,RUNNING,MULTICAST,IPv4>mtu
1500 index 3
       inet 192.168.5.70 netmask ff000000 broadcast
10.255.255.255
       ether 8:0:20:e5:95:c4
```

5. Make the configuration persist across system reboots.

   Assigning IP addresses by using the ifconfig command does not create a persistent configuration. If you reboot the system, the configuration is discarded. To make the configuration persistent, you must add the configuration information to specific configuration files.

   a. Add the IP address 10.0.5.20/24 to the /etc/hostname.ce0 file.

   b. Add the IP address 192.168.5.70/26 to the /etc/hostname.bge0 file.

```
# echo 10.0.5.20/24 > /etc/hostname.ce0
# echo 192.168.5.70/26 > /etc/hostname.bge0
```

c.   Add the new IP addresses and the corresponding interface names to the
/etc/hosts file. For example:

```
127.0.0.1            local host
10.0.5.20/24         everest-10050     # interface xyz
192.168.5.70/26      everest-1921685-65 # interface sales
```

The two IP interfaces are given names to distinguish which interface
connects to a corresponding network segment. You can also add comments to
further identify the interfaces.

6.   In Everest's /etc/defaultrouter file, add the IP address of the NAT box
Gobi, whose IP address is 10.0.5.150.

10.0.5.150

The default router of the sales domain is Everest. However, the sales domain
connects to the 10.0.5.0 segment (the xyz.com domain) by using Gobi.

7.   Add Everest's domain to the /etc/defaultdomain file.

sales.xyz.com

8.   Enable packet forwarding on the router.

 # svcadm enable ipv4-forwarding

9.   Start a routing protocol.

 # svcadm enable route:default

10. Perform a reconfiguration reboot.

 # reboot -- -r

You have successfully configured Everest to route traffic for the sales domain.

10.2.2.2 How to Configure Client Hosts in the Sales Domain

In the following procedure, a system that is given the host name Kilimanjaro will
be used as the sample client. Assume that Kilimanjaro has a single IP interface,
hme0.

1.   As superuser or an administrator with the proper RBAC privileges on Kilimanjaro, configure the interface with a valid IP address for its subnetwork.

 # ifconfig hme0 plumb 192.168.5.75/26 up

2.   Create a persistent configuration by adding the network information to the
appropriate configuration files.

a.   Add the IP address 192.168.5.75/26 to the /etc/hostname.hme0 file.

 # echo 192.168.5.75/26 > /etc/hostname.hme0

b. Add the address and host information to the `/etc/hosts` file.
   For example:

   192.168.5.75/26   kilimanjaro

3. Make sure that an empty `/etc/defaultrouter` file exists in the system.

4. Add the domain name to the `/etc/defaultdomain` file.
   # **echo sales.xyz.com > /etc/defaultdomain**

5. Check whether packet forwarding is enabled on Kilimanjaro.

```
# routeadm
Configuration          Current
                       Option        Configuration    Current
                                                       System State
-------------------------------------------------------------------
                       IPv4 routing  enabled          disabled
                       IPv6 routing  disabled         disabled
              IPv4 forwarding         enabled          disabled
              IPv6 forwarding         disabled         disabled
              Routing services 'route:default rping:default'
```

6. Disable packet forwarding.
   # **svcadm disable ipv4-forwarding**

7. Perform a reconfiguration reboot
   # **reboot -- -r**

   You have completed the configuration of this client host. The next procedure describes how to configure a system with static routing.

10.2.3 Configuring the Accounting Domain

This section describes the configuration of `acctg.xyz.com`, the second domain in the XYZ, Inc. network. The procedures in this section describe the following.

- Section 10.2.3.1, "How to Configure the Router for the Accounting Domain," describes how to configure the router to provide networking services. This router is also designated to become the DHCP server. Thus, a separate procedure to prepare the router for this purpose is also included.

- Section 10.2.3.3, "How to Configure Client Hosts in the Accounting Domain," describes how to prepare the client hosts to connect to the network. The accounting domain will use the DHCP service. Thus, a separate procedure to set the client hosts to use the service is also included.

10.2.3.1 How to Configure the Router for the Accounting Domain

The router for the accounting domain is Tigris. Similar to the configuration of Everest for the sales domain, the general steps to configure Tigris are as follows.

- Configure IP interfaces.
- Add information to configuration files for persistent configuration.
- Enable packet forwarding and start a routing protocol.

Assume that Tigris has qfe0 and qfe1 as interfaces.

1. Configure each IP interface with IP addresses that will connect to the respective segments of the network. For example:

```
# ifconfig qfe0 plumb 192.168.5.10/26 up
# ifconfig qfe1 plumb 10.0.5.10/24 up
```

2. Make the configuration persistent by adding the IP address information on their corresponding hostname.*interface* configuration files.

   a. /etc/hostname.qfe0 would contain 192.168.5.10

   b. /etc/hostname.qfe1 would contain 10.0.5.10.

```
# echo 192.168.5.10/26 > /etc/hostname.qfe0
# echo 10.0.5.10/24 > /etc/hostname.qfe1
```

3. Add host-IP address information on the /etc/hosts file.

```
127.0.0.1 local host
192.168.5.10/26  tigris-1921685-0 # interface acctg
10.0.5.10/24  tigris-10050   # interface xyz
```

4. Add Gobi's IP address to the /etc/defaultrouter file.
   10.0.5.150 # gobi (NAT box)

5. Add the domain name to the /etc/defaultdomain file.
   # echo acctg.xyz.com > /etc/defaultdomain

6. Start a routing protocol.
   # svcadm enable route:default

7. Enable packet forwarding.

   ```
   # svcadm enable ipv4-forwarding
   ```

8. Perform a reconfiguration reboot.

   ```
   # reboot -- -r
   ```

   You have completed the configuration of Tigris.

10.2.3.2 Setting Up a DHCP Server

In addition to managing routes for the accounting domain, Tigris will also be configured to provide the dynamic host configuration protocol (DHCP) service. This section describes the procedures to set up the server.

How to Configure Tigris as a DHCP Server   As preparation for this procedure, you need to decide the following:

- Data-store type: binary files, text files, or NIS+

  For XYZ, Inc.'s network, the data-store type is binary. The network uses traditional NIS service. However, traditional NIS does not support fast incremental updates. Consequently, this name service is not offered as a data-store option in DHCP. Networks that use NIS should either use text files or binary files for the data store.

- Configuration parameters for the data-store type you select.

- Name service to update host records, if any (`/etc/hosts`, NIS+, DNS).

- Lease time: As a guideline, specify a time that is twice the predicted downtime of a system.

- DNS domain name and IP address of DNS servers, if any.

1. As superuser or an administrator with the proper RBAC privileges on Tigris, start the DHCP Manager.

   ```
   # /usr/sadm/admin/bin/dhcpmgr &
   ```

2. Choose **Configure** as a DHCP Server.

   The DHCP Configuration wizard appears.

3. Choose **options,** or provide required information that you prepared beforehand.

   For the data-store type, select binary files.

4. Click **Finish** to complete the server configuration.

   The Start Wizard Address prompt appears.

5. Click **Yes** to begin configuring the first set of IP addresses that DHCP would manage.

   For the sample company XYZ, Inc., this set would include the IP addresses for the `acctg.xyz.com` domain.

6. After reviewing the information, click **Yes** to add the set of IP addresses to the network table.

7. Start the DHCP service by choosing **Start** from the Service menu.

8. Reboot the server.

9. Add other sets of IP addresses to be managed by DHCP by starting the DHCP Manager and choosing **Network wizard.**

10.2.3.3 How to Configure Client Hosts in the Accounting Domain

In the following procedure, a system with the given host name Mekong will be used as the sample-client host in this domain.

The steps that follow are common to all the clients in the the domain. Thus, you must perform the same procedure on the other clients in `acctg.xyz.com`. Assume that Mekong has a single IP interface, `bge0`.

1. Make sure that the following files exist in the system and that they do not have any entries.

   ▪ `/etc/hostname.bge0`

   ▪ `/etc/dhcp.bge0`

   In the accounting domain, the DHCP server will provide the IP addresses to the client hosts. Thus, no IP addresses should be added to the `/etc/hostname.`*`interface`* file.

2. Make sure that the `/etc/defaultrouter` has no entry.

   Client hosts in the accounting domain use dynamic routing. By keeping the file empty, the system is forced to use dynamic routing.

3. As superuser or an administrator with the proper RBAC privileges on Mekong, make sure that routing protocols are running on the system.

   For example:

```
# routeadm
Configuration Current                            Current
            Option        Configuration System State
------------------------------------------------------------
            IPv4 routing      disabled      disabled
            IPv6 routing      disabled      disabled
            IPv4 forwarding   enabled       disabled
            IPv6 forwarding   disabled      disabled
            Routing services  'route:default rping:default'
# svcadm enable routing:default
```

4. If packet forwarding is enabled in the system, then disable it.
   ```
   # svcadm disable ipv4-forwarding
   ```

5. Perform a reconfiguration reboot.
   ```
   # reboot -- -r
   ```

10.2.3.4 How to Prepare the Client Hosts to Use the DHCP Service

Perform this procedure on the client hosts in the accounting domain.

> **Note**
>
> The option to enable the DHCP service is available during the installation of the Solaris 10 OS. If you did not enable this service at installation, then you must perform the following procedure to enable the DHCP client on the system.

1. Make sure that you are superuser or an administrator with the proper RBAC privileges on the client host.

2. Perform one of the following substeps depending on the indicated condition.
   The conditions refer to the method you used when you installed the Solaris 10 OS on the system. In an *interactive configuration,* you provide configuration information as you are prompted by the installation program. In *preconfiguration,* you specify all the configuration information in a sysidcfg file that you manually create before you start the installation. The installation program uses this file when it installs the OS. With this method, you would no longer need to answer prompts during installation. Refer to *Solaris 10 10/08 Installation Guide: Basic Installations* (http://docs.sun.com/app/docs/doc/820-5236?l=en) for more information.

   a. If the system uses interactive configuration, proceed directly to step 3.

   b. If the system uses preconfiguration, add the dhcp subkey to the network_interface keyword in the sysidcfg file.

   The location of the file depends on where you created it on the system.
   For example, if the client host has qfe0 as the interface, then in the sysidcfg file, you would include the following line:
   ```
   network_interface=qfe0{dhcp}
   ```

3. Unconfigure the system.
   ```
   # sys-unconfig
   ```

4. Reboot the system.
   In an interactive configuration, you are prompted to use DHCP to configure network interfaces. In preconfiguration, the system automatically uses DHCP based on the information in the sysidcfg file.

5. If you are using interactive configuration, specify **Yes** when you are prompted to use DHCP.

10.2.4 Configuring the Multihomed Host

Amazon, the multihomed host in XYZ, Inc.'s network will be configured to connect the accounting and sales domain. This system will also act as a name server. Thus, the section describes three procedures:

- Configuration of the multihomed host's interfaces
- Configuration of the host to provide naming services
- Adding users to the NIS domain

In the Solaris OS, a system with more than one interface is considered a *multi-homed host*. A multihomed host does not forward IP packets. However, you can configure this host to run routing protocols. With multiple interfaces that are configured, a multihomed host can allow connections among multiple networks.

The following types of systems are typically configured as multihomed hosts.

- NFS servers, particularly those that function as large data centers, can be attached to more than one network to share files among a large pool of users. These servers do not need to maintain routing tables.
- Database servers can have multiple network interfaces to provide resources to a large pool of users, just like NFS servers.
- Firewall gateways are systems that provide the connection between a company's network and public networks such as the Internet. Administrators set up firewalls as a security measure. When configured as a firewall, the host does not pass packets between the networks that are attached to the host's interfaces. However, the host can still provide standard TCP/IP services such as ssh to authorized users.

10.2.4.1 How to Configure the Multihomed Host

Assume that the multihomed host has qfe0 and qfe1 as interfaces.

1. Configure the two interfaces, each with IP addresses for the two domains. For example, qfe0 might have 192.168.5.50/26 and qfe1 might have 192.168.5.90/26.

```
# ifconfig qfe0 plumb 192.168.5.50/26 up
# ifconfig qfe1 plumb 192.168.5.90/26 up
```

2. Add relevant information to the appropriate configuration files:

   a. /etc/hostname.*interface* files

   ```
   # echo 192.168.5.50/26 > /etc/hostname.qfe0
   # echo 192.168.5.90/26 > /etc/hostname.qfe1
   ```

   b. /etc/hosts file
       For example:

   ```
   192.168.5.50/26   amazon-19216850   # interface acctg
   192.168.5.90/26   amazon-19216865   # interface sales
   ```

   c. /etc/defaultdomain

   # echo acctg.xyz.com > /etc/defaultdomain

3. Enable dynamic routing.

   # svcadm enable route:default

4. Check if packet forwarding is enabled.

   # svcs ipv4-forwarding
   ```
   STATE      STIME     FMRI
   online    12:14:12  svc:/network/ipv4-forwarding:default
   ```

5. Disable packet forwarding if it is enabled.

   # svcadm disable ipv4-forwarding

6. Perform a reconfiguration reboot.

   # reboot -- -r

10.2.4.2 How to Configure a System for Naming Services

Naming services is a feature that resolves system names and their respective IP addresses. Using naming services facilitates network administration because names of systems are easier to remember than the systems' IP addresses. You must configure a name server to manage and match systems with specific names.

Naming services also provide the advantage of storing naming-service information in centrally located files, maps, or database tables. Thus, you would not need to maintain this information in every system on the network.

The corporate network of XYZ, Inc. will be configured to use the Network Information Service (NIS). Normally, the recommended setup is to configure one NIS server for each domain. In bigger networks, you would also configure slave-domain servers as backups to the main, or master, server. However, in this chapter's sample network, only one NIS server will be configured to serve both the accounting and sales domains.

For more details about setting up the NIS server, as well as information about other naming services that are available in the Solaris OS, see Chapter 13, "Using Naming Services." For more details about configuring naming services, see *System Administration Guide: Naming and Directory Service (DNS, NIS, and LDAP)* (http://docs.sun.com/app/docs/doc/816-4556).

Setting up the NIS server involves three major steps:

- Preparing the source files
- Modifying the /var/yp/Makefile script based on how the source files are prepared
- Setting up the name server

Amazon will provide naming services to both the sales and accounting domain. Thus, an added step is necessary to enable Amazon to serve multiple domains.

The naming services to the sales domain will be prepared first. Then Amazon will be further configured to serve the accounting domain.

10.2.4.3 Preparing the Source Files

These source files contain the information about all individual client hosts in the network. NIS uses the following source files to provide naming services.

- auto.home or auto_home
- auto.master or auto_master
- bootparams
- ethers
- group
- hosts
- ipnodes
- netgroup
- netmasks
- networks
- passwd
- protocols
- rpc
- service

- shadow
- user_attr

In this procedure, you will prepare appropriate directory locations to store the source files.

1. As superuser or an administrator with the proper RBAC privileges on Amazon, create a directory for the source files of the sales domain.

    By default, the source files are located in the /etc directory. However, this location is undesirable because the same directory also contains the contents of the local files on the master server. All users would have access to the master-server maps, and the root password would be passed to all NIS clients by using the passwd map. Consequently, problems might arise for passwd and shadow files. Thus, a different location is recommended.

    In the case of XYZ, Inc., all the domains share only one name server, Everest. Therefore the source files of each domain should be stored in separate locations. However, the accounting and sales domains will share a single hosts file that lists all the systems in the entire XYZ, Inc. network.

    The source files for the sales domain will be in /var/yp/sales/etc.

    ```
    # cd /var/yp
    # mkdir sales; mkdir sales/etc
    ```

2. Copy all the source files, except the hosts file, to the new directory.

    The hosts file is shared by both domains. Thus, this file does not require a separate location and can remain in the /etc directory.

    ```
    # cp /etc/source-files /var/yp/sales/etc
    ```

3. Copy audit_user, auth_attr, exec_attr, and prof_attr files to the same directory.

    These files are used by RBAC in the Solaris OS.

4. Make sure that the contents of the source files in the newly created directory are correct.

    For example, the /var/yp/sales/etc/networks file should contain the IP addresses of the sales domain.

    The /etc/hosts file should contain all the IP addresses and corresponding host or system names in the entire XYZ, Inc. network.

    For more detailed information about these files and their contents, refer to the corresponding man page for each file.

10.2.4.4 Preparing the `Makefile` Script

The `Makefile` script prepares the name server to provide name services by using the information that is contained in the different source files.

1. Using a text editor, open the `/var/yp/Makefile` script.
2. On the appropriate lines in the file, specify the new directory locations of the specific source files.
    For example:

```
DIR=/var/yp/sales/etc
PWDIR=/var/yp/sales/etc
```

3. Enable domain name services (DNS) to provide naming services to the Internet.
    NIS does not perform naming services for systems that are not in the domain, such as systems on the Internet. Thus, you need to use DNS to resolve names when the client hosts in the two domains access the Internet.

    a. Add the comment mark (#) at the beginning of the line `B=`.
    b. Remove the comment mark at the beginning of the line `B=-b`.

    The lines in the script should appear as follows:

```
# B=
B=-b
```

4. Save the new information, and exit the text editor.

10.2.4.5 Setting Up the Name Server

This procedure creates the maps with information that the NIS server uses to resolve names and systems on the network.

1. Copy the `nsswitch.files` file to the `nsswitch.conf` file.
    The `nsswitch.files` file is the template whose contents are used to initially set up the name server. The contents of this file are copied to the `nsswitch.conf` file. The `nsswitch.conf` file is the actual configuration file that is used by the scripts to perform the initial setup.

    `# cp /etc/nsswitch.files /etc/nsswitch.conf`

2. Edit the `nsswitch.conf` file by inserting the following information to the `netmasks` line:
    `netmasks:files nis`

This line establishes NIS's lookup order when resolving system names. Specifically, local files are searched first before the NIS maps.

3. Build the new maps on the server by issuing the `ypinit` command.

   # **/usr/sbin/ypinit -m**

   You will need to provide certain information for the script to complete the process.

   - Machines to become NIS slave servers. Specify **Amazon** and its IP address.

   - Action to take at the first nonfatal error. Choose to terminate at the first nonfatal error. This option will force `ypinit` to exit upon encountering the first problem. You can then fix the error and restart `ypinit`. This option facilitates troubleshooting, especially if you are using `ypinit` for the first time.

   - Action to take on existing files in the `/yp/var/domainname` directory. Specify your preferred option. Note that this information is requested by the script only if you have previously installed NIS.

4. Enable NIS as the naming service.

   # **cp /etc/nsswitch.nis /etc/nsswitch.conf**

5. Start the server to enable DNS forwarding.

   # **svcadm restart network/nis/server:everest**

   With this command, the `ypserv` service automatically starts with the `-d` option to forward requests to DNS.

10.2.4.6 Enabling the Name Server to Support Multiple Domains

This procedure enables Amazon to provide naming services to the accounting domain in addition to the sales domain.

1. As superuser or an administrator with the proper RBAC privileges on Amazon, create a directory for the source files of the accounting domain. For example:

```
# cd /var/yp
# mkdir acctg; mkdir acctg/etc
```

2. Copy the source files, except the `hosts` file, to the new directory.
   # **cp /etc/**_source-files_ **/var/yp/acctg/etc**

3. Make sure that the contents of the source files are correct.

   For example, the `networks` file should contain the IP addresses of the accounting domain. You have already provided the content for the `/etc/hosts` file when you prepared the source files for the sales domain.

4. Push the source file data of the accounting domain, including the `passwd` file, so that the data is included in the NIS database.

   Note that the entire command should be typed in a single line.

   ```
   # make DOM=acctg.xyz.com DIR=/var/yp/acctg/etc PWDIR=/var/yp/acctg/etc passwd
   ```

5. Push the common `hosts` file that is shared by both domains so that the information is included in the NIS database.

   ```
   # make DOM=sales.xyz.com hosts
   # make DOM=acctg.xyz.com hosts
   ```

   The `hosts` file is in the default directory `/etc`. Thus, specifying the location is not necessary.

   After you complete this procedure, then Amazon as a name server can support both the accounting and sales domains of the XYZ, Inc. network.

10.2.4.7 How to Add NIS Users to the NIS Domain

After the NIS server and client hosts have been set up, you can add users to use the domains. Amazon is the NIS server for two domains. To prevent confusion, create users in one domain first, and then proceed to the next domain.

1. As superuser or an administrator with the proper RBAC privileges on Amazon, create a new user's login ID by using the `useradd` command.

   # **useradd** _userID_

   userID is the login ID of the new user. This command creates entries in the `/etc/passwd` and `/etc/shadow` files.

2. Issue the `passwd` command to create the new user's initial password.

   # **passwd** _userID_

3. At the prompt, provide a password for the new user.
   This password will serve as a temporary password for the user.

4. Copy the new entry to Amazon's `passwd` map input files.
   The map input files are located in the directories you created for the domains. Suppose that you are creating users for the sales domain. You would copy the new lines from the `/etc/passwd` and `/etc/shadow` files to the `/var/yp/sales/etc/passwd` file and `/var/yp/sales/etc/shadow` file, respectively.
   For example, if you added the new user `brown`, the line from the `/etc/passwd` file that you would copy to the password input file would look like the following:

   ```
   brown:x:123:10:User brown:/home/brown:/bin/csh:
   ```

   The line for `brown` that you would copy from the `/etc/shadow` file to the shadow input file would look like the following:

   ```
   brown:W12345GkHic:6445::::::
   ```

5. Delete the new user entry from the NIS server's local `/etc/passwd` and `/etc/shadow` files.

   ```
   # userdel userID
   ```

   Caution

   For security reasons, do not keep user entries in the NIS server's `/etc/passwd` and `/etc/shadow` files.

6. Make sure that the `/var/yp/Makefile` script correctly defines the directory where the password input files reside, depending on the domain for which you create users.
   For example, if you are creating users for the sales domain, then the `DIR` and `PWDIR` parameters in the `Makefile` script should specify the directory where the source files for the sales domain are located. When you create users for the accounting domain, change the `DIR` and `PWDIR` definitions so that they point to the directory where the source files for the accounting domain reside.

7. Update the `passwd` maps by issuing the `make` command on the source file directory.

   ```
   # cd /var/yp/sales/etc
   # /usr/ccs/bin/make passwd
   ```

8. Inform the user of the login ID and the temporary password you assigned. The user can change the password to a permanent one anytime by logging in with the temporary password and issuing the `passwd` command from a terminal window.

9. Follow the same steps to create users for the accounting domain.

10.2.4.8 How to Prepare a Client Host to Use the Naming Service

After you have configured the server to provide a naming service, you need to configure the clients in the domain to use the service. You must perform this procedure in each client system in the domain.

Perform the following steps:

1. As superuser or an administrator with the proper RBAC privileges on the client host, issue the following command.

   `# ypinit -c`

2. When prompted to list the NIS server, specify **Amazon**.

10.2.5 Setting Up a System for Static Routing

This section discusses static and dynamic routing as an introduction to configure Denali to use static routing.

10.2.5.1 Overview of Static and Dynamic Routing

Information about network routes can be provided to a system either manually or automatically. If a system's routing information is maintained manually, that system is configured with *static routing*. If routing information is provided to the system dynamically, then that configuration is called *dynamic routing*. In dynamic routing, the routing information is updated automatically by relying on routing protocols such as RIP for networks that use IPv4 addresses.

The Solaris OS supports both static and dynamic routing. You can configure either routing type on a single system. Within a single network, you can deploy a combination of both types of routing, where some systems use static routing while others use dynamic routing. Typically, dynamic routing is used because routing tables are updated dynamically.

Table 10.2 compares static, dynamic, and the combination of both types of routing, and for which network setup each type of routing can best be used.

Table 10.2 Types of Routing

Routing Type	Best Used On
Static	Small networks, hosts that obtain their routes from a default router, and default routers that are configured to detect only one or two routers on the next few hops.
Dynamic	Large networks, routers on local networks with many hosts, and hosts on large autonomous systems. Dynamic routing is the best choice for systems on most networks.
Combined static and dynamic	Routers that connect a statically routed network and a dynamically routed network, and border routers that connect an interior autonomous system with external networks.

10.2.5.2 How to Configure Denali with Static Routing

In XYZ, Inc.'s network, Denali in the sales domain is designated to be configured with static routing. This specific type of configuration requires an additional procedure that is not performed on the rest of the clients in the sales domain. This procedure consists of disabling routing in Denali and updating its routing table manually with additional static routes.

1. As superuser or an administrator with the proper RBAC privileges on Denali, configure this system by following the same steps used to configure Kilimanjaro in the sales domain.

   The following list summarizes those steps:

   a. Configure Denali's interface with a valid IP address for the sales domain.

   b. Create a persistent configuration by adding the information to the appropriate configuration files.

   c. Add Denali's domain name to the /etc/defaultdomain file. Denali belongs to the sales.xyz.com domain.

   d. Disable packet forwarding on Denali.

2. Add the router's default static route to the set of static routes. Edit the /etc/defaultrouter file by adding the IP address of Everest to the file.
   ```
   # route -p add default 192.168.5.70
   ```

3. Add an entry for the default router in Denali's /etc/hosts file.

   The file should already contain information from when you first created the persistent configuration. Suppose you assigned 192.168.5.76 to Denali. With the additional default router entry, the file should appear as follows:

   ```
   127.0.0.1      localhost loghost
   192.168.5.76   denali
   192.168.5.70   everest
   ```

4. Check whether routing is enabled on the system.

   ```
   # routeadm
   Configuration  Current                               Current
                  Option          Configuration         System State
   -----------------------------------------------------------------
                  IPv4 routing    enabled               disabled
                  IPv6 routing    disabled              disabled
                  IPv4 forwarding disabled              disabled
                  IPv6 forwarding disabled              disabled
                  Routing services 'route:default rping:default'
   ```

   The command output shows that routing is enabled.

5. Disable routing on Denali.

   # **svcadm disable route:default**

6. Perform a reconfiguration reboot.

   # **reboot -- r**

   Now that routing is disabled on Denali, any new routes need to be added to the routing table manually.

10.2.5.3 How to Add Routes Manually to the Routing Table

You perform this procedure anytime new routes are created on XYZ, Inc.'s network. Specifically for Denali, two new routes that traverse the 10.0.5.0 network need to be added.

- Route to the accounting domain using the multihomed host that you just configured.
- Route to Gobi, the NAT Box, whose IP address is 10.0.5.150.

1. View the current state of Denali's routing table.

```
# netstat -rn
Routing Table: Ipv4
Destination     Gateway         Flags   Ref   Use    Interface
-----------     --------------  ------  ----  -----  ----------
default         192.168.5.70    UG      1     249    bge0
224.0.0.0       192.168.5.70    U       1     0      bge0
127.0.0.1       127.0.0.1       UH      1     57     lo0
```

The routing table indicates only one route, which is the route to Everest on the 192.168.5.0 subnetwork. The IP address listed for the gateway in the default route belongs to Everest. The second route is still the 192.168.5.0 subnetwork, but the IP address is the subnetwork's multicast address. The third route in the table is for the loopback routing (127.0.0.1).

2. Add a route to Gobi by using its IP address.

```
# route -p add -net 10.0.5.0/24 -gateway 10.0.5.150/24
add net 10.0.5.0: gateway 10.0.5.150
```

3. Add a route to the accounting domain by using Amazon, the multihomed host.

```
# route -p add -net 192.168.5.0/26 -gateway 192.168.5.50/26
add net 192.168.5.0: gateway 192.168.5.50
```

This shorter route that uses the multihomed host helps reduce network congestion on the 10.0.5.0 network by not using the default route for packets destined to the accounting domain.

4. View the routing table.

The table now shows the two routes to the 10.0.5.0 network.

```
# netstat -rn
Routing Table: IPv4
Destination     Gateway         Flags   Ref   Use    Interface
-----------     --------        -----   ----  -----  ---------
default         192.168.5.70    UG      1     249    ce0
224.0.0.0       192.168.5.70    U       1     0      bge0
192.168.5.0     192.168.5.50    U       1     78     bge0
10.0.5.0        10.0.5.150      U       1     375    bge0
127.0.0.1       127.0.0.1       UH      1     57     lo0
```

10.2.6 Configuring the Corporate Domain

The xyz.com domain consists of the combination of all the components of the network, specifically the two domains, accounting and sales. The NAT box with the assigned name Gobi is a Solaris system that connects the internal corporate network to the rest of the Internet.

10.2.6.1 How to Configure the NAT Box

The following procedure describes how to configure the border router, with the assigned name Gobi.

1. As superuser or an administrator with the proper RBAC privileges on Gobi, determine which interfaces are physically installed.

    ```
    # dladm show-link
    ce0             type: legacy     mtu:1500    device:ce0
    bge0            type: non-vlan   mtu:1500    device:bge0
    ```

    The command output indicates that Gobi has two installed interfaces: ce0 and bge0.

2. Configure the interfaces with IP addresses to connect to the external and internal networks, respectively.

    ```
    # ifconfig ce0 plumb 123.45.67.89/8 up
    # ifconfig bge0 plumb 10.0.5.150/24 up
    ```

3. Verify the network configuration.

    ```
    # ifconfig -a
    lo0: flags=1000849 <UP,LOOPBACK,RUNNING,MULTICAST,IPv4> mtu 8232
    index 1
            inet 127.0.0.1 netmask ff000000
    ce0: flags=1000843<UP,BROADCAST,RUNNING,MULTICAST,IPv4>mtu 1500
    index 2
            inet 123.45.67.89 netmask ff000000 broadcast 192.255.255.255
            ether 8:0:20:c1:1b:c6
    bge0: flags=1000840<UP,BROADCAST,RUNNING,MULTICAST,IPv4>mtu 1500
    index 3
            inet 10.0.5.150 netmask ff000000 broadcast 10.255.255.255
            ether 8:0:20:e5:95:c4
    ```

4. Make the configurations persist across system reboots.

    a. Add the IP address 123.45.67.89/24 to the /etc/hostname.ce0 file.

    b.   Add the IP address `10.0.5.150/24` to the `/etc/hostname.bge0` file.

```
# echo 123.45.67.89/24 > /etc/hostname.ce0
# echo 10.0.5.150/24 > /etc/hostname.bge0
```

5.   Add the new IP addresses and the corresponding host names to the `/etc/hosts` file.
    For example:

```
127.0.0.1      local host
123.45.67.89  gobi-123456789 # interface external network
10.0.5.150  gobi-10050# interface xyz domain
```

    The two IP interfaces are given names to distinguish which interfaces connect to their corresponding networks.

6.   Add domain information in the `/etc/defaultdomain` file.
    For example:

xyz.com

7.   Enable packet forwarding and a routing protocol.

```
# svcadm enable ipv4-forwarding
# svcadm enable route:default
```

8.   Perform a reconfiguration reboot.

    `# reboot -- -r`

10.2.6.2 How to Configure Network Address Translation in the NAT Box

The NAT Box Gobi needs to be configured to perform network address translation. This feature maps the source addresses of the packets whose destinations are outside the company network to the company's externally visible `123.45.67.89` address. This mapping will allow those external recipients to reply to the NAT box without needing to know about the local or private addresses used within the company. The NAT box receives those replies and uses stateful-translation tables to map back to the original host.

    For more information about network address translation, see the `ipnat`(4) man page.

    To enable NAT, perform the following steps.

1. Navigate to the `/etc/ipf` directory.

2. Create the `ipnat.conf` file.

3. Add the following lines to the file:

```
map 192.168.5.0/26 --> 123.45.67.89/24
map 192.168.5.64/26 --> 123.45.67.89/24
map 10.0.5.0/24 --> 123.45.67.89/24
```

    With these rules, the XYZ, Inc. network can connect to systems on the Internet. However, the reverse is not true in order to implement security.

4. Enable the Solaris IP filter daemon.

    The daemon activates the feature that translates IP addresses according to the manner that the rules define.

    `# svcadm enable network/ipfilter`

    You can also define different IP filter rules to further enhance security on the corporate network. Refer to the appropriate *Solaris System Administration Guide* for more information. These reference guides will be listed at the end of the chapter.

10.2.7 Testing the Network Configuration

This section describes commands that you use to test the network and to ensure that client hosts can communicate with each other within their own subnetwork, with other clients in the other subnetworks, and finally to the Internet.

The following commands provide information about the general status of the network and its components:

-   `ping`

    Use this command to send ICMP echo requests from any selected host system. If the host replies, then traffic can flow between your system and the host. If the host does not respond, then the network is not passing traffic at all.

    By using the `-s -i` option, you can specify the `ping` command to send one datagram per second from a specific interface and then collect statistics.

    For more information about this command and its options, see the `ping`(1M) man page.

```
# ping www.google.com
www.google.com is alive
# ping -s -i hme0 www.google.com
PING www.google.com (74.125.19.147): 56 data bytes
64 bytes from 74.125.19.147: icmp_seq=0. time=3.59 ms
64 bytes from 74.125.19.147: icmp_seq=1. time=3.12 ms
64 bytes from 74.125.19.147: icmp_seq=2. time=3.66 ms
64 bytes from 74.125.19.147: icmp_seq=3. time=3.11 ms
64 bytes from 74.125.19.147: icmp_seq=4. time=3.01 ms
64 bytes from 74.125.19.147: icmp_seq=5. time=3.05 ms
^C
----www.google.com PING Statistics----
6 packets transmitted, 6 packets received, 0% packet loss
round-trip (ms)  min/avg/max/stddev = 3.01/3.26/3.66/0.29
```

- getent

  Use this command to obtain a list of entries from a given database. The information generally comes from one or more of the sources that are specified for the database in the /etc/nsswitch.conf file. Thus, this command can indicate if /etc/nsswitch.conf has been correctly set up. For more information, see the getent(1M) man page.

```
# getent hosts
127.0.0.1        localhost
192.168.5.70     everest
10.0.5.150       gobi
...
```

- nslookup

  This command starts a program to query name servers, including name servers on the Internet. The command indicates whether the /etc/resolv.conf file has been configured correctly. For more information, see the nslookup(1M) man page.

  Suppose that you issue the command from a client host with the IP address 192.168.5.13. The first example queries the system Tigris in XYZ, Inc.'s network. The second example queries a server external to XYZ, Inc.'s network.

```
# nslookup tigris
Server:         192.168.5.13
Address:        192.168.5.13#53

Name:   tigris.xyz.com
Address: 192.168.5.10
```

continues

```
# nslookup google.com
Server:         192.168.5.13
Address:        192.168.5.13#53

Non-authoritative answer:
Name:   google.com
Address: 74.125.45.100
Name:   google.com
Address: 209.85.171.100
Name:   google.com
Address: 72.14.205.100
```

10.3 Monitoring Network Performance

You can monitor the performance of your network by using the following common commands that provide information about the network:

- dladm
- ifconfig
- netstat
- snoop
- traceroute

10.3.1 dladm Command

The dladm command is used on the data-link layer of the TCP/IP networking stack. The two most common forms of this command are the dladm show-dev command and the dladm show-link command to show existing links on the system.

```
# dladm show-dev
LINK  STATE SPEED     DUPLEX
eri0  up    100Mb     full
```

The dladm show-dev command displays the current network devices that are installed on your system, their current state, speed, and duplex mode, which can be either half or full.

```
# dladm show-link
ce0    type: legacy     mtu:1500     device:ce0
bge0   type: non-vlan   mtu:1500     device:bge0
bge1   type: non-vlan   mtu: 1500    device: bge1
```

The `dladm  show-link` command lists links that are configured on top of the devices in your system. The command also shows the maximum packet size for transmission (MTU) and the type of device. The link names take the name of their corresponding device names. Thus, in the sample output, the `ce0` link is configured over the `ce0` device. For an introduction, see Section 10.1.1, "Overview of the TCP/IP Networking Stack," at the beginning of this chapter.

10.3.2 `ifconfig` Command

The `ifconfig` command can also be used to obtain information about interfaces on the IP layer of the TCP/IP stack. Use `ifconfig *interface*` to obtain information about a specific interface, or use `ifconfig  -a` to see information about all the interfaces.

```
# ifconfig -a
lo0: flags=2001000849<UP,LOOPBACK,RUNNING,MULTICAST,IPv4,VIRTUAL> mtu 8232 index 1
        inet 127.0.0.1 netmask ff000000
e1000g0: flags=1000843<UP,BROADCAST,RUNNING,MULTICAST,IPv4> mtu 1500 index 2
        inet 129.145.154.95 netmask ffffff80 broadcast 129.145.154.127
```

The command output also indicates whether a specific interface is UP. If the UP flag does not appear for a given interface, then that interface cannot receive or transmit network traffic. The `ifconfig` command also displays the IP address that is assigned to an interface.

10.3.3 `netstat` Command

The `netstat` command shows network status and protocol statistics. You can display the status of TCP, SCTP, and UDP endpoints in table format. Likewise, you can display routing table and interface information.

You issue the `netstat` command by using the syntax `netstat  *options*`. The command displays various types of network data, depending on the selected command line option. If you combine an option with another option such as `-n`, then network addresses will be displayed as numbers instead of symbols.

Table 10.3 lists selected options that might be most useful for monitoring the network. For detailed information about these options and other options you can use with the command, refer to the `netstat`(1M) man page.

The following examples show output that is generated by the `netstat` command when it is combined with different options.

Table 10.3 Options for the Netstat Command

Option	Displayed Information
-s	Statistics per protocol. All protocols are included in the command output, such as IP, IGMP, IPMP, RAWIP, SCTP, TCP, and UDP.
-P protocol	Statistics about the specified protocol.
-i	Status and other information about each network interface on the system.
-a	Status of sockets on the local system.
-f inet | inet6	Statistics about a family of addresses, either IPv4 addresses if you specify inet, or IPv6 addresses if you specify inet6.
-r	Routing-table information.
-D	Status of interfaces that are configured for DHCP.
-n	Used in combination with any of the previously listed options where applicable. Displays network addresses as numbers instead of symbols.

- **netstat -rn**

```
Routing Table: IPv4
Destination          Gateway              Flags    Ref    Use      Interface
--------------------  --------------      -----    ----   -----    -----------
default              192.168.5.70         UG       1      249      ce0
224.0.0.0            192.168.5.70         U        1      0        bge0
10.0.5.0             10.0.5.10            U        1      78       bge0
10.0.5.0             10.0.5.150           U        1      375      bge0
127.0.0.1            127.0.0.1            UH       1      57       lo0
```

- **netstat -P *transport-protocol***

```
TCP: IPv4
Local Address Remote Address           Swind Send-Q Rwind Recv-Q State
------------- ---------------          ----- ------ ----- ------ -----
lhost-1.login abc.def.local.Sun.COM.980      49640      0 49640      0 ESTABLISHED
lhost.login   ghi.jkl.local.Sun.COM.1020 49640      1 49640      0 ESTABLISHED
remhost.1014  mno.pqr.remote.Sun.COM.nfsd 49640      0 49640      0 TIME_WAIT

TCP: IPv6
Local Address   Remote Address   Swind Send-Q Rwind Recv-Q State If
-------------   --------------   ----- ------ ----- ------ --------
localhost.38983 localhost.32777 49152      0 49152      0 ESTABLISHED
localhost.32777 localhost.38983 49152      0 49152      0 ESTABLISHED
localhost.38986 localhost.38980 49152      0 49152      0 ESTABLISHED
```

- `netstat -i`

```
Name Mtu   Net/Dest  Address    Ipkts    Ierrs   Opkts   Oerrs   Collis   Queue
lo0  8232  loopback  localhost   142        0     142       0       0       0
hme0 1500  host58    host58    1106302      0   52419       0       0       0
```

- `netstat -f inet`

```
TCP: IPv4
Local Address  Remote Address   Swind Send-Q  Rwind  Recv-Q   State
------------   --------------   ----- ------   -----  ------   -------
host58.734     host19.nfsd      49640     0    49640       0   ESTABLISHED
host58.38063   host19.32782     49640     0    49640       0   CLOSE_WAIT
host58.38146   host41.43601     49640     0    49640       0   ESTABLISHED
host58.996     remote-host.login 49640   0    49206       0   ESTABLISHED
```

10.3.4 `snoop` Command

You can use the `snoop` command to monitor the state of data transfers. The command captures network packets and displays their contents in the format that you specify. Packets can be displayed as soon as they are received, or saved to a file. You must assume the Network Management role or become superuser to use the snoop utility.

To capture `snoop` output into a file, use the `-o` *filename* option, as follows:

`# snoop -o /tmp/s-log`

Then, to view the contents of the log, use the `-i` *filename* option. The contents would be similar to the following example:

```
# snoop -i /tmp/s-log
1 0.00000 fe80::a00:20ff:fee9:2d27 -> fe80::a00:20ff:fecd:4375 ICMPv6 Neighbor adver-
tisement
2 0.16198 farhost.com -> myhost RLOGIN C port=985
3 0.00008 myhost -> farhost.com RLOGIN R port=985
10 0.91493 10.0.0.40 -> (broadcast) ARP C Who is 10.0.0.40, 10.0.0.40 ?
34 0.43690 nearserver.here.com -> 224.0.1.1 IP D=224.0.1.1 S=10.0.0.40 LEN=28,
ID=47453, TO =0x0, TTL=1
35 0.00034 10.0.0.40 -> 224.0.1.1 IP D=224.0.1.1 S=10.0.0.40 LEN=28, ID=57376, TOS=0x0,
TTL=47
```

More options for this command can be obtained in the snoop(1M) man page.

10.3.5 `traceroute` Command

The `traceroute` command traces the route an IP packet follows to a remote host. You use the `traceroute` command to uncover any routing misconfiguration and routing path failures. If a particular host is unreachable, you can use `traceroute` to see what path the packet follows to the remote host and where possible failures might occur.

The `traceroute` command also displays the round-trip time for each hop along the path to the target host. This information can be useful for analyzing whether traffic is slow between the two hosts.

The following example displays a packet's route from the local system to the remote system `farhost`. The output shows the seven-hop path the packet follows from the local system. The output also shows the time it took for a packet to traverse each hop.

```
% traceroute farhost.faraway.com
traceroute to farhost.faraway.com (172.16.64.39(, 30 hops max, 40 byte packets
1 frbldg7c-86 (172.16.18.1) 1.516 ms 1.283 ms 1.362 ms
2 bldg1a-001 (172.16.1.211) 2.277 ms 1.773 ms 2.186 ms
3 bldg4-bldg1 (172.16.4.42) 1.978 ms 1.986 ms 13.996 ms
4 bldg6-bldg4 (172.16.4.49) 2.655 ms 3.042 ms 2.344 ms
5 ferbldg11a-001 (172.16.1.236) 2.636 ms 3.432 ms 3.830 ms
6 frbldg12b-153 (172.16.153.72) 3.452 ms 3.146 ms 2.962 ms
7 farhost (172.16.64.39) 3.430 ms 3.312 ms 3.451 ms
```

To trace all the routes from the local system, use the option `-a`, as follows:

```
% traceroute -a local-host
```

For more technical details about the `traceroute` command, see the `traceroute`(1M) man page.

References

man pages section 1: User Commands
(http://docs.sun.com/app/docs/doc/816-5165)

man pages section 1M: System Administration Commands
(http://docs.sun.com/app/docs/doc/816-5166)

Solaris 10 10/08 Installation Guide: Basic Installations
(http://docs.sun.com/app/docs/doc/820-5236?l=en)

System Administration Guide: IP Services
(http://docs.sun.com/app/docs/doc/816-4554)

System Administration Guide: Naming and Directory Service (DNS, NIS, and LDAP) (http://docs.sun.com/app/docs/doc/816-4556)

11

Solaris User Management

The Solaris Operating System (Solaris OS) utilizes user accounts for authentication at login. These accounts are also used to grant permissions to access files and to run programs. A user account can be specific to a particular system or for a group of systems on a network. In an enterprise environment, a system administrator typically manages the users and groups for the enterprise by using a centralized naming service or directory service, such as LDAP or NIS. In a smaller environment, user account data is more likely to be stored in local files.

This chapter includes information about managing user accounts and groups and briefly describes the relationship between users and roles. This chapter also includes examples that show how to manage users, groups, and roles.

11.1 Solaris Users, Groups, and Roles

A *user* is an individual who can access a system and its resources. To gain access to a system, a user must log in. The login process includes an authentication step where the user specifies his or her user name and password. The information supplied at login is compared to authentication information that is stored on the system or in a centralized naming service. If the user name and password match, the user is granted access to the system. If the user name and password do not match, the user is denied access to the system.

In addition to authentication, the Solaris OS bases access to files and programs on the user. File and directory permissions determine whether a user can access a resource and run particular programs.

Most Solaris users are unprivileged. Such users can only access their own files and public files, and they can run unprivileged programs that do not affect the running of the system. The Solaris OS also has privileged users, most notably the `root` user, who is also known as superuser. *Superuser* can access any file or run any program on the local system. Superuser has more privileges than needed to perform many privileged operations.

The Solaris OS also uses special accounts called roles. A *role* is like a user, but it cannot directly access the system and can only be assumed by users who are granted the right to do so. When permitted, an unprivileged user can assume a role to perform limited privileged operations based on the rights that are granted to that role. Rights might include the ability to execute programs as privileged user IDs or group IDs or by using additional Solaris privileges or authorizations that enable certain functions in applications, such as the Solaris Management Console (`smc`). Roles can be used to divide administrative tasks into several smaller tasks. A user can assume a particular role to manage that task, such as Printer Administration, User Administration, and so on.

A *group* is a collection of users that is typically used for setting group owner-ship on files and directories. Groups are divided into two types: primary groups and supplementary groups. Each user must be a member of a primary group, which is `staff` by default. Supplementary groups are optional, and a user can belong to several such groups. For example, all employees belong to the `staff` group, which is the primary group. All employees who are staff members in the sales group can also belong to the `sales` supplementary group. When accessing files and directories that have the `sales` group owner, the group file permissions are checked to determine whether to permit or deny access. For information about file permissions, see Section 11.1.1, "File System Object Permissions."

By default, users, groups, and roles are managed in local files on the system. When running a networked environment, you might consider using a naming ser-vice to store account information. A *naming service*, also called a *directory service*, is a centralized repository in which to store account information for users, groups, and roles. The service provides this account information to all systems on the net-work. For multisystem installations, using a naming service is more efficient than maintaining these accounts locally on individual systems. The Solaris OS supports the LDAP and NIS naming services. For more information, see Chapter 13, "Using Naming Services."

11.1.1 File System Object Permissions

Access to file system objects such as files, directories, and devices depend on user and group information as well as access modes. Each file system object has a user owner, a group owner, and a mode. The mode determines what kind of access can be granted to the user owner, group owner, and others who attempt to access that object.

For example, the sandy user has created a file called /home/sandy/readme. The file's ownership, permissions, size, modification time, and number of links are shown by using the ls -l command:

```
$ ls -l /home/sandy/readme
-rw-r--r--   1 sandy staff       3637 Oct  1 14:10 /home/sandy/readme
$
```

The output shows that sandy is the user owner of the /home/sandy/readme file and that staff is the group owner. The output also shows the mode of the file, which is represented by the following ten bits: -rw-r--r--. The first bit indicates the type of file entry. In this example, the first bit, -, indicates that the entry is an ordinary file. The remaining bits are grouped into three sets of three bits. The first set represents the access mode for the user owner, the second set is for the group owner, and the third set is for others. The example shows that sandy can read and write the file (rw-), while the staff group and others can only read the file (r--r--). The third bit in each set represents the execute bit. For example, the /bin/cat executable has permissions that give read and execute access to the user owner, the group owner, and others: -r-xr-xr-x.

For information about the ls command and file permission modes, see the ls(1) and chmod(1) man pages. You can also view man pages by using the man command (see the man(1) man page). For example, run the following command to see the man page for the ls command:

$ **man ls**

If you own a file system object, you can use the chmod command to manipulate the mode to ensure that the object has appropriate read, write, and execute permissions. If you do not own the file or directory, however, then access to the object depends on the following:

- Permissions specified for group or other
- Whether you or your groups are listed in an access control list (ACL) that is associated with that object (see the getfacl(1) man page)

11.1.2 User Account Components

Solaris user accounts are comprised of several components including user names, group names, user and group IDs, and so on. This section describes the principal user account components. Most of this information is specified in the user account repository, which on local systems is the `/etc/passwd` file. Encrypted passwords for each user account are stored in the `/etc/shadow` file, and group information is stored in the `/etc/group` file.

A *user name* is the name by which a user accesses a system and its resources. A user name is also referred to as a *login name*. A user name can be from two to eight characters in length and can include alphanumeric characters. The first character of a user name must be an alphabetic character, and at least one character must be a lowercase letter.

A *password* is a secret character sequence that is associated with the user's login name. The user should avoid creating a password that is easy to guess or that appears in a dictionary. At login, a user authenticates his or her user name and password to gain access to the system. The length of the password depends on the hash algorithm, which is configured in the `/etc/security/policy.conf` file. The password complexity rules, history, and password-aging defaults are specified in the `/etc/default/passwd` file. For more information, see the Solaris 10 *System Administration Guide: Security Services* on `http://docs.sun.com`.

A *user ID (UID)* is a unique numerical ID that is associated with a specific user name. A UID for a regular user can be between 100 and 2147483647 (except for 60001, 60002, and 65534). UIDs 0–99, 60001, 60002, and 65534 are reserved for use by the Solaris OS. Also, avoid using UIDs over 60000 because they are not compatible with some Solaris features. To avoid file ownership problems between systems on a network, ensure that each user name matches the same UID for all systems. For information about reserved UIDs and UID incompatibility issues with some Solaris features, see the Solaris 10 *System Administration Guide: Basic Administration* on `http://docs.sun.com`.

A *group name* is the name of a user group, which is a collection of users. When a user account is created, the user is assigned to a primary group by specifying the group ID (GID) of the group. The default user group is `staff`, which uses GID 10. A user can also belong to other, supplementary groups by adding the user name to the appropriate group entry in the `/etc/group` file. To change a user's primary group, you must modify the GID in the user's account.

A *group ID (GID)* is the unique numerical ID that is associated with each group. To view existing group information, see the `/etc/group` file. Typically, GIDs are assigned from the unused integers between 100 and 60000.

A *home directory*, or *login directory*, is the space allocated to each user for storing files. The home directory can be on a local system or on a file server so that it can be made available to other systems on the network.

The *login shell* is the shell program that the user runs by default. If no shell is specified, the shell is /usr/bin/sh.

Users can customize their environment by configuring *user profiles* that are stored in their home directory. Depending on the user's shell, the .profile, .login, or .cshrc file is read at login to set up the customized environment. For more information about user profiles, see the various shell man pages (such as sh(1), ksh(1), bash(1), and csh(1)). For information about customizing a user's environment, see the Solaris 10 *System Administration Guide: Basic Administration* on http://docs.sun.com.

11.1.3 User Management Tools

The Solaris OS has several tools for managing users, groups, and roles. The Solaris Management Console (smc) uses a graphical user interface (GUI) while the following tools use a command line interface (CLI):

- useradd, usermod, userdel—Add, modify, and delete a local user account, respectively
- groupadd, groupmod, groupdel—Add, modify, and delete a local group, respectively
- roleadd, rolemod, roledel—Add, modify, and delete a local role, respectively
- smuser, smgroup, smrole—Manage local or NIS user accounts, groups, and roles, respectively

For examples that show how to use some of these commands, see Section 11.2, "Managing Users and Groups," and Section 11.3, "Managing Roles." For detailed information about the syntax that is used by these commands, see the useradd(1M), usermod(1M), userdel(1M), groupadd(1M), groupmod(1M), groupdel(1M), roleadd(1M), rolemod(1M), roledel(1M), smuser(1M), smgroup(1M), smrole(1M), and smc(1M) man pages.

11.1.4 User Management Files

The following files are used to store information related to users, groups, and roles:

- /etc/passwd—Stores user account information, such as the user name, UID, GID of the user's primary group, home directory, and login shell
  The following are some example /etc/passwd entries:

```
sandy:x:1003:102:Sandy D.:/export/home/sandy:/usr/ksh
terry:x:1004:103:Terry M.:/export/home/terry:/usr/ksh
```

- `/etc/shadow`—Stores password information for user accounts, such as the user name, encrypted password, and password-aging criteria
  The following are some example `/etc/shadow` entries:

```
sandy:x7AMq48Sr92:13879:2:365:30:90:14244
terry:Qx20RsM36c5:13980:2:365:30:90:14255
```

- `/etc/group`—Stores group information, such as the group name, an optional password, GID, and a list of users who are members of the group
  The following are some example `/etc/group` entries:

```
sales::102:sandy
tech::103:terry
```

- `/etc/user_attr`—Stores the list of authorizations and profiles associated with users and roles
  The following are some example `/etc/user_attr` entries:

```
operadm2:::::profiles=Media Restore,Operator;type=role
root:::::auths=solaris.*,solaris.grant;profiles=Web Console
Management,All;lock_after_retries=no;type=role
```

For more information about the structure of these files, see the `passwd`(4), `shadow`(4), `group`(4), and `user_attr`(4) man pages.

11.2 Managing Users and Groups

This section includes examples that show how to manage Solaris user accounts and groups.

11.2.1 Starting the Solaris Management Console

To start the Solaris Management Console, run the following command:

```
# /usr/sbin/smc &
```

Figure 11.1 shows the User Tool of the Solaris Management Console. From the User Tool, you can manage user accounts, user templates, rights, roles, groups, and mailing lists.

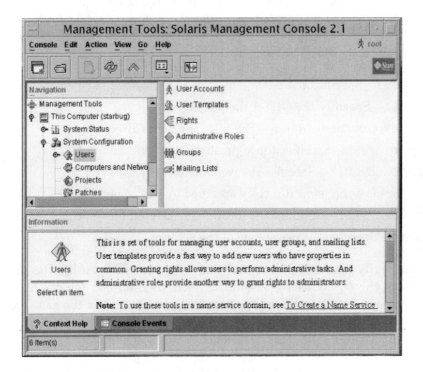

Figure 11.1 Solaris Management Console

For more information, see the smc(1M) man page. For information about using the Solaris Management Console GUI to manage users and groups, see the Solaris 10 *System Administration Guide: Basic Administration* on http://docs.sun.com.

11.2.2 Adding a Group and a User to Local Files

The following example shows how to use the groupadd and useradd commands to add the group sales and the user sandy to files on the local system. These commands cannot be used to manage users and groups in an environment that uses a naming service.

Before you create a group or a user, first determine the group name or user name, and the associated GID or UID, respectively.

First, use the groupadd command to create the new sales group, which has a GID of 102. You can verify that the group has been created by using the grep command to find the sales group entry in the /etc/group file.

Next, create the sandy user account. When you create a user account, you need to specify the relevant account information. The following describes the useradd syntax that is used to create the sandy user account:

- -u 1003—Specifies the UID
- -g 102—Specifies the GID of the primary group
- -d /export/home/sandy—Specifies the home directory
- -s /bin/ksh—Specifies the login shell
- -c "Sandy D."—Specifies the real name of the user
- -m—Creates the home directory specified by the -d option
- -k /etc/skel—Specifies the location of skeleton files, such as .profile
- sandy—Specifies the user name of the account

You can verify that the user account has been created by using the grep command to find the sandy user entry in the /etc/passwd file. You can also use the grep command to see that the sandy user is now a member of the sales group by checking the /etc/group file.

The following shows the commands used by the example:

```
# groupadd -g 102 sales
# grep "^sales" /etc/group
sales::102:
# useradd -u 1003 -g 102 -d /export/home/sandy -s /bin/ksh \
-c "Sandy D." -m -k /etc/skel sandy
64 blocks
# grep "^sandy" /etc/passwd
sandy:x:1003:102:Sandy D.:/export/home/sandy:/usr/ksh
# grep "^sales" /etc/group
sales::102:sandy
#
```

For more information, see the groupadd(1M) and useradd(1M) man pages.

11.2.3 Adding a Group and a User to an NIS Domain

The following example shows how to use the smgroup and smuser commands to add the tech group and the terry user to the starlite host of the solar.com NIS domain.

First, create the new tech group, which has a GID of 103. The following describes the smgroup options that are used to create the tech group:

- -D nis:/starlite/solar.com—Specifies the default domain
- -- —Specifies that the following options are for the smgroup add subcommand:
  - -g 103—Specifies the GID of the group
  - -n tech—Specifies the group name of the account

You can verify that the group has been created by using the grep command to find the tech group entry in the /etc/group file.

Next, create the terry user account. When you create a user account, you need to specify the relevant account information. The following describes the smuser options that are used to create the terry user account:

- -D nis:/starlite/solar.com—Specifies the default domain
- -- —Specifies that the following options are for the smuser add subcommand:
  - -u 1004—Specifies the UID
  - -n terry—Specifies the user name of the account
  - -c "Terry M."—Specifies the real name of the user
  - -d /export/home/terry—Specifies the home directory
  - -s /bin/ksh—Specifies the login shell
  - -g tech—Specifies the name of the primary group

You can verify that the user account has been created by using the grep command to find the terry user entry in the /etc/passwd file. You can also use the grep command to see that the terry user is now a member of the tech group by checking the /etc/group file.

The following shows the commands used by the example:

```
# /usr/sadm/bin/smgroup add -D nis:/starlite/solar.com -- -g 103 -n tech
# grep "^tech" /etc/group
tech::103:
# /usr/sadm/bin/smuser add -D nis:/starlite/solar.com -- -u 1004 \
-n terry -c "Terry M." -d /export/home/terry -s /bin/ksh -g tech
# grep "^terry" /etc/passwd
terry:x:1004:103:Terry M.:/export/home/terry:/usr/ksh
# grep "^tech" /etc/group
tech::103:terry
#
```

For more information, see the smgroup(1M) and smuser(1M) man pages.

11.3 Managing Roles

This section includes examples that show how to manage roles. The first example shows how to change the root user to a role. The second example shows how to list the configured roles on the system, and the third example shows how a user can assume a role.

11.3.1 Changing root from a User to a Role

This example shows how to change root from a login user to a role.

When root is a role, root can no longer directly log in to the system except in single-user mode. To become root, a user must first log in to the system and assume the root role. As a result, the user's login ID, not the "anonymous" root user, is logged by the Solaris auditing service.

Before you can change a user to a role, you must have sufficient privileges to perform user management tasks. In this example, the primaryadm role has sufficient privileges.

Next, ensure that no one is already logged in as the root user. If root is logged in, then have the root user log out. Then, use the usermod command to change the root user into a role and use the grep command to verify that the root role is listed in the /etc/user_attr file. The -K type=role option changes the specified user into a role.

As a failsafe measure, ensure that at least one local user is assigned the root role. The example uses the usermod command to assign the root role to local user jan. The -R root option specifies which role to assign to the specified user.

Next, the example shows how to use the su command to become the jan user. The roles command shows a list of roles, if any, that the specified user can assume. If no user is specified, the roles command shows the roles for the logged-in user.

Finally, the `jan` user uses the `su` command to assume the `root` role. The following shows the commands used by the example:

```
$ su - primaryadm
Password: primaryadm-password
# who | grep "^root"
# usermod -K type=role root
# grep root /etc/user_attr
root:::::type=role;auths=solaris.*,solaris.grant;profiles=Web Console
# usermod -R root jan
# exit
$ su - jan
Enter password:   jan-password
$ roles
root
$ su - root
Enter password:   root-password
#
```

For more information, see the `usermod(1M)` man page. For information about using the Solaris Management Console GUI to manage roles, see the Solaris 10 *System Administration Guide: Security Services* on `http://docs.sun.com`.

To configure the `root` role in an environment that uses a naming service, see "How to Make `root` User Into a Role" in the Solaris 10 *System Administration Guide: Security Services*.

Like the `root` user, the `root` role has a lot of power, so the Solaris OS offers a more fine-grained privilege model called *role-based access control (RBAC)*. For information about RBAC, see the Solaris 10 *System Administration Guide: Security Services*.

11.3.2 Viewing the List of Roles

The following example shows how to use the `smrole list` command to view the list of configured roles. Note that you must include the `--` option to show the list of roles.

```
$ /usr/sadm/bin/smrole list --
Authenticating as user: primaryadm

Type /? for help, pressing <enter> accepts the default denoted by [ ]
Please enter a string value for: password :: primaryadm-password

Loading Tool: com.sun.admin.usermgr.cli.role.UserMgrRoleCli from starlite
Login to starlite as user primaryadm was successful.
Download of com.sun.admin.usermgr.cli.role.UserMgrRoleCli from starlite was successful.
root                0                Superuser
primaryadm          100              Most powerful role
sysadmin            101              Performs non-security admin tasks
operadm             102              Backup Operator
operadm2            103              Backup/Restore Operator
$
```

For more information, see the `smrole(1M)` man page.

11.3.3 Assigning a Role to a Local User

In this example, the `usermod` command assigns the `operadm2` role to user `dana`. The `operadm2` role administers backup and restore operations. The `-R operadm2` option specifies the role to assign to user `dana`. After assigning the role to a user, use the `svcadm` command to restart the naming service cache daemon.

Next, the `root` user uses the `su - dana` command to become the `dana` user. User `dana` then assumes the `operadm2` role to perform the backup and restore operations for the system.

```
# usermod -R operadm2 dana
# svcadm restart system/name-service-cache
# su - dana
Password: dana-password
% su - operadm2
Password: operadm2-password
Confirm Password: operadm2-password
$ /usr/ucb/whoami
operamd2
$
```

For more information, see the `usermod(1M)` man page. For information about using the Solaris Management Console GUI to manage roles, see the Solaris 10 *System Administration Guide: Security Services.*

12

Solaris Zones

This chapter describes basic Solaris Zones concepts and provides common procedures for using this feature.

12.1 Overview

The Solaris 10 Operating System (Solaris 10 OS) introduced an operating system-level virtualization feature called *Solaris Zones*, also known as *Solaris Containers*. Resource management features available in the operating system are used with zones to form containers, referred to simply as zones. Zones impose little or no overhead. A non-global zone is a virtualized operating system environment created within a single instance of the Solaris Operating System, known as the global zone. Thus, the global zone is the Solaris 10 OS.

The zones software partitioning technology provides an isolated environment for running applications. This isolation prevents processes that are running in one zone from monitoring or affecting processes running in other zones. A process assigned to a zone can manipulate, monitor, and directly communicate with other processes that are assigned to the same zone. The process cannot perform these functions with processes that are assigned to other zones in the system or with processes that are not assigned to a zone.

A zone also provides an abstract layer that separates applications from the machine's physical attributes, such as physical device paths. Zones provide a virtualized environment that can hide details such as physical devices and the system's primary IP address and host name from applications.

Zones can be used on any machine that is running at least the Solaris 10 release. The upper limit for the number of zones on a system is 8192. The number of zones that can be effectively hosted on a single system is determined by the total resource requirements of the application software running in all of the zones.

As shown in Figure 12.1, zones are ideal for environments that consolidate a number of applications on a single server. The cost and complexity of managing numerous machines make it advantageous to consolidate several applications on larger, more scalable servers. Zones allow you to delegate some administrative functions while maintaining overall system security.

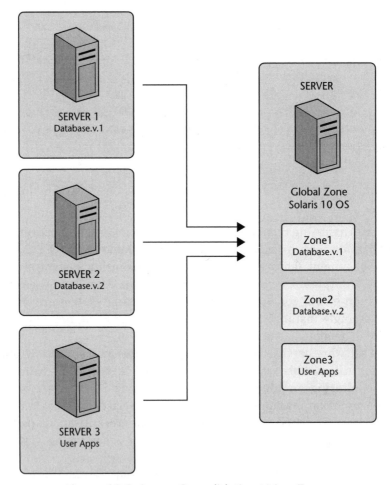

Figure 12.1 Server Consolidation Using Zones

12.2 How Zones Work

Every Solaris system contains a global zone. The global zone is the Solaris operating system instance. After installing Solaris 10 on a system, if no non-global zones are created, all processes run in the global zone. The global zone has a dual function. It is both the default zone for the system, and the zone used for system-wide administrative control. After you create a running non-global zone, it has processes that are associated with that non-global zone and no other zone. Any processes created by a process in a non-global zone are also associated only with that zone.

A non-global zone can be thought of as a box. One or more applications can run in this box without interacting with the rest of the system. Zones isolate software applications or services by using flexible, software-defined boundaries. Applications that are running in the same instance of the Solaris Operating System can then be managed independently of one other. Thus, different versions of the same application can be run in different zones, to match the requirements of your configuration. Each zone can provide a customized set of services. A non-global zone looks like a separate Solaris instance to users or applications in the zone.

Unprivileged processes in the global zone might be able to perform operations not allowed to privileged processes in a non-global zone. For example, users in the global zone can view information about every process in the system. If this capability presents a problem for your site, then you can restrict access to the global zone.

A zone provides isolation at almost any level of granularity you require. A zone does not need a dedicated CPU, a physical device, or a portion of physical memory. These resources can either be multiplexed across a number of zones running within a single domain or system, or allocated on a per-zone basis using the resource management features available in the operating system. This allows the use of zones both on large systems, where dedicated resources might be most appropriate, and on smaller ones, where a greater degree of sharing is necessary. It also allows administrators to make appropriate tradeoffs based on the relative importance of resource isolation versus utilization.

There are two models for the operating system file layout for a Solaris non-global zone. The default zone model is called the *sparse-root* zone. Sparse-root zones optimize physical memory and disk space usage by sharing some directories with the global zone. Only a subset of the packages installed in the global zone is installed directly into the non-global zone. Read-only loopback file systems, identified as `inherit-pkg-dir` resources, are used to gain access to other files. Sparse-root zones have their own private file areas for directories such as `/etc` and `/var`.

The second zones model, the *whole-root* zone, enhances configuration flexibility, but increases resource usage. These zones do not use shared file systems for `/lib`, `/platform`, `/sbin`, and `/usr`. The advantages of this model include the capability for global administrators to customize their zone's file system layout. This would be done, for example, to add arbitrary unbundled or third-party packages.

The zone model is two-level: One global zone and one or more non-global zones. Non-global zones are created from the global zone, and each non-global zone must be contained within the global zone.

12.3 Branded Zones

All zones have an associated brand, including default native zones created on a Solaris 10 system. The branded zone (BrandZ) framework extends the Solaris Zones infrastructure to include the creation of brands. The term *brand* can refer to a wide range of operating environments. BrandZ enables the creation of non-global zones that contain non-native operating environments used for running applications. The brand type is used to determine the scripts that are executed when a zone is installed and booted. In addition, a zone's brand is used to properly identify the correct application type at application launch time. All brand management is performed through extensions to the current zones structure.

Using the appropriate brand module, it is possible to run binaries that were built for another operating system. For example, the `lx` brand uses the branded zones framework to enable Linux binary applications to run unmodified on a machine with a Solaris Operating System kernel.

12.4 Network Interfaces in Zones

Zone network interfaces configured by the `zonecfg` command to provide network connectivity will automatically be set up and placed in the zone when the zone is booted. The Internet Protocol (IP) layer accepts and delivers packets for the network. This layer includes IP routing, the Address Resolution Protocol (ARP), IP security architecture (IPsec), and IP Filter.

Two IP types are available for networked non-global zones, shared-IP and exclusive-IP. Both shared-IP zones and exclusive-IP zones can be used on the same machine.

The shared-IP zone shares a network interface with the global zone, and the exclusive-IP zone must have a dedicated network interface. Full IP-level functionality is available in an exclusive-IP zone. Exclusive-IP zones always communicate with each other over the physical network. That communication can be restricted by using the IP Filter from within such zones, just as it can for a separate system. Traffic between two shared-IP zones stays in the computer unless a default router is assigned for one or both zones. Traffic from a zone with a default router goes out to the router before coming back to the destination zone. Only shared-IP network configurations are supported in an lx branded zone.

12.5 Devices in Zones

The set of devices available within a zone is restricted to prevent a process in one zone from interfering with processes running in other zones. For example, a process in a zone cannot modify kernel memory or modify the contents of the root disk. Thus, by default, only certain pseudo-devices that are considered safe for use in a zone are available. However, if required, additional devices can be made accessible for use within a specific zone by using the zonecfg utility.

The devfs file system is used by the Solaris system to manage /devices. Each element in this namespace represents the physical path to a hardware device, pseudo-device, or nexus device. The namespace is a reflection of the device tree. As such, the file system is populated by a hierarchy of directories and device special files.

The /dev file hierarchy, which is today part of the / (root) file system, consists of symbolic links, or logical paths, to the physical paths present in /devices. Applications reference the logical path to a device presented in /dev. The /dev file system is loopback-mounted into the zone using a read-only mount. Subsystems that rely on /devices path names are not able to run in non-global zones until /dev path names are established.

12.6 Packages and Patches in a Zones Environment

The packaging and patch tools work in a zones-enabled environment. The root file system for a non-global zone can be administered from the global zone by using the Solaris packaging and patch tools. The Solaris packaging and patch tools are supported within the non-global zone for administering bundled, unbundled, or third-party products.

Only a subset of the Solaris packages installed on the global zone is completely replicated when a non-global zone is installed. For example, many packages that contain the Solaris kernel are not needed in a non-global zone. All non-global zones implicitly share the same Solaris kernel from the global zone. However, even if a package's data is not required or is not of use in a non-global zone, the knowledge that a package is installed in the global zone might be required in a non-global zone. The information allows package dependencies from the non-global zones to be properly resolved with the global zone.

Packages have parameters that control how their content is distributed and made visible on a system with non-global zones installed. The parameters are set to true or false.

- The SUNW_PKG_ALLZONES package parameter defines the **zone scope** of a package. The scope determines the type of zone (global or non-global) in which an individual package can be installed.
- The SUNW_PKG_HOLLOW package parameter defines the *visibility* of a package if that package is required to be installed on all zones and be identical in all zones.
- The SUNW_PKG_THISZONE package parameter defines whether a package must be installed in the current zone only.

The pkgparam command can be used to view the values for these parameters. Packages that do not define values for zone package parameters have a default setting of false. When a patch is generated for any package, the parameters must be set to the same values as the original package.

All patches applied at the global zone level are applied across all zones. When a non-global zone is installed, it is at the same patch level as the global zone. When the global zone is patched, all non-global zones are similarly patched. This action maintains the same patch level across all zones.

A patch can be added to a non-global zone in the following cases:

- The patch does not affect any area of the zone that is shared from the global zone.
- All packages in the patch are set SUNW_PKG_ALLZONES=false.

12.7 Administering Zones

To use administrative tools from the global zone, you must be logged in as the global administrator, the root user.

A set of administrative tools developed to manage zones allows the zones to be

- Configured
- Installed
- Booted and rebooted independently, without affecting the other environments on the system
- Patched
- Upgraded

- Cloned
- Moved to a different location on the same system
- Migrated to a different system
- Halted

Zone administration operations can be divided into two parts:

- Global zone administration tasks, such as creating a zone
- Non-global zone administration tasks, such as configuration, within a zone

12.7.1 Zone Configuration

Resources that can be controlled in a zone include the following:

- Resource pools or assigned CPUs, which are used for partitioning machine resources.
- Resource controls, which are used for the constraint of system resources. Resource management features are available in the operating system and are used with zones to form containers.
- Scheduling class, which enables you to control the allocation of available CPU resources among zones through relative shares. Using the fair share scheduler (FSS) you can express the importance of the workloads in a given zone through the number of shares of CPU resources that you assign to that zone.

A zone is created on a system by using the Solaris `zonecfg` command from the global zone. For all zones tools used from the global zone, you must be logged in as the global administrator, the root user. There is also an interactive interface for zone creation.

The configuration describes resources and properties that are needed for the zone to operate. Note that the only required elements to create a non-global zone on the Solaris 10 OS are the `zonename` and `zonepath` properties. Other resources and properties are optional. Some optional resources also require choices between alternatives, such as the decision to use either the `dedicated-cpu` resource or the `cpu-shares` property.

- The `zonename` is the name you choose for the zone.
- The `zonepath` to the zone root is required. The path is the directory in the global zone where all of the zone's operating system files will be contained, for example, `/export/home/newzone`. The root directories of the non-global zones are one directory lower. This is summarized in Table 12.1.

Table 12.1 Non-Global Zone Root Path and Directory Structure

Path	Description
/export/home/newzone	`zonecfg zonepath`
/export/home/newzone/root	Root of the zone
/export/home/newzone/dev	Devices created for the zone

- The zone is automatically booted when the global zone is booted if the optional autoboot value is set to true. The default value is false. Note that for the zones to be booted automatically, the zones service `svc:/system/zones:default` must also be enabled.

- The optional `dedicated-cpu` resource specifies that a subset of the system's processors should be dedicated to a non-global zone while it is running.

- The optional `capped-cpu` resource provides an absolute fine-grained limit on the amount of CPU resources that can be consumed by a project or a zone. FSS is used to ensure fair CPU allocations when multiple workloads (multiple zones) share a set of CPUs.

- The optional `capped-memory` resource sets limits for physical, swap, and locked memory.

- The optional *net* resource configures network connectivity. For exclusive IP zones, you must also specify `ip-type=exclusive` in the configuration.

- Each zone can have various mounted file systems, which generally include the set of file systems mounted when the virtual platform is initialized, and the set of file systems mounted from within the zone application environment itself.

- Access to devices in the global zone can be configured.

- Permitted additions or deletions to a default set of safe privileges can be included in the configuration.

You can use a script to configure and boot multiple zones on your system. Alternatively, you can create a zone named `newzone` from the shell prompt in the global zone by typing the following:

```
global# zonecfg -z newzone "create ; set zonepath=/export/home/
newzone"
```

The following example creates a simple zone configuration using the `zonecfg` command:

1. As the root user or administrator with the required RBAC privileges on the host, configure a zone with the zone name you have chosen. The name `new-zone` is used in this example procedure.

    ```
    global# zonecfg -z newzone
    newzone: No such zone configured
    Use 'create' to begin configuring a new zone.
    ```

2. Create the new zone configuration. This example uses the Sun default settings. Note that the prompt changes to a `zonecfg` prompt with the name of the zone being configured.

    `zonecfg:newzone>` **create**

3. Set the zone path, `/export/home/newzone` in this example.

    `zonecfg:newzone>` **set zonepath=/export/home/newzone**

4. Optionally, add a file system.

    `zonecfg:newzone>` **add fs**

    a. Set the zone mount point for the file system, `/usr/local` in this example. Note that the prompt has expanded to show the name of the resource being configured.

        `zonecfg:newzone:fs>` **set dir=/usr/local**

    b. Specify that `/usr/local` in the global zone is to be mounted as `/usr/local` in the zone being configured.

        `zonecfg:newzone:fs>` **set special=/usr/local**

    c. Specify the file system type, `lofs` in this procedure.

        `zonecfg:newzone:fs>` **set type=lofs**

    d. End the file system specification.

        `zonecfg:newzone:fs>` **end**

5. Optionally, add a network interface for a shared-IP zone.

    `zonecfg:newzone>` **add net**

    a. Set the IP address for the network interface.

        `zonecfg:newzone:net>` **set address=192.168.0.1**
        You can also set the IP address in the form ***ip address of zone/netmask***, for example, `10.6.10.233/24`.

   b. Set the physical device type for the physical interface, for example, hme.
      `zonecfg:newzone:net>` **`set physical=hme0`**

   c. End the file system specification.
      `zonecfg:newzone:net>` **`end`**

6. Optionally, dedicate one CPU for this zone.
   `zonecfg:newzone>` **`add dedicated-cpu`**

   a. Set the number of CPUs.
      `zonecfg:newzone:dedicated-cpu>` **`set ncpus=1-2`**

   b. (Optional) Set the importance. The default is 1.
      `zonecfg:newzone:dedicated-cpu>` **`set importance=10`**

   c. End the specification.
      `zonecfg:newzone:dedicated-cpu>` **`end`**

7. Verify the zone configuration for the zone.
   `zonecfg:newzone>` **`verify`**

8. Commit the zone configuration for the zone.
   `zonecfg:newzone>` **`commit`**

9. Exit the `zonecfg` command.
   `zonecfg:newzone>` **`exit`**

Note that even if you did not explicitly type `commit` at the prompt, a `commit` is automatically attempted when you type `exit` or an EOF occurs.

You can change the brand of a zone that is in the configured state. Once a branded zone has been installed, that brand cannot be changed or removed.

A zone configuration can be changed by using the `zonecfg` command. You can also use `zonecfg` to clear a property type or revert to a zone configuration. After modifying the configuration, you can view the changes by typing `info` at the `zonecfg` prompt, as shown in the next section.

The following example changes zone-wide resource control values for the number of LWPs assigned to a zone to prevent it from affecting other zones. Note that the contents of `inherit-pkg-dir` resources cannot be modified or removed after the zone has been installed with `zoneadm`.

```
global# zonecfg -z newzone
zonecfg:newzone> select rctl name=zone.max-lwps
zonecfg:newzone:rctl> remove value (priv=privileged,limit=80,action=none)
zonecfg:newzone:rctl> add value (priv=privileged,limit=100,action=deny)
zonecfg:newzone:rctl> end
zonecfg:newzone> exit
```

Temporary limits that last only until the system is rebooted can be specified through the `prctl` command.

12.7.2 Viewing a Zone Configuration

Type `info` at the `zonecfg` prompt to view the zone's configuration.

```
zonecfg:newzone> info
zonename: newzone
zonepath: /export/zones/newzone
autoboot: false
pool:
inherit-pkg-dir:
        dir: /lib
inherit-pkg-dir:
        dir: /platform
inherit-pkg-dir:
        dir: /sbin
inherit-pkg-dir:
        dir: /usr
net:
        address: 192.168.0.1
        physical: hme0
```

12.7.3 Zone Installation and Booting

The `zoneadm` command is the primary tool used to install and administer non-global zones. Operations using the `zoneadm` command must be run from the global zone. After you have configured a non-global zone and verified that the zone can be installed on your system's configuration, you can then install the zone. The files needed for the zone's root file system are installed by the system under the zone's root path. The following tasks can be performed using the `zoneadm` command:

- Verify a zone
- Install a zone
- Uninstall a zone
- Boot a zone, which is similar to booting a regular Solaris system
- Display information about a running zone
- Halt a zone
- Reboot a zone
- Relocate a zone from one point on a system to another point on the same system

- Provision a new zone based on the configuration of an existing zone on the same system through cloning
- Migrate a zone, used with the `zonecfg` command

Install the configured zone `newzone` by using the `zoneadm` command with the `-z install` option.

```
global# zoneadm -z newzone install
```

A successfully installed zone is ready for booting. Booting a zone transitions the zone to the running state. You can log in to a zone that is in the running state.

Boot the installed zone `newzone` by using the `zoneadm` command with the `-z boot` option.

```
global# zoneadm -z newzone boot
```

12.7.4 Zone Login Using the `zlogin` Command

After installation, the zone is in an unconfigured state. The zone does not have an internal configuration for naming services, its locale and time zone have not been set, and various other configuration tasks have not been performed. Therefore, the Solaris `sysidtool` programs are run the first time the zone console login is used. The process can be automated by placing an `/etc/sysidcfg` file in the zone before the zone is booted for the first time. For more information, see the `sysidtool`(1M) man page.

Each zone maintains a virtual console, `/dev/console`. Performing actions on the console is referred to as console mode. The zone console is closely analogous to a serial console on a system.

```
global# zlogin -C newzone
```

When the zone console displays, log in as `root`, press Return, and type the root password when prompted.

To log in to the zone with a user name, use the `zlogin` command with the `-l` option, the user name, and the name of the zone.

```
global# zlogin -l jane newzone
```

To exit the zone in a non-virtual console zone login, type `exit`.

```
newzone# exit
```

To disconnect from a non-global zone console, type the tilde (~) character and a period.

```
newzone# ~.
```

For additional information about zone login options, see the Solaris zlogin(1M) man page.

12.8 Halting, Uninstalling, Moving, and Cloning Zones

To halt a zone, use zoneadm halt.

```
global# zoneadm newzone halt
```

The uninstall procedure must be used with caution. The action is irreversible.

To uninstall a zone, halt the zone and use zoneadm uninstall. This will return the zone to the configured state.

```
global# zoneadm -z newzone uninstall
```

A zone can be moved from a source host system to a target host system by specifying a new, full zonepath. The zone must be halted.

```
global# zoneadm -z newzone move /zones/zone_roots/newzone
```

Cloning is used to provision a new zone on a system by copying the configuration data from a source zonepath to a target zonepath. The source zone must be halted while it is cloned.

```
global# zonecfg -z zone1 export -f /export/zones/master
```

Edit the file master. Set properties and resources for the components that cannot be identical for different zones, such as the zone path and IP addresses. You could also create a new zone using the zonecfg command.

```
global# zonecfg -z zone2 -f /export/zones/master
```

Install the new zone by cloning the source zone, zone1.

```
global# zoneadm -z zone2 clone zone1
Cloning zonepath /export/home/zone1...
```

When both the source and target zones reside on ZFS and are in the same pool, the `zoneadm` clone command automatically uses ZFS to clone the zone. You can still request that a zone be copied instead of using ZFS when cloned. You cannot use manual ZFS snapshots to replace the `zoneadm` process.

12.9 Migrating a Zone to a New System

The `zonecfg` and `zoneadm` commands can be used to migrate an existing non-global zone from one system to another. The zone is halted and detached from its current host. The `zonepath` is moved to the target host, where it is attached.

The global zone on the target system must be running the same Solaris release as the original host. To ensure that the zone will run properly, the target system must have the same versions of the following required operating system packages and patches as those installed on the original host:

- Packages that deliver files under an `inherit-pkg-dir` resource
- Packages where `SUNW_PKG_ALLZONES=true`

Other packages and patches, such as those for third-party products, can be different.

The `zoneadm detach` process creates the information necessary to attach the zone on a different system. The `zoneadm attach` process verifies that the target machine has the correct configuration to host the zone. If the target host has later versions of the zone-dependent packages and their associated patches, those packages can be updated to match the new host. This option also enables automatic migration between machine classes, such as from `sun4u` to `sun4v`. Specified patches can be backed out during the attach. There are many ways to create an archive of the `zonepath`. For example, you can use the `cpio` or `pax` commands described in the `cpio(1)` and `pax(1)` man pages. There are also several ways to transfer the archive to the new host. The mechanism used to transfer the `zonepath` from the source host to the destination depends on the local configuration. In some cases, such as a SAN, the `zonepath` data might not actually move. The SAN might simply be reconfigured so the `zonepath` is visible on the new host. In other cases, the `zonepath` might be written to tape, and the tape mailed to a new site.

For these reasons, this step is not automated. The system administrator must choose the most appropriate technique to move the `zonepath` to the new host.

In the following example, the source host is identified as `host1`, and the target host is identified as `host2`. Note that you will need to make any required adjustments to the configuration on the target machine. For example, the network physical device will be different on the new host, and devices that are part of the configuration might have different names on the new host.

1. As the root user or administrator with the required RBAC privileges on the hosts, halt the zone to be moved.

    ```
    host1# zoneadm -z newzone halt
    ```

2. Detach the zone. The zone will then be in the configured state.

    ```
    host1# zoneadm -z newzone detach
    ```

3. Create an archive of the zonepath, for example, by using the cpio or pax commands. Then, move the zonepath for newzone to the new host. The mechanism used to transfer the zonepath from the source host to the destination depends on the local configuration. In some cases, such as a SAN, the zonepath data might not actually move. The SAN might simply be reconfigured so the zonepath is visible on the new host. In other cases, the zonepath might be written to tape, and the tape mailed to a new site. For these reasons, this step is not automated. The system administrator must choose the most appropriate technique to move the zonepath to the new host.

4. On the new host, configure the zone.

    ```
    host2# zonecfg -z newzone
    newzone: No such zone configured
    Use create to begin configuring a new zone.
    ```

5. To create the zone on the new host, use the zonecfg command with the -a option and the zonepath on the new host.

    ```
    host2# zonecfg -z newzone
    zonecfg:newzone> create -a /export/zones/newzone
    ```

6. Make any required adjustments to the configuration.

7. Commit the configuration and exit.

8. Attach the zone on the new host using one of the following methods:

    - Attach the zone with a validation check. The system administrator is notified of required actions to be taken if required packages and patches are not present on the new machine or if the software levels are different between machines.

    ```
    host2# zoneadm -z newzone attach
    ```

- Attach the zone with a validation check and update the zone to match a host running later versions of the dependent packages or having a different machine architecture.

  host2# **zoneadm -z newzone attach -u**

  If the source system is running an older version of the Solaris system, then it might not generate a correct list of packages when the zone is detached. To ensure that the correct package list is generated on the destination, you can remove the SUNWdetached.xml file from the zonepath. Removing this file will cause a new package list to be generated by the destination system.

  Also, use the -b option to back out specified patches, either official or IDR, during the attach. You can use the -b option independently of the -u option.

```
host2# zoneadm -z newzone attach -u -b DR246802-01 -b 123456-08
```

- Force the attach operation without performing the validation. This method is useful in certain cases, such as backup and restore operations, but it does require that the system be properly configured to host the zone. An incorrect configuration could result in undefined behavior later.

  host2# **zoneadm -z newzone attach -F**

12.10 Deleting a Zone

The following commands remove a zone from a system.

```
global# zlogin newzone shutdown
global# zoneadm -z newzone uninstall -F
global# zonecfg -z newzone delete -F
global# zoneadm list -iv
ID    NAME      STATUS    PATH          BRAND   IP
0     global    running.../            native  shared
```

12.11 Listing the Zones on a System

This procedure lists the zones on the system.

```
global# zoneadm list -iv
ID    NAME      STATUS    PATH                    BRAND   IP
0     global    running.../              native  shared
1     newzone   running.../export/home/newzone native  shared
```

12.12 Zones Usage Examples

This section provides examples for customizing and troubleshooting the zones running on your system.

12.12.1 Adding a Dedicated Device to a Non-Global Zone

Even though the set of devices available within a zone is restricted, additional devices can be made accessible for use within a specific zone by using the zonecfg utility.

For example, assume that a zone will be created for the purpose of training students. The root account will only be used by the global administrator. The system will be attached to a LAN that is not connected to any other networks. The instructor needs access to the audio device. There are very few risks associated with such access, and it is not likely that the audio device will suffer a failure. Even if the audio device did fail, it would be unlikely to affect other zones.

```
global# zonecfg -z training
zonecfg:training> add device
zonecfg:training:device> set match=/dev/sound/*
zonecfg:training:device> end
zonecfg:training> exit
```

12.12.2 How to Export Home Directories in the Global Zone into a Non-Global Zone

You can export home directories or other file systems from the global zone into non-global zones on the same system. The file systems are added by using the loop-back-mounted file system. The dir path specifies the mount point for the file system, and special specifies the directory in the global zone.

```
global# zonecfg -z newzone
zonecfg:newzone> add fs
zonecfg:newzone:fs> set dir=/export/home
zonecfg:newzone:fs> set special=/export/home
zonecfg:newzone:fs> set type=lofs
zonecfg:newzone:fs> set options=nodevices
zonecfg:newzone:fs> end
zonecfg:newzone> exit
```

12.12.3 Altering Privileges in a Non-Global Zone

Processes are restricted to a subset of privileges. Privilege restriction prevents a zone from performing operations that might affect other zones. The set of privileges limits the capabilities of privileged users within the zone. When a zone is booted, a default set of *safe* privileges is included in the configuration. These privileges are considered safe because they prevent a privileged process in the zone from affecting processes in other non-global zones on the system or in the global zone.

Optional privileges that are not part of the default set of privileges can be specified through the limitpriv property. Required privileges must be included in the resulting privilege set. Prohibited privileges cannot be included in the resulting privilege set.

To view the privileges available in a zone, use the ppriv utility with the -l and the -v options from the global zone.

```
global# ppriv -l -v zone
```

The following zonecfg entry adds the ability to set the system clock to the default set of privileges in the zone newzone.

```
zonecfg:newzone> set limitpriv="default,sys_time"
```

To display the list of privileges available within a given non-global zone, log in to the zone and use the ppriv utility with the -l and the -v options.

```
newzone# ppriv -l -v zone
```

12.12.4 Checking the Status of SMF Services

You can check the status of SMF services from the command line in the global zone or from within the non-global zone. The following command can be used to check the status in newzone from the global zone.

```
global# zlogin newzone svcs -a
```

To check the status from the non-global zone, log into the zone using zlogin and type:

```
newzone# svcs -a
```

12.12.5 Modifying CPU, Swap, and Locked Memory Caps in Zones

The prctl(1M) command can be used to temporarily modify CPU, swap, and locked memory caps until the next reboot of the zone. These resources are set permanently using zonecfg. For CPU caps, 100 equals 1 CPU.

Add a cap to a zone with no cap:

```
global# prctl -n zone.cpu-cap -t privileged -v 200 -s -i zone newzone
```

View the current cap on a zone:

global# **prctl -n zone.cpu-cap -i zone newzone**

Replace the existing cap with a new cap:

global# **prctl -n zone.cpu-cap -v 200 -r -i zone newzone**

Remove the existing cap:

global# **prctl -n zone.cpu-cap -x -i zone newzone**

Swap and locked memory caps are in bytes. M and G modifiers can be used, such as:

```
global# prctl -n zone.max-swap -t privileged -v 1G -s -i zone newzone
```

12.12.6 Using the Dtrace Program in a Non-Global Zone

DTrace programs that require only the dtrace_proc and dtrace_user privileges can be run in a non-global zone. The providers supported through dtrace_proc are fasttrap and pid. The providers supported through dtrace_user are profile and syscall. DTrace providers and actions are limited in scope to the zone. To add these privileges to the set of privileges available in the non-global zone, use the zonecfg limitpriv property.

```
global# zonecfg -z newzone
zonecfg:newzone> set limitpriv="default,dtrace_proc,dtrace_user"
zonecfg:newzone> exit
global# zoneadm -z newzone boot
global# zlogin newzone
newzone# dtrace -1
```

Using Naming Services

The primary function of a naming service is to translate human readable domain names and network devices into "machine language," while rendering IP addresses as human-friendly names. Generally, this means translating hostnames into IP addresses. A naming service makes it easy to connect with network devices both on a local system and on the World Wide Web.

A naming service talks to databases that store information about host names and addresses, including the following:

- *User names*
- *Passwords*
- *Access permissions*
- *Group membership, printers, etc.*

Without a naming service, each machine would have to maintain its own copy of this information. Naming service information can be stored in files, maps, or database tables. If you centralize all naming service data, then administration tasks are much easier.

13.1 Using Naming Services (DNS, NIS, AND LDAP)

The Solaris operating system (Solaris OS) provides the following naming services: DNS, NIS, and LDAP. Most modern networks use two or more of these services in combination. When more than one service is used, the services are coordinated by the `nsswitch.conf` file. The `nsswitch.conf` file is explained in detail later.

- *DNS* (Domain Name System) is an Internet-wide naming system used for resolving host names to IP addresses and IP addresses to host names.
- *NIS* (Network Information Services)
- *LDAP* (Lightweight Directory Access Protocol)

13.1.1 Naming Service Cache Daemon (`nscd`)

On Solaris systems, the `nscd` is started at boot. It is a process that does lookups and keeps a cache of lookups for the most common naming service requests including NIS and LDAP. For the most part, `nscd` is automatic and doesn't typically require much configuration, if any.

For performance reasons, it is usually a good idea to keep `nscd` running. See the man page for `nscd.conf` for more information.

13.1.2 DNS Naming Services

The *Domain Naming System* (DNS) is an Internet service for TCP/IP networks. The DNS service translates human-readable computer hostnames (`www.example.com`) into IP addresses (`111.222.333.444`). Thus, workstations on the network can be identified with common names instead of Internet addresses. Virtually all information resources (host names) are resolved to their Internet protocol (IP) addresses through DNS.

The collection of networked workstations that use DNS is referred to as the DNS namespace. The DNS namespace can be divided into a hierarchy of domains. A DNS domain is simply a group of workstations. Each domain is supported by two or more naming servers: a principal server and one or more secondary servers. Each server implements DNS by running a daemon called `in.named`.

On the client's side, DNS is implemented through the *resolver*. The resolver's function is to resolve user queries from a server. The resolver queries a naming server that returns either the requested information or a referral to another server.

13.1.3 NIS Naming Services

The *Network Information Service* (NIS) was developed by Sun independently of DNS. Whereas DNS focuses on making communication simpler by using workstation names instead of numerical IP addresses, NIS focuses on making network administration more manageable by providing centralized control over a variety of network information.

NIS stores information about the network, machine names and addresses, users, and network services. This collection of network information is called the NIS namespace, and this namespace information is stored in NIS maps. These NIS maps are designed to replace UNIX /etc files and other configuration files. NIS maps store much more than names and addresses. As a result, the NIS namespace has a large set of maps.

NIS uses a client-server arrangement similar to DNS. Replicated NIS servers provide services to NIS clients. The principal servers are called *master* servers, and for reliability, they have backup, or *slave* servers. Both master and slave servers use the NIS information retrieval software and both store NIS maps.

13.1.4 LDAP Naming Services

The Internet protocol LDAP (Lightweight Directory Access Protocol) is used by computer applications to look up information from a server. LDAP is more scalable and offers better security features than NIS.

Like a phone book, LDAP servers index data entries and filter data to find and return useful information. LDAP isn't a database but rather is a protocol used to access information stored in an information directory, also known as an LDAP directory.

LDAP is excellent for using directory-like information to do fast lookups. The following LDAP Commands manipulate directory entries directly:

- `ldapsearch(1)`
- `ldapmodify(1)`
- `ldapadd(1)`
- `ldapdelete(1)`

13.1.5 Organizational Use of Naming Services

Sun's NIS was one of the first UNIX-based distributed naming services, and it is still widely used today; however, in recent years the popularity and utility of LDAP has caused many organizations to adopt LDAP as their preferred naming service. NIS remains popular with many organizations, including Sun, because it is tried and true. It is also easy to maintain, and this validates the truism, "If it ain't broke why fix it?" Furthermore, NIS works well to store host names and IP addresses of computers within an organization, while DNS can scale much better.

Many organizations store the host names and IP addresses in NIS maps while using DNS to look up names of computers outside of the network. To enable the two naming services, include DNS in the `nsswitch.conf` file that is described in detail later in this chapter.

Sun is committed to LDAP as a naming service. You can enable support of NIS clients that use naming information stored in the LDAP directory. You can also use the N2L (NIS to LDAP) service to completely transition from the NIS naming service to the LDAP naming service. Sun currently supports the N2L service in conjunction with the Sun Java System Directory Server, LDAP v2 and v3 protocols. Deployments of LDAP still use DNS for structuring the topmost levels of the hierarchy.

If you do not implement NIS, LDAP, or DNS, then the network uses local files as the name service. If you are only interested in local data, this is the only naming service you need. The term "local files" refers to the files in the `/etc` directory required for network databases.

In conclusion, virtually all organizations use DNS to resolve top-level domain names on the Internet. In addition, most organizations choose either NIS or LDAP as a naming service. Although NIS functions well for small to medium-large organizations, many large organizations prefer LDAP. The better security and scalability it offers justifies the increased complexity.

From their point of view, the users of NIS and/or LDAP see very little difference in the functionality of these two naming services.

13.1.6 Network Database Sources

Networks that use local files for their name service use files in the `/etc/inet` and `/etc` directories. NIS uses databases that are called NIS maps. DNS uses records with host information.

The network databases are files that provide information needed to configure the network. The configuration for your network database depends on the type of name service you select for your network. For example, the `hosts` database contains at least the host name and IPv4 address of the local system and any network interfaces that are directly connected to the local system. However, the `hosts` database could contain other IPv4 addresses and host names, depending on the type of name service on your network.

There is an entry in the `/etc/nsswitch.conf` file for each database. The common network databases are

- `passwd`
- `group`
- `hosts`

- netmasks
- ethers
- protocols
- services
- networks

The following list provides a brief description of each of these common Solaris naming service databases.

- passwd
  - The passwd database contains information about user accounts.
  - The following get entries command provides user information that is partially encrypted:

  getent passwd <userID>

- group
  - The group database contains a list of group names, encrypted passwords, and privileges.

  getent group <userID>

- hosts
  - The hosts file is a local database that associates the names of hosts with their Internet Protocol (IP) addresses. The hosts file can be used in conjunction with, or instead of, other hosts databases, including the DNS and the NIS hosts map.
  - The hosts file contains the host name and IPv4 address of the local system and any network interfaces that are directly connected to the local system.
  - The hosts file may contain DNS as a name service to search. You can also list more than one name service, such as NIS and files.
  - The hosts file has one entry for each IP address of each host. If a host has more than one IP address, it will have one entry for each, on consecutive lines.

  getent hosts <userID>

The following is an example of the host table.

```
#
# Internet host table
#
123.456.789.98    sr1-usa-99    loghost
::1 localhost
```

- netmasks
  - If your network runs NIS or LDAP, the servers for these name services maintain netmasks databases. For networks that use local files for name service, this information is maintained in the /etc/inet/netmasks file.
  - Make sure that the file /etc/netmasks exists and that, at a minimum, it contains the following three entries:

```
128.197.0.0 255.255.255.0
168.122.0.0 255.255.255.0
155.41.0.0 255.255.255.0
```

  - These entries define the Class B subnets that make up the BU domains and their associated netmasks. You only need the one entry that is relevant for the subnet the boot server is on, but it doesn't hurt to have all three.
  - If you set up subnetting (allows for more networks), edit the netmasks database as part of network configuration. The netmasks database consists of a list of networks and their associated subnet masks.
  - If a netmask 255.255.255.0 is applied to the IP address 129.144.41.101, the result is the IP address of 129.144.41.0.

    129.144.41.101 & 255.255.255.0 = 129.144.41.0

  - In the example above, the system looks for a network number of 129.144.41 instead of a network number of 129.144.

The file /etc/netmasks is a symbolic link to /etc/inet/netmasks. The example below shows the contents of this file:

```
# The netmasks file associates Internet Protocol (IP) address
# masks with IP network numbers.
#
# network-number netmask
#
# Both the network-number and the netmasks are specified in
# ''decimal dot'' notation, e.g:
#
# 128.32.0.0 255.255.255.0
129.144.0.0 255.255.255.0
```

- ethers
  - The ethers database contains Ethernet numbers—machine names and Ethernet addresses. The Ethernet address is the key in the map.
- bootparams
  - The bootparams file contains a list of client entries that diskless clients use for booting.

- protocols
  - The protocols database contains a list of Internet protocols such as IP, TCP, and numerous others.
    getent protocols
- services
  - The services database contains a list of "well-known" services along with corresponding port numbers and the protocols the services use. A few examples are kerberos, hostnames, printer, bootpc, etc.
    getent services
- networks
  - A database file that associates IP addresses with official network names and aliases.
    getent networks

13.2 Name Service Switch File

The name service switch file determines which naming services a system uses to search for information. It also determines the order in which naming services are searched. All Solaris systems use the /etc/nsswitch.conf as the name service switch file. The nsswitch.conf file is loaded with the contents of a template file during the installation of the Solaris OS, depending on the name service that is selected.

The /etc/nsswitch.conf file includes a list of databases that are sources of information about IP addresses, users, and groups.

The following four templates are used during a Solaris installation and when you need to change a name service:

- Local files /etc/nsswitch.files
- DNS /etc/nsswitch.dns
- NIS /etc/nsswitch.nis
- LDAP /etc/nsswitch.ldap

13.2.1 Configuring the Name Service Switch File

Name service lookups are attempted on specified databases in the order in which the items are listed in the naming service, nsswitch.conf file. There is an entry in the nsswitch.conf for each database. This file is copied to or replaced by a specific naming service file—such as DNS, NIS, or LDAP—as shown in the following examples.

13.2.1.1 Example of the Switch File

The following `nsswitch.conf` example is configured to use NIS in conjunction with local files.

```
# /etc/nsswitch.nis:
#
# An example file that could be copied over to /etc/nsswitch.conf; it
# uses NIS (YP) in conjunction with files.
#
# "hosts:" and "services:" in this file are used only if the
# /etc/netconfig file has a "-" for nametoaddr_libs of "inet"
# transports.

# NIS service requires that svc:/network/nis/client:default be enabled
# and online.

# the following two lines obviate the "+" entry in /etc/passwd and
# /etc/group.

passwd:     files nis
group:      files nis

# consult /etc "files" only if nis is down.

hosts:      files nis dns

# Note that IPv4 addresses are searched for in all of the ipnodes
# databases before searching the hosts databases.

ipnodes:    nis [NOTFOUND=return] files

networks:   files nis
protocols:  files nis
rpc:        files nis
ethers:     files nis
netmasks:   files nis
bootparams: files nis
publickey:  files nis

netgroup:   nis

automount:  files nis
aliases:    files nis

# for efficient getservbyname() avoid nis

services:   files nis
printers:   user files nis

auth_attr:  files nis
prof_attr:  files nis
project:    files nis
```

13.2.1.2 Abbreviated Example of an LDAP Configured Switch File

The following example is configured to use LDAP in conjunction with local files. The only difference in this example is that LDAP is added to the search sequence.

According to the search sequence shown here, local files are searched first for the object and then the LDAP database is searched.

```
#
networks:    files ldap
protocols:   files ldap
rpc:         files ldap
ethers:      files ldap
netmasks:    files ldap
bootparams:  files ldap
publickey:   files ldap
#
```

13.2.2 Database Status and Actions

Based on the results of a search, either a "return" action or a "continue" action is possible. The status is the result of a call to a lookup function. The format for status and action is:

Status = Action

- SUCCESS = return The requested entry was found. The default action is return.
- UNAVAIL = continue The source is either unresponsive or unavailable. The default action is continue.
- NOTFOUND = continue The source (table, map, or file) was accessed but the needed information was not found. The default action is continue.
- TRYAGAIN = continue The source was busy. It was found but could not respond to the query. The default action is continue.

Examples include the following:

- **Example 1**

  `passwd: files nis`

  In this example, the designated files in the /etc directory are searched for the corresponding password entry. If the entry is not found, the NIS maps are searched for the entry. If no entry is found in the NIS maps, an appropriate error is returned, and no further information sources are searched.

- **Example 2**

  `hosts: nis [NOTFOUND=return] files`

  In this example, the lookup continues to files if nis is UNAVAIL. In other words, try files only if nis is down.

13.3 DNS Setup and Configuration

The client piece of the DNS architecture is known as a *resolver*, and the server piece is known as a *name server*. Resolvers retrieve information associated with a domain name, and domain name servers store various pieces of information about the domain space and return information to the resolvers upon request. The resolver program is a set of routines that are built into the operating system.

A developer or system administrator is concerned with the human readable and editable files explained in this section.

13.3.1 Resolver Files

The Solaris client resolver code is controlled by the following two files:

- The `resolv.conf` file contains IP addresses of DNS nameservers that are to be resolved. Generally, queries are done in the order listed in the file.

- The `/etc/resolv.conf` file contains keywords and directives. The following are the three major directives:
  - `domain`: local domain name
  - `search`: list of host names (in order of lookup)
  - `nameserver`: Internet address of name server

An example of the `resolv.conf` file follows:

```
#Domain name resolver config file
domain xxx.xxx.com
search xxx.xxx.com xxx.xxx.xom
nameserver 129.xxx.xxx.xxx
nameserver 129.xxx.xxx.xxx
nameserver 129.xxx.xxx.xxx
```

13.3.2 Steps DNS Clients Use to Resolve Names

The following simplified sequence of steps is typically used by a DNS client to resolve a name to an address.

1. The client computer consults the `/etc/nsswitch.conf` file to determine the name resolution order. For example, `file dns`.
2. The client computer consults the local `/etc/inet/host` file first, then it sends a recursive (waits for an answer) DNS query. The local DNS server first checks the contents of its cached data for recent queries.

3. The DNS server returns the response, if the connection was successful.

4. The client computer connects with the remote server.

13.4 NIS Setup and Configuration

There are three types of NIS machines.

- Master servers
- Slave servers
- Clients on NIS servers

Any machine can be an NIS client, but only machines with disks should be NIS servers, either master or slave. Servers are also clients, typically of themselves. Before configuring your NIS namespace, you must do the following:

- Install the properly configured `nsswitch.conf` files on all machines that will be using NIS.
- Plan your NIS domain.

Use the Service Management Facility to manage an NIS service. Administrative actions on this service, such as enabling, disabling, or restarting can be performed by using the `svcadm` command. See the `svcadm(1M)` man page for more information.

13.4.1 Setting Up NIS Clients

The two methods for configuring a client machine to use NIS as its naming service are explained below:

- **Method 1:** `ypinit`
  To configure a client machine to use NIS, log in to the machine as root or superuser and run the `ypinit -c` command.
  When you use this command, you are asked to name NIS servers from which the client obtains naming service information.

- **Method 2:** broadcast
  The broadcast method uses an option in the `ypbind` command. Log in to the machine as root or superuser and set the domain name with the `domainname` command; then run `ypbind`.

ypstart will automatically invoke the NIS client in broadcast mode (ypbind – broadcast), if the /var/yp/binding/'domainname'/ypservers file does not exist.

```
# domainname doc.com
# mv /var/yp/binding/'domainname'/ypservers /var/yp/binding/'domainname'\
```

> **Note**
>
> The Solaris operating system does not support a configuration in which an NIS client and a Native LDAP client coexist on the same client machine.

Running the ypbind command starts a search of the local subnet for an NIS server. If the search finds a subnet, ypbind binds to it. This search is referred to as broadcasting. If the search does not find an NIS server on the client's local subnet, ypbind fails to bind, and the client machine is not able to obtain namespace data from the NIS service.

13.4.2 Working with NIS Maps

Maps are constructed from standard text files by associating an index key with a value. For example, the information in the master server's /etc/hosts file is used to create a map that uses each host name as a key and the IP address as the value. The key and value pairs (also known as records) that are created from the entries in the /etc/hosts file comprise the hosts.byname map. In addition to the hosts.byname file, a hosts.byaddr file is also provided for reverse name resolution. For these two functions, name resolution and reverse name resolution, a total of four files are needed:

- hosts.byname.dir
- hosts.byname.pag
- hosts.byaddr.dir
- hosts.byaddr.pag

> **Note**
>
> Files ending in .dir contain an index in the .pag files containing the key/value pair for faster searching. An NIS record has a maximum size of 1024 bytes, and this limitation applies to all NIS map files. For example, a list of users in a group can contain a maximum of 1024 characters in single-byte character set file format. NIS cannot operate correctly with map files that exceed this maximum.

13.4.2.1 Obtaining Map Information

Obtain map information by using the ypcat, ypwhich, and ypmatch commands. The most commonly used maps have nicknames that some commands can translate into map names.

You do not have to be superuser to use ypcat, ypwhich, and ypmatch. In the following examples, mapname refers to both map names and nicknames.

ypcat The ypcat command displays the values in a NIS map. The following list provides some uses of the command:

- Use the ypcat -x command (without mapname) to produce a list of available maps and nicknames.

```
Use   "passwd"    for map   "passwd.byname"
Use   "group"     for map   "group.byname"
Use   "project"   for map   "project.byname"
Use   "networks"  for map   "networks.byaddr"
Use   "hosts"     for map   "hosts.byname"
Use   "ipnodes"   for map   "ipnodes.byname"
Use   "protocols" for map   "protocols.bynumber"
Use   "services"  for map   "services.byname"
Use   "aliases"   for map   "mail.aliases"
Use   "ethers"    for map   "ethers.byname"
```

- Use the ypcat -k mapname command to list both the keys and the values for a specific map.
- Use the ypcat mapname | grep *item* command, where *item* is the information for which you are searching. To obtain information about other domains, use the -d domainname options.

ypwhich The ypwhich command is used to determine which server is the master of a particular NIS map. Some uses of the ypwhich command follow:

- Use the ypwhich command, without arguments, to show the NIS server for the local machine you are currently bound to.
- Use the ypwhich -m command to show the master NIS server for a map.
- Use the ypwhich -m mapname command to show the master NIS server for a specific map.

This command provides similar information to ypcat.

ypmatch The ypmatch command is used to find a specific entry in a NIS map.

- Use the ypmatch key mapname command to find the value of one or more keys in an NIS map.

The following example matches individual host entries.

```
# ypmatch beta localhost hosts
192.123.45.67 beta
127.0.0.1 localhost loghost
```

13.4.2.2 Managing NIS maps

System information should be updated when you modify an NIS map. After edit-ing a source file such as /etc/hosts for example, update the NIS maps on the master server and then propagate the changes to the slave servers. The only excep-tion to this rule is when users change their password with the yppasswd command.

For example, when editing /etc/hosts, add a server to the file; then update the file. To update the NIS maps on the master server, complete the following steps:

1. Update the text files in your source directory (typically, /etc, unless it was changed in the Makefile file).

2. Change to the /var/yp directory.

3. Refresh the NIS database maps using the make utility (/usr/ccs/bin/make).

13.4.2.3 Updating the NIS Slave Server Map

The following steps manually update the NIS timezone map on the master server and propagate all maps to the slave servers:

1. Edit the source file on the NIS master, for example vi /etc/timezone

2. Remake and push the NIS maps to the slave servers.
   cd /var/yp; /usr/ccs/bin/make

3. If the push from the master fails, the following commands run on the slave server and manually "pull" only the timezone map from the master server
   /usr/lib/netsvc/yp/ypxfr timezone.byname

4. To pull all of the maps from the master server at once use the command
   ypinit -s nis_master

Sometimes maps fail to propagate. To ensure periodic updating and propagat-ing of NIS maps on slave servers, you can run ypxfr as a cron job. Because maps have different rates of change, scheduling a map transfer by using the crontab command enables you to set specific propagation intervals for individual maps.

The Solaris OS provides several template scripts in the /usr/lib/netsvc/yp directory that you can use and modify to meet your local site requirements. These scripts are useful when slave servers are down during NIS map propagations. When slave servers are down, they might not receive the update until the cron script runs again unless you run a "safety valve" script on startup. Sun provides the ypxfr_1perhour script that can be run hourly by cron as an example of a "safety valve" script

```
PATH=/bin:/usr/bin:/usr/lib/netsvc/yp:$PATH
export PATH
# set -xv
ypxfr passwd.byname
ypxfr passwd.byuid
```

13.4.2.4 Creating the List of Slave Servers on the Master

The initial conversion of source files into maps on the master server is done using the command:

```
/usr/sbin/ypinit -m
```

The ypinit command prompts for a list of NIS slave servers. Type the name of your current server, along with the names of your NIS slave servers.

- The ypinit command asks whether you want the procedure to terminate at the first nonfatal error or continue despite nonfatal errors. You should answer Yes.

- The ypinit command can also ask whether the existing files in the /var/yp/domainname directory can be destroyed. This message is displayed only if NIS has been previously installed. You should answer Yes in order to be able to install a new version of NIS maps.

After the ypinit command has constructed the list of servers, it invokes the make command.

This program uses the instructions contained in the Makefile file (either the default one or the one you modified) located in the /var/yp directory. The make command strips any remaining comment lines from the source files and runs the makedbm function on them, creating the appropriate maps and establishing the name of the master server in each map.

13.5 LDAP Setup and Configuration

The `ldapclient` is a utility used to set up LDAP clients in the Solaris system. The name service requests are satisfied by retrieving information from the LDAP server.

The Solaris operating system does not support a configuration in which a NIS client and a Native LDAP client coexist on the same client machine. See `ldapclient`(1M) man page for information about setting up a client of an LDAP namespace.

The credential level for the Solaris LDAP client is the credential used by the client to authenticate and retrieve information from the LDAP server. The Solaris LDAP client supports the following three types of credential levels:

- **Anonymous**: The client accesses information from the LDAP server without using any credentials.
- **Proxy Credentials**: The client authenticates to the LDAP server using a proxy account.
- **Per-User or Self-Credentials**: The client authenticates to the LDAP server using the credential of the user who is actually making the name service request.

There are two main ways to set up a client by using `ldapclient`.

- **Profile**—At a minimum, you need to specify the server address containing the profile and domain you want to use. If no profile is specified, the default profile is assumed. The server will provide the rest of the required information, except for proxy and certificate database information.

  If a client's credential level is proxy or proxy anonymous, you must supply the proxy bind DN and password.

  You must install and configure the server with the appropriate profiles before you can set up clients.
- **Manual**—You configure the profile on the client itself, which means you define all parameters from the command line. When you use manual setup, the profile information is stored in cache files and is never refreshed by the server.

> **Note**
>
> Although you can manually configure clients, it is not recommended. Instead use the configuration profiles to decrease the complexity and the cost of managing clients.

13.5.1 Initializing a Client Using Per-User Credentials

There are two client configuration files—ldap_client_cred and ldap_client_file. Use the ldapclient command to create or modify the content of these files. Do not edit either of the client configuration files directly with an editor.

13.5.1.1 How to Initialize a Client Using Per-User Credentials

To use Per-User credentials, the client must use the sasl/GSSAPI authentication method. The only GSSAPI mechanism currently supported by the client is Kerberos V5. See kerberos(5) for details. In addition, DNS must be used for host name resolution.

Before you set up an LDAP client with per-user credentials, the following items must already be configured.

On the DNS server, at least one DNS server must be configured and running. On the Kerberos KDC:

- One or more Kerberos KDC servers must be configured and running.
- Kerberos host principal for the directory server must be set up in the KDC.
- Kerberos principals must be set up in the KDC for all users of the Solaris LDAP client.

On the LDAP server:

- The LDAP server must be installed and configured to support the sasl/GSSAPI.
- Appropriate identity mapping configurations must exist.
- idsconfig must have been run on the directory server and an appropriate per-user gssapi profile (such as gssapi_EXAMPLE.COM) must have been created.
- The directory server must be pre-loaded with (at a minimum) the users of this client machine, the client host, and necessary auto_home LDAP entries. See other sections of this book for details on how to add entries using ldapaddent.

On the LDAP client:

- /etc/nsswitch.ldap must be configured to use DNS for hosts and ipnodes like this:

```
host:      files dns
ipnodes:   files dns
```

(Modify the nsswitch file with an editor as necessary)

- `/etc/resolv.conf` must be configured and the DNS SMF service must be running.
- Kerberos on the LDAP client machine must be configured and enabled. See `kclient`(1M) for details.

13.5.1.2 Configuring the LDAP Client Using Per-User Credentials

Once these items have been configured, you are ready to initialize the LDAP client. Use the following procedure to configure and test the client.

1. Run `ldapclient init` to initialize the client using the `gssapi` profile

```
# /usr/sbin/ldapclient init -a profilename=gssapi_SPARKS.COM -a \
domainname=example.com 9.9.9.50
```

2. Attempt to log in as a user.
3. Run `kinit -p user`.
4. Run `ldaplist -l passwd user` in user's login session and you should see "userpassword."

   But `ldaplist -l passwd bar` can get the entry without `userpassword`. By default, root can still see `userpassword` of everybody.

13.5.1.3 Troubleshooting

If you encounter the following `syslog` message, it is likely that Kerberos is not initialized or its ticket has expired:

```
libsldap: Status: 7 Mesg: openConnection: GSSAPI bind failed - 82 Local error.
Run klist to browse it. Run kinit -p foo or kinit -R -p foo and try again.
```

You can add `pam_krb5.so.1` to `/etc/pam.conf` so it will automatically `kinit` when you log in.

For example:

```
Login      auth optional pam_krb5.so.1
rlogin     auth optional pam_krb5.so.1
other      auth optional pam_krb5.so.1
```

- If a user is kinited (has obtained an initial ticket-granting credential for a principal) and the syslog message indicates Invalid credential, then the problem could be that the host entry (root) or user entry is not in the LDAP directory, or the mapping rules are not correct.

- When ldapclient init is executed, it checks to see if the LDAP profile contains the self/sasl/GSSAPI configuration.

  If it fails at the /etc/nsswitch.ldap check, then the reason is usually that dns was not added to the host: and ipnodes:. If it fails because the DNS client is not enabled, then you should run svcs -l dns/client to see if the /etc/resolv.conf is missing or if it is just disabled. If it is disabled, run svcadm enable dns/client to enable it.

- If the check fails because of sasl/GSSAPI bind, check syslog to find out what went wrong.

13.5.2 Configuring an LDAP Client

This section explains how to configure clients that run the Solaris 10 OS.

1. Verify that the following Solaris 10 native LDAP phase II packages are installed on the client system:

   SUNWnisu
   SUNWcsr
   SUNWcsu
   SUNWcsl

Note

The following steps configure SSL for communication between the Solaris 10 clients and the directory servers. These steps assume that the directory servers have been configured for SSL.

2. Verify that the server name in the cn attribute of the server certificate matches the name of the directory server that the client is connecting to. If it does not, change the defaultServerList or the preferredServerList attribute to match the cn attribute of the server certificate.

Note

The Solaris 10 OS comes with a bundled certutil utility in the /usr/sfw/bin directory. Unlike Solaris 8 and 9 clients, Solaris 10 clients expect a cert8.db database.

3. To create the certificate database and add the certificates execute the following commands:

```
# /usr/sfw/bin/certutil -N -d /var/ldap
# chmod 644 /var/ldap/*.db
```

The following commands assume that the certificate file is in ASCII format. If it is in binary format, remove the -a option from the commands.

```
# /usr/sfw/bin/certutil -A -a -i <path to root CA cert>
-n "RootCA" -t "CT" -d /var/ldap
# /usr/sfw/bin/certutil -A -a -i <path to sub CA cert>
-n "SubCA" -t "CT" -d /var/ldap
```

4. Configure the client using the ldapclient utility:
   a. Back up the /etc/pam.conf and /etc/nsswitch.conf files:

```
# ldapclient init -a profileName=COMPANYprofile -a
domainName="COMPANY.com" -a proxyDN="cn=proxyagent,ou=profile,
dc=COMPANY,dc=com" -a proxyPassword=<proxy_password>
<primary directory server IP address>
```

If ldapclient fails, check the Directory Server ACIs. For the ldapclient command to succeed, the ACIs should allow for anonymous access.

   b. Verify the configuration on the client:

   ```
   # ldapclient list
   ```

   c. The ldapclient initialization modifies the /etc/nsswitch.conf hosts line to point to LDAP. Change the hosts line as follows before proceeding:

   ```
   hosts:  files dns
   ```

5. Configure /etc/pam.conf as follows:

```
# Not complete. All services have not been defined. Only   changes are
# documented here.
#
login    auth requisite      pam_authtok_get.so.1
login    auth required       pam_dhkeys.so.1
login    auth required       pam_unix_cred.so.1
login    auth required       pam_dial_auth.so.1
login    auth binding        pam_unix_auth.so.1 server_policy
login    auth required       pam_ldap.so.1

other    auth requisite      pam_authtok_get.so.1
other    auth required       pam_dhkeys.so.1
other    auth required       pam_unix_cred.so.1
other    auth binding        pam_unix_auth.so.1 server_policy
other    auth required       pam_ldap.so.1

passwd   auth binding        pam_passwd_auth.so.1 server_policy
passwd   auth required       pam_ldap.so.1

other    account requisite   pam_roles.so.1
other    account required    pam_projects.so.1
other    account binding     pam_unix_account.so.1 server_policy
other    account required    pam_ldap.so.1

other    password required   pam_dhkeys.so.1
other    password requisite  pam_authtok_get.so.1
other    password requisite  pam_authtok_check.so.1
other    password required   pam_authtok_store.so.1 server_policy
```

6. To use netgroups to restrict access to the systems, do the following:

Note

This step describes how to configure one server. Make similar changes to other servers, as needed.

a. Add a netgroup to the Directory Server. Add the following line to the end of the /etc/password file on the Solaris client:

+@<netgroup>

b. Add the following line to the end of the /etc/shadow file on the Solaris client:

+@<netgroup>

Note

Due to a limitation in the `pam_ldap` authentication module, ensure that there are no trailing colons (:) on the lines you add to the `/etc/password` and `/etc/shadow` files.

7. If you will use netgroups to limit access to systems, configure `/etc/nsswitch.conf` as follows:

```
passwd:              compat
shadow:              compat
passwd_compat:       ldap
shadow_compat:       ldap
group:               files ldap
netgroup:            ldap
```

8. Ensure that the following line exists in the `sshd` configuration file: `/etc/ssh/sshd_config`: `PAMAuthenticationViaKBDIntyes`

13.5.3 Using Profiles to Initialize an LDAP Client

To initialize an LDAP client, first become superuser.

1. Become superuser or assume an equivalent role. Roles contain authorizations and privileged commands.

2. Run `ldapclient` with `init`.

```
# ldapclient init \
-a profileName=new \
-a domainName=thisisan.example.com 123.456.1.1
System successfully configured
```

13.5.4 Using Proxy Credentials to Initialize an LDAP Client

To Initialize a Client Using Proxy Credentials, become superuser. Do not edit either of the client configuration files directly. Use `ldapclient` to create or modify the content of these files.

1. Become superuser or assume an equivalent role. Roles contain authorizations and privileged commands.

2. Run `ldaplient` (defining proxy values).

```
# ldapclient init \
-a proxyDN=cn=proxyagent,ou=profile,dc=thisisan,
   dc=example,dc=com \
-a domainName=thisisan.example.com \
-a profileName=pit1 \
-a proxyPassword=test1234 123.456.0.1
System successfully configured
```

13.5.5 Initializing an LDAP Client Manually

Superusers or administrators with an equivalent role can perform manual client configurations. However, many of the checks are bypassed during the process, so it is easy to misconfigure your system. In addition, you must change settings on every machine, instead of changing settings in one central place, as is done when using profiles.

1. Become superuser or assume an equivalent role. Roles contain authorizations and privileged commands.

2. Use `ldapclient manual` to initialize the client.

```
# ldapclient manual \
-a domainName=dc=thisisan.example.com \
-a credentialLevel=proxy \
-a defaultSearchBase=dc=thisisan,dc=example,dc=com \
-a proxyDN=cn=proxyagent,ou=profile,dc=thisisan,dc=example,dc=com \
-a proxyPassword=testtest 123.456.0.1
```

3. Use `ldapclient list` to verify.

```
NS_LDAP_FILE_VERSION= 2.0
NS_LDAP_BINDDN= cn=proxyagent,ou=profile,dc=thisisan,dc=example,dc=com
NS_LDAP_BINDPASSWD= {NS1}1a2345e6c654321f
NS_LDAP_SERVERS= 123.456.0.1
NS_LDAP_SEARCH_BASEDN= dc=thisisan,dc=example,dc=com
NS_LDAP_CREDENTIAL_LEVEL= proxy
```

13.5.6 Modifying a Manual LDAP Client Configuration

To modify an LDAP client configuration follow these steps:

1. Become superuser or assume an equivalent role. Roles contain authorizations and privileged commands.

2. Use the following `ldapclient mod` command to change the authentication method to `simple`:

   ```
   # ldapclient mod -a authenticationMethod=simple
   ```

3. Use `ldapclient list` to verify the change was made.

```
# ldapclient list
NS_LDAP_FILE_VERSION= 2.0
NS_LDAP_BINDDN= cn=proxyagent,ou=profile,dc=thisisan,dc=example,dc=com
NS_LDAP_BINDPASSWD= {NS1}1a2345e6c654321f
NS_LDAP_SERVERS= 192.168.0.1
NS_LDAP_SEARCH_BASEDN= dc=thisisan,dc=example,dc=com
NS_LDAP_AUTH= simple
NS_LDAP_CREDENTIAL_LEVEL= proxy
```

13.5.7 Troubleshooting LDAP Client Configuration

You cannot change some attributes of an LDAP client configuration by using the `mod` subcommand. For example, you cannot change the `profileName` and `profileTTL` attributes. To change these attributes, create a new profile by using the `ldapclient init` command.

13.5.8 Uninitializing an LDAP Client

The command `ldapclient uninit` restores the client name service to what it was prior to the most recent `init`, `modify`, or `manual` operation. In other words, it performs an "undo" on the last step taken. An example of its use follows:

```
# ldapclient uninit
System successfully recovered
```

13.5.9 Initializing the Native LDAP Client

Native LDAP is the integration of LDAP as a name service for the Solaris OS. Once configured, Native LDAP is another name service option within `nsswitch.conf(4)` designed to complement `/etc` files and DNS. It is used in the same way as NIS.

To configure a Solaris 10 Native LDAP client for use with an OpenLDAP server you should be familiar with the operation of LDAP and already have a working LDAP tree in place. The tree should have user data in a form that works with `nss_ldap` and `pam_ldap`.

The Solaris LDAP client differs in some key ways from the PADL LDAP client that comes bundled with nearly every modern Linux distribution. The most visible difference is Sun's dedication to the NIS-type domain convention. When configuring a Solaris host for LDAP you must also change the system's domain name to match the information stored in LDAP. Despite the differences, the basic schema for storing the name service databases is consistent enough for Solaris and Linux to coexist.

13.5.9.1 Prepare the LDAP Server

To use OpenLDAP with Solaris 10, you will need to make three changes.

- Fix an interoperability problem between Solaris' `ldapclient` and OpenLDAP server. A patch may be applied to OpenLDAP that enables the use of Solaris' `ldapclient init` function.
- Add two schema files necessary for storing the data Solaris needs to manage user accounts.
- Seed the directory with data to make it do something useful.

If you elect to skip the first step, make sure you follow the instructions for configuring Solaris with `ldapclient` manual syntax or else the `ldapclient init` mechanism will not work. You may then skip the third step of this section that deals with initializing profile information.

13.5.9.2 Patching OpenLDAP

Make sure you have applied the necessary patches to the OpenLDAP server for the Solaris `ldapclient init` utility to configure properly.

13.5.9.3 Installing the Schema

Solaris relies on objectclasses and attributes from two schemas, DUAConfigProfile and Solaris, in addition to the schema that comes bundled with OpenLDAP. To use the new schema, just drop the schema files in your schema directory, add the two appropriate lines to `slapd.conf` and restart `slapd`.

13.5.9.4 Initializing the Directory Structure

Using the patched version of the OpenLDAP server, you can use a feature of `ldapclient` to store all the information necessary to configure the LDAP client in LDAP. You will see in the set of steps given that it is easy and quick to provision and reprovision LDAP clients.

The following sample LDIF file creates the `ou=profiles` hierarchy with one example profile underneath `example.com` domain. You will need to substitute the base DN through the LDIF before adding it to your directory.

```
# Example profile LDIF:
dn: ou=profile,dc=example,dc=com
objectClass: top
objectClass: organizationalUnit
ou: profile

dn: cn=Solaris,ou=profile,dc=example,dc=com
objectClass: top
objectClass: DUAConfigProfile
cn: Solaris
defaultServerList: ldap1.example.com ldap2.example.com
defaultSearchBase: dc=example,dc=com
defaultSearchScope: one
searchTimeLimit: 30
bindTimeLimit: 2
credentialLevel: anonymous
authenticationMethod: simple
followReferrals: TRUE
profileTTL: 43200
```

Whether or not you choose to create profiles, one more important change is necessary. In order for Solaris to process domain searches, it expects the base DN to have the objectclasses "domain" and "domainRelatedObject" and the attribute "associatedDomain." The "associatedDomain" attribute must contain the name of the domain for the Solaris environment.

For example, if you are Example Company using the domain example.com, your base DN might be dc=example,dc=com and your associatedDomain entry would be "example.com."

```
dn: dc=example,dc=com
objectClass: top
objectClass: domain
objectClass: domainRelatedObject
objectClass: nisDomainObject
domainComponent: example
associatedDomain: example.com
nisDomain: example.com
```

13.5.9.5 Configure the Client

After preparing the server with Solaris specific tweaks, the client needs to be brought online. For Solaris 10 no reboot is required.

13.5.9.6 Prepare Configuration Files

When editing the `nisswitch.ldap` file, keep a few things in mind. Since LDAP is defaulted to resolve hosts, in some circumstances this could cause an infinite loop when the name service switch goes to look up the LDAP host to connect with. Use DNS as your primary host naming system with a fallback to `/etc/hosts` files.

Generally list `files` first and then `ldap`, except for `hosts` and `ipnodes`. For `hosts` and `ipnodes`, list `files` first and then `dns`. Refer to the example below.

```
# New:
hosts:          files   dns
ipnodes:        files   dns

# Old:
hosts:          ldap [NOTFOUND=return]   files
ipnodes:        ldap [NOTFOUND=return]   files
```

When editing `nisswitch.ldap`, make sure it is `nisswitch.ldap` and not `nisswitch.conf` because `ldapclient` will overwrite `nsswitch.conf` with `nis-switch.ldap` during the conversion process.

Aside from `hosts` and `ipnodes`, set all the other name service definitions to `files ldap`. This forces lookups to check local overrides first (e.g., `/etc/passwd`; `/etc/group`). DNS should be configured in the same way (e.g., `/etc/hosts`).

13.5.9.7 Verify Required Packages

The following package installations are required for the Sun LDAP client. In the case of `sendmail` and `autofs`, there may still be some questions unanswered, but this configuration should work.

```
SUNWnisu        #provides ldapclient
SUNWnisr
SUNWspnego      #gss-api related libs
SUNWsndmr       #see note below
SUNWatfsr       #see note below
SUNWlldap
```

> **Note**
>
> `sendmail` and `autofs` packages are required because `ldapclient` calls those services to be restarted as it configures the host. When they are not present, `ldapclient` detects the error stopping/starting the services and does not make the changes to the system.

13.5.9.8 Configure the Client Using a Profile

If you installed a patched version of OpenLDAP and installed the profile template, you will be able to use a much more simplified method of configuring the host for LDAP.

Unless a proxyDN and a proxyPassword are specified, the `ldap` service may refuse to start. In this case you can provide those credentials. In the following sample, configuration `ldapclient` did enough syntax checking to make sure that the DN was at least syntactically valid, but did not attempt to bind because the credentials supplied were not technically valid for the LDAP server. If your directory allows for anonymous searches of the `ou=profile` branch, then you should be able to execute the following:

```
# Make sure the domainname is set before running ldapclient
host# domainname
example.com
host# ldapclient -v init -a proxyDN=cn=fake,ou=People,dc=example,dc=com \
-a proxyPassword=xxxx ldap1.example.com
# lots of output snipped here
start: system/filesystem/autofs:default... success
start: sleep 100000 microseconds
start: sleep 200000 microseconds
start: system/name-service-cache:default... success
start: sleep 100000 microseconds
start: sleep 200000 microseconds
start: network/smtp:sendmail... success
restart: sleep 100000 microseconds
restart: sleep 200000 microseconds
restart: sleep 400000 microseconds
restart: milestone/name-services:default... success
System successfully configured
host#
```

13.5.10 LDAP API Entry Listings

See the following site for LDAP API listings: `http://publib.boulder.ibm.com/iseries/v5r1/ic2924/info/apis/dis.pdf`

13.5.11 Troubleshooting Name Service Information

Each name service provides a tool for acquiring information stored within it. The information that is displayed is specific to a particular name service without consideration of the `/etc/nsswitch.conf` file.

By using the `getent` utility, you can search several name service databases in the order they are specified in the `/etc/nsswitch.conf`. You may want to try using the `getent` utility instead of service specific utilities such as `nslookup`, `dig`, or `ypmatch`. This can save troubleshooting time in isolating name service malfunctions.

14

Solaris Print Administration

The printing software in the Solaris Operating System (Solaris OS) provides a variety of tools, services, and protocols that you can use to set up and manage print servers and print clients, both locally and on a network. This chapter explores planning for printing in your environment, setting up printers with the Solaris Print Manager graphical user interface (GUI), and using the LP print commands to perform routine print administration tasks.

14.1 Overview of the Solaris Printing Architecture

The Solaris print subsystem consists of print commands, a print spooler, any over-the-wire protocols, and the underlying technologies that move a print request from the client to the server, or to the printer.

At the core of the Solaris print subsystem is a UNIX System V (R4) based spooler. The term *spooler* is an acronym for *Simultaneous Peripheral Operations On-line*. The spooler software intercepts a print request and then sends it to disk or memory, where the request is held until the printer is ready to print the request.

In addition, client applications in the print subsystem make requests of and manage the spooler, as well as manage filters that perform document translation, back-end processing software that performs final document transformation, and device (printer) communication. To utilize the complete functionality of the print subsystem, all of these resources are required.

Starting with the Solaris 10 5/08 OS, the printing software implements the Open Standard Print Application Programming Interface (PAPI), which is a single API that interacts with the print services. The PAPI consists of a front-end API implementation that dynamically loads back-end print service or protocol modules that communicate directly with the print services. The PAPI makes it possible to layer applications, toolkits, and the print commands themselves on top of a print service, protocol-neutral interface.

14.2 Key Concepts

To better understand printer setup and print administration in the Solaris OS, an understanding of the following basic concepts is essential.

14.2.1 Printer Categories (Local and Remote Printers)

Printers can be divided into two categories, local and remote. These terms refer to the print queue configuration, rather than to how or where the printer is connected. A *print queue* refers to the setup and configuration of a printer, either on a print server or on a print client.

A *local* printer is a print queue that has been configured on a system that is local to you. A *remote* printer is a print queue that is configured anywhere *but* your local system. These terms do not imply that the printer is physically attached to a system or to the network.

14.2.2 Printer Connections (Directly Attached and Network Attached)

Another way to categorize printers is by how they are physically connected to the world. Some printers are directly attached to a system (print server) by a wire. These printers are referred to as *directly attached* printers. If a printer is connected to the network, rather than to a system, the printer is referred to as a *network-attached* printer.

The terms "directly attached" and "network attached" refer specifically to the physical connection of the printer hardware. The terms "local" and "remote" refer solely to the print queue configuration. Sometimes, these terms are used interchangeably, but the difference should be noted, as it can be helpful in determining what information is required prior to setting up a new printer.

14.2.3 Description of a Print Server and a Print Client

A *print server* is a system on which a print queue is configured. The print server makes the printer available to other systems on the network. A single system can be the print server for several printers.

A *print client* is a system that utilizes configured print queues. When planning for printer setup, you will need to decide which systems will be the print servers. Note that print servers and print clients can run different versions of the Solaris software.

14.3 Solaris Printing Tools and Services

The Solaris 10 OS provides several printing tools and services that can be used to set up and manage printers. Some tools and services are more appropriate for specific uses, while others can be used for all, or most, printing tasks that you might perform.

The following sections briefly describe these tools and services and how they are used in the Solaris 10 OS.

14.3.1 Solaris Print Manager

Solaris Print Manager is a Java technology-based graphical user interface (GUI) that is used to set up and manage printers on a local system or on a network.

Solaris Print Manager is the preferred method for managing printer access because the tool centralizes information for printers that are set up on a network, in a naming service environment. When you use Solaris Print Manager to manage printers, the appropriate databases are updated automatically.

Solaris Print Manager also contains a command-line console that you can enable to show the LP print command equivalent when a print queue is added, deleted, or modified.

Note that Solaris Print Manager cannot be used for all print administration tasks, for example, managing print requests or disabling printers. For these tasks, you will need to use the print command-line interface.

14.3.2 LP Print Service

The Solaris line printer (LP) subsystem print service is a command-line interface (CLI) that includes all of the print commands and a set of software utilities that enable you set up and manage your printing environment. The print service also consists of the LP print service software, any print filters that you might provide, and the hardware, such as the printer, system, and network connections.

14.3.3 PostScript Printer Definitions File Manager

The PostScript Printer Definition (PPD) File Manager, `/usr/sbin/ppdmgr`, is a command-line utility that was introduced in the Solaris 10 5/08 release. This utility is used to administer PPD files and the cache of printer information on a Solaris system. PPD File Manager can also be used to add new PPD files to the system.

For more detailed information, see *System Administration Guide: Solaris Printing* on `http://docs.sun.com`.

14.4 Network Protocols

Network protocols are used for communications between print clients and print servers, and between print servers and printers. The Solaris printing architecture enables the use of several different network protocols for both types of communications. Each network printing protocol has its own set of strengths and weaknesses that should be evaluated before you determine which protocol best fits your needs. When setting up a network-attached printer, first consult the printer vendor documentation for information about which network protocol to use.

The following sections briefly describe the network protocols that are supported in the Solaris 10 OS.

14.4.1 Berkeley Software Distribution Protocol

By default, the Solaris print subsystem uses the Berkeley Software Distribution (BSD) protocol to communicate with printers. If you are setting up a network-attached printer with Solaris Print Manager, BSD is the default protocol. The BSD protocol is also sometimes referred to as the "LPD protocol" or the "RFC-1179 protocol."

14.4.2 Transmission Control Protocol

The Transmission Control Protocol (TCP) is the basic communication protocol of the Internet. TCP is a robust protocol that is most often used for printing on a network. TCP enables applications to communicate with each other as though they were connected by a physical circuit. Because of its reliability and robustness, a raw TCP socket is preferred over the BSD protocol for server-to-printer communications. If you are setting up a network-attached printer with Solaris Print Manager, TCP is one of the options that you can select.

14.4.3 Internet Printing Protocol

Because it enables interoperability with the Common UNIX Printing System (CUPS) and Windows print clients, the Internet Printing Protocol (IPP) is a network printing protocol that is rapidly becoming the industry standard for printing.

IPP is used for client-to-server and server-to-printer communications. In the Solaris 10 OS, both types of IPP support are provided. Server-side support is provided by a listening service that is embedded under the Apache Web Server software. Starting with the Solaris 10 5/08 OS, client-side support is implemented through the PAPI.

Printer support for IPP is available through a device Uniform Resource Identifier (URI) interface script. A URI is an addressing technology that identifies resources on the Internet or a private intranet. When setting up printers that use IPP with Solaris Print Manager, select the URI protocol option. This option is also new in the Solaris 10 5/08 OS.

For detailed information about configuring and using IPP, including instructions on how to specify a device URI when setting up a network-attached printer, see *System Administration Guide: Solaris Printing* on `http://docs.sun.com`.

14.4.4 Server Message Block Protocol

The Server Message Block (SMB) network protocol, through Samba, is an implementation that enables interoperability between Linux and UNIX servers, and Windows-based clients.

14.5 Planning for Printer Setup

When planning for printer setup in your environment, keep the following requirements and guidelines in mind.

14.5.1 Print Server Requirements

You can attach a printer to a stand-alone system or to a system on the network. Any system on the network with a printer can be designated as a print server, as long as the system has the resources to manage the printing load. Before setting up printers in your environment, first determine which systems will be the print servers. Keep in mind that a system that has been designated as a print server should meet the following guidelines and requirements:

- **Spooling space**

    Spooling space is the amount of disk space that is used to store and process requests in the print queue. Spooling space is the single most important factor to consider when deciding which systems to designate as print servers. When users submit files for printing, the files are stored in the /var/spool/lp directory until the files are printed. The size of the /var directory depends on the amount of available space on the device or the ZFS volume (zvol) where it resides. Spooling space can be allocated in the /var directory on the print server, or mounted from a file server and accessed over the network. Note that if not created as a separate file system, the /var directory uses space in the root (/) file system. The root (/) file system might be insufficient on a print server.

- **Memory requirements**

    A system does not need additional memory to function as a print server. However, more memory improves performance for managing print requests.

- **Swap space**

    The swap space allocation on the print server should be sufficient to handle all LP print service requirements.

For additional information about allocating disk space and mounting file systems, see *System Administration Guide: Devices and File Systems* on http://docs.sun.com.

14.5.2 Locating Information About Supported Printers

Before beginning the process of printer setup, determine if the printer you are adding is supported. The /usr/share/lib directory contains the terminfo database. This database includes information about terminal settings and printer capabilities. The printer you are adding must correspond to an entry in the terminfo database. Each printer is identified in the terminfo database with a short name.

The following example shows the entries in the terminfo database:

```
$ pwd
/usr/share/lib/terminfo
$ ls
1   3   5   7   9   B   H   P   a   c   e   g   i   k   m   o   q   s   u   w   y
2   4   6   8   A   G   M   S   b   d   f   h   j   l   n   p   r   t   v   x   z
$
```

Each subdirectory contains compiled database entries for terminals or printers. The entries are organized by the first letter of the printer or terminal type. For example, if you have an Epson printer, look in the `/usr/share/lib/terminfo/e` directory to determine if your particular model of Epson printer is supported.

```
$ cd /usr/share/lib/terminfo/e
$ ls
emots           ep2500+high    ep48          ergo4000       exidy2500
env230          ep2500+low     epson2500     esprit
envision230     ep40           epson2500-80  ethernet
ep2500+basic    ep4000         epson2500-hi  ex3000
ep2500+color    ep4080         epson2500-hi80 exidy
$
```

14.5.3 Locating Information About Available PPD Files

A PPD file describes the fonts, paper sizes, resolution, and other capabilities that are standard for a particular printer. Support for setting up and administering printers with PPD files has been incorporated into the Solaris print subsystem. Two interface scripts, `standard_foomatic` and `netstandard_foomatic`, provide a generic Solaris interface between the Solaris spooler and the back-end process of the Solaris print server.

PPD files are stored in repositories on the system. If you are running a Solaris 10 release prior to the Solaris 10 5/08 release, you can locate available PPD files in the `/usr/lib/lp/model/ppd/system` directory.

Starting with the Solaris 10 5/08 release, PPD files are stored in any of the following four repositories on the system:

- `/usr/share/ppd`—Specifies the `system` repository
- `/usr/local/share/ppd`—Specifies the `admin` repository
- `/opt/share/ppd`—Specifies the `vendor` repository
- `/var/lp/ppd`—Specifies the `user` repository

You can also check Solaris Print Manager to determine if your printer make, model, and driver (PPD file) are supported.

14.5.4 Adding a New PPD File to the System

If the Solaris software does not provide the appropriate PPD file for your printer, you can download the file and add it to your system by using the PPD File Manager utility (`ppdmgr`).

PPD files can be downloaded from the following locations:

- Printer vendor's Web site
- Openprinting Web site at `http://openprinting.org/printer_list.cgi`
- Foomatic database at `http://www.linuxfoundation.org`

In the following example, a PPD file for an HP LaserJet 4350 printer is downloaded and then added to the system by using the `ppdmgr` command.

1. Open a Web browser and then go to the following URL:

    `http://openprinting.org/printer_list.cgi`

2. To locate the PPD file, do the following:

    a. Select the printer make: HP

    b. Select the printer model: LaserJet 4350

    c. Click Show.

    d. Locate or select the Recommended driver option, then click the Custom PPD link.

    e. Save the PPD file to your system: Select File -> Save Page As.

Note

Before copying the PPD file to your system, make sure that the file requires no other drivers. If the file requires additional drivers, check that the driver is supported in the Solaris OS.

---

3. Add the PPD file to your system by using the `ppdmgr` command with the `-a` option.

    `# ppdmgr -a /home/username1/ppdfiles/HP_LaserJet_4350.ppd`

    The PPD file is copied to the following path:

    `/usr/share/model/ppd/system/foomatic/HP/HP_LaserJet_4350
    .ppd.gz`

    Note that the `.gz` extension is added when the PPD file is copied to your system.

4. Check the Printer Driver field in Solaris Print Manager to determine if the driver is listed.

If the PPD file does not appear in the list of available drivers, update the `ppdcache` file for all of the repositories on the system. If Solaris Print Manager is running, quit and restart the application, then check for the file again.

```
# ppdmgr -u
```

For a description of the `ppdmgr` command, including all of the available options, see *man pages section 1M: System Administration Commands* on `http://docs.sun.com`.

14.5.5 Adding Printers in a Naming Service

The Solaris print subsystem can be configured to use a naming service such as NIS, LDAP, or NIS+, to advertise printers. NIS is the naming service that is most commonly used. Adding printers to a naming service enables users, systems, and applications to communicate across the network. In addition, printer configuration and maintenance is simplified because the naming service stores printer configuration information for every printer on the network.

The naming service maps are created on the naming service server by the system administrator. To set up printers that are added to a naming service, you must have access privileges for managing the naming service database. For more information, see *System Administration Guide: Naming and Directory Services* on `http://docs.sun.com`.

Note that if a naming service is not specified during printer setup, the printer information is only added to the print server's configuration files. Subsequently, print clients will not automatically detect the printer, unless you manually add the information to each print client that needs to use the printer.

14.5.6 Printer Support in the Naming Service Switch

The `printers` database, which resides in the naming service switch file, `/etc/nsswitch.conf`, provides centralized printer configuration information to print clients on the network. By including the `printers` database and corresponding sources of information in the naming service switch file, print clients automatically have access to printer configuration information without users having to manually add this information to their own systems.

In addition, users can direct their systems to the source of information about printers in the order preferred. Places to define printers are user, files, and the naming service that is implemented at your site, for example, NIS. The order in which the printer configuration information for each print client is searched is determined by the information that is in this file.

The following example shows the `printers` entry in an `/etc/nsswitch.conf` file. Here, the search order is user, files, then NIS, which means the user's

$HOME/.printers file is checked for printer configuration information first, followed by the /etc/printers.conf file. Lastly, the printers.conf.byname table is checked for the printer information.

```
#
.
.
.
printers:   user files nis
```

14.5.7 Enabling Network Listening Services

In the Solaris 10 OS, the print subsystem is managed by the Service Management Facility (SMF). Several printing services, such as the print scheduler (lpsched), and the listening services for the IPP, RFC-1179, and SMB protocols, are managed by using the svcadm command. If you are planning to set up printers that use any of these protocols, you must first enable these services.

The following example shows how to enable the IPP listening service:

```
# svcadm enable application/print/ipp-listener
# svcs application/print/ipp-listener
STATE          STIME    FMRI
online         12:09:16 svc:/application/print/ipp-listener
```

In the preceding example, application is the service name category, print is the service name, and ipp-listener is the service instance or protocol.

The following example shows how to disable the IPP listening service:

```
# svcadm disable application/print/ipp-listener
# svcs application/print/ipp-listener
STATE          STIME    FMRI
disabled       13:20:14 svc:/application/print/ipp-listener
```

Note

Some network printing services, for example IPP, require additional configuration before you can enable the service. For complete instructions, see the Solaris 10 *System Administration Guide: Solaris Printing* on http://docs.sun.com.

For more information about managing services by using SMF, see Chapter 2, "Boot, Service Management, and Shutdown."

14.6 Setting Up Printers with Solaris Printer Manager

You can use Solaris Print Manager to add, modify, and delete printers. To configure printers with the tool, you must be logged in to the system and running Solaris Print Manager as the `root` user.

Adding printers to a naming service during printer setup also requires access privileges for managing the naming service database at your site.

14.6.1 Assigning Printer Definitions

The task of setting up a printer with Solaris Print Manager includes defining the attributes of the printer. Each attribute is referred to as a *printer definition*. Table 14.1 describes all of the printer definitions that you can set with Solaris Print Manager. Use this information to help you determine what information is required to set up printers.

Table 14.1 Printer Definition Descriptions

Printer Definition	Description	Required or Optional
Printer Name	A unique name that identifies the printer. Printer names can have up to 255 alphanumeric characters and can include dashes, underscores, and dots (.).	Required for the setup of all printers
Print Server	The name of the print server for the printer. The default setting is Use localhost for Printer Server.	Required for the setup of all printers and to add access to a printer. Information for this field is provided by the tool.
Description	A user-defined string that provides information to assist users in identifying the printer.	Optional
Printer Port	A device to which the printer is attached.	Required for the setup of a directly attached printer
Printer Type	The type of printer. The default is PostScript.	Required for the setup of all printers that do *not* use PPD files
File Contents	The content to be printed.	Required for the setup of all printers that do *not* use PPD files
Printer Make	The printer manufacturer, for example, Lexmark.	Required for the setup of all printers that use a PPD file

continues

Table 14.1 Printer Definition Descriptions (*continued*)

Printer Definition	Description	Required or Optional
Printer Model	The printer model, for example, Lexmark Optra 3E12.	Required for the setup of all printers that use a PPD file
Printer Driver	The driver specified by the PPD file that the printer uses.	Required for the setup of all printers that use a PPD file
Fault Notification	Specifies how to notify the user of errors, for example, Mail to Superuser.	Optional
Default Printer	Sets the printer as the default printer when selected.	Optional
Banner	Specifies options for printing banner pages.	Optional
User Access List	List of users that are allowed to print on the print server. The default is all.	Optional

For information about setting other printer definitions or using the `lpadmin` command to set printer definitions, see *System Administration Guide: Solaris Printing* on `http://docs.sun.com`.

14.6.2 Starting Solaris Print Manager

To start Solaris Print Manager, the system must have a bit-mapped display monitor and be an X Window System.

You can start Solaris Print Manager in one of the following ways:

- From the desktop: Launch -> Preferences -> System Preferences -> Add/Remove Printer.

- From the command line:

```
# /usr/sbin/printmgr&
Java Accessibility Bridge for GNOME loaded.
```

14.6.3 Setting Up a New Directly Attached Printer With Solaris Print Manager

The following example describes how to set up a new attached printer `luna03` on the print server `gadzooks`. The printer is a Lexmark 1855 S that is attached to the parallel printer port on the print server. Note that in this example, the printer does not use a PPD file.

1. Connect the printer to the print server, then power on the printer.
2. On the print server, log in as the `root` user, and then start Solaris Print Manager.
3. In the naming service window, select the naming service. In this example, files is selected.
4. From the Print Manager menu, deselect the Use PPD files option, and check that the Use localhost for Printer Server default option is selected.
5. From the Printer menu, choose New Attached Printer.
6. In the New Attached Printer window, provide the information that is required to configure the printer, as shown in Figure 14.1.

Figure 14.1 illustrates the setup of a new attached printer, `luna03`. The printer attributes, such as the printer name, description, and printer port, are defined here. Because the printer does not use a PPD file, a printer make and model is not required. Instead, information about the printer type and file contents is provided. In this example, the printer is designated as the default printer. For this configuration, the remaining options use the Solaris Print Manager default settings.

1. To verify that the printer was successfully set up, check Solaris Print Manager. The printer should now appear in the list of available printers.
2. Verify that the printer can print requests.

```
# lp -d luna03 test
request id is luna03-973 (1 file)
```

14.6.4 Setting Up a New Network-Attached Printer with Solaris Print Manager

Before you begin the task of setting up a new network-attached printer, consult the vendor documentation for which protocol to use. Network-attached printers might

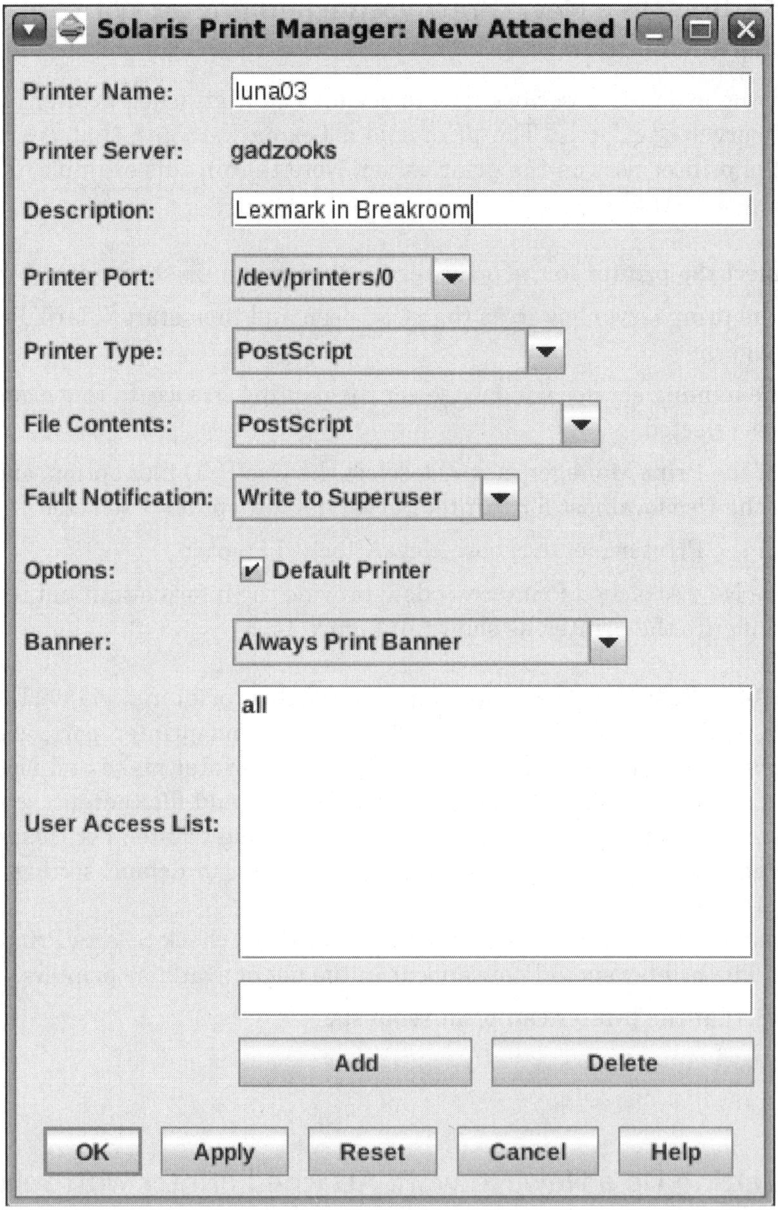

Figure 14.1 Solaris Print Manager: New Attached Dialog Box

use one or more special protocols that require a vendor-supplied printing program. The procedures that are used to set up the vendor-supplied printing program can vary. If vendor-supplied support is not provided for the printer, Solaris network printer support can be used with most devices. However, use the printer vendor-supplied software, whenever possible.

The following example describes how to set up a new network-attached printer on the print server gadzooks. The printer is an HPLaserJet 4300 that is connected to the network. The printer has been added to the naming service. Note that in this configuration, the printer also uses a PPD file.

1. Connect the printer to the network, then power on the printer.
2. On the system that is the print server, log in as the root user.
3. Start Solaris Print Manager.
4. In the Naming Service window, select the naming service. In this example, the naming service is NIS.
5. From the Print Manager menu, check that the Use PPD files and Use local-host for Printer Server default options are selected.
6. From the Printer menu, choose New Network Attached Printer.
7. In the New Network Attached Printer window, provide the information that is required to configure the printer, as shown in Figure 14.2.

Figure 14.2 illustrates the setup of hp4300_pr502, a new network-attached printer. The printer attributes, such as the printer name and description, are defined here. The printer uses a PPD file, so the printer make and printer model are selected, rather than a printer type and file contents. Note that the Printer Driver field is automatically populated with the correct driver and PPD file information *after* the printer make and model are selected. Because the printer is directly connected to the network, a destination and protocol are specified. The destination format depends on the protocol type that is used. Here, TCP is the network protocol, so the destination is specified as hp4300_pr502:9100. The printer is designated as the default printer. In this configuration, the remaining options use the Solaris Print Manager default settings.

1. To verify that the printer was successfully set up, check Solaris Print Manager. The printer should now appear in the list of available printers.
2. Verify that the printer can print requests.

```
# lp -d  hp4300_pr502 test
request id is hp4300_pr02-996 (1 file)
```

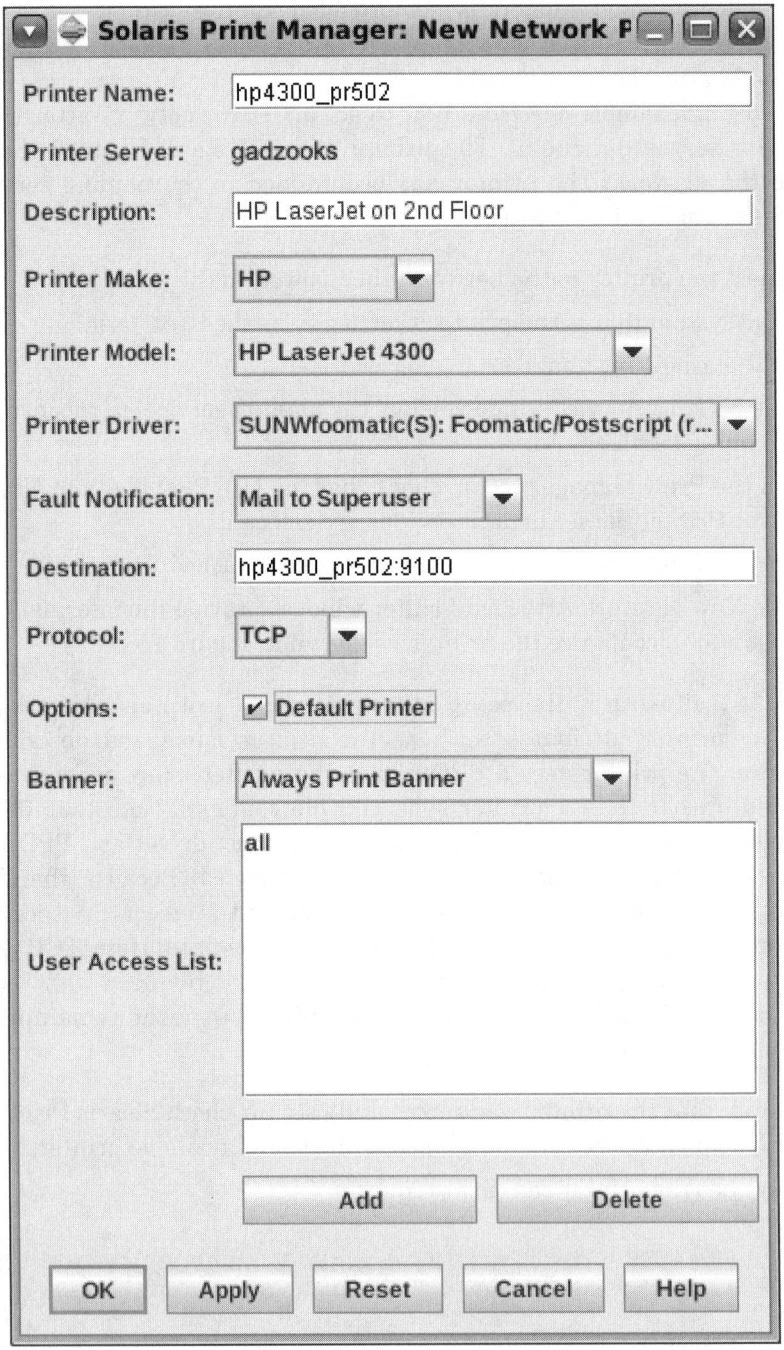

Figure 14.2 Solaris Print Manager: New Network Dialog Box

14.7 Setting Up a Printer on a Print Client with Solaris Print Manager

A print client is a system that is *not* the server for the printer. Yet, this system has access to the printer through the configuration of a remote print queue. A print client uses the services of the print server to spool, schedule, and filter print requests. A system can be a print server for one printer and a print client for another printer.

Access to a printer can be configured on a domain-wide basis or on a per-system basis. If you add the printer information to the naming service database, access is configured on a domain-wide basis.

14.7.1 Adding Printer Access With Solaris Print Manager

In the following example, access to the printer homeprt1 is added to a print client. The server for the printer is Zeus.

1. On the system where you want to add access to the printer, log in as the root user, and then start Solaris Print Manager.

2. From the Printer menu, choose Add Access to Printer.

3. Provide the required information for the following attributes:

   - Printer Name: homeprt1

   - Printer Server: Zeus

   - Description: Home print queue

4. To set the print queue as the default, select the Default Printer check box.

5. After applying your changes, check Solaris Print Manager.
   The printer should now appear in the list of available printers.

6. Verify that the printer can print requests.

```
# lp -d homeprt1 test
request id is homeprt1-1 (1 file)
```

14.8 Administering Printers by Using LP Print Commands

This section includes some of the tasks that you might need to perform after setting up your printing environment. With the exception of deleting a printer, all of these tasks can *only* be performed by using the LP print commands.

14.8.1 Frequently Used LP Print Commands

The following frequently used LP print commands are described in this section:

- `accept`—Accepts print requests
- `cancel`—Cancels print requests
- `disable`—Deactivates a printer and disables it from printing requests
- `enable`—Activates a printer and enables it to print requests
- `reject`—Rejects print requests
- `lp`—Submits print requests (SysV UNIX)
- `lpadmin`—Configures the print service
- `lpmove`—Moves a print job from one printer to another printer
- `lpr`—Submits print requests (BSD UNIX)
- `lpsched`—Starts the LP print service
- `lpstat`—Prints information about the print service

Note that the `lp` and `lpr` commands are essentially the same. The `lp` command has its origin in SysV UNIX, whereas the `lpr` command has its origin in BSD UNIX.

For more information about all of the available LP print commands, see *System Administration Guide: Solaris Printing* on `http://docs.sun.com`.

14.8.2 Using the `lpstat` Command

The `lpstat` command is used to obtain status and other helpful information about printers. In the following examples, information about the printer `luna03` is displayed.

For more information about using the `lpstat` command, see *man pages section 1: System Administration Commands* on `http://docs.sun.com`.

To display a system's default printer, use the `lpstat` command with the `-d` option.

```
$ lpstat -d
system default destination: luna03
```

To display the status of a printer, use the `lpstat` command with the `-p` option.

```
$ lpstat -p luna03
printer luna03 is idle. enabled since Jul 12 11:17 2005 available.
```

To view more details about a printer's attributes, such as its status, the connection type, and whether the printer uses a PPD file, use the `lpstat` command with the `-p` and `-l` options, as shown here:

```
$ lpstat -p luna03 -l
printer luna03 is idle. enabled since Thu Jul 12 15:02:32 PM PDT
                Form mounted:
                Content types: postscript
                Printer types: PS
                Connection: direct
                Interface: /usr/lib/lp/model/standard
                PPD: none
                .
                .
                .
```

14.8.3 Disabling and Enabling Printers

As a system administrator, you might need to disable printers from time to time for various reasons. The `/usr/bin/disable` command is used to disable printers.

For example, to disable the printer Lexmark_prt05, you would type:

disable Lexmark_prt05

The `/usr/bin/enable` command is used to enable a printer. For example, to enable the printer Lexmark_prt05, you would type:

```
# enable Lexmark_prt05
printer "Lexmark_prt05" enabled
```

To verify that the printer is enabled, use the `lpstat` command. For example:

```
# lpstat -p Lexmark_prt05
printer Lexmark_prt05 is idle. enabled since Jul 15 12:31 2008. available.
```

14.8.4 Accepting or Rejecting Print Requests

The `accept` and `reject` commands enable you to turn on or off a print queue that stores print requests. When you use the `reject` command, no new print requests can enter the print queue on the print server. However, any print requests that are still in the queue will be printed.

To stop a printer from printing requests that are already in the queue, you need to use the `disable` command.

The following example shows how to stop the printer luna03 from accepting print requests:

```
# reject -r "luna03 is down for repairs" luna03
destination "luna03" will no longer accept requests.
```

This example shows how to set the printer luna03 to accept print requests:

```
# accept luna03
destination "luna03" now accepting requests.
```

14.8.5 Canceling a Print Request

Use the cancel command to cancel print requests that are in print queues or to cancel print requests that are already printing. Print requests can be canceled in one of three ways:

- By request ID
- For a specific user
- For a specific printer

When you use the cancel command, a message lets you know the request was canceled and that the next request in the queue is being printed.

You can cancel a print request *only* under the following conditions:

- You are the user who submitted the request, and you are logged in to the system where the request was submitted.
- You are the user who submitted the request on any client system, and the print server has the user-equivalence option configured for the printer in its etc/printers.conf file.
- You are logged in as the root user or have assumed an equivalent role on the print server.

To cancel a specific print request, you need to provide the request ID. The request ID contains the name of the printer, a dash, and the number of the print request.

To list the request IDs for a printer, use the `lpstat` command with the `-o` option. For example, to list the request IDs for the printer `lucille`, you would type:

```
# lpstat  -o lucille
lucille-230
lucille-231
```

To cancel a print request by specifying its request ID, you would type:

```
# cancel lucille-230
request "lucille-230" cancelled
```

To verify that the print request was canceled, you would type:

```
# lpstat -o lucille
lucille-231
```

14.8.6 Moving Print Requests from One Printer to Another Printer

The `lpmove` command is used to move print requests from one printer to another printer. Moving requests from one printer to another printer requires `root` user privileges.

In this example, the requests for the printer `lucille` are moved to the printer, `Lexmark_prt05`.

1. List the IDs of the print requests on the original printer, `lucille`.

```
# lpstat -o lucille
lucille-188
lucille-189
lucille-190
```

2. Check that the destination printer is accepting print requests by using the `lpstat` command with the `-a` option.

```
# lpstat -a Lexmark_prt05
Lexmark_prt05 accepting requests since Nov 25 13:58 2008
```

3. Move the print requests from the original printer to the destination printer.

   `# lpmove lucille lexmark_prt05`

4. Start accepting new requests from the original printer.

```
# accept lucille
destination "lucille" now accepting requests.
```

5. Check for any remaining print requests in the original printer's queue, and if necessary, move those requests.

```
# lpstat -o lucille
lucille-185
```

14.8.7 Deleting a Printer

As a system administrator, you might need to delete printers from time to time. The task of deleting a printer involves removing it from the print service, removing printer access from the print client, and removing the printer information from the print server.

The following example shows the steps that are required to delete a printer. Note that this example includes several individual tasks that were previously described, for example, rejecting print requests, disabling a printer, and canceling and moving print requests.

1. On the print client that has access to the printer you want to delete, log in as the `root` user.

2. Delete the information for the printer on the print client by using the `lpadmin` command with the `-x` option.

```
# lpadmin -x lucille
Removed "lucille".
```

3. On the system that is the print server for the printer `lucille`, log in as the `root` user.

4. Stop accepting print requests for the printer.

```
# reject -r "queue deletion" lucille
destination "lucille" will no longer accept requests
```

This step prevents any new requests from being added to the printer's queue while you are in the process of removing the printer. The `-r` option is used to provide a reason.

5. Stop the printer by using the `disable` command with the appropriate options.

disable -c -r "queue deletion" lucille

The `-c` option cancels the current print job, and then disables the printer. The `-r` option is used to provide a reason.

You can optionally use the `-w` option instead of the `-c` option to direct the system to wait until the current print job has finished before disabling the printer.

6. Move any print requests that are still in the print queue to another printer.

7. Use the `lpstat` command with the `-o` option to determine the request IDs of the print requests on the original printer.

```
# lpstat -o lucille
lucille-185
lucille-186
```

- Check that the new destination printer is accepting requests by using the `lpstat` command with the `-a` option.

```
# lpstat -a luna03
luna03 accepting requests since Nov 25 14:19 2008
```

- Move the print requests from the printer that you are deleting to the destination printer. In this example, print requests from the printer `lucille` are being moved to a new printer, `luna03`.

lpmove lucille luna03

8. To delete the printer from the print server, use the `lpadmin` command with the `-x` option.

```
# lpadmin -x lucille
Removed "lucille".
```

9. Verify that the printer was successfully deleted.

```
# lpstat -p lucille
lucille: unknown printer
```

14.9 Troubleshooting Printing Problems

This section includes some basic tips for troubleshooting printing problems. For more detailed troubleshooting procedures, see *System Administration Guide: Solaris Printing* on `http://docs.sun.com`.

14.9.1 Troubleshooting No Output (Nothing Prints)

When nothing prints, there are three general areas to check: the printer hardware, the network, and the LP print service.

- Check that you are logged in as the `root` user or have assumed an equivalent role on the system.
- Check the hardware.

    The hardware is the first area to check. Make sure that the printer is plugged in and turned on. Refer to the manufacturer's documentation for information about hardware settings.

    The printer hardware includes the printer, the cable that connects the printer to the system, and the ports into which the cable connects at each end. As a general approach, work your way from the printer to the computer.

- Check the network.

    Problems are more common with remote print requests that are going from a print client to a print server. Make sure that network access between the print server and print clients is enabled.

- Check the LP print service.

The print scheduler must be running on the print server. See the following section for information about checking that the print scheduler is running. Also, the printer must be up and running and accepting print requests. Use the `lpstat` command to check whether a printer is up and running. See the previous section for instructions.

14.9.2 Checking That the Print Scheduler Is Running

In the Solaris 10 OS, the print scheduler is managed by SMF.

To determine if the print scheduler is running on the print server, use the `svcs` command. For example, you would type:

```
# svcs application/print/server
STATE          STIME    FMRI
disabled       Aug_12   svc:/application/print/server:default
```

From the previous output, you can see that the print scheduler is disabled. To enable the print scheduler, you would type:

```
# svcadm enable application/print/server
STATE          STIME    FMRI
# svcs application/print/server
STATE          STIME    FMRI
online         Aug_12   svc:/application/print/server:default
```

To disable the print scheduler, you would type:

```
# svcadm disable application/print/server
STATE          STIME    FMRI
# svcs application/print/server
STATE          STIME    FMRI
disabled       Aug_15   svc:/application/print/server:default
```

14.9.3 Debugging Printing Problems

Enabling the `lpr.debug` log within the `/etc/syslog.conf` file provides a variety of useful information for pinpointing printing problems. However, because a large volume of information is provided, this feature should only be enabled when you are debugging printing problems.

1. On the system that you want to debug printing problems, log in as the `root` user.

2. Enable the `lpr.debug` log within the `/etc/syslog.conf` file:

   ```
   # echo "lpr.debug /var/tmp/lpr.debug" >>/etc/syslog.conf
   ```

> **Caution**
>
> The white space between `lpr.debug` and `/var/tmp/lpr.debug` **must** be a tab.

3. Create the `lpr.debug` file by using the `touch` command.

   ```
   # touch /var/tmp/lpr.debug
   ```

4. Restart the syslog SMF service.

   ```
   # svcadm restart system.log
   ```

14.9.4 Checking the Printer Network Connections

Check that the network connection between the print server and the print client is set up correctly. For example:

```
zeus# ping bastion2
bastion2 is alive
bastion2# ping zeus
zeus not available
```

The `ping` command sends ECHO_REQUEST packets to hosts on a network. If the system is reachable, the return message indicates that the system is *alive*, which means that the network is up. The message also indicates that a naming service or the local `/etc/hosts` file has translated the host (system) name that you specified into an IP address.

If the return message indicates that the system is not available, check that the naming service is working properly at your site. See *System Administration Guide: Naming and Directory Services* on `http://docs.sun.com`.

Index

A

ABI (application binary interface), 47
accept command, print requests, 387
accumulation, patch, 97
ACLs (access control lists), 112–113
actions, database status and, 349
add_drv command, 255–256
add_install_client, 15
alternative service restarter, 43–44
Analyze menu, partition table, 215–217, 221–222
ancestry of process, Process Manager, 170–171
anonymous memory, 136
application binary interface (ABI), 47
application-independent shut down, 46
application-specific shut down, 46
architecture, Solaris print, 369–370
archive file systems, 124
at command
    checking jobs in queue, 176–177
    controlling access to, 178
    creating at job, 175–176
    defined, 175
    removing existing at job, 177–178
atq command, 176–177

attributes
    extended file, 115
    fields displayed with ps command, 148
    rules file, 15
autofs command, 101, 131
AUTOFS file system, 100
auto_home map, 132–133
auto_master file, 131
automatic log rotation, Fault Management, 185–186
automation tools, patch, 86–88
automount command, 131
automountd daemon, 131
automounting file systems, 130–133
    overview of, 130–131
    using direct maps, 132
    using indirect maps, 132–133
    using master maps, 131

B

backing up file systems
    defined, 107
    UFS, 107–108, 115–116
    before upgrading, 24
    ZFS, 120
backslash (\) character, 15

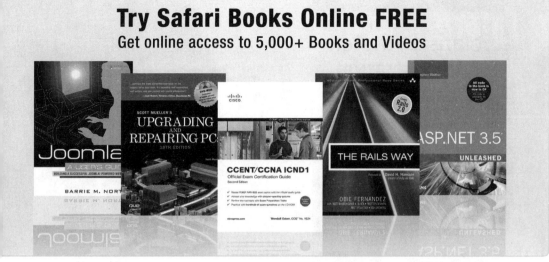

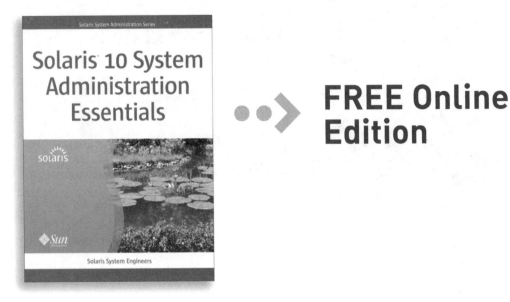

FREE Online Edition

Your purchase of **Solaris™ 10 System Administration Essentials** includes access to a free online edition for 45 days through the Safari Books Online subscription service. Nearly every Prentice Hall book is available online through Safari Books Online, along with more than 5,000 other technical books and videos from publishers such as Addison-Wesley Professional, Cisco Press, Exam Cram, IBM Press, O'Reilly, Que, and Sams.

SAFARI BOOKS ONLINE allows you to search for a specific answer, cut and paste code, download chapters, and stay current with emerging technologies.

Activate your FREE Online Edition at www.informit.com/safarifree

> **STEP 1:** Enter the coupon code: GCGAXWA.

> **STEP 2:** New Safari users, complete the brief registration form.
> Safari subscribers, just log in.

If you have difficulty registering on Safari or accessing the online edition, please e-mail customer-service@safaribooksonline.com